THE RENAISSANCE SOCIETY OF AMERICA
RENAISSANCE TEXT SERIES IV

TWO LATIN COMEDIES BY
JOHN FOXE THE MARTYROLOGIST

IOHANNES FOXVS.

Colligit vt FOXVS Sanctorum gesta Virorum
Digna facit Sanctis Plurima martijribus.

B

John Foxe at about age seventy (from Henry Holland, Herωologia, 1620 [Short Title Catalogue, No. 13582], f. 201). Courtesy Harvard University Library.

TWO LATIN COMEDIES BY JOHN FOXE THE MARTYROLOGIST

Titus et Gesippus

Christus Triumphans

EDITED WITH INTRODUCTION,
TRANSLATION, AND NOTES BY

JOHN HAZEL SMITH

PUBLISHED IN ASSOCIATION WITH
THE RENAISSANCE SOCIETY OF AMERICA BY

CORNELL UNIVERSITY PRESS

ITHACA AND LONDON

120993

First published 1973 by Cornell University Press.
Published in the United Kingdom by Cornell University Press Ltd., 2-4 Brook Street, London W1Y 1AA.

International Standard Book Number 0-8014-0730-3
Library of Congress Catalog Card Number 72-3950

Composition by St. Catherine Press, Ltd.

Printed in the United States of America

Librarians: Library of Congress cataloging information appears on the last page of the book.

For Mary Jean

Contents

Illustrations

Acknowledgments

This work was begun under a fellowship from the John Guggenheim Memorial Foundation and was completed under a grant from the American Council of Learned Societies. Brandeis University also provided significant financial support for preparation of the manuscript. The British Museum kindly permitted the use and the reproduction of its manuscript materials. To each of these institutions I express my profound gratitude.

Among the individuals who have aided my work I must single out Samuel Schoenbaum, who brought the manuscript of *Titus et Gesippus* to my attention; Douglas J. Stewart, who translated Laurence Humphrey's Greek poem in the front matter of *Christus Triumphans* and who tolerated my constant questions with a patience and wisdom which would do credit to the Greeks; David S. Wiesen, who read every word of my translations and who saved me from many errors; J. V. Cunningham, who offered helpful criticism on a portion of the work; and George B. Parks, whose efforts and counsel were crucial to the publication of this volume.

J. H. S.

Newton Lower Falls, Massachusetts

TWO LATIN COMEDIES BY
JOHN FOXE THE MARTYROLOGIST

Introduction

The Biographical Environment of *Titus et Gesippus*

In the summer of 1545, when he was about twenty-eight, John Foxe resigned the fellowship which he had held for seven years in Magdalen College, Oxford. Many biographies, including the earliest, which purports to be by a son of Foxe,[1] have contended that Foxe was forced to resign, though the official register states that he (and five others) resigned willingly for sufficient cause.[2] There is no question that Foxe felt pressure of some sort, from his colleagues if not from his superiors, for among his papers is the draft of an appeal to the President of Magdalen, Owen Oglethorpe, against some anonymous detractors. They had accused him of such improprieties as missing Mass in order to read books, and laughing during services—indeed, all of the charges apparently were concerned with Foxe's religious practices. Some charges Foxe admits, usually offering extenuations; some he denies. But fundamentally he feels that he is being unfairly persecuted:

My life has many flaws and several vices which deserve, not only an overseer, but also a castigator. But it is one thing to castigate a life and

---

[1] It survives in manuscript in British Museum Lansdowne MS. 388, ff. 2-51v; its Latin text was edited, with an English translation (slightly modified in places), in the Introduction to *The Second Volume of the Ecclesiasticall History: Containing the Acts and Monuments of Martyrs* (London, 1641). Traditionally thought to be by Samuel Foxe, but widely distrusted as spurious since the nineteenth century, the Life has been plausibly defended as the work of John Foxe's other son, Simeon, by J. F. Mozley, *John Foxe and His Book* (London, 1940), pp. 1-11.

[2] See *Dictionary of National Biography*. Mozley (p. 25), however, interpreted this (following Anthony à Wood) as indicating a resignation to avoid expulsion. My brief memoir of Foxe's life depends largely on these two sources and on the manuscript letters in Lansdowne MS. 388.

I

another to hunt for crimes. If pious men do it out of love, I certainly applaud their pious and honest motives. But why so anxiously, I wonder, why so curiously do they pry into my life? or why into my life alone and not also into others'? Is it because others do not have faults, or because these people love only me? Far from it. Rather it's because they do not hate others, do not wish to harm them. For they do wish to harm me, not to do me a kindness.

As Foxe sees it, their motive is that they suspect him of following a "certain new religion," because he is an avid reader of scriptures (*sacris literis*). But he emphatically denies their suspicion: "One faith, one truth, one Jesus Christ, one salvation of the whole world: I neither belong to nor follow any other sect."[3] We may doubt the ingenuousness of this statement, of course; in admitting, for instance, that he sometimes missed formal services, he asserts that, like St. Basil, he was reading as a form of prayer—"and here I would argue with them about the true mode of praying."[4]

Whether there is any direct connection between the circumstances described in this appeal and Foxe's departure from Magdalen cannot be determined. But the church of Henry VIII in 1545 was substantially the same as the Roman church had been in 1525, except for its head, and Foxe was antipathetic to that church throughout his life. Whether Foxe was forced out or not, then, we may well

---

[3] Lansdowne MS. 388, f. 56r-v: "Habet vita mea, confiteor, flagitia multa vitiaque plurima, quae non modo observatorem sed et castigatorem desiderant: verum aliud est castigare vitam, aliud venari crimina. Quod si zelo faciant pii homines, pios profecto praetextus et honestos laudo. Sed quaeso, cur tam anxie, cur tam curiose in vitam inquirunt meam? aut cur solum in meam, in aliorum non item? An quia caeteri non habent crimina, aut me solum isti diligant? Minime. Sed quia caeteros non oderunt, non uolunt laedere. Mihi quia fauere nolunt, volunt laedere. ... quia me suspicantur nouae cujusdam religionis esse. ... Quid ergo? Quia frequentiorem me in sacris literis uident. ... Vnna [*sic*] fides, vna ueritas, vnus Iesus Christus, vna salus totius mundi: aliam ego factionem nec sector nec affecto." This and other Foxe letters are somewhat inaccurately printed in Josiah Pratt, "Life of the Martyrologist," *The Church Historians of England: Reformation Period: The Life and Defence of John Foxe*, I, Pt. 1 (London, 1870), Appendix XVIII, pp. 56]-[65.

[4] Lansdowne MS. 388, ff. 53v-54: "Sed dicitis missarum tempore me libris incumbere: si arguitis omnino, nego; si interdum, fateor; sed sacris tamen, quorum ego lectionem precationi, ne uacillet animus, intermisceo; quemadmodum et Basilius ille magnus consueuit: ibique de uero precandi modo cum illis contenderem." The old Life of Foxe claims that Foxe had already undergone conversion, but concealed it out of fear of the Six Articles.

believe that many in the College were happy to have him go. Presumably President Oglethorpe was among them, for he was an ecclesiastical conservative: later Oglethorpe was preferred to a bishopric under Queen Mary; still later, though he crowned Queen Elizabeth (when senior bishops made themselves unavailable), he regretted the act throughout his life.[5] Apparently Foxe was not himself unhappy at going, for, though he later maintained a warm interest in the College, in the letters of 1545 he calls Oxford a prison (*Collegiorum haec ergastula*) and a cloister (*haec Collegiorum coenobia*) and, in describing his disaffection to a friend, is reduced to clichés: "All things that glitter are not gems; you don't know how the shoe pinches me here."[6]

The specific reason which Foxe gives for leaving is that to retain his followship he must, under the statutes of the College, enter holy orders by Michaelmas, 1545. Some have claimed that the rule was not always insisted on in other cases,[7] and that may be so, but Foxe's references to the rule do not allege discrimination. In rejecting the "priestly business" (*presbiteralem*),[8] he uses language far more personal, more overtly sexual. To one Dr. Hensey of Exeter he explains, "Under a statute of our College, I may not stay here beyond Michaelmas unless—unless I would castrate myself and plunge into the priestly sort";[9] and he tells a friend named Hedley, "Michaelmas is drawing near, and you know the force of our statute; and I am not of a mind to be circumcised this year."[10] How much of his hostility to the priesthood was personal and how much ideological I do not know, but the combination, in his images, of being emasculated and of undergoing a non-Christian rite suggests that both factors were in his mind. It is interesting, therefore, to find him telling Hensey in a later letter that he would accept a "priestly and shaven crown if either you were the bishop who could

[5] See *D. N. B.*
[6] Lansdowne MS. 388, f. 117.
[7] See Mozley, pp. 24-25.
[8] Lansdowne MS. 388, f. 82.
[9] Lansdowne MS. 388, f. 80v: "Neque enim hic ultra Michaelis statuto collegii nostri commorari licebit, nisi, nisi in sacerdotale genus memet castrari ac praecipitare velim."
[10] Lansdowne MS. 388, f. 117: "Michaelis iam festum appetit, et nosti statuti nostri decretum, neque libet mihi hoc anno circumcidi."

give it to me or I were so tolerant of cold that I thought I could get one by such a great loss of hair." But we should not take this too seriously, for Foxe admits that he is joking, with a pun on the crown (money) which Hensey has sent him.[11]

Once Foxe had made up his mind, after what he claimed was a careful weighing of the pros and cons,[12] he wrote to a number of acquaintances asking them for help in finding a job. The letters to Hensey and Hedley were a part of that correspondence; drafts of letters also survive addressed to (John?) Tindall, to John Cheke, and to one Richard Benetus.[13] Apparently there were other letters which have not survived, for Foxe tells Tindall that Hugh Latimer has asked him to stay with him for a few months;[14] Foxe has turned down this opportunity because he is intent on getting a teaching position in a school or (as he says in other letters) as a tutor: remuneration is not important ("by nature I am a great despiser of money and ambition"[15]), and if all else fails he will become a bishop of sheep.[16]

Apparently Foxe had less than overwhelming success with his applications. As we can judge from Foxe's later replies, Hensey sent him a crown (five shillings) along with the news that Exeter (whether the Oxford College or the School in Devon is not clear, though Foxe uses the term *scholae*) had just hired a teacher and that Hensey's personal circumstances did not permit him to take another mouth into his family as a tutor;[17] and Hedley sent him advice,

[11] Lansdowne MS. 388, f. 82: "Scholasticorum auiditatem vt non defendo, ita nec coronam recuso tuam (vir liberal[issime]); quam neque ita rursus affecto sordide vt non multo tamen libentius presbiteralem illam rasamque quam tu appellas sim recepturus, si aut tu episcopus esses qui posses mittere, aut ego tam frigoris patiens ut tanta pilorum jactura mihi accersendum arbitrarer (patere vicissim jocari tecum)."

[12] Lansdowne MS. 388, f. 117.

[13] Lansdowne MS. 388, ff. 119r-v, 111 and 118, and 83v. The reading *Benetus* is doubtful, but seems much more likely than "Beritius" (i.e., Richard Bertie), the reading of Pratt (p. [63]). I follow Mozley (p. 18), who also suggests *Benitius*.

[14] Lansdowne MS. 388, f. 119v. The whereabouts of Latimer, who had earlier resigned as Bishop of Worcester, are unknown at this time (*D. N. B.*).

[15] Lansdowne MS. 388, f. 80v: "Stipendium nullum capto, pecuniarum ac ambitionis semper natura contemptor maximus."

[16] Lansdowne MS. 388, f. 117: "Si scholae praefecturam nusquam contingat adipisci, equidem fiam alicubi Episcopus ouium."

[17] Lansdowne MS. 388, f. 82: "Scholae Exoniensi praefectum esse honestum

which Foxe firmly rejected, to reconsider his decision.[18] Foxe did get a job, though, as the tutor at Charlecote, Warwickshire, to the son of William Lucy—Thomas Lucy, whose deer the young Will Shakespeare is alleged to have poached more than forty years later. In his letter to Tindall, Foxe describes a two-day visit to Charlecote, presumably to be interviewed, and he rhapsodizes about the people there:

I do not so much approve of as marvel at the character and manners of the man [William Lucy]: I never in my life saw a man more splendid and golden. And the household is altogether like its head, so pleasing that I long for one just like it. In sum, there is nothing which is not up to the taste and sentiment of my spirit.

In the event, Foxe found further reason for happiness at Charlecote, for he met Agnes Randall there and married her in 1547. But the physical environment seems to have been another matter, as Foxe describes it in the same letter:

You know the house is totally isolated, almost completely shut off by mountains from the light of day and the traffic of men. Besides, it has a bordering stream, but its waters are almost always stagnant—except that once a year it washes the house itself as the Nile does Egypt. Finally, Faulkner [presumably Foxe's predecessor] has a little room which smells so unsavory, not of a goatish armpit but of the privy, that whoever lives there should have his nose cut off.[19]

In any case, Foxe did not stay at Charlecote long. By the summer of 1547 he was in London, according to the old biography a fugitive because of his Protestant views. There he almost perished until a

---

virum gaudeo. ... De familia quod scribis facile accipio excusationem tuam, agnosco enim temporum horum tempestates et angustias."

[18] Lansdowne MS. 388, f. 117.

[19] Lansdowne MS. 388, f. 119r-v: ". . . hominis ingenium ac mores non tam probo quam admiror, quo numquam in vita quicquam vidi magis candidum ac magis aureum. Nec minus illa placet capiti suo respondens per omnia familia, talis qualem optare queam, denique nihil non ad votum atque sententiam animi mei faciens. Sed nosti domum illius situm quam vndique deserta, montibus lucisque ab omni pene luce hominumque confluxu interclusa. Deinde vicinum habet amnem quidem, sed vndis perpetuo ferme stagnantibus, nisi quod singulis annis semel domum ipsam perluit, ut Nilus Aegiptum. Postremo habet Fauknerus cubiculum quod non hircum sed cloacam olet tam insuaviter, ut opus sit exectis naribus quisquis ibi habitare velit."

dramatic event occurred in St. Paul's. As the impoverished Foxe, now about thirty years old, sat there, "spent vvith long fasting, his countenance thinne, and eyes hollovv, after the gastfull manner of dying men; every one shunning a spectacle of so much horror," suddenly a stranger thrust money into his hand and assured him that within a few days his lot would change for the better. It did. Within three days, Foxe was summoned to live in the home of Mary Fitzroy, Duchess of Richmond, where he found a sympathetic environment and friends such as John Bale. He became the tutor to the three eldest children of Henry Howard, Earl of Surrey, who had been executed in 1547, and after a time moved to Reigate Castle with them. Meanwhile, Henry VIII had died, and the crowning of Edward VI brought new hope for religious dissenters like Foxe. In 1550, Foxe was ordained a deacon by Nicholas Ridley, Bishop of London. But by this time political rivalries had dimmed the hopes of all of Edward's subjects, including Foxe. When Queen Mary ascended the throne in 1553, she was welcomed by most Englishmen irrespective of her Catholicism, but the new realm very soon affected Foxe adversely. Among the political prisoners released immediately were Stephen Gardiner, Bishop of Winchester and scourge of reformers, who was made lord chancellor, and the Duke of Norfolk, grandfather of the Howard children who were Foxe's charges. By September, Foxe had lost his position; by the spring (probably) of 1554 he had joined the Marian exiles on the Continent.

Titus et Gesippus

When Foxe made the decision in 1545 which ultimately led him along this path, and when he was writing those letters of application, he attempted to demonstrate his qualifications for a teaching position by sending to his correspondents samples of his writing. This was a common practice. For instance, Nicholas Grimald in 1547, applying for a position at Christ Church, Oxford, sent a copy of his *Archipropheta* to Richard Cox, the dean of the College.[20] Foxe was wont to send such gifts on other occasions as well, if we may judge

---

[20] F. S. Boas, *University Drama in the Tudor Age* (Oxford, 1914), p. 34.

from his surviving letters, and he once or twice cited Seneca's counsel that it is less important for a gift to be good than for it to be appropriate to its recipient.[21] To Cheke he sent something theological, to Benetus he promised to send (apparently) an inspirational tract and a comedy, and to Hedley and Hensey he sent *Titus et Gesippus*. Why he thought it an appropriate gift for them I do not know, for I have not identified them beyond the meager information which Foxe gives about them: Hensey, the intended dedicatee, is at Exeter; Hedley, a recent grandfather, knows about the Magdalen statutes.[22]

In any case, Foxe's references to the play permit us to date it with some precision. To Hedley he wrote, "I took this comedy of Titus and Gesippus into hand and completed it this autumn; indeed, I devoted scarcely more than two months to it. But I still have it under hand and will give it a second polishing. God willing, I intend to give it to Dr. Hensey."[23] And to Hensey he sent "a little comic gift, such as it is, of a poem. I wrote the comedy this autumn, and I'll call it back now for a second polishing during this Lent. God willing, I mean it to be dedicated to you."[24] Clearly, then, Foxe wrote the play in the autumn of 1544 and intended to revise it before April of 1545 (Easter fell on April 5 that year).

The letters quoted are drafts which Foxe kept and took away from Oxford with him. They passed to his heirs and eventually came into the possession of John Strype, the church historian, who planned to write a life of Foxe.[25] The manuscript of *Titus et Gesippus*, preserved in the same volume, has the same provenance. It too is a

---

[21] Lansdowne MS. 388, ff. 81v, 82v.

[22] Josiah Pratt (VIII, 599) mentioned a Richard Hedley who in 1556 was accused in St. Peter's parish of being "a seller of heretical books." Whether this might be Foxe's Hedley I have not determined.

[23] Lansdowne MS. 388, f. 120: "Comoediam illam de Tito et Gesippo hoc autumno in manus coepimus et perfecimus. Huic vix plus profecto duobus mensibus dedimus. Verum adhuc sub manum secundam limam subituram premimus eamque Doctori Henseo, si Deus volet, destinauimus."

[24] Lansdowne MS. 388, f. 80v: ". . . ne omnino vacuus literarum ad te veniret, oblata ista occasiuncula perfunctorie saltem te salutare ac comicum hoc interim qualecunque carminis donusculum missitare libuit. Comoediam autumno hoc a nobis conscriptam, ad secundam nunc limam hac quadragesima reuocabimus, tibique, Deo annuente, destinabimus."

[25] See *D. N. B.*, s.v. "Foxe."

draft, and it is heavily revised. Conceivably there were earlier drafts, for some pages are relatively clean; but the surviving text must be a very early draft, perhaps the very first, and I cannot believe that it represents the play as Foxe sent it to Dr. Hensey. For one thing, the revisions seem like the tinkerings of an author in the process of composing: very few of them materially alter the substance, and most of them seem like phraseological fussing. More significantly, though the play is complete, it is not really finished. Sometimes Foxe has rewritten a clause without troubling to integrate the new version into the sentence; and Foxe's prosody, deficient even in the best of circumstances, in this play often defies analysis. As it stands, then, it would scarcely be a persuasive demonstration of Foxe's competence to teach Latin. Probably the best evidence of the earliness of this draft, however, is in the names of the characters. There is at times profound confusion in those names: *Titus* appears once or twice where we expect *Gesippus*; Titus is once called Pamphilus; Gesippus' mother is called Sostrata in one scene and Sophrona in the scene immediately following; and Stylpho and Crito are confused in Act III.[26] If indeed Foxe carried out his intention to revise the play, he presumably would have eliminated these flaws.

If the confusions of names argue against the surviving version's being the gift that Foxe sent, they are also, *a fortiori*, strong evidence that the surviving version was not acted. As likely as not, the play was first written as an academic exercise and was pulled out for refurbishing only when Foxe needed gifts in some numbers for his correspondents. On the other hand, such dramatic exercises were probably often (or even usually) performed. In his mind's eye, at least, Foxe evidently saw the play on the Magdalen boards, for he ended it with Phormio addressing the audience in a teasing fashion and regretting the insufficiency of the refreshments (*epulae*) to supply everyone: surviving records indicate that such *epulae* were standard after programs at Magdalen.[27] I should not be surprised to learn that a revised version of *Titus et Gesippus* was acted at Magdalen

[26] See the Textual Notes.

[27] R. E. Alton, ed., "The Academic Drama in Oxford: Extracts from the Records of Four Colleges," *Collections* V, Malone Society Reprints (Oxford, 1959 [1960]), entries for 1551-52, 1552-53, 1553-54.

sometime in 1545. Although early records of dramatic productions there have been lost, F. S. Boas has stated that Magdalen was "one of the greatest centres of academic acting."[28]

Whether acted or not, the writing of *Titus et Gesippus* at Oxford in 1544-1545 is noteworthy, for this is a romantic comedy with important Terentian additions. It is thus an epitome of English Renaissance comedy, but quite an early specimen. The immediate source was English, but the play is only one step removed from the wellspring of all the sixteenth-century versions of the Titus-Gesippus story, the eighth tale of the tenth day of Boccaccio's *Decamerone*. We may be forced, then, to modify Boas' statement that the "first University play with a plot of undoubted Italian origin" was *Hymenaeus* in 1579.[29] Mary A. Scott counted thirty-three Elizabethan plays with Boccaccian plots,[30] but those plays were written considerably later than *Titus et Gesippus*; as F. P. Wilson wrote, "England did not become Italianate until Elizabeth's reign was well under way,"[31] but *Titus et Gesippus* was written while Henry VIII sat on the throne. To be sure, we now have considerable evidence of romantic plays earlier than had once been suspected. A version of *Gl'Ingannati*, for instance, was performed at Cambridge in 1546-7 (F. P. Wilson called that "astonishingly early"[32]); long ago, John Bale reported a play by Ralph Radcliffe on the friendship of Titus and Gesippus written between 1547 and 1553,[33] and L. J. Mills speculated on even earlier dramatic versions of the story.[34] Besides, our traditional distinction between classical and romantic is an oversimplification. Terence's plays are not without romantic interest, however the term be defined; and when the very type of classical stoicism, Cato the younger, reputedly gave up his wife Marcia so that his friend Hortensius might marry her, his act was not so remote in spirit from that of Gesippus in our play. Elyot told the Titus-Gesippus story in the same section of *The Governor* in which he told

[28] Boas, p. 385.

[29] *Ibid.*, pp. 134-135.

[30] *Elizabethan Translations from the Italian* (Boston, 1916), p. 93.

[31] *The English Drama 1485-1585*, ed. G. K. Hunter (Oxford, 1969), p. 113.

[32] *Ibid.*, p. 114.

[33] See below, n. 46.

[34] See below, p. 13. Cf. C. R. Baskervill, "Some Evidence for Early Romantic Plays in England," *MP*, XIV (1916), 229-251, 467-512.

the stories of such "classical" friends as Orestes and Pylades, and Damon and Pythias, and within a few years after Foxe's play was written the Boccaccian pair was included without apology in numerous formulaic lists of prototypical friends.[35] Still, these facts merely qualify, they do not destroy, the correctness of our belief that romantic comedy in England is largely to be associated with the period after 1560. Perhaps we should not feel astonishment, but we are entitled to be surprised, that in 1544 Oxford produced a play merging Boccaccian and Terentian matter. Perhaps, too, we shall have to modify Boas' conclusion that Cambridge was more interested in comedy than Oxford was: "In comedy," he said, "Tudor Oxford has left nothing of first-rate interest."[36] When Oxford comedy was represented by the likes of Nicholas Grimald's *Archipropheta* and *Christus Redivivus*—and when the Oxonian John Foxe's only known dramatic work was another *comoedia sacra*, *Christus Triumphans*—that was perhaps a fair conclusion. But I suspect that our conclusions have been based upon far less than a representative sample of what was actually produced, at Oxford and elsewhere, and that any general conclusion is therefore suspect.

Perhaps as surprising as anything else about this romantic comedy is that it was written by John Foxe the martyrologist. Although very few people today have read the entire Book of Martyrs, everyone recognizes it as a work which can be called comic only in some specialized sense, if at all, and Foxe is so completely identified with that work that his name is seldom mentioned without the distinctive title "martyrologist." Few other men are so thoroughly identified with a genre in which they wrote.

None of Foxe's previously known works could be called imaginative literature; for instance, his pieces published before his exile in 1554 include translations from the German of sermons by Luther and Oecolampadius and of a tract on Christian faith by Urbanus Regius, an original tract opposing the death penalty, and a few

---

[35] Laurens J. Mills, *One Soul in Bodies Twain* (Bloomington, Indiana, 1937), pp. 112-113, 402.

[36] Boas, p. 347. He did note, however, the fact that some number of Oxford comedies have been lost; significant among these are Nicholas Grimald's *Troilus* (before 1557), and Richard Edwardes' *Palamon and Arcyte* (1564), both in English, both based on Chaucer, and both presumably romantic. The latter, of course, dealt with a theme of love and friendship.

other controversialist pieces. Some years after writing *Titus et Gesippus*, Foxe himself described his writing as "literary labours on behalf of the Christian republic."[37] Even his one previously known comedy, *Christus Triumphans*, is not so recognizably comic by later standards, or so different in spirit from the Book of Martyrs, that anyone would have thought of Foxe as a comedian. So pervasive is Foxe's reputation as a religious controversialist that the only two scholars I know of who have referred to *Titus et Gesippus* both assumed that it belonged to the same class of comedy as *Christus Triumphans*. Josiah Pratt, in his note to Foxe's letter, cited earlier, which names the play, stated where the "said Comedy, or rather Sacred Drama," could be found;[38] and J. F. Mozley, also citing the location of the play, identified it as one of the "Latin plays on religious subjects" which Foxe wrote at Oxford.[39]

Though Pratt and Mozley must both have looked at the play, perhaps they may be forgiven their misjudgment. Like most other scholars who have worked on Foxe's papers, they were looking for biographical or historical information, not literary works. Perhaps, too, they were misled by several pages of the *Titus et Gesippus* manuscript which are headed by prayerful crosses and, in one instance, by the name *Jesus*. Even the old biography supposed to be by Foxe's son failed to distinguish more than one kind of comedy:

It should seem he designed the first over branchings of an early wit, to the exercises of Poetry, and wrote divers Latine Comedies. . . . But even then he began to give earnest of what he afterward proved, for that neither those first flourishes of his youth were spent, but in holy Histories of the Bible: nor followed he that vein long.[40]

Besides the two plays which survive, moreover, Foxe's letter to Benetus, cited earlier, refers to the "argument of a comedy" which

[37] Mozley, p. 50, translating a letter from Foxe to Oporinus in British Museum Harleian MS. 417, f. 98.
[38] Pratt, p. 64].
[39] Mozley, p. 20.
[40] *The Second Volume of the Ecclesiasticall History* (London, 1641), sig. A4. The original Latin is in Lansdowne MS. 388, f. 5v. The manuscript said that some comedies were extant (*Extant Comoediae*); the 1641 translation contradicted this by speaking of "divers Latine Comedies yet to be seen."

he has extracted from "Solomon's Ecclesiastes"[41] unless this is a reference to *Titus et Gesippus*, the subject of the comedy must have been religious. Conceivably Foxe might have taken some such verse as Ecclesiastes 11.1 ("Cast thy bread upon the running waters, for after a long time thou shalt find it again") as the "argument" of *Titus et Gesippus*, but the possibility seems remote. Among the other "exercises of Poetry" found in Foxe's unpublished papers are one or two attempts at religious nondramatic poetry,[42] and the printed edition of *Christus Triumphans* includes a prefatory religious poem by Foxe.[43]

There is, however, another ingredient in Foxe's critical temper —seen, for instance, in the occasional witticisms in his correspondence and in an unpublished poem, written about the same time as *Titus et Gesippus*, which laughs epigrammatically at the discomfiture of a Magdalen master, John Harley, whose cloak was stolen while he was out walking one day at dawn. Though the calamities of the age and the hardships of his own life perhaps impelled Foxe to write mostly serious and controversialist pieces, there was a comedian Foxe. Yet we do not really need to seek a wholly different temper to understand the existence of *Titus et Gesippus*. It is not a play of which a man with Foxe's moral proclivities would need to feel ashamed, for it is informed with ethical principles which were perfectly orthodox in the Renaissance. Unlike *Christus Triumphans*, it does not have a prologue, but, if it did, Foxe might very well have included a statement of the Horatian principle echoed by the prologue of the later play: "Placere actores omnibus; / Prodesse poeta, nocere studet nemini" (ll. 33-34). In Boccaccio, the tale fulfills the requirement of the tenth day for stories about generosity in love, and after telling the story Fiammetta comments on its theme of sacred friendship; we hear, moreover, that a common social game in Italy was to debate whether Titus or Gesippus (to use Foxe's forms of their names) had shown the greater generosity.[44]

[41] Lansdowne MS. 388, f. 83v: "Spero me habere ex Solomonis Ecclesiaste argumentum Comoediae nec invtile nec inamaenum, quod simulatque lambendo paululum conformabimus tibi perpoliendum atque absoluendum committemus."

[42] Lansdowne MS. 388, ff. 78-79v.

[43] See below, pp. 222-225.

[44] Louis Sorieri, *Boccaccio's Story of* Tito e Gisippo *in European Literature* (New York, 1937), pp. 75-76.

And Sir Thomas Elyot's version is frankly told as a "goodly example" to "minister to the readers singular pleasure and also incredible comfort to practise amity."[45] No doubt Foxe (or perhaps his mentor at Oxford) chose the story for the same reason and, having written his version, Foxe then used it to demonstrate his competence as a teacher of the young.

Foxe was not the only playwright to be attracted to the story, but his is the earliest play discovered so far that treats Titus and Gesippus by those names. Jacopo Nardi's *Comedia de Amicitia* (c. 1510), in Italian rimed verse, is based on the Boccaccian tale (and is the earliest dramatization of it which is known), but Nardi changed all the names. Within a few years after Foxe there were several Titus-Gesippus plays. In England, Ralph Radcliffe wrote a *De Titi et Gesippi Firmissima Amicitia* (c. 1547-1553) for his boys at Hitchen School, and in 1577 the Children of Paul's performed a *Titus et Gesippus* at Whitehall; both of these plays (if they are two) are lost.[46] In Germany we find plays on the subject by Hans Sachs (1546), Leonhard Schwartzenbach (1551), and Martin Montanus (after 1557); both Sachs (in 1531) and Montanus (in 1557) had also narrated the story in nondramatic versions. As I have noted, L. J. Mills postulated "several" early friendship plays, and in particular felt that Elyot's version in *The Governor* was probably based on a play.[47] Such speculation cannot be confirmed or denied with our present evidence, but at least one early play on the theme is now known to exist, and it would not be surprising to find others earlier than Foxe's, by men attracted as Foxe no doubt was by the combination of romance and ethical lesson.

For the simple fact is that the combination of romance and moral lesson in the Titus-Gesippus story made it throughout Europe one

[45] *The Book Named the Governor*, ed. S. E. Lehmberg (New York, 1962), p. 136. My later quotations from Elyot are from this edition.

[46] The former was listed by John Bale, *Scriptorum . . . Catalogus* (Basel, 1557-1559), p. 700; see Herbert G. Wright, *Early English Versions of the Tales of Guiscardo and Ghismonda and Titus and Gisippus from the Decameron*, Early English Text Society, Orig. Ser. No. 205 (London, 1937), cii. For the latter see E. K. Chambers, *The Elizabethan Stage*, IV (Oxford, 1923), 93. The 1577 production was a masque. The possibility is remote that it was a revival of Radcliffe's play, and even more remote that it could have been Foxe's.

[47] Mills, pp. 102, 146.

of the most popular stories in the sixteenth century: as Herbert G. Wright said, "Few stories can have been better known."[48] When Foxe was writing in 1544, the *Decamerone* had not been translated into English (the first such translation appeared in 1620), but it was available in numerous printings in Italian or in translations into German and French (the latter was published in 1544). The Titus-Gesippus story had been plucked out for several Continental tellings: in Latin, by Filippo Beroaldo (1491) and by Matteo Bandello (1509); in French, by Nicholas de Troyes (1536) and by Bertrand de la Borderie (1544); and in German, by Hans Sachs (1531), by Sebastian Frank (1531), and by Christoph Bruno (1541). In English, there were William Walter's verse translation of Beroaldo, published by Wynkyn de Worde under the title *History of Tytus & Gesyppus* (n.d.), and Sir Thomas Elyot's *The Governor*, 11.12 (1531).[49]

Foxe used Elyot's exemplum as his principal, and probably his only, source. In a number of ways Elyot had altered the story so that his version is fundamentally different from all other known versions: in consequence, we cannot be certain about Elyot's source, though no one except perhaps Mills has radically disputed Wolff's conclusion that Elyot used Boccaccio or Beroaldo or both.[50] In any case, for our present purposes we may conveniently classify the versions available to Foxe into two types: Elyot's and (essentially including all others) Boccaccio's. Foxe did not follow Elyot in all details, including one or two very important ones; in a few places we find parallels between Foxe and Boccaccio; in many more places we see unprecedented innovations in Foxe. Yet the number and

[48] Wright, p. ci.

[49] See Johannes Bolte, ed., Martin Montanus' *Schwankbücher* (*1557-1566*), Bibliothek des Litterarischen Vereins in Stuttgart, CCXVII (Tübingen, 1899), 580-581; Sorieri, *passim*; Scott, pp. 96, 226-227; Wright, pp. lxxvii-cvi; Domenico Maria Manni, *Istoria del Decamerone di Giovanni Boccaccio* (Florence, 1742), pp. 561-600. Cf. my "Sempronia, John Lyly, and John Foxe's Comedy of *Titus and Gesippus*," *PQ*, XLVIII (1969), 554-561.

[50] S. L. Wolff, "A Source of *Euphues. The Anatomy of Wyt*," *MP*, VII (1910), 577-585. Clement T. Goode thought that Elyot had used, in addition, Petrus Alphonsus' *Disciplina Clericalis* ("Sir Thomas Elyot's *Titus and Gysippus*," *MLN*, XXXVII [1922], 8), but Mills (p. 100), while acknowledging that Elyot could not simply have translated either Boccaccio or Beroaldo, disagreed with Goode. Cf. S. E. Lehmberg, *Sir Thomas Elyot Tudor Humanist* (Austin, 1960), p. 68 n., and John M. Major, *Sir Thomas Elyot and Renaissance Humanism* (Lincoln, Nebraska, 1964), pp. 256-258.

quality of the parallels between Foxe and Elyot, as shown in the accompanying chart, make it virtually certain that Foxe knew Elyot.

Correspondences between		Corresponding Details in
Elyot	*Foxe*	*Boccaccio*
Titus' father, Fulvius, is a Roman Senator.	Titus' father (unnamed) is apparently a Roman Consul. (Foxe added a second consul, named Fulvius.)	Tito's father, Publio Quinto Fulvio, is only a Roman gentleman.
Gisippus' father is named Chremes.	Gesippus' father is named Chremes. (Only in Foxe is he still alive at the time of the deception.)	Gisippo's father is named Chremete.
Titus and Gisippus cannot be distinguished: they are alike in "years, . . . stature, proportion of body, favour, and colour of visage, countenance and speech."	Titus and Gesippus cannot be distinguished: they are alike in age, height, complexion—in everything except clothing.	Tito and Gisippo are not said to look identical (the bride is deceived, apparently repeatedly, by an exchange in a darkened bedroom).
Gisippus does not hesitate to give up his bride.	Gesippus does not hesitate to give up his bride.	Gisippo gives up his bride only reluctantly.
A dowry and a wedding feast are referred to.	A dowry and a wedding feast are planned.	Neither a dowry nor a wedding feast is mentioned.
On the wedding day, Gisippus goes to the bride's house (to complete arrangements), but Titus goes through both the public ceremony and the bedroom ritual.	On the wedding day, Gesippus goes to the bride's house (to hurry her along), but Titus goes through both the public ceremony and the bedroom ritual.	Gisippo goes through the wedding ceremony, and Tito is substituted for the bedroom ritual. No one goes to the bride's house on the wedding day.
Titus is called home (by friends in the Senate) and offered "advancement to the highest dignities."	Titus is called home to succeed his father as consul.	Tito is called home to look after his private affairs.
Titus leaves Athens very soon after the wedding night.	Titus leaves Athens very soon after the wedding night.	Tito remains in Athens for some time after the wedding night.
In Rome, the exiled Gisippus sees both Titus and his bride come from Titus' house.	In Rome, the exiled Gesippus sees both Titus and his bride come from Titus' house.	In Rome, the exiled Gisippo sees Tito alone returning from the forum.
Gisippus considers stabbing himself.	Gesippus considers stabbing himself.	Gisippo does not consider stabbing himself.
As Gisippus sleeps, a single thief robs and murders a citizen in some other location.	As Gesippus sleeps, a single thief robs and (almost) murders a citizen in some other location.	As Gisippo watches, two thieves fall out and one kills the other.

The murderer plants physical evidence on Gisippus (bloodying his knife).	The assailant plants physical evidence on Gesippus (exchanging knives with him).	The only physical evidence is the body, near Gisippo.
When arrested, Gisippus denies nothing, desiring to to be thought guilty.	When arrested, Gesippus denies nothing and speaks ambiguously; he is taken to have confessed.	Gisippo allows himself to be arrested and then falsely confesses.
Titus, a consul ("or in other like dignity") is present officially when Gisippus is arraigned before the Senate.	Titus, a consul, is one of the judges before whom Gesippus is arraigned. (During the trial, the Senate is consulted.)	Tito, a private citizen, happens by when Gisippo is being sentenced by the praetor, Varro.
Titus does not recognize Gisippus until a pregnant look during an answer brings recognition.	Titus does not recognize Gesippus until Gesippus' refusal to answer him arouses his suspicion. (Titus is not sure until later.)	Tito recognizes Gisippo immediately at the trial.
After the villain confesses, he is freed when Titus appeals to the Senate for him.	After the villain confesses, he is freed (and becomes Titus' servant) when Gesippus and Titus plead to Fulvius for him.	After the murderer confesses, he is freed by the emperor; Tito and Gisippo do not plead for him.

The list of parallels between Foxe and Boccaccio is much briefer, though one or two parallels involve very important elements.

Corresponding Details in	Correspondences between	
Elyot	*Foxe*	*Boccaccio*
The bride's father is not mentioned. (Other Athenians become angry when Titus and Gisippus tell them of the deception.)	The bride's father (Simo) becomes angry when he hears of the deception (from a servant who sees Titus leave).	The bride's father (unnamed) becomes angry when he hears of the deception (from the angry bride).
There is no mention of the bride's ever being told of the substitution.	We do not know when the bride learns of the substitution, but in Rome she discusses it with Titus. (She is not angry.)	The bride is told of the substitution when Tito must return to Rome. (She becomes angry and tells her father.)
Titus and Gisippus lead an army to Athens and destroy Gisippus' enemies. The possibility of Gisippus' marrying another girl is never mentioned.	Though invited home (and in the Argument described as going home), Gesippus apparently stays in Rome, enriched by Titus, and marries Fulvius' daughter Pamphila (Titus' former sweetheart, in whom Gesippus had expressed interest even as he was about to marry Sempronia).	Gisippo stays in Rome (in Tito's house), enriched by Tito, and marries Tito's sister, Fulvia. (Gisippo had earlier told Tito that he could find another girl.)

On this evidence I see no reason to believe that Foxe knew any Boccaccian version. Although he was an avid reader, his reading, from what we know of it, was not in works like the *Decamerone*; Terence, whom he had certainly read, was a school text, and Boccaccio was not. The departures from Elyot are best explained as Foxe's inventions which happen to coincide with Boccaccio. For one thing, they are like Boccaccio only in a general way; in each case the specific details are different. We can see, moreover, why a man treating the story dramatically would alter Elyot's nondramatic exemplum in precisely these ways. The introduction of the bride's father, Simo, for instance, like the inclusion of Chremes (who dies in all other versions), permits Foxe to show us some Terentian fathers —men worried about their social and financial status, gleeful over their successes, peevish when thwarted by their juniors. Raising the question of the bride's response to the situation corrects a serious flaw in Elyot from a dramatic viewpoint, though in his treatise it would perhaps be irrelevant. The invention which is easiest of all to explain is the finding of a bride for Gesippus: comedies, after all, are supposed to end in marriage. Elyot elected to show the vindication of the true friend politically, for in his version (like Boccaccio's) politics is important: Gisippus is exiled from Athens by political enemies whose hand is strengthened by resentment of the Athenian's giving up his bride to a Roman. Foxe, however, eliminated all references to tension between Athens and Rome and included no political elements except one or two speeches by Fulvius about the need for a public figure to ignore private considerations: in the play, Gesippus must leave Athens because his father disowns him. The true friend must be vindicated, of course, but it is no denial of the virtues of friendship to have the friend succeed in love as well. Indeed, Foxe invented a situation to make Gesippus' love-interest ironically parallel that of Titus: Pamphila, whom Gesippus finally marries, is a former sweetheart of Titus whom Gesippus would have wooed long ago but for the hurt it would have caused his friend.

Probably the best argument for calling these departures from Elyot inventions rather than borrowings is the number of other variations that Foxe could not have found in any known source. Some are trivial, some crucial. Foxe's Gesippus, for instance, falls asleep in a public road (near Titus' house, apparently) rather than

in a barn (as in Elyot) or in a cave (as in Boccaccio); and his heroine
is called Sempronia rather than Sophronia. These alterations are
not so readily explained as some of the other inventions. The decision, for instance, to keep the victim of Martius' robbery alive is
what we would expect in a comedy—though we would hope for
a more artful revelation of his survival than Foxe achieves. The
omission of the political elements that are so important in Elyot
tightens up the play's unity. So do several other omissions, including
those of details preceding Gesippus' proposed wedding day: the
reasons for Titus' being in Athens, the length of his stay, Gesippus'
courtship of Sempronia, and the meeting of Titus and Sempronia.
A strict neoclassicist would presumably have striven for even tighter
unity by setting the whole action at Rome, thus avoiding the serious
disunity of time and place of which Foxe's play is guilty. From the
technical terms which Foxe uses in these plays we can be certain
that he had been exposed to critical works which discussed such
questions,[51] but he (and the presumed tutor for whom he may have
written this play) obviously did not believe that plays must observe
the minor unities. Interestingly, John Airy, the tutor of Foxe's
fellow Oxonian Nicholas Grimald, did not either: commenting on
Grimald's *Archipropheta*, he found classical precedents for violation
of the unity of time, and he expressed approval of the unity of place
solely on the grounds of theatrical convenience.[52] The minor unities,
in fact, did not become law until a generation later, with Castelvetro,
and Foxe did not concern himself with them. But he did begin *in
medias res* to avoid excessive diffuseness.

Some of Foxe's most significant alterations are in the characters.
He supplied names for several characters who are nameless in the
sources: Martius, the cutthroat; Cratinus, a member of the Roman
posse which arrests Gesippus; and Simo, father of the bride. And he
adds several new characters: Crito, who travels to Rome with a
message for Gesippus; Stylpho and his daughter Phrygia, who are
involved in a plan for a marriage with Gesippus; Trebatius, a
messenger from Rome; and a number of comic characters: Dromo,
Midas, Stephanio, and Pythias, all slaves; and Marsias and Misenus,

[51] See below, p. 40, and *Titus et Gesippus* 11.2.47. Cf. T. W. Baldwin, *Shakespere's
Five-Act Structure* (Urbana, 1947), pp. 355-356.
[52] Boas, p. 28.

musicians. Most of these names seem to have been chosen for some relevant association: Martius suggests Mars, the fighting god; Marsias, the piper, was presumably named for Marsyas, the satyr who challenged Apollo on the flute; the name of Misenus, another musician, recalls that of Aeneas' trumpeter, the son of Aeolus; and Trebatius, who performs the quasi-legal function of informing Titus of his father's death, may have been suggested by the name of a lawyer friend of Cicero. All the other names listed are Terentian: Stephanio looks after the kitchen in both *Adelphoi* and *Titus et Gesippus*; Simo is an old man in Foxe and in the *Andria*; Dromo and Syrus are slaves in Foxe and Terence; and Sophrona, the old mother in our play, is an old nurse in several Terentian plays.

The most important Terentian addition by Foxe was Phormio, who functions here as he does in Terence: there he is a scheming adventurer; here he is the clever slave who manipulates affairs on behalf of his master. For a time in *Titus et Gesippus*, Phormio is the dominant figure. Foxe clearly was aiming not only at making his play Terentian, but also at improving its effectiveness, and Phormio was his way around a dilemma inherent in his story.

If one accepts the orthodox Renaissance (and Platonic) view that friendship is a nobler relationship than heterosexual love, Gesippus' sacrifice of his bride almost at the altar is both noble and understandable; Elyot tried to emphasize this attitude by making Gisippus woo Sophronia in secret at first, as though his romantic interest were a betrayal of his friendship for Titus. But if one accepts the theory, Titus' longing for the girl like a medieval courtly lover is more than a social flaw: it is a gross violation of a most fundamental principle of morality. On the other hand, if one does not accept the theory, Gesippus' gesture, though noble, becomes psychologically incomprehensible. In the former case, one protagonist loses moral stature in a way which is difficult to overcome; in the latter, the other protagonist suffers even more serious loss of intellectual stature. To describe such a dilemma is not to deny the facts of the Renaissance philosophy, but to assert the conflict between humanist theory and human thought. Theoreticians from Bembo to Bacon exalted friendship over love, and imaginative works from *Damon and Pythias* to *Euphues* and *The Two Gentlemen of Verona* explicitly or implicitly endorsed the theory. But the authors of these works recognized practical difficulties in the philosophy and built their dramatic conflicts around those difficulties: Valentine, after all, does not sacrifice Sylvia to Proteus, and no one in the audience expects him to. In Lyly's *Endymion*, Eumenides finally accepts Geron's argument that "Love is but an eyeworm, which only tickleth the head with hopes and wishes; friendship the image of eternity, in which there is nothing movable, nothing mischievous." But before doing so he has to fight down his own natural desires: "The love of men to women is a thing common and of course; the friendship of man to man infinite and immortal," he says, and then recoils, "Tush! Semele doth possess my love." Claudio in *Much Ado About Nothing* puts the conflict more simply: "Friendship is common in all other things / Save in the office and affairs of love." Commenting on Elyot's version of the Titus-Gesippus story, L. J. Mills put this conflict into historical perspective: "For the first time in the sixteenth century the medieval emphasis on love and the classical doctrines of friendship came into dramatic conflict in English literature—but not the last."[53]

Foxe did not want to eliminate this conflict, and his philosophic bias is apparently orthodox. Yet he did want to make his characters' behavior credible, and the Titus-Gesippus story is one of the very few that call for the friend to sacrifice his love interest so completely. That Foxe was aware of a problem is shown by a soliloquy which he gives to Gesippus during the off-stage union of Titus and Sempronia (III.1): Gesippus expresses the orthodox theory, but only after he has voiced his fear that people will think him a stupid weakling for surrendering his bride. Judging from his father's reaction to the sacrifice, Gesippus' fear is well founded, but Foxe tried to keep the audience from such a reaction. Early in the play we see Gesippus impatiently hurrying along the wedding preparations: he is clearly eager to marry Sempronia, whose beauty he rapturously praises. But even before he knows of Titus' love for Sempronia, we also hear him confess that he has a strong interest in another girl, whom he would have carried off as Paris did Helen if she were not (as he thinks) Titus' sweetheart. This device cleverly maintains the nobility of Gesippus' sacrifice even as it makes that sacrifice more under-

[53] Mills, p. 103.

standable. Even more important in serving this end is Phormio. As
Phormio becomes the dominant figure for a time, and thus gives
the comedy a properly Terentian tone, he also assumes much of the
onus of guilt. He overhears Gesippus' confession of interest in
Pamphila, and it encourages his efforts on behalf of Titus. It is
Phormio who describes the deadly nature of Titus' disease, Phormio
who allows Gesippus to uncover its cause, Phormio who subtly
implants the idea of Gesippus' sacrifice, and Phormio who devises
the scheme to make it work.

The effect of Phormio's machinations on Titus is even more
marked. Titus does not have to confess to Gesippus the nature of his
illness (Gesippus' visit to his sick friend occurs offstage). More
importantly, Titus does not even know what Phormio is doing. In
the opening scene, Titus admits his problem to Phormio and asks
for help; but the help he specifies is for Phormio to kill him or to
arrange a postponement of Gesippus' wedding so that Titus can
leave town, and it is entirely Phormio's idea to promote the substitution while telling Titus that nothing can be done. The go-
between, who comically emphasizes the importance of his function
in a hyperbolic soliloquy (I.5.1 ff), thus assumes most of the moral
guilt that adheres to Titus in other versions. Not all of it, however,
for Foxe deliberately includes certain details that make Titus appear
insensitive: though Titus does not know that Gesippus is listening
to his exultation after the consummation of the union with the girl
whom Gesippus was to have married (II.2.1 ff), yet the juxtaposition
of this scene with Gesippus' unhappy soliloquy in II.1 adversely
affects Titus' impression on the audience. So does his precipitous
departure from Athens (II.5), which we hear about from Gesippus,
who is fearful of its consequences: Titus' departure, we realize from
Trebatius' news (II.3), is motivated by a desire to collect an
inheritance, and we sense the unfairness of fortune's workings. In
the end, Titus proves his worth as a friend, but before then he fails
one more time: his failure to recognize Gesippus is perhaps dramatically justified, since Gesippus is in rags and at first does not speak
(III.8) and since, at the trial, Titus is convinced that the man
before him has committed an act of which Gesippus is incapable;
yet Titus' instinctive coldness toward a less fortunate mortal (a
difference in fortune which is emphasized by Titus' rich appearance

and his materialistic conversation with Sempronia) seems a character flaw, and by contrast Phormio recognizes Gesippus the instant he sees him (IV.7).

By this time in the play, the protagonists have come to dominate the action. Phormio is still active in Rome, but nothing comes of most of his activity. He is sent to see Gesippus in prison and confirm Titus' fears about the Athenian's identity (IV.5), but the confirmation comes before Phormio returns when Crito arrives from Athens (IV.6). After Titus and Gesippus are both confined for the murder, Phormio runs to tell Sempronia what has happened (IV.7), but it is Martius' confession that resolves the difficulty. The one useful purpose which Phormio serves in Rome is to promote the wedding of Pamphila and Gesippus. In an effective scene (IV.4), Phormio finds Pamphila somewhat testily resentful of Titus for abandoning her and apparently of Gesippus for helping him to do so. But Phormio cleverly persuades her to entertain the idea of marrying Gesippus by noting his resemblance to Titus and by alluding to her as a spinster. Otherwise, Phormio's continuing presence in the play after the action moves to Rome is dramatically useless.

Though Phormio is not consistently useful, on the whole Foxe has improved his play by adding him. Foxe's general conception, moreover, and the broad structural outlines of his play are effective. But there are structural flaws. When Foxe first introduced the idea that Titus had once loved Pamphila, it prepared for Gesippus' sacrifice of Sempronia and, as we have seen, set up an ironic parallel to the Titus-Sempronia-Gesippus triangle. That parallel could not be carried on after Gesippus learned that Titus loved Sempronia rather than Pamphila, but at least the matter was brought to fruition in the final arrangement between Gesippus and Pamphila. The addition was a happy one, moreover, if only for the opportunity it gave to Foxe to create an impressive vignette of Pamphila. Not all of his additions worked out so neatly. Most glaring is the unresolved situation in Athens. There, Chremes and Simo become reconciled and actually arrange a new marriage for Gesippus, to Simo's niece Phrygia. Phrygia is brought onstage and Gesippus is sent for. But of course he does not come (though the Argument indicates that he will), for he finds a Roman bride; we do not learn

Chremes' response to this, and we may wonder why Foxe included Phrygia at all.

Foxe's handling of Sempronia also raises questions. Her role in the play is larger than in the sources, but her only real contribution to the dramatic action is to send Phormio for Pamphila (IV.2) in order to help Gesippus' romantic cause. Her appeal to Fulvius to spare Gesippus (V.2) is the sort of scene which was later used to good effect by Shakespeare in *Measure for Measure* and *Coriolanus*, but in this play it comes to naught and carries little emotional weight. After her first appearance in III.8, she says all the right things but is not a little vapid; this is especially true in her first scene as she answers Titus' questions about her feelings. It is a little surprising that she does not appear earlier in the play, since all of the action in the first two acts revolves around the question of whom she will marry. On the other hand, Foxe avoided showing the two friends together throughout the first two acts, too, even though the theme of the play concerns friendship. I have attempted to explain the latter omission by noting the dramatic importance of Phormio in those acts. Perhaps the failure to show Sempronia has a similar explanation. By raising the question (in III.8) of how Sempronia had reacted to the substitution of Titus for Gesippus, Foxe showed a concern for the feelings of the bride which Elyot had not shown at all. Boccaccio had deliberately emphasized the bride's feelings in his version by having her become furious and complain to her family about the deception, but Foxe did not want to complicate an already difficult problem by suggesting that both Titus and Gesippus were acting inhumanely in ignoring the wishes of the girl. He may have consciously decided, then, that if the audience did not see Sempronia until late in the play, until he had allowed time for the fully developed love marriage which it sees in III.8, it would not think of the possible harm to the bride's sensitivities. Conceivably he could have shown a scene in which Titus and Sempronia fall in love with each other, but such scenes do not seem to appear until some time later in English drama. For instance, in Gascoigne's *Supposes* (1566), taken from Ariosto's *Suppositi*, there are no Polynesta-Erostrato scenes, and we do not even see Polynesta between the first scene and the last.

Most of the structural flaws in *Titus et Gesippus* are in the middle of the play. As I have attempted to show, the beginning is effectively structured. The ending is reasonably effective also. The thrust of the action in Rome is toward the discovery of Gesippus' identity. Here too Foxe was burdened with a difficult fundamental problem: Gesippus' initial decision, not really comprehensible, to conceal his identity. Given that inherent defect, Foxe invents details which effectively bring on the gradual discovery: the ironic mistaking of Gesippus for a vagabond (III.8) and Gesippus' refusal to answer Titus in the first trial scene (IV.3) are the most notable. The innovation of suspending the trial so that Titus can investigate the case (IV.3), and later of postponing sentencing so that Fulvius can go on a fruitless trip to consult the Senate (V.2), allows time for Martius' guilt to develop and make his confession somewhat less surprising than in the sources. But far too many key decisions are revealed in soliloquies. Much of the dialogue of the play, especially in comic scenes, is very good, but the piling up of soliloquies in places such as I.4-I.5, I.9-II.1, and IV.7-V.1 shows an inconsistent concern for developing naturalistic dialogue and an occasionally expedient decision.

A significant nonstructural addition by Foxe is the comic business. Two scenes involving musicians (I.6 and II.4) are largely irrelevant, though there is some irony in their preparation for an expected wedding which will not occur. The first of these scenes, with its long discussion of musical modes, is too long, but the tricking of Syrus into thinking that the music of the spheres is being played is a nice comic bit, at least for a (possible) university audience. In the other scene, the comic by-play between Pythias, who wants to go on dancing, and the musicians who are ready to leave is a homely and sophisticated touch. One joke in this scene requires comment. As Misenus emerges from a doorway, he utters a Terentian appeal to Juno Lucina and claims that the house is giving birth to him; Marsias answers by parodying Horace's dictum, "A mountain in labor produces a ridiculous mouse (*mus*)": "A house in labor produces a ridiculous man (*mas*)." No doubt the Magdalen audience thought that funny, and it anticipates some of the courtly wit found in later comedy: one thinks, for instance, of the *mas-mass-Mars* and *as-ass-ars* trick which Dares and Samias play on Sir Tophas in *Endymion*. Equally esoteric is the humor when Phormio appeals to a large

group of beings for help in his difficult task: beginning simply enough
with the names of some gods, he moves through practitioners of
mythological magic to end with references to Plato, Aristotle, and
Pythagoras. Far more effective, I think, is the humor resulting from
Chremes' and Crito's rage at being outwitted by Gesippus, for this
is germane to the play and comes from the naturalistic conversation
of two silly old men.

When we consider the nature of the material with which Foxe
burdened himself and the status of the comic art when he was
writing, we must conclude that Foxe wrote a more than creditable
play. If it has flaws, it also has positive virtues. It is clearly a better
play than *Christus Triumphans*. Perhaps, if we had Foxe's final revision, we would find some of the flaws eliminated, for we must
remember that we are dealing with a draft play. On the other hand,
the completely revised state of *Christus Triumphans* does not indicate
that Foxe's revisions necessarily removed all faults, and it is perhaps
best not to speculate on the quality of a revision which we cannot
now see.

The Biographical Environment of *Christus Triumphans*

When Foxe fled from England in 1554, he went to Antwerp,
Rotterdam (where he visited the house in which Erasmus was born),
Frankfurt (where he met the Basel printer, Froben), and Strassburg,
the earliest haven for exiles from Mary's England. His stay in Strassburg was brief, but was long enough to see the publication in
September, 1554, of a work which he had written in England,
*Commentarii rerum in ecclesia gestarum, maximarumque per totam Europam
persecutionum a Wiclevi temporibus ad hanc usque aetatem descriptio*. This is
the first version of the work which would later make Foxe famous,
the Book of Martyrs, but it is only a fraction of the later work in size
and scope: it is concerned mostly with the Lollards, for the Marian
persecutions which inspired the continuation had not yet reached
major proportions: burnings did not begin until February, 1555.

By the autumn, Foxe had moved to Frankfurt, apparently as a
preacher. Throughout his exile Foxe was very poor: he had dedicated
his *Commentarii* to a German nobleman whom he did not know in
the hope of financial return and, getting no response, had followed

it up with a personal letter of entreaty. Later he would work as a proofreader in Basel to make ends meet for his wife and (ultimately) two daughters, and several of his letters from Basel contain requests for money. It is likely that a paying position lured Foxe from Strassburg to Frankfurt. On the other hand, he may merely have accepted an invitation which the Frankfurt congregation of exiles sent to all other English exiles to move to Frankfurt and unite in one great church. In any case, Foxe stayed in Frankfurt for about a year, until September, 1555. It was a year that saw that congregation rent by a serious dispute over the form of the prayer book to be used in the worship service. Foxe took part in some of the activities of that year—a year that ended just six months before the publication of *Christus Triumphans*.

The English exiles were not a monolithic political or ecclesiastical group. Some were royalists, some republicans; some were Calvinists, others orthodox Anglicans; and some who were conservative on one issue were radical on another. The majority at Frankfurt, led by William Whittingham, were Calvinists when Foxe arrived there in 1554, and they favored a prayer book similar to that which Calvin had worked out at Geneva. There was also, however, a party which favored the Edwardian Book of Common Prayer, which was in use at Zurich and Strassburg. A political compromise had been reached, and the prayer book in use at Frankfurt was based on the Book of Common Prayer but departed from it in several respects. In a further attempt at harmony two pastors were chosen, John Knox to satisfy the Calvinists, and Thomas Lever the conservatives. An attempt was made, moreover, to bring in Peter Martyr as a lecturer in divinity; Foxe wrote a letter in October urging Martyr to accept the invitation, but the appeal was unsuccessful. Continuing disagreement led Knox and Whittingham to write to Calvin for his opinion of the Book of Common Prayer, and his partially negative response provoked the radicals (Foxe among them) to try to adopt Calvin's liturgy. When the conservatives resisted, another compromise was worked out, and a revised liturgy, but one still based on the Book of Common Prayer, was adopted for a limited trial in February, 1555.

Within a month, however, the balance of power was suddenly altered by the arrival of a group of conservatives led by Richard Coxe. Once Coxe had gained control, he contrived, in a rather unsavory episode, to have Knox accused of treason and driven from Frankfurt; the congregation then adopted the Book of Common Prayer. A few months later, on August 27, some twenty radicals, including Whittingham and Foxe, signed a letter of secession, and when they failed to win concessions from the majority, most of them left in September. Many went to Geneva. Foxe went to Basel.

In Frankfurt, Foxe had lived with one of the radicals, Antony Gilby, and though not a leader had himself been identified with the radical position. Although he seceded, however, he was repelled by the bitterness which led to such a breach. In a letter to Peter Martyr he claims to have been nearly neutral and characterizes the participants as lacking charity.[54] Foxe was not averse to bitter ideological controversy, as we know from the bulk of his writings, but he shrank from personal encounters. No doubt this was a temperamental trait, but perhaps it was in part pragmatically motivated. For one as poor as Foxe, and as dependent upon patronage, it would have been singularly unwise to antagonize people unnecessarily, and it is remarkable that, despite Foxe's forthrightness, he seldom won a personal enemy. Interestingly—and in justification of our spending so much time on this Frankfurt quarrel—within six months after leaving Frankfurt, Foxe named several Frankfurt merchants in the dedicatory epistle of *Christus Triumphans*. He was confessedly attempting to win their patronage, and it is possible, I think, to see a pattern in the persons he named. The full significance of the pattern will be visible only if we consider some events which occurred after Foxe's secession.

After the expulsion of Knox, the pastor in Frankfurt was Robert Horne, formerly a chaplain to Edward VI and reforming Dean of Durham, and still basically a structural authoritarian (in 1561 he was to become Bishop of Winchester). His congregation held somewhat different views. Though they were split on the question of church structure, a majority were less conservative on that question than in their liturgical views. Accordingly, in January 1557, less than a year after the publication of Foxe's play, the congregation voted into being a "new discipline," in which the congregation was "aboue the pastor and not the pastor aboue the churche"—in

<hr/>

[54] Mozley, pp. 46-47.

Garrett's words, "a Bible Commonwealth in which there would be no place for bishops."[55] Refusing to accept this insurrection, Horne, who was also suspected of financial mismanagement, resigned, and some of his followers withdrew from active participation in the affairs of the congregation. How well defined this division had become before Foxe seceded, or even before he wrote the dedicatory epistle to *Christus Triumphans* in March, 1556, and how much Foxe would have known of it from Basel is open to question. But the persons whom Foxe names seem to cover the political spectrum. John Binks lived with Robert Horne and opposed the "new discipline" so strongly that he refused to serve the congregation after its adoption; Garrett gives no information about his views in the prayer book quarrel, but if he was in Frankfurt at the time he did not sign the letter of secession.[56] Binks, then, may have been a conservative on both issues. John Escot also opposed the "new discipline"; in the earlier quarrel, however, he had sided with the radicals and had signed the letter of secession; but he had not left Frankfurt and had, in fact, continued to live in the Kornmarck in the house of Henry Parry, whom Knox identified as a leading opponent.[57] Escot seems to have been a middle-of-the-roader. John Kelke, who also lived in the Kornmarck (with Lawrence Kent, another merchant), had been a member of Whittingham's party in the 1555 quarrel, but he had not seceded; in 1557 he signed the "new discipline."[58] Kelke was a radical on both issues, but not enough of a radical to secede. These three men are the dedicatees of Foxe's book. Only one major class seems to be omitted from the list—those who actually seceded— and in the nature of things no such person could be included among the society of merchants still in Frankfurt. Early in his letter, then, Foxe seems to have corrected that omission by stating that he would have liked to include one Walton, probably William Walton, who had been a strong supporter of Knox and had seceded with Whittingham in 1555.[59]

[55] Christina H. Garrett, *The Marian Exiles: A Study in the Origins of Elizabethan Puritanism* (Cambridge, 1938), p. 329.

[56] *Ibid.*, p. 90.

[57] *Ibid.*, p. 151.

[58] *Ibid.*, p. 202. Garrett lists two Kelkes and only tentatively identifies John as a merchant, but Roger, a student and gentleman, did not go to Frankfurt.

[59] *Ibid.*, p. 320. The identification is uncertain because William Walton (the

Perhaps this is an accidental congruence of circumstances—and indeed one or two of the identifications are not beyond question. But it would clearly make sense for Foxe, interested for both financial and didactic reasons in gaining support for his work from more than one group, to appeal to all political factions in Frankfurt. Early in the dedication, moreover, Foxe also refers favorably to the English merchants of Strassburg, and this may have been another political gesture. As Frankfurt was, at one time or another, radical in liturgy and in ecclesiastical structure, Strassburg was a bastion of conservatism. When the first Frankfurt exiles had invited the exiles at Strassburg to join them, the latter had refused to come unless the Book of Common Prayer were adopted in its entirety. The leader of the Strassburg congregation, moreover, was (until his death in August 1556) Richard Ponet, formerly Bishop of Winchester and still an advocate of Anglican orthodoxy. Garrett suggests that it may have been Ponet who sent Coxe to Frankfurt in 1555 to bring Knox down.[60] His congregation apparently sympathized with Ponet's views, and where Frankfurt was working toward a democratic structure, Strassburg was looking to "aristocratic hegemony among the English colonies."[61] With fine impartiality, Foxe praised both.

However that may be, Foxe certainly was looking for financial support in the publication—and probably also in the writing—of *Christus Triumphans*. Although Garrett has shown that many of the exiles were men of some means,[62] Foxe was not. Indeed, he may have been among the poorest, for he was poor in the best of times. Now, in Basel, apparently living with a number of other families in the Klarakloster, a former cloister across the Rhine from the main part of Basel, he had another mouth to feed: his first daughter, Christiana, was apparently born almost immediately after his arrival there. Baptized on September 22, she was a small infant when *Christus Triumphans* was published in the following March. Presumably out of

---

only Walton listed by Garrett) is not called a merchant; moreover, he did not turn up in any other congregation after signing the secession, and Garrett thinks that he died abroad. If so, Foxe could not name him for that reason.

[60] Garrett, p. 135.

[61] *Ibid.*, p. 329.

[62] *Ibid.*, p. 41.

penury, Foxe was allowed to matriculate without fee at the University.[63] There are records of financial gifts to Foxe, and letters in which Foxe solicits other gifts. But he still had to secure gainful employment. Like his friends John Bale and Laurence Humphrey, he became a proofreader for Basel printers. Most of Foxe's work was for Oporinus, who printed Protestant tracts and Neo-Latin plays, including a number of Foxe's writings, *Christus Triumphans* among them. According to Strype, Foxe lived with Oporinus and was paid only bread and water for his labor, but Mozley judiciously disputes both assertions. Though Mozley speaks of Foxe's "severe labour as proofreader,"[64] it would appear that Foxe had enough leisure to do considerable writing, and we may wonder how demanding Oporinus was. As a case in point, if Foxe proofread his own *Christus Triumphans*, he overlooked a number of printing errors.

Among the writings which occupied Foxe at this time, besides *Christus Triumphans*, were a translation of a tract on the eucharist written by Cranmer (Foxe began it in Frankfurt and completed it in 1557, but it was apparently never published); a curious volume of pages, blank except for commonplace headings under which students of the University of Basel were supposed to compile appropriate phrases (1557); a translation of a work about the martyrdom of John Philpot; and the Book of Martyrs. Most of Foxe's attention, of course, was directed to this last work, and his manuscripts are filled with letters and other documents which he compiled during these years at Basel. He finished his work on it in 1559 (he had delayed his return to England following Elizabeth's accession), and it was published in Latin in August of that year by Oporinus and another Basel printer, Nicholas Brilinger.

In October of 1559, Foxe and his family (now including a one-year-old daughter, Dorcas) returned to England. He soon established a long-standing relationship with the important London printer John Daye; was ordained a priest (1560); had two sons, Samuel and Simeon (1560 and 1568); and became famous with the publication in English of the *Acts and Monuments of these latter and perilous days* (1563). But that work and those later times are beyond the scope of the present study.

[63] *Ibid.*, p. 357; Mozley, p. 52.
[64] Mozley, p. 53.

Christus Triumphans

The first edition of Foxe's apocalyptic comedy of Christ triumphant was published by Oporinus in Basel in March, 1556. A number
of writers have listed a first printing in London in 1551;[65] T. W.
Baldwin, singling out a reference by P. Bahlmann, thought that
"the circumstantial details given by Bahlmann concerning it make
it reasonably certain that [such an edition] once existed."[66] Such
evidence as exists in Bahlmann's (and others') lists, however, suggests
the opposite: the entry is certainly based on the title page of the 1556
Basel edition including the identification of the author as "Anglo."
Why would an English publication of a book written by an English-
man who was still in England go to such pains to identify his
nationality?

The question is important for its implications concerning the
date of the play. There seems to have been a tacit general assumption
that *Christus Triumphans* was written shortly before its 1556 publication; but if there was a 1551 printing, then of course the date of
composition is pushed back several years. Baldwin, in fact, thought
the play earlier than 1551. Taking 1538 as the *terminus a quo* (because
of the publication in that year of Thomas Kirchmeyer's *Pammachius*,
which many scholars think influenced Foxe's play), he thought it
probable that Foxe wrote it "in this university period, 1539-1545,
and that he wrote it for university presentation."[67] He noted the
play's allusion to Bocardo, the Oxford prison (V.2.31), and asked,
"Why this localization to Oxford?" But the reference to Bocardo
proves merely that the author knew Oxford and presumably
expected his audience to know what he was referring to; it does not
prove that the play was *written* at Oxford. For a staunch protestant
such as Foxe, the most obvious time to refer to Bocardo was after
March, 1554, when Latimer, Ridley, and Cranmer were imprisoned

---

[65] E.g., Paul Bahlmann, *Die Lateinischen Dramen von Wimphelings Stylpho bis zur
Mitte des sechzehnten Jahrhunderts. 1480-1550* (Münster, 1893), p. 107. E. K.
Chambers hesitantly accepted the date but noted that Sidney Lee, in his *D. N. B.*
account of Foxe, could cite only Thomas Tanner as authority for it. William
Winters printed the date without question in *Biographical Notes on John Foxe the
Martyrologist* (Waltham Abbey, 1876), p. 4.

[66] *Shakespere's Five-Act Structure* (Urbana, 1947), p. 353.

[67] *Ibid.*, p. 354.

there. Baldwin rejected the idea that Foxe had those protestant martyrs in mind, pointing out from other references to Bocardo that the Oxford prison was notorious before it received its most famous occupants. The very structure and purpose of Foxe's play, however, make an association with Latimer and Ridley almost inescapable. Though his chronicle traces Ecclesia's tribulations through millennia of persecutions, by Act V she has become identified with the English church's suffering under Mary.[68] Hierologus and Theosebes are seized by agents of the pope, Pseudamnus, and the only real question is whether the reference is to the arrest of Latimer and Ridley in March, 1554, or to their execution on October 16, 1555. If taken literally, V.3.29 implies that they are still alive, for Anabasius says they are in chains (*Vinctus*); the Chorus at V.5.84 uses the same word in anticipating the joy of Hierologus and Theosebes when they hear of Ecclesia's marriage. But there is an ominousness in Anabasius' statement, and (except in eschatological terms) a pathetic irony in the Chorus', which clearly suggest that Foxe is talking of men already known to be matryrs. That there are only two men in Bocardo in Foxe's play is perhaps also significant: in fact, Cranmer was there along with Latimer and Ridley, but he was not executed until March 21, 1556, just about the time when *Christus Triumphans* was published. When Foxe was writing, he apparently knew of only two bishops' martyrdoms, not three, and accordingly he allowed Pseudamnus to enchain only two men.

Other internal evidence makes a date very early in 1556 almost certain. The golden rose and the sword in a golden sheath which are sent to Dynastes and Dynamicum (V.3.15-16) are a clear allusion to the papal honors conferred on Mary and Philip by Julius III in a letter dated January 27, 1555.[69] But this is less useful to us than the linsey-woolsey pallium sent to Nesophilus (V.3.17-18). A note by the Genevan translator of Foxe's play, Jean Bienvenu, correctly identifies Nesophilus (when he is referred to again at V.3.60) as Cardinal Pole, and the pallium is of course the symbol of an arch-

---

[68] See the notes to Act V for the specific allusions which Foxe makes to events of concern to Englishmen.

[69] *Calendar of State Papers (Spanish)*, XIII, 137. Gaetano Moroni Romano said the letter was dated January 26 (*Dizionario di Erudizione Storico-Ecclesiastica*, LIX [Venice, 1852], 131).

bishop's office. Pole succeeded Cranmer as Archbishop of Canterbury. He did not receive the pallium until March 22, 1556, but he had taken over the administration of the archbishopric on December 11, 1555, when Cranmer was officially deprived.[70] One could argue, perhaps, that Foxe was merely anticipating the ultimate replacement of the imprisoned Cranmer by Pole (who had returned to England in November, 1554, as papal legate after years of exile on the Continent) and was not referring to a dignity already conferred. For my part, this seems less satisfactory than the view that Foxe knew of Pole's elevation when he was writing.

If a *Christus Triumphans* was published in London in 1551, then, it was not the play which has come down to us, and there is no evidence that there was an earlier one. Foxe's draft manuscript of this play survives, and it contains all of the allusions cited above and must have been written shortly before March, 1556.[71] It was certainly written at Basel, for it is found among the papers which Foxe worked on in Basel, not among his "Letters and Writings in [Oxford] University." The play may have been written for a university performance, as Baldwin judiciously argued, but if so it was for the University of Basel, in which Foxe matriculated in 1555. I do not know whether it was performed there or not—or whether the stage at Basel could handle the elaborate machinery of Act V— but Foxe does refer in his Prologue to "spectatores noui" (l. 3), probably meaning a young audience (though it could also refer to the recentness of Foxe's arrival in Basel); and in the Dedicatory Epistle printed in the 1556 edition he speaks of the play as one of the exercises of his studies (see p. 209 below).

Christus Triumphans has not been kindly received by modern critics. Most have ignored it, and those who have commented on it have found it seriously deficient. C. H. Herford called it a "strange and lurid drama" rivaling "the crudest of the mysteries in naïve prolixity of form, and it must be added, in essential barrenness of thought"; he thought it crowded "with unnecessary figures,

---

[70] See *D. N. B.*, s.v. "Reginald Pole."

[71] It is found in British Museum Lansdowne MS. 1045, ff. 132-155v. Besides these allusions, the manuscript contains an earlier reading at V.1.38 which seems a clear reference to Mary, whose chief residence was at Greenwich: "S[ATAN]. Adsumus / E Grynwico serui Dei."

confused in structure, unimaginative in conception, and alternately undignified and pedantic in style."[72] Sidney Lee, in his account of Foxe in the *Dictionary of National Biography*, called it a "crude and tedious mystery play." J. F. Mozley put his view more bluntly: "the play has no poetic merit."[73] Even such a biased reporter as the Rev. John Stoughton could find nothing kinder to say about this "Latin poem of considerable length, of a very different order of genius from the *Divina Commedia* of Dante," than to call it a "singular composition."[74] Yet it was not always thus. In 1561, Jean Bienvenu of Geneva thought enough of the play to translate it into French: except for omitting (presumably as indecorous) the scene (II.2) in which Saul quarrels with Polyharpax, adding five scenes between V.3 and V.4 as a "petit discours de la maladie de la Messe," and making some of the language more topical (e.g., having Psychephonus call Ecclesia a "Lutherienne" rather than an Origenist at IV.8.54), it is a reasonably close translation into French verse, mostly rhymed couplets.[75] In 1562, Foxe's friend and fellow exile Laurence Humphrey, author of some prefatory verses printed in the 1556 edition of *Christus Triumphans*, in his capacity as newly elected President of Magdalen College asked Foxe's permission to produce the play at Magdalen. Foxe gave his permission, but there are no records to show whether it was in fact acted at Magdalen.[76] In 1562-63, it was performed at Trinity College, Cambridge.[77]

[72] *Studies in the Literary Relations of England and Germany in the Sixteenth Century* (Cambridge, 1886), pp. 139, 143.

[73] Mozley, p. 53.

[74] "Life of John Foxe," in *The Acts and Monuments*, ed. Josiah Pratt, 4th ed., I (London, [1900]), 17.

[75] *Le Triomphe de Iesus Christ: Comedie Apocalyptique* (Geneva, 1562). Bienvenu, a citizen of Geneva, was active in both politics and literature. His best-known original work seems to have been the *Comédie du monde malade* (1568), which I have not seen but which has been described as an allegorical satire on the various estates, especially medicine, and on current political affairs. It is said to have won him a number of enemies. See Virgile Rossell, *Histoire de la Littérature hors de France* (Lausanne, 1895), pp. 55-57; and *Biographie Universelle Ancienne et Moderne* (Paris, 1843), s.v. "Jacques Bienvenu." The translation of Foxe's play is summarized by the *Bibliotheque du Théatre Francois depuis son Origine* (Dresden, 1768), III, 236, which compares it to Thrasibule Phénice's (i.e., Theodore de Beza's) *Comédie du Pape Malade* (1561) and calls it a "comble de l'extravagance."

[76] We know of Humphrey's request because of Foxe's reply, which survives in British Museum Harleian MS. 416, f. 140v.

[77] Boas, p. 387.

In 1579, the prose panegyric which Foxe appended to the play was translated by John Daye, and the translation was several times reprinted.[78] In 1590, an edition of the play appeared in Nuremberg. And as late as 1672, the play was edited as a school text by one T. C. of Sidney Sussex College, Cambridge; the pages of this edition were reissued with an altered date in 1676. The editor, perhaps Thomas Comber, later Dean of Durham,[79] praised the play for the singular elegance of its style, worthy of scholastic emulation, and for its morality and recommended it as an instrument for teaching pupils to be grammarians, poets, and Christians: here are no pagan oaths (except when Satanic characters are speaking); no matter from Ovid's "Art of Vileness", no Plautine slaves to set a bad example by their wiles; no impurities from Apuleius, Petronius, and Martial; and no barbarisms such as the utterance of Aristophanes' frogs, βρεκεκεκὲξ, κοὰξ, κοάξ. T. C. included a crabbed poetic address to schoolmasters in praise of Foxe, whom he compared to Aesop's fox as a many-talented person (μυριοτεχνίτης):

> Eia, agite, o mystae ludi, qui ducitis agmen
> Aetatis tenerae per pascua ab amne rigata,
> Jordanis potius quam Nili visite ripas.
> Hicce animae ipsa salus laeto cum gramine crescit;
> Hoc flumen lumen, numenque immiscet in herbis;
> Reddet et hoc aptos coelique solique ad Athenas.
> Mentem animamque simul luci sacrabitis altae,
> Quaeque phrases sugent Latium Solymamque decentes.
> Ictu uno actuque sales ediscere Plauti,

[78] A number of writers have incorrectly described Daye's work as a translation of Foxe's comedy itself: e.g., Wilhelm Creizenach, *Geschichte des Neueren Dramas*, III (Halle, 1903), 528; and Sidney Lee, in the *D. N. B.* life of Foxe.

[79] In response to a query by R. Inglis, the editor of *N. & Q.*, 2nd ser., VII (January 15, 1859), 47n., said that an edition of the *Memoirs of Dean Comber* (1799), p. 68, contained the following note: "These initials were thought by many judicious persons to stand for Thomas Comber, and the intention of its publication was worthy of him; but as no memorandum of this appears among such of his MSS. as are now extant, we cannot vouch for its being brought out by him." Another possible candidate is Thomas Calvert (B.A. 1626), vicar of Holy Trinity at York until his ejection in 1662; see E. Calamy, *Nonconformist Memorials*, ed. Palmer (1775), II, 582. Calvert was the author of sermons published in 1647 and 1660 and of *The Blessed Jew of Marocco . . . the true Messias. Now Englished* (1648).

Et Christi hisce datur. Mora quae vos, quidve timetis,
Quum scriptis scriptura praeest divina prophanis?
Si tulit is punctum, qui miscuit utile dulci,
Sic tulit hic punctum, qui miscuit utile sacro.
Tempus ad aeterna est bufonis sanguis Iesu
Sanguine libratus. Parnassi noscere res est
Monte datum: at Zionis noscere spes est
Monte datum, mundi cana ultra secla beatas.
Quid levitas? Aura est. Gravitas accedit ad auram
Cum simili ac aequo. Tenerae possessio mentis
Luce sui et Christi praecludit inania mundi,
Mire animam tingit, quae mane imbuta juventae,
Ad senium et coelum gratum servabit odorem.
Amputat obscaenae Foxus praeputia scenae;
Baptizat Musas coeli, sine sordeque coeni,
Lympha, quae mentem mundat simul et labra purgat.
Nae catus ipse vir es, seu Romae pingere mores
Seu Solymae eloquio te accingas scribere sacra:
Digne quae scribis Monumenta ac Acta vocantur.

Oh come, ye priests of the school, who lead a troop of tender youth through pastures washed by a stream, go to the banks of the Jordan rather than the Nile. Amid joyous grass here grows the very health of the soul: this river intermingles light and divinity with its herbs. It will make men fit for the Athens of heaven and earth. You will consecrate at once both their minds and their souls to that exalted light, and they will suck phrases appropriate for both Latium and Jerusalem. In one stroke, one strike you may learn the wit of Plautus and with it that of Christ. Why hesitate? What do you fear, since divine scripture has preeminence over profane scripts? If he who mixed the useful with the sweet won the applause, so does this one, who mixed the useful with the sacred. Time, to eternity, is as the blood of a toad balanced against the blood of Jesus. It is given by Mt. Parnassus to know things, but it is given by Mt. Zion to know hopes blessed beyond the hoary ages of the world. What is comic pleasure? Air. And tragic pleasure is just as much like the air. But the possession of a compliant mind, by its own light and by Christ's, shuts out the empty pleasures of the world and colors the soul miraculously; implanted early in youth, it will preserve its pleasing savor into old age and heaven. Foxe cuts off the foreskins of the lewd stage and baptizes the muses with the water of heaven, free from the filth of sin, water which cleanses the mind even as it purifies the lips. You are a wise man indeed, whether you undertake to paint the manners of Rome or, with the eloquence of Jerusalem, to write sacred things: worthily are your writings called Monuments and Acts.

It is not my purpose to refute the opinions of scholars such as Herford and to embrace those of Comber. By any but the most partisan standards, *Christus Triumphans* is seriously flawed. In political outlook, Humphrey and Bienvenu were obvious partisans of Foxe, and Comber's bias is suggested by his association with Sidney Sussex, "nursery of Puritanism" as it has been called and the college of Oliver Cromwell. Echoes of Horace and references to Plautus notwithstanding, it is hard to believe that anything but special pleading for a political bias could have motivated Comber's praise of the play for its elegance of style: the frequent nonclassical usages in both diction and grammar make this a curious school text. Yet even if, by modern tastes, *Christus Triumphans* is a bad play, it is not, I think, so bad as Mozley thinks it. It makes even more effective use of the language of Roman comedy than *Titus et Gesippus* does in the creation of some very vital dialogue. If it contains some hopeless lines such as Maria's "Quidue os saliua distillans composita?" (I.2.12) and some hopeless scenes such as the theological discussion between Ecclesia and Paul (III.5), it also has some effective speeches (less of the action depends on soliloquies than in *Titus et Gesippus*) and some effective scenes (for instance, the opening of V.2, with Psychephonus timorously saying his spurious prayers to prevent exposure even though the characters who have entered are his allies; or the opening of IV.4, in which Satan bounds onto the stage expecting to be exuberantly welcomed only to find the stage empty.) If honorable characters (e.g., Europus and Africus, not to mention Ecclesia herself) are flat and uninteresting—a trait not unique to this play—many of the villains are considerably more than stereotypes. There are perhaps too many characters for theatrical effectiveness, but few if any of them are unnecessary for what Foxe had in mind. As he confesses in his Prologue, this is a big play with a very wide scope. Part of the reason the play fails for us is that Foxe attempted to do too much. In his dedicatory epistle he states his aim as to follow the Apocalyptic history and "to transfer as far as possible from the sacred writings into the theater those things which pertain primarily to ecclesiastical affairs"— in other words to write a chronicle history based upon Apocalypse; in the draft version he called the work history. Accordingly, he telescopes within a few moments in Act I the fall of Satan from heaven and the redemption of Christ (and recalls the fall of man as though it were a recent occurrence), and in subsequent acts moves swiftly through fifteen hundred years to the reign of Mary, unabashedly noting the passing of a millennium between Acts I and IV and the passing of three hundred years within a handful of scenes in Act III. Though Ecclesia remains the central figure throughout, she is exposed to a wide variety of enemies, and she represents at various times the pre-Christian church, the early post-Christian church, and finally the English church—all of these being one true church, of course, but the oneness gets clouded over. Despite this major flaw, the play provides some pleasures, at least to the reader: some of the comic scenes are effective in themselves, and there is the overall pleasure of detecting the meaning of Foxe's allegorical representations. Whether this pleasure is a proper *dramatic* pleasure is no doubt open to debate, but *Christus Triumphans* is not the only play which has attempted to appeal to that pleasure: in the twentieth century, Bertolt Brecht's *Arturo Ui*, for instance, is an allegory similar in some limited ways to Foxe's play.

But our main interest in *Christus Triumphans* is certain to be historical rather than esthetic. Whatever we may think of the play, it merits some of our attention because it won the praise of men in three countries and two centuries, and must therefore represent some part of the critical current of its time. Besides that, *Christus Triumphans* belongs to a class of plays which hold no small place in a transitional period of English drama.

Herford and others are certainly right in comparing *Christus Triumphans* to the mysteries. The telescoping of time mentioned above (perhaps what Herford meant by the phrase "naïve prolixity of form") clearly recalls medieval drama. The source of the play is Biblical: as the subtitle indicates, the major source is the Book of Apocalypse, especially Chapters 12-13 and 17-21; significant portions of the second and third acts are taken from the Book of Acts. This Biblical material, moreover, is amplified in ways familiar

from the old mystery plays. Saul is provided with a motive for going
to Damascus to persecute Christians and with a dramatic context
for the trip (the need to get authorization from the Jewish leaders,
and then the earthy comic scene in which he quarrels with Polyharpax). Again, a comic Satan is thrown out of heaven and stands
verbally (and probably physically) shaking his fist at Michael in
enraged frustration. I know of no specific medieval parallels to these
scenes, but the tone is not without parallel. At the other extreme, the
long theological discussion between Ecclesia and Paul in III.5,
based largely on Paul's epistles, had many precedents in medieval
morality plays. So too did the inclusion of allegorical abstractions
like Ecclesia and Psyche. *Christus Triumphans* is not, I think, directly
related to medieval drama, but it clearly owes something to that
earlier dramatic tradition.

Yet the play is not formless. T. W. Baldwin could not fit it into
the five-act formula which post-classical critics derived from their
analysis of Terentian comedy,[80] but *Christus Triumphans* was divided
into five acts, if not according to the method at least according to
the example of Roman comedy as Renaissance theoreticians saw it.
More strikingly influential was the language of Roman comedy, for
despite many late Latin words and some transliterations from Greek,
there are enough Plautine phrases so that any Renaissance academic
audience would have been aware of them. The purpose of the play,
as the Prologue states it, is also classical: to mix profit and pleasure
(Prologue 32-33). The play is, then, a mixture of classical and
medieval. The names of the characters are an interesting reflection
of this mixture. The names are all descriptive of the characters'
functions in the dramatic action, as many names are in morality
plays; but it was also a humanist practice to name characters in this
way, the difference being that the humanists used names formed from
classical, especially Greek, roots. This is Foxe's method. Again,
the denouement of the play, a preparation for a wedding, is a clear
use of a long theological tradition inherited from the apocalyptic
source and from some Roman comic practice.

Other elements in *Christus Triumphans* are not from Roman
comedy. Despite Foxe's disavowal, in the dedicatory epistle, that

[80] Baldwin, *Five-Act Structure*, p. 355.

he is flagellating, "in the manner of the Old Comedy, the several types of vices and the grosser shames of the mob," parts of the play seem almost Aristophanic in their satire. I do not know whether Foxe meant the phrase "Old Comedy" to refer to Aristophanes (the only example he cites is the modern one of Macropedius' *Asotus*) or even whether he knew Aristophanes (though Aristophanes was available at Oxford[81]), but the parody of Catholic ritual in places is closer to the parody of Socrates in Aristophanes than to anything in Terence.[82] On the other hand, the doleful monologues by Eve, Mary, and Ecclesia (these reminded Herford of Hecuba's speeches[83]); the deaths (apparently) of Hierologus and Theosebes; the central concern with the persecution of Ecclesia by Jews, Caesars, and popes; and the mingling of exalted and historical figures with mean and fictional ones—these are foreign to the classical comic tradition altogether. Some of them seem rather the matter of tragedy.

Foxe clearly knew what he was doing, for he repeatedly called attention to his indecorous mixture and at times obstrusively made his audience aware of critical theories of the drama. The subtitle, *comoedia apocalyptica*, is itself a mixture, and this combination of comic theatrical language and of theological language is not uncommon. The dedicatory epistle frankly yokes the dramatic "Farewell, and applaud" and other diction drawn from dramatic theoreticians with the apocalyptic "It is finished." The prologue confesses that Foxe is presenting sacred matters as if they were a play. The epilogical final chorus uses more theatrical imagery in alerting the audience to the "final catastrophe [on] our stage," the second coming of Christ. At IV.2.25-28, Anabasius, the messenger from hell, tells Dioctes, the persecutor, to "play your part after the manner of the stage. As in comedies plays don't end altogether the same if the story doesn't permit it, so think of this world as a sort of drama school, where you must play the role not as you wish but as it's assigned to you." Evidently Foxe meant what he said in the Prologue,

---

[81] See T. W. Baldwin, *William Shakespere's Small Latine & Lesse Greeke* (Urbana, 1944), I, 103, 106 *et passim*.

[82] Note the litany-like name-calling, mostly by Psychephonus, in IV.8 and the parodies of the breviary in V.1 and V.2.

[83] Herford, p. 144.

but his emphasis on dramatic imagery calls attention to the indecorousness of what he was doing by calling to mind the critical theoreticians whose rules he was violating.

This technique could perhaps have been motivated by a desire to ward off puritanical attacks on the very act of writing, or staging, plays: the Prologue, for instance, is at some pains to equate watching sacred plays with attendance at church. (We may recall Foxe's unorthodox "prayers" at Magdalen, which consisted of reading books rather than attending mass.) Along the same lines, Humphrey's commendatory poems obtrusively summon the readers to Foxe's Christian play as if that were itself an act equivalent to taking up Christ's cross. But that sort of defensiveness does not explain all that Foxe did. His reference (Prologue 38-40) to the gaps and bogs and to the "warring elements" which it was impossible to tie together is a defense against dramatic critics, not moral ones; and the mock quarrel between Humphrey and Foxe in the prefatory poems concerns, not the appropriateness of writing plays, but the question whether this play is tragic or comic. Foxe's answer, that it is comic, is implicitly elaborated on by the Prologue's opening sentences, in which the play is called "new." It seems clear that Foxe knew he was writing neither a tragedy nor a comedy in the pure sense, but a tragicomedy.

Marvin Herrick's admirable study of tragicomedy discusses Foxe's play as an exemplar of the Christian Terence, and he emphasizes the contributions which that tradition made to the development of tragicomedy. When Foxe called his play "new," he seems to have been using what had become almost a technical term for a play which was neither tragedy nor comedy, for many Christian Terence predecessors had used the word. What they described as "new" were plays having some or most of the characteristics which I have described in *Christus Triumphans*. It is scarcely necessary to review Herrick's lucid chapter on the development of Christian Terence tragicomedy from about 1500 on; but his summary of the process will indicate the significance of plays like *Christus Triumphans* in the transition from medieval to modern drama:

. . . the playwrights of the Christian Terence imposed the formal structure of classical comedy upon the loosely-made medieval drama, the mysteries, moralities, farces, and tried to purify dramatic diction by imitating the easy but elegant style of Terence. Their plays were usually arranged in five acts and developed from protasis through epitasis to catastrophe. The Latin dialogue was conversational, often homely, sometimes lively and full-flavored, and yet literary. At the same time the authors of the Christian Terence were fully aware that they should not imitate Terence slavishly; they were trying to reform classical drama [from its immorality] as well as medieval [from its formlessness], for they believed that western Europe in the sixteenth century needed a new kind of drama, one that was adapted to a new religion, new manners, new customs. Therefore they reformed Terence and modified the classical rules of both comedy and tragedy. . . . The sacred dramatists often set aside the traditional prescription that the plot of tragedy should be based upon history (*res gestae*) and that the plot of comedy should be a *fictio*. The "sacred and new comedies" were *historiae* from Holy Writ. . . . These Neo-Latin playwrights also broke down the traditional prescription that tragic characters should be well-known, important personages while comic characters should be unknown, common folk. They freely mingled high with low. Kirchmeyer's *Pammachius*, for example, has historical persons like Christ and the Emperor Julian, fictitious characters like Pammachius and Dromo, and the allegorical figure of Truth. They also carried on the medieval practice of inserting comic scenes in a serious argument. . . . Finally, the Christian Terence, for all its devotion to the dramaturgy of Terence, often ignored the classical economy of time and place. . . . The result was a drama that was neither pure comedy nor pure tragedy, but a mixed form. The result was truly a *drama novum*, and an important forerunner of the modern drama. . . . The plays of the Christian Terence anticipated almost every characteristic, save the pastoral machinery, of the secular tragicomedy that flourished in western Europe at the close of the sixteenth and the beginning of the seventeenth centuries.[84]

It is certain that Foxe knew some of the plays of Christian Terence. In the dedicatory epistle, as we have seen, he refers to *Asotus* (1537), by the German Catholic author Georgius Macropedius. At III.3.10, he seems to have echoed Nicolas Bartholemaeus' *Christus Xylonicus* (1531).[85] He is likely to have known the plays of his fellow Oxonian

---

[84] Marvin T. Herrick, *Tragicomedy: Its Origin and Development in Italy, France, and England*, Illinois Studies in Language and Literature, 39 (Urbana, 1955), 61-62.

[85] See note *ad loc.*

Nicholas Grimald, *Christus Redivivus, Comoedia Tragica, sacra et nova* (1543) and *Archipropheta* (1547), and perhaps some now lost, like *Christus Nascens*. In Basel he had easy access to a large number of German Latin plays, especially in two large anthologies: *Comoediae ac Tragoediae Aliquot ex Novo et Vetere Testamento Desumptae* (Basel: Nicolaus Brylinger, 1540), in which *Pammachius* and *Christus Xylonicus* are contiguous; and *Dramata Sacra Comoediae atqve Tragoediae* (Basel: J. Oporinus, 1547); both of these printers were involved in bringing out Foxe's Latin version of the Book of Martyrs in 1559.

One of the Christian Terence plays, Thomas Kirchmeyer's (in Latinized Greek: Naogeorgius') *Pammachius* (1536), requires special notice. Critics from Herford to Herrick are convinced that Foxe knew and used *Pammachius* in the writing of *Christus Triumphans*. *Pammachius* is a four-act play (the fifth act was unwritten, says the epilogue, because the Son of God will come and provide his own catastrophe) which attacks the papacy as violently as does *Christus Triumphans* and which, like Foxe's play, is an "attempt to give dramatic form to the Protestant version of the Antichrist."[86] The Protestant version, of course, reflecting a view expressed by Luther and earlier reformers identifies the Antichrist, not with the Caesars or the Turks, but with the papacy—in Kirchmeyer's play, Pope Pammachius; in Foxe's, Pseudamnus. *Pammachius* was acted at Christ's College, Cambridge, in early 1545, just before Foxe left Oxford, and he may very well have heard of it then, for it became a *cause celebre* when Bishop Gardiner, unhappy at the staging of such a radical play, launched an investigation into the circumstances of the production.[87] Foxe's friend, John Bale, moreover, had translated the play into English.[88] The circumstantial evidence for Foxe's

[86] Herford, p. 124. As Herford points out (p. 124 n.), in none of the medieval treatments does the Antichrist assume the role of Pope. Leicester Bradner calls to my attention another play, of interest because it was translated in 1550 by Thomas Hoby of Cambridge, in which the Pope is found to be the Antichrist: Francesco Negri's *Libero Arbitrio* (1546). Hoby's translation was not published; a translation by Henry Cheeke (S.T.C. 18419) entitled *Freewyl* was published ca. 1573. The details of the play, which has a number of morality-type characters (Lady Grace Justifying, King Freewyll, Dame Falsehood), are not like those in *Christus Triumphans*, but the author's interest parallels Foxe's.

[87] Herford, pp. 129-131; Boas, pp. 22-23.

[88] Herford, p. 131. The translation, done before 1548, has not survived. Bale's *Kyng Johann* is usually thought to have been strongly influenced by *Pammachius*.

knowing the play is very strong. Foxe's epilogue, moreover, seems to echo Kirchmeyer's anticipation that Christ will provide his own catastrophe. Herford notes other incidental parallels: the surprise of Satan at not being met on his return from hell; allegorical heroines (Veritas in Kirchmeyer, Ecclesia in Foxe); councils of the infernal characters (*Christus Triumphans* IV.4, *Pammachius* IV.5); the villains' amazement on hearing news of the Reformation; the appearance of reformed teachers and the "angry interrogations about their doctrine"; and the final withholding of the dramatic climax of Christ's second coming.[89] To Herford, these parallels "yield a strong presumption that the younger writer, in spite of his silence, owed much of the form of [*Christus Triumphans*] to the greater artist and equally fervid theologian who had led the way." The case is strong, and I cannot refute it. But, as Herford himself admits, the details in all these incidents are different, and there are almost no verbal parallels between the two plays. In the earlier manuscript version of Foxe's play, moreover, and thus the version which presumably would have been most directly influenced by *Pammachius*, the central figure was not Ecclesia, but Sarcobius (that is, living flesh), brother of Psyche; that conception was more remote from *Pammachius* than is the revised version. It seems very likely that Foxe got certain broad ideas from Kirchmeyer, but his execution was essentially original.

The Texts

The format of this edition is self-explanatory except for the bracketed reference numbers appearing to the right of the Latin texts, e.g., [*f. 145v*] or [*p. 53*]. These numbers refer to the leaves in the manuscripts of *Titus et Gesippus* and *Christus Triumphans* (identified as folio numbers) or to the pages in the first printed edition of *Christus Triumphans* (identified as page numbers). In the translation, which is as close to being literal as readability would permit, I have not reproduced the formal characteristics of the Latin texts: thus, I have silently provided entrances and exits at appropriate places (the Latin texts have only lists of characters at the beginning

---

[89] Herford, pp. 144-148.

of each scene); I have interpolated a few stage directions to clarify
stage business; I have not translated metrical headings, etc. The
notes to the Latin text record mainly my emendations and comments
on Foxe's unusual diction, together with some conjectural emendations which I have not adopted. Most of the abbreviations used in
those notes are explained in the headnote to the Textual Notes,
where a complete textual history is presented. Additional abbreviations used only in the notes to the Latin text are the following:

DuCange   *Glossarium Mediae et Infimae Latinitatis.*

L-S   *A Latin Dictionary,* ed. C. T. Lewis and Charles Short
           (Oxford, 1879); this has been my principal lexico-
           graphic source, supplemented by the other works
           listed here and by Thomas Cooper, *Thesavrvs*
           Lingvae Romanae & Britannicae (London, 1573).

LTL   *Lexicon Totius Latinitatis,* ed. Aegidio Forcellinus *et al.*
           (Padua, 1940).

TLL   *Thesavrvs Lingvae Latinae* (Leipzig, 1900-date).

The notes to the Latin text do not normally record Foxe's
phraseological borrowings from earlier writings. There are hundreds
of such borrowings, mostly from Latin comedy but also from Cicero
(e.g., *Titus et Gesippus* III.9.3) and others, and a text constructed
on the principles of the great tradition of classical editing would
have noted them. Such a record here would have expanded the size
of the work beyond reasonable limits without, I think, materially
enhancing the usefulness of the work for those who will use it. The
notes to the translation occasionally point to Foxe's material sources,
particularly in *Christus Triumphans,* where Foxe (or his first editor)
included some marginal references, not always accurate, to scriptural
chapters; wherever possible I have narrowed these latter references
by including in square brackets the specific verses echoed. The notes
to the translation, moreover, besides glossing historical allusions and
pointing out certain dramatic features, also record some of the more
significant differences between Foxe's final readings and his earlier
drafts.

In the Latin texts I have aimed at a conservative edition. I have
not reproduced Foxe's diacritical markings and have silently nor-
malized capitalization and punctuation; I have silently spelled out

abbreviated speech prefixes, -*que* for -q_3, nasal macrons, etc.;
I have corrected palpable errors which might seriously interfere
with the sense, noting the emendations in the notes to the Latin
text and in the Textual Notes but (except for speech prefixes and
character lists) not enclosing the emendations in square brackets.
Otherwise, I have tried to reproduce Foxe's wording even if that
wording is imperfect by classical standards of grammar or metrics.

My copy text for *Titus et Gesippus* is, perforce, the only known
version of that play, in British Museum Lansdowne MS. 388.[90]
Though I have argued elsewhere that John Lyly may have known
the play,[91] there is no evidence that it was ever printed. The manuscript, Foxe's foul papers, presents extraordinary editorial problems.
Only occasionally is there any serious difficulty in reading the words
of the manuscript, and most such difficulties involve canceled
readings. But it is often impossible to determine with certainty how
Foxe intended later revisions to be combined with earlier wording:
he often failed to cross out words which he intended to delete, and
in many revised passages, especially those involving multiple revision, more than one combination is possible. Metrical patterns
provide little assistance. Even in his finished *Christus Triumphans*,
where the metrical patterns are labeled, Foxe revealed frequent
irregularities; in *Titus et Gesippus*, the patterns are both unlabeled
for the most part and very rough, and the revised wording is often
metrically unequal with the original wording. Many times Foxe
apparently set down a thought without taking the time to integrate
it with the earlier version. In general, I have adopted Foxe's latest
thoughts (one or two exceptions are recorded in the notes to the
Latin text), and as far as possible I have tried to fit them into the
established metrical and syntactic patterns. But many of the resulting
lines are nonmetrical, and a few of the sentences are syntactically
awkward. I have not undertaken to improve Foxe's Latin. The
redaction which Foxe sent to Dr. Hensey was probably formally

[90] Ff. 121-146, 112-116v in the latest of three numberings (the pages are out of
order in all three). The leaves measure about 19.8 cm by 14.5 cm. Several
exemplars of one watermark appear, very similar to Briquet No. 11370 (C. M.
Briquet, *Les Filigranes* [Paris, 1907], III).

[91] See "Sempronia, John Lyly, and John Foxe's Comedy of *Titus and Gesippus*,"
PQ, XLVIII (1969), 554-561.

better than the version which has survived; but, having no access to that redaction, I have attempted merely to reproduce Foxe's final intentions as of the time when he last touched the surviving version. I acknowledge the likelihood that other eyes may see better ways of combining some of these words metrically or grammatically than I have seen, but I can hope that the text which I present is at least substantially correct.

The editorial problems in *Christus Triumphans* are of a different sort. I have adopted as my copy text the octavo edition printed in March, 1556, by Ioannes Oporinus. The variant manuscript version, found in Lansdowne MS. 1045,[92] is in Foxe's own hand, whereas the octavo has passed through at least one other person's hands, the compositor's. But the manuscript is an early draft, Foxe's foul papers, and the octavo is an authorial revision later than the manuscript: dozens of revisions in the manuscript show the abandonment of an earlier reading in favor of the reading which appears in the octavo. Since Foxe worked for Oporinus (with whom, in later years, he had a close personal relationship), it is a virtual certainty that the lost manuscript from which Oporinus worked was given to him by Foxe himself and was in Foxe's hand. On the other hand, the octavo contains a number of palpable errors which cast doubt on the total reliability of that text. If Foxe proofread the work, he did not proofread very carefully; but someone did proofread it, for there are some press variants and there is an errata page (sig. 15v). A number of errors remain, however, and I have accordingly used the manuscript as an invaluable source of corrections. Sometimes I have followed the manuscript even when the printed text has a possible reading, but only when I have had some reason for believing that Oporinus misread his manuscript. All such departures from the copy text are recorded in the notes to the Latin text and in the Textual Notes.

The surviving manuscript omits everything after V.5.67, but in Act II it presents two scenes omitted from the octavo. After II.1 is a 34-line scene in which Eve and Mary rejoice at the good news of

---

[92] Ff. 132-155v. The leaves measure about 29.3 cm by 19.9 cm. The watermark found on several leaves, a gothic P surmounted by a quatrefoil, is similar to Briquet No. 8653 (vol. III), but Briquet has none identical and notes that the class of this watermark is quite varied.

Psyche's deliverance and Christ's transcendence; this is a natural follow-up of the scenes in Act I in which Eve and Mary are shown grieving over their children, but it adds little to the play and I see no reason to suspect that its omission was anything but deliberate. After the present II.2, the manuscript has an 18-line scene in which Sarcobius is summoned to Mark's house by a boy named Rhodus to pray for Peter, who is said to be in Herod's prison. This is an obvious preparation for the scene (II.3 in the octavo) in which Peter, newly freed, goes to Mark's house; the name of Rhodus is clearly inspired by the name of the maid, Rhoda, in the Biblical passage which Foxe was following for this episode (Acts 12.13). The deletion of this scene must have been deliberate: it was part of an overall revision which materially altered the direction of the play. From numerous canceled passages in the manuscript it is clear that Foxe at first conceived of Sarcobius as the central figure of much of the play; his name, presumably meaning living flesh (from σάρξ and βίος) suggests that he occupied the place which Soma holds in the revised version, and like Soma he is the father of Europus, Africus, and Asia. But Soma does not appear in the revised version, and the emphasis has been shifted from the father to the suffering mother, Ecclesia. Several of Sarcobius' speeches could be transferred to the new protagonist with only minor changes, like changes in the gender of pronouns; others required more drastic revision (see the Textual Notes to III.1 and III.2). Foxe apparently decided that the short scene after II.2 did not suit Ecclesia and accordingly abandoned it. He may also have wanted to shorten the play a bit: the Prologue (l. 37) apologizes for the length of the play, and following the revision the second act is now somewhat shorter than the other acts.[93]

I have collated completely three copies of the 1556 octavo of *Christus Triumphans* (copies owned by the British Museum, Harvard,

---

[93] I have spoken of the manuscript as though it were of a piece, but there is some evidence of stratification. On f. 145v, for instance, Soma is the only name used for Ecclesia's husband (see IV.3.1, Textual Note). Again, some pages are much more heavily revised than others, and a few of these—especially toward the end of the play—remain, even in their final versions, more remote from the printed text than most. It is possible, then, that some pages survive from, say, the first draft and that other first-draft pages were discarded after recopying.

and the University of Illinois), and I have partially collated the Bodleian copy. Ignoring insignificant pieing of type, I have found press variants in three forms:[94]

Signature	Uncorrected	Corrected
C1, l. 25	hoc (Bodleian)	hoc,
D5v, catchword	AC*Y*. (Harvard)	ACT.
D6, l. 15	Et si (Harvard)	Etsi (E tsi in Bodleian)[95]
E8, l. 1	inuasse (Harvard)[96]	iuuasse

I have also collated one copy of each of two later editions of *Christus Triumphans*. The 1590 Nuremberg octavo, printed from the 1556 octavo without reference to manuscript, is a very sound edition, and a number of the emendations made by the unnamed editor are confirmed by Foxe's draft manuscript. The 1672 London edition, by T. C. (Thomas Comber?), is a somewhat inaccurate reprint of the 1556 octavo. Substantive variants in these editions are recorded in the Textual Notes.[97]

[94] I have completely collated only the text of the play, not the front matter. One press variant in the front matter is noted; see Humphrey's "De Infirmo Christo et Scandalo Crucis," l. 22.

[95] This change may have been caused by mere pieing of type after the form was loosened for the correction on D5v.

[96] If I have correctly identified the corrected and the uncorrected states, the corrected state is wrong; see note *ad loc.*

[97] Also recorded there are some (probably sixteenth-century) manuscript notes from the Harvard copy. Not recorded are some curious defacements of the Illinois copy, in which scores of lines (or parts of lines) are methodically crossed out without explanation or apparent pattern.

TITUS ET GESIPPUS

Latin text and
English translation
(on facing pages)

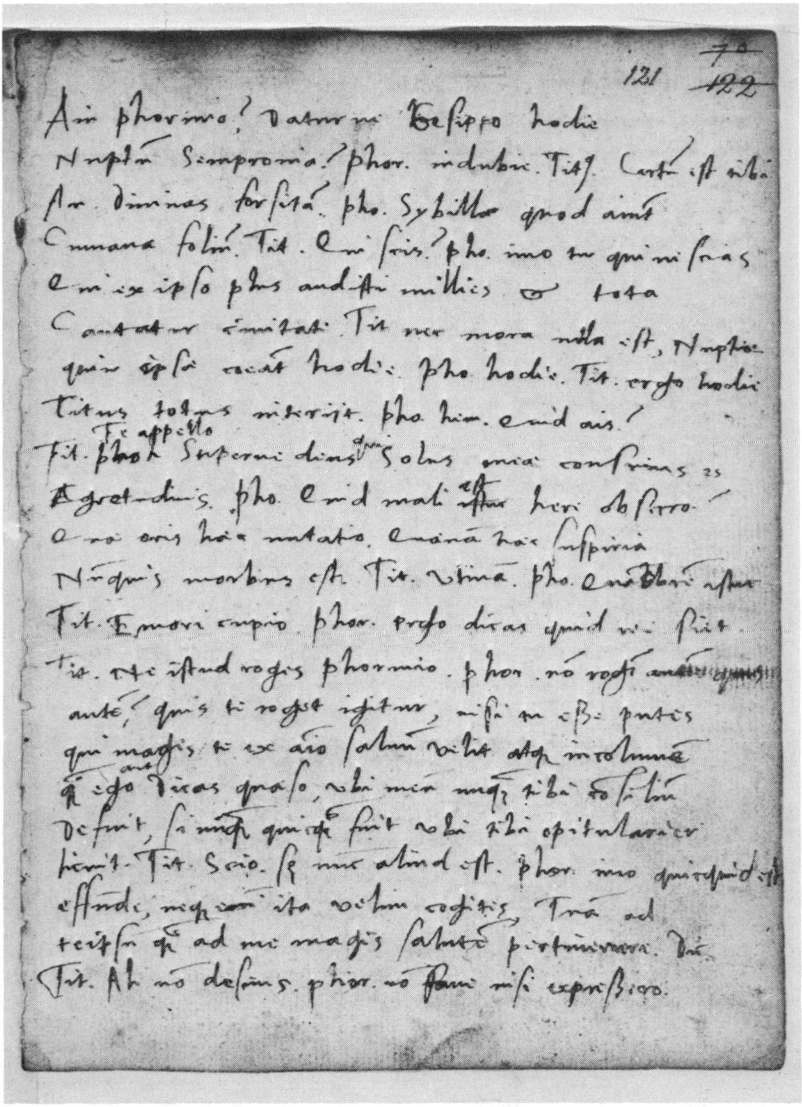

Figure 1. The opening lines of *Titus et Gesippus* (Lansdowne MS. 388, f. 121).

[DRAMATIS PERSONAE[1]

GESIPPUS
TITUS
CHREMES
PHORMIO
SIMO
CRITO
STYLPHO
FULVIUS
MARTIUS
MARSIAS
MISENUS
DROMO
SYRUS

MIDAS
STEPHANIO
TREBATIUS
CRATINUS

SOPHRONA
SEMPRONIA
PHRYGIA
PAMPHILA
PYTHIAS

CHORUS MIMICUS
TURBA EXPLORATORUM
POPULUS ROMANUS]

[1] *Gesippus*] in all other versions I have seen, the first syllable is spelled *Gi-* (or *Gy-*).

Titus] in the sources, Titus is sent to Athens to study; Foxe does not indicate why Titus is in Athens. For other differences, see Introduction, p. 17. Foxe once calls the character Pamphilus by mistake.

Chremes] a Terentian name used for this character by both Boccaccio (*Chremete*) and Elyot. But in those sources he is dead before the deception.

Phormio] the titular figure in Terence's *Phormio* provided Foxe with this name and in large part the character, which is not in the sources.

Simo] the bride's father is nameless in Boccaccio and is absent from Elyot; Foxe borrowed the name from old men in Terence's *Andria* and in several Plautine plays.

Crito] no such character appears in the sources. Foxe at first called him Albertus Discus (III.2.40), then Stylpho. Discus is the name of a freedman in Terence's *Eunuchus;* Crito is found in Terence's *Phormio* and *Andria*.

Stylpho] no such character appears in the sources; his name is taken from a reference in Terence's *Phormio*.

Fulvius] in Elyot, the name of Titus' father, who does not appear in this play.

Martius] the character is unnamed in the sources; Foxe probably chose the name from the Roman god of war.

DRAMATIS PERSONAE

GESIPPUS, an Athenian youth.

TITUS, a Roman youth, friend to Gesippus, later a Roman consul.

CHREMES, an Athenian, father of Gesippus.

PHORMIO, slave to Titus.

SIMO, an Athenian, friend to Chremes.

CRITO, an Athenian merchant.

STYLPHO, an Athenian, brother of Simo.

FULVIUS, Roman consul.

MARTIUS, Roman cut-throat.

MARSIAS and MISENUS, Athenian musicians.

DROMO, slave to Simo.

SYRUS, MIDAS, and STEPHANIO, slaves in the household of Chremes.

TREBATIUS, a messenger from Rome.

CRATINUS, a Roman.

SOPHRONA, an Athenian woman, wife of Chremes.

SEMPRONIA, an Athenian girl, daughter of Simo; at first betrothed to Gesippus, and later wife of Titus.

PHRYGIA, an Athenian girl, daughter of Stylpho.

PAMPHILA, a Roman girl, daughter of Fulvius; formerly in love with Titus, later betrothed to Gesippus.

PYTHIAS, slave in the household of Chremes.

CHORUS OF MIMES.

POSSE COMITATUS.

ROMAN PEOPLE.

Marsias] a character invented by Foxe and presumably named for Marsyas, the satyr who invented the flute and was flayed alive after challenging Apollo to a musical competition which Apollo won.

Misenus] another invented character, perhaps named for Aeneas' trumpeter, the son of Aeolus.

Dromo, Syrus, Midas, Stephanio] all added characters. Dromo and Syrus are both Terentian slaves; Midas is referred to in Terence's *Phormio*, Stephanio in Terence's *Adelphi* (as looking after the kitchen, like Foxe's Stephanio).

Trebatius] historically, the name of a lawyer and friend of Cicero. No comparable character appears in the sources.

Cratinus] an added character, whose name is found in Terence's *Phormio*.

Sophrona] the bride's mother is not referred to in the sources, in which the heroine is called Sophronia. Originally Foxe called this character Sostrata (a Terentian name); Sophrona is also Terentian, the name of several old nurses.

Sempronia] see Introduction, pp. 18 and 23 and n. 91.

Phrygia] an added character; her name is alluded to several times in Terence.

Pamphila] a Terentian name. No comparable figure appears in Elyot, but, in Boccaccio, Gisippo is married to Fulvia, a sister of Tito.

Pythias] an added character; her name is that of a nurse in Terence's *Eunuchus*.

55

[TITUS ET GESIPPUS, COMOEDIA]

[PERIOCHA]

Tito Gesippus amico amatam coniugem   [*f. 136v*]
Concedens, offenso patre patria pellitur,
Qui tum Romam ad amicum flectens, ab eo quia
Inagnitus primum, propterea se putans
Contemni, luctu confectus sese parat   5
Conficere. Ibi tum cuiusdam astu latrunculi
In somno oppressus pro latrone stringitur.
Titus re tandem cognita ut amicum videt
Gesippum, vt seruet suum se crimini obiicit.
Quorum egregiam miseratus amicitiam latro   10
Re prodita illis seruat, vitam exorat suam.
Gesippus meliorem accipit aliam, Semproniae
Opera, rursusque reuocante patre rediit domum,
Non sine plausu magno: omnia strepunt gratiis.

[ACTUS PRIMUS. SCENA PRIMA.]

[*Titus. Phormio.*]

[TITUS.]

Ain Phormio? Daturne Gesippo hodie   [*f. 121*]
Nuptum Sempronia?
PHORMIO.   Indubie.
TITUS.   Certum est tibi
An diuinas forsitan?
PHORMIO.   Sybillae quod aiunt
Cumanae folium.

Periocha 14. *gratiis*] emended from *gratis*, the apparent reading in MST.
    I.i.S.H. and P.H.] omitted in MST. Except for act divisions, Foxe omitted
all S.H.'s, and hereafter I shall not note their omission.
    1. S.P.] omitted in MST. Foxe normally omitted S.P.'s at the beginnings of
scenes, and I shall not hereafter note such omissions.

THE COMEDY OF TITUS AND GESIPPUS

ARGUMENT

After Gesippus gives up his beloved bride to his friend Titus, he is driven from the land by his angry father. When he goes to Rome to see his friend and is not recognized at first, he thinks himself scorned and, consumed with grief, prepares to kill himself. Through the cunning of a certain robber, he is surprised while asleep and bound as a robber. When Titus finally realizes the truth as he recognizes his friend Gesippus, he charges himself with the crime to save his friend. Moved to compassion for their great friendship, the robber saves their lives by confessing, and then begs for his own. With the help of Sempronia, Gesippus receives another girl who is more pleasing to him, and when his father summons him home, he goes,[1] not without great applause. Everything resounds with thanksgiving.

[I.1]   *Enter Titus and Phormio.*

TITUS. What, Phormio? Sempronia is marrying Gesippus today?
PHORMIO. Without a doubt.
TITUS. Are you sure, or maybe you're guessing?
PHORMIO. As they say, it's a leaf of the Sibyl at Cumae.[2]

---

[1] Though Gesippus is summoned home by his father, who wants him to marry Phrygia (III.2-6), there is no indication at the end of the play that Gesippus will return, for he intends to marry Pamphila, a Roman girl. See the Introduction.
[2] The celebrated prophetess at Cumae who wrote her oracles on leaves; the phrase is proverbial, meaning to utter certainties.

TITUS.   Qui scis?

PHORMIO.   Imo tu qui ne scias
  Qui ex ipso plus audisti millies quam tota   5
  Cantatur ciuitate.

TITUS.   Nec mora ulla est, nuptiae
  Quin ipsae coeant hodie?

PHORMIO.   Hodie.

TITUS.   Ergo hodie
  Titus totus interiit.

PHORMIO.   Hem, quid ais?

TITUS.
  Te appello qui solus meae conscius es
  Aegretudinis.

PHORMIO.   Quid mali est, here, obsecro?   10
  Quae oris haec nutatio? Quaenam haec suspiria?
  Numquis morbus est?

TITUS.   Vtinam.

PHORMIO.   Quamobrem istuc?

TITUS.
  Emori cupio.

PHORMIO.   Ergo dicas quid rei siet.

TITUS.
  Ne istud roges, Phormio.

PHORMIO.   Non rogem
  Autem? Quis te roget igitur, nisi tu esse putes   15
  Qui magis te ex animo saluum velit atque incolumem
  Quam ego? Aut dicas, quaeso, vbi meum unquam tibi consilium
  Defuit, si unquam quicquam fuit vbi tibi opitularier
  Licuit.

TITUS.   Scio, sed nunc aliud est.

PHORMIO.   Imo quicquid est
  Effunde, neque enim ita velim cogites, tuam ad   20
  Teipsum quam ad me magis salutem pertinere. Dic.

TITUS.
  Ah non desinis.

9. *qui*] perhaps Foxe intended *superne deus qui,* though the reading would be hypermetrical; see Textual Notes.

17. *Quam ego*] perhaps intended for deletion in revision.

TITUS. How do you know?

PHORMIO. But how would you not know, since you've heard from Gesippus himself a thousand times more than is sung about in the whole city?

TITUS. Is there no delaying the wedding from happening today?

PHORMIO. It's today.

TITUS. Then today is Titus totally undone.

PHORMIO. Well! What are you saying?

TITUS [*to the heavens*]. I call upon you, who alone know of my sickness.

PHORMIO. What on earth is wrong, master? What's this shaking of your head? What are these sighs? Is this some sickness?

TITUS. I wish it were.

PHORMIO. Why?

TITUS. I want to die.

PHORMIO. Then tell me what's the matter.

TITUS. Don't ask me that, Phormio.

PHORMIO. Don't ask indeed! Who should ask you, then, unless you think there's someone more sincere than I am in wishing you safe and sound? Or tell me, please, when was my counsel ever wanting to you if there was ever any way at all in which I could help you?

TITUS. I know, but this is different.

PHORMIO. Well, whatever it is, out with it. I wouldn't want you to think that your well-being means more to you than to me. Tell me.

TITUS. Ah, you don't stop.

PHORMIO.   Non sane nisi expressero.
  Dic.   [*f. 121v*]
TITUS.   Obtundis.
PHORMIO.   Sane si medelam speres—
TITUS.
  Neque faciam.
PHORMIO.   Minus torquebit te.
TITUS.   Nihil
  Est.
PHORMIO.   Quasi non prodat te vultus tuus,   25
  Index satis locuples.
TITUS.   Nihil est inquam.
PHORMIO.   Age,
  Age, si nihil est quin eas ad sodales intro
  Atque Gesippo tuo adsis ut par est in nuptiis.
TITUS.
  Veh misero mihi, nequeo continere amplius.
PHORMIO.
  Iamdudum desiderari scio praesentiam tuam.   30
TITUS.
  Mi Phormio.
PHORMIO.   Quid ais?
TITUS.   Nae ego
  Inauspicato natus sum in vitam hanc.
PHORMIO.   Deus
  Bonus mala prohibeat.
TITUS.   Qui vtinam
  Quoquo pacto peremptus essem cum huc primum
  Tetulissem pedem!
PHORMIO.   Miror quidnam sit rei.   35
TITUS.
    Vis dicam tibi?
PHORMIO.   Si lubet.

---

25. *Quasi*] ?read *Etiam quasi*, which would yield a six-foot line (the first two feet being dactyls); but *Etiam* was apparently deleted.
  28. *Gesippo*] emended from *Tito*.
  29. *Veh*] = *Vae*.

PHORMIO. Not until I've wrung it out of you. Tell me.

TITUS. You keep hammering away.

PHORMIO. Well, if you would look for a cure——

TITUS. I won't.

PHORMIO.——it will torture you less.

TITUS. It's nothing.

PHORMIO. As if your face weren't a sure sign to betray you.

TITUS. It's nothing, I say.

PHORMIO. Come, come, if it's nothing, why not go in to your companions to be with your friend Gesippus at his wedding, as is proper?

TITUS [*aside*]. Oh woe is me, I can't hold it in any longer.

PHORMIO. I know they wanted you there long ago.

TITUS. My Phormio——

PHORMIO. What?

TITUS. Truly I was born under an evil star.

PHORMIO. May the good lord prevent evil.

TITUS. Would that I had been killed somehow as soon as I came here.

PHORMIO. I wonder what's the matter.

TITUS. You want me to tell you?

PHORMIO. If you will.

TITUS.   Dicam. Semproniam
  Illam Gesippo hodie meo nupturam nostin',
  Phormio?
PHORMIO.   Quid ni?
TITUS.   Os illius, habitum
  Atque formam—sed quid eam praedicem tibi?
PHORMIO.   Audio.
TITUS.
  Deinde Gesippum illum vnice animo meo   40
  Semper charissimum, huic qui datur in coniugem?
PHORMIO.
  Perge.
TITUS.   Qui nisi is esset, facile ego in hac
  Re prospicerem mihi.
PHORMIO.   Quid tum postea?
TITUS.   Vah, tardus es,
  Phormio.
PHORMIO.   Au, perquam pol Tite ut ais
  Tardus sum. Iam intelligo. Ausculta in aurem.   45
TITUS.   [*f. 122*]
  Ita amet me deus, Phormio.
PHORMIO.   Et me. Sed quid hic
  Me iam velis facere?
TITUS.   Gladio me tuo
  Interimas atque eximas miseriis.
PHORMIO.   Istud
  Hostibus meis fiet potius.
TITUS.   Aut siquid aliud,
  Aliud innire queas remedii.
PHORMIO.   Conclamatum est.   50
TITUS.
  Saltem ut proferantur nuptiae in diem alterum
  Dum aliquo me concedam praecipitatum.
PHORMIO.   Here,
  Non tam bardus nec tardus sum qui incendia
  Tua non intelligam. Vtinam tam facile dare

44. *Tite*] emended from *Pamphile*.
50. *innire*] = *inire*.

TITUS. I'll tell you. Phormio, you know Sempronia, who is marrying my friend Gesippus today?

PHORMIO. Of course.

TITUS. Her face, her bearing, her figure—but why should I praise her to you?

PHORMIO. I'm listening.

TITUS. Then you know that Gesippus, who's marrying her, has always been singularly dear to my heart.

PHORMIO. Go on.

TITUS. If it weren't he, I'd look after my own interests in this matter without any hesitation.

PHORMIO. Go on.

TITUS. Bah, you're slow, Phormio.

PHORMIO. Oh! I'm very slow indeed, as you say, Titus. Now I understand. Listen. [*He whispers in Titus' ear.*]

TITUS. Yes, Phormio, god love me.

PHORMIO. And me. But now, what would you like me to do about it?

TITUS. Kill me with your sword and deliver me from my miseries.

PHORMIO. That would be better done by my enemies.

TITUS. Or, if you can devise something else, some other remedy——

PHORMIO. It's hopeless.

TITUS. At least if the wedding were put off to another day while I run off somewhere——

PHORMIO. Master, I'm not so stupid or so slow[1] that I don't understand what's burning you; would that I could as easily give you

---

[1] The Latin rhyme (*tardus-bardus*) cannot be effectively captured in English.

Lenimen queam. Quin agam sedulo   55
Manibus pedibusque facturus omnia quo iuuem
Te. Tu quiesce interim et da cogitandi locum.
Titus.
    Fiet.
Phormio.   Ego consulam locos meos dialecticos.

[Actus Primus. Scena Secunda.]
Gesippus. Dromo. Syrus. [*Pythias. Stephanio.*]

[Gesippus.]
    Quis tandem finis cerimoniarum? Citius decem
Elephanti pariunt quam vnas isti parturiunt nuptias.
Tam sancti sunt in nugis, ipsa in re remisissimi.
Quin mihi aut cito dent aut non dent vxorem prorsus?
Me enecant isto taedio. Nec pater usquam apparet gentium   5
Nec quicquam paratum dum ad nuptias manus non admolior.
Atqui iam opus est ut faciam. Heus, heus, Dromo
Et Syre, exite ad me ilico.
Dromo.   Quis euocator hic?
    Here, tun' accersisti?   [*f. 122v*]
Syrus.   Here adsumus. Numquid imperas?
Gesippus.
    Syre, Stephanio et Pythias fac sis huc vocentur ocyus.   10
Syrus.
    Abeo.
Gesippus.   Tu, Dromo, curriculo perfuge ad forum, obsonium
E macello comportatum ad nuptias. Cape argentum hoc atque,
Audin'? si quas rariores nosti gulae delicias, nihil
Desit lautitiarum ita vti scis conuenire conuiuio.
Dromo.
    Factum puta.
Gesippus.   Stephanio, te praeficimus rei   15
    Culinariae.
Stephanio.   Accipio.

---

    58. *dialecticos*] apparently a separate line in MST, though Foxe probably meant
it merely as a runover of l. 58.
    P.H. *Pythias. Stephanio*] omitted in manuscript.
    3. *ipsa . . . remisissimi*] see Textual Notes.

a balm. But I'll set to work, hand and foot, doing everything I can to help you. Meantime you be calm and allow yourself room for thought.

TITUS. All right.

PHORMIO. I'll consult my places of logic.[1]   [*Exeunt.*

[I.2]   *Enter Gesippus.*

GESIPPUS. Is there any end of these ceremonies? Ten elephants bear young faster than these people produce one wedding. They're as neglectful of the substance of the business as they are scrupulous about trivia. Oh, that they would either give me a wife quickly or not give me a wife straightaway. They're killing me with this irksome delay. My father is nowhere to be seen, and nothing is prepared unless I put my own hands to work on the wedding. But now I must do it.—— [*Shouts.*] Hey there, Dromo and Syrus, come out here to me.

Enter Dromo and Syrius.

DROMO. Who's calling? Master, did you call?

SYRUS. Master, here we are. What is your command?

GESIPPUS. Syrus, call Stephanio and Pythias here at once.

SYRUS. I'm on my way.   [*Exit.*

GESIPPUS. Dromo, you run to the forum on the double to get provisions for the wedding from the butcher. Take this silver, and—— are you listening?——if you know of any rare delicacies for our palates, let no luxury be wanting that you know is suitable for our banquet.

DROMO. Consider it done.   [*Exit.*

Enter Syrus, Stephanio, and Pythias.

GESIPPUS. Stephanio, I place you in charge of kitchen operations.

STEPHANIO. I accept.

---

[1] The grounds of proof in argument, which Magdalen students would know very well from their work in grammar school and university. Phormio later finds a solution in the place of similitude (the physical resemblance of Titus and Gesippus).

GESIPPUS.   Syre, adduc nobis qui choraules siet
  Et hymenaeum cantitet, deinde qui choreas saltitent
  Et tripudia. Vt omnia perstrepent hilaritate.
SYRUS.   Curabitur.
GESIPPUS.
  Tua, Pythia, cura est ut intus niteant omnia
  Splendeantque in aedibus; componantur ad munditiem; rosas
      ac lilia quoqueversum   20
  Interspergito. Limina sertis ornentur, et atria
  Fronde. Fument accensis thura Sabea focis. Tum
  Peristroma illud ex Arabia e cistula euoluas ac
  Thoro insternas geniali, quod mea adueniens
  Demeretur Sempronia. Deinde quid aliud volui   25
  Dicere? Sed nihil refert. Haec interim exequitor.
PYTHIAS.
  Fiet, domine.
GESIPPUS.   Abite. Nunc pater mihi vbi
  Vbi est conquirendus est, vt conueniam, nec satis
  Vbi quaeram scio. Atque eum quam opportune cum socero
  Advenientem.   30

[ACTUS PRIMUS. SCENA TERTIA.]
Simo. Chremes. Gesippus.   [*f. 123*]

[SIMO.]
  Quin tu istas gratias omitte, Chreme, quasi hactenus
  Inter nos non norimus, aut quasi gratiae id mihi
  Adponi aequum sit pro officio ego quod facio. Siquid meum
  Vsquam vides tibi aut tuis quod expetendum sit, uel id
  Deberi a me tibi, Chreme, credito——itque pro mutua   5
  Ac inueterata hac uitae simul quae mihi iam diu
  Tecum incoepit consuetudine.
CHREMES.   Perbenigne et dicis et facis,
  Simo. Eandemque vicissim tibi cantionem recino: si quid fortuna
      habet

---

18. *perstrepent*] the correct reading would be *perstrepant*.
20. *componantur ad munditiem*] see Textual Notes.
5. *itque*] a dubious reading; the dash could be a *v* (?read *vic'que*).
8. *cantionem recino*] see Textual Notes.

GESIPPUS. Syrus, bring me the flute player and the singer of the wedding hymn and the dancers. How everything will resound with merrymaking.

SYRUS. It will be taken care of.

GESIPPUS. Pythias, your job is to see that everything in the house is shiny and sparkling and elegantly arranged. Scatter roses and lilies everywhere. Decorate the doorways with garlands and the halls with boughs. Make Sabaean[1] incense smoke in the burning hearths. Unroll the Arabian carpet from its basket and spread it on the bridal couch, because my Sempronia deserves it when she comes. Then what else did I want to tell you? Well, nothing important. For now, look after these things.

PYTHIAS. It will be done, my lord.

GESIPPUS. Get going.———   [*Exeunt all but Gesippus.*
Now I must hunt for my father to speak to him, wherever he is—and I don't quite know where to look. But just in time he's coming with my father-in-law.

[I.3]   *Enter Simo and Chremes*

SIMO. Never mind the thanks, Chremes. As if we didn't know this between ourselves long ago, or as if it were right to attribute to my graciousness what I do out of duty. If you see anything at all of mine which you or your family should want, please consider that I owe it to you, Chremes———that's the result of this mutual and long-standing familiarity which began between your life and mine at the same time long ago.

CHREMES. Your words and actions are very kind, Simo, and I sing the same refrain to you in turn: if it is my good fortune to have

---

[1] Saba (the Biblical Sheba) in Arabia Felix was famous for its frankincense and myrrh. Then, as now, Arabia was also noted for its carpets, to which Gesippus refers in the next sentence.

Nostra vbi quid tibi gratiae referre possumus, me rebusque
Meis vtere vt voles. Numquid nunc rei aliud restat reliquum? 10
GESIPPUS.
    Cesso compellare.
CHREMES.   Quis hic loquitur? Gesippe?
GESIPPUS.   Pater,
    Teipsum querito.
CHREMES.   Qua de re?
GESIPPUS.   Hodie vis vxorem me ducere
    Annon? Iam advesperascit.
CHREMES.   Ohe vt hic prurit ad nuptias!
    Quin iam venio. Tu interim praecurre domum, ibi vt
    Concinnentur omnia ita vt decet conviuas excipi luculenter.
GESIPPUS.   Hanc 15
    Modo edictionem dedi Pythiae ad accurandum!   [*f. 123v*]
CHREMES.   Laudo. Nunc
    Ad Semproniam ergo ingredere, vt sese exornet ne sit in
    Mora cum opus sit accersier.
GESIPPUS.   Admodum.
CHREMES.   Sed heus
    Insuauem fortassis tibi operam praecipimus. Ibit
    Pro te, censeo, alius. Tu parcas calcibus.
GESIPPUS.   Ne paueas, pater!   20
    Ego hoc defungar optime!
SIMO.   Gesippe, etiam respicis.
    En Gesippe, pactas hic tecum decem argenti drachumulas,
    Quid ais?
GESIPPUS.   Quidnam facturus?
SIMO.   Ea lege, ad me rursum vti
    Redeas absque osculo.
GESIPPUS.   Quin hercle dato.
SIMO.   Enimvero hercle accipe.
GESIPPUS.
    Nolim tantum tibi damni, Simo.
SIMO.   Viden' vero?

13. *Annon*] emended from *Anno.*
19. *Insuauem*] ?read *Gesippe insuauem*; see Textual Notes.

anything by which I may show something of my gratitude toward you, use me and my goods as you wish. Now, does anything else remain to be done?

GESIPPUS [*aside, coming forward*]. I'll speak to them.

CHREMES. Who's speaking here? Gesippus?

GESIPPUS. Father, I've been looking all over for you.

CHREMES. What about?

GESIPPUS. Do you want me to get married today or not? It's almost evening already.

CHREMES. Oho, how he itches for the wedding! Well, I'm coming now. Meantime you run on home to arrange everything there as it should be for receiving guests splendidly.

GESIPPUS. I've just ordered Pythias to see to that.

CHREMES. Very good. Now then, go have Sempronia get dressed so she won't keep us waiting when it's time to call her.

GESIPPUS. Yes indeed.

CHREMES. But alas, maybe we're rushing you off on an unpleasant task. I think someone else will go for you. You save your shoes.

GESIPPUS. Have no fear, father. I'll take care of this best.

SIMO. Gesippus, look here now. Here's a deal with you for ten silver drachmas,[1] Gesippus, what do you say?

GESIPPUS. What do I have to do?

SIMO. The condition is that you come back to me without giving her a kiss.

GESIPPUS. Well, by Hercules, give them to me.

SIMO. Well, by Hercules, take them.

GESIPPUS. I wouldn't want to do you such an injury, Simo. [*Exit.*

SIMO. Did you see that?

---

[1] A small silver coin, equivalent to the Roman denarius and worth slightly more than sixteen cents.

CHREMES.   Mira res,   25
  Quid fert adolescentia.
SIMO.   Ita est.
CHREMES.   Satis iam Simo a nobis, quod ad
  Hanc rem attinet, spero esse definita omnia, nisi te quid aliud
  Moratum habet.
SIMO.   Nihil.
CHREMES.   De dote uti dudum conventum est.
SIMO.
  Dos ut dixi triginta talenta tibi: accersas vbi lubet.
CHREMES.   [*f. 124*]
  Cedo dextram. Porro hoc te rogo, Simo, ut haec inter nos
    affinitas   30
  Stabili nunc foedere inita, magis magisque augescens indies,
  Perpetua postmodum aetate cum nostra succrescat simul.
SIMO.
  Imo sic opto et volo, Chreme.
CHREMES.   Sed quando supputabimus?
SIMO.
  Tuo fiat arbitratu.
CHREMES.   Quin iam censeo opportunissimum,
  Intus si velis apud nos.
SIMO.   I prae, consequar.   35

[ACTUS PRIMUS. SCENA QUARTA.]
Phormio.

[PHORMIO.]
  Pas, Iupiter, Saturnus, virgula Mercurii,
  Vulcani retia, arcus Cupidinis, Gygis
  Annulus, Syrenarum cantus, Cyrcaea
  Pocula, Medeae herbae, Medusae caput,
  Ungula Pegasi, lupi oculus, vos denique   5

---

   1. *Pas*] I take this as a transliteration of the Greek πᾶς. The word is repeated
in l. 7, twice alone and twice with Latin prefixes which yield no meaning; cf. the
nonsense prefix *schm* in American slang, as in *everything—schmeverything.*

CHREMES. It's miraculous what youth does.[1]

SIMO. It certainly is.

CHREMES. Simo, I hope we've finished everything that we have to do in this matter—unless there's something else to hold you back.

SIMO. Nothing else.

CHREMES. The dowry is as we agreed before?

SIMO. As I said, a dowry of thirty talents for you.[2] Ask for it whenever you wish.

CHREMES. Let's shake on it. And, Simo, I beg you that this alliance between us, begun now in this firm contract, may increase from day to day, growing more and more firm even as our days do grow, and on in perpetuity.

SIMO. I earnestly hope so too, Chremes.

CHREMES. When shall we do our reckoning?

SIMO. Whenever you wish.

CHREMES. Well, I think now is a very good time if you want to go into my place.

SIMO. Lead on, I'll follow. [*Exeunt.*

[I.4]   *Enter Phormio.*

PHORMIO. The whole crew of you! Jupiter, Saturn, Mercury's rod,[3] Vulcan's net,[4] Cupid's bow, Gyges' ring,[5] the Sirens' song, Circe's cup,[6] Medea's herbs,[7] Medusa's head,[8] Pegasus' hoof,[9]

---

[1] Gesippus' integrity is thus established, to the surprise of his elders, in that he refuses to accept money that he could easily keep without living up to the terms of the bet.

[2] The talent contained, usually, 6,000 drachmas and was worth around $1,000.

[3] The caduceus.

[4] The net with which Vulcan, god of fire and metal-working, captured his wife Venus *in flagrante delicto* with Mars.

[5] The ring by means of which Gyges, a king of Lydia, could make himself invisible.

[6] The cup with which Circe turned men into beasts.

[7] The herbs, etc., with which the sorceress Medea rejuvenated Aeson, Jason's father.

[8] The gorgon Medusa's head, cut off by Perseus and fixed in Minerva's aegis, had serpents for hair and eyes which turned men to stone.

[9] Pegasus, the winged horse of Bellerophon, born of Medusa's blood; mounted on Pegasus, Bellerophon conquered the Chimaera. Pegasus' hoof kicked the Muses' Mt. Helicon and produced the soul-inspiring fountain Hippocrene.

Platonis ideae, exalationes Aristotelis,
Numeri Pythagorae; pas, hehi pas repas
Compas! Proh diuum atque hominum fidem!
Quam duram coepi ego prouinciam hodie,
Et quam audax facinus, plusquam facinus, hodie   10
Agressus sum! Quod nunc superi superaeque
Omnes tantam mihi potestatem astutiae
Infulciant ut queam perficere. Quippe non
Humanam sed diuinam opem res haec prorsus   [*f. 124v*]
Postulat, adeo meas longe machinas   15
Omnes superat: principio senes duo
Fallendi simul, virginis incantandus
Animus, Gesippi expugnandus amor—
Quod quam sit difficile nihil dico nunc—
Populo vniuerso oblinendi oculi.   20
Tum temporis punctum ad res istas datur mihi,
Tum solus sum, sine Theseo veluti in
Labyrintho situs. Etiamnum nonnullum per
Transsennam veluti filum habere videor,
Quo scilicet hinc me elabi pacto oporteat.   25
Consului enim locos meos oraculis
Ceu pro Delphicis dialecticos.
Inde vt alius ex alio, vt fit, in mentem incidit
Locus mox offert se similitudinis.
Hinc prehendi argumentum meo quam graphice   30
Appositum molimini. At vna haec est mihi
Cautio, nequid huius suboleat herunculo
Quem in maerore haerere adhuc satius est.

8-9.] see Textual Notes.
23-27.] see Textual Notes for the special problems in these lines.

the wolf's eye,[1] and finally you too, Plato's Ideas,[2] Aristotle's exhalations,[3] and Pythagoras' numbers[4]—hey, every one of you, all withall and wherewithall![5] Oh the faith of gods and men! How hard the duty I've undertaken today! How audacious the crime, worse than a crime, I've begun today! May all the gods and goddesses stuff me now with the power of their wisdom that I may bring this off, for it surely demands resources not human but divine, so far does it exceed all my devices. First two old men must be deceived at the same time, and the mind of the girl must be charmed. Gesippus' love must be taken by storm, and how difficult that is I pass over for the present. Everyone's eyes must be blinded. Now is the time for me to do all this, and now I'm on my own as if I were in the Labyrinth without Theseus.[6] But even now, through the lattice,[7] I seem to have a thread, as it were, with which I should certainly be able to get out of this spot. For delphic oracles, so to speak, I have consulted my places of logic: of these, the place of similitude instantly presents itself, just as one thing happens to come into the mind from another. Hence I've seized upon a theme which is beautifully appropriate to my task. But I must be careful not to let any of this leak out to my young master. It's better for him to remain

[1] Referring to an old Roman belief that if a wolf saw a man before the man saw the wolf, the man would become dumb.

[2] The archetypal ideals of Platonic philosophy.

[3] Aristotle's πνεῦμα σύμφυτον, "some type of hot, foamy substance analogous in composition to the element of which the stars are made. . . . It starts from the heart and its function is to provide the sensitive and kinetic link between the physical organs and the *psyche*. . . . The *pneuma* is present in the sperm and transmits the nutritive and sensitive soul from progenitor to offspring" (F. E. Peters, *Greek Philosophical Terms: A Historical Lexicon* [New York, 1967], p. 161); see A. L. Peck, tr., *Generation of Animals*, Loeb Classical Library (London, 1953), pp. 578-593. Literally, πνεῦμα means wind (Aristotle's *De Meteorologia, passim*).

[4] Pythagoras reduced the basic intervals of music to mathematical ratios, which he "extended to the principle that things are, in effect, numbers" (Peters, p. 25). Aristotle says the Pythagoreans saw "the elements of numbers to be the elements of everything, and the whole universe to be a proportion of number" (*Metaphysics*, 986a, Hugh Tredennick, tr., Loeb Library [London, 1947], I, 33).

[5] See the note to the Latin text on *Pas* (l. 1).

[6] Theseus escaped from Minos' Labyrinth in Crete with a thread provided by Ariadne. In *Christus Triumphans* Satan desires some Theseuses to help him.

[7] Cf. *Christus Triumphans*, Prologue 11; Foxe's draft reading, *per nebulas* (through the clouds), may be taken as a gloss on this Ciceronian phrase.

Quo nostrae procedant vt volumus astutiae.
Atque opportune huc ut volumus incedit obuiam. 35
Vide animi maestus: admiranda res amor
Quid facit. Atqui hunc libido est gustare sermonem.

[Actus Primus. Scena Quinta.]
Titus. Phormio. *[f. 125]*
Dimetri.

[Titus.]
Nunc illud est profecto quod
Si sexcenti Aesculapii,
Cumque his Salus ipsa, omnia
In unum omnes sua simul
Narthecia opesque conferant 5
Huic iam malo antidoti nihil
Quicquam adferant, quin perditus
Perpetuo prorsus perierim.
Vah intimis adeo miser
Medullis totus aestuo 10
Penitissime, cui neque pudor
Neque consilium neque ratio
Quicquam subseruit. O mea
Sempronia, mea suauitas,
Vsque adeo meum haec ingens tuae 15
Formae vis perstringit iecur.
O faciem illam pulchram, o genas
Lubentes, o collum eburneum,
O formarum delicium ac decus
Rarum. Ergo praeter te, mea *[f. 125v]* 20
Sempronia, aliud rerum nihil
Mihi omnium volo. Sola tu
Vel mors vel vita mea, quam nisi
Fiet in coniugem ut duxero
Vnum pol spirare nequeo 25
Praeterea diem. Nec qua id pote est
Fieri video, namque quod

23. *Vel mors*] ?read *Mors.*

still mired in his grief. In that way my wiles may proceed as I wish. And just as I wished, here he comes toward me. See how sad he is. It's remarkable what love does! But I'm eager to hear what he has to say.

[I.5]   *Enter Titus.*

TITUS. Now indeed I have that sickness for which six hundred Aesculapiuses along with Salus herself,[1] if they rolled all their medicines and all their skills into one, could supply no antidote to prevent me from dying straightaway, utterly beyond recovery. Alas, wretch that I am, my very heart is so completely on fire that neither shame nor good counsel nor reason can help me at all. Oh my Sempronia, my sweet, how continually the great power of your beauty squeezes at my liver![2] Oh that beautiful face, those lovely cheeks, that ivory neck! Oh the delight and the rare grace of your charms! Besides you, then, I want nothing else in the world, my Sempronia. You alone are life or death to me: unless I marry you I cannot breathe even one day more. And I don't see how it can be done, for what Phormio has

---

[1] Aesculapius was god of medicine; Salus (the Greek Hygeiea), i.e., health, was his helper.

[2] In Renaissance physiology, the liver was thought the seat of love.

Mihi est pollicitus Phormio
Magis solandi ergo mei
Quam quod quicquam habeat.   30
Factum certo scio.

PHORMIO.

Quasi de improuiso ingeram me. Prorsus haec
Res extra salutem est quantum video
Nisi deus succurrat quispiam an diuina virgula.
Quippe humanos cuneos nodus hic omnes superat.   35
Miseret me heri.

TITUS.   Occidi. Quid ais,
Phormio?

PHORMIO.   Here, tu' hic eras? Teipsum querito.

TITUS.

Quid ais? Ecquid vitae est an nihil, Phormio?

PHORMIO.

Here, in re immedicabili non arte sed patientia
Opus est. Laboratum est sedulo, ac si pro capite   40
Here hercle sudandum sit, meo, si quid industria
Confici potuisset. Verum cum eo res in loco
Est ut nusquam sit consilio locus,
Consilium hoc iam solum superest: tua vt   [*f. 126*]
Occurras patientia quando mutarier   45
Id aliter non potest. Det locum voluntas
Necessitati.

TITUS.   Veh mortuo mihi.
Vt animus antehac in spe atque in timore
Detentus fuit, ita nunc spes postquam adempta est
Vita vna adempta est simul. Hah, Phormio,   50
Huccine fretus praesidio tuo?

PHORMIO.   Fretus meo?
Nam quid queso te in hac re vt facerem?
Si quidem prius id mihi indicasses, fateor,
Verum alienam vxorem nunc in ipsis nuptiis
Tum in aliena regione velle ducere   55
Fieri non potest. Tu dijudica.

TITUS.   Quin
Romam ergo abiens commenda me parentibus.

promised me is more to console me than that he really has anything, I'm quite sure of that.

PHORMIO. [*aside*]. I'll come up as if I were just arriving. [*Aloud, as
if to himself.*] As far as I can see, this business is completely
beyond saving unless some god or some divine wand helps us.
This knurl really defies all human wedges. I feel sorry for my
master.

TITUS. I'm dead. What are you saying, Phormio?

PHORMIO. Master, were you here? I've been looking for you.

TITUS. What do you say, Phormio, is there hope for my life or not?

PHORMIO. Master, when a disease is incurable, one needs patience,
not skill. I've worked hard, master, just as if I had to sweat for
my own neck—my own, by Hercules—and as if anything could
have been done through my industry. But when matters are in
such a state that there is no room for a plan, the only plan remaining is this: meet the situation with patience when it can't
be altered. Let your will give way to necessity.

TITUS. Or to my death! As my life had been prolonged up to now
in hope and fear, so now, when my hope has been ripped away,
my life has been ripped away with it. Oh Phormio, is this where
I've got by relying on your help?

PHORMIO. Relying on my help! For heaven's sake, what could I
do about it? If indeed you had told me about it earlier, I
confess——. But now, to want to marry another man's wife at
the very moment of his wedding, and in the other man's country
to boot—it can't be done. You be the judge.

TITUS. Well, then, go to Rome and commend me to my parents.

PHORMIO.

Here, quaeso quo nunc agis te?

TITUS.   In lectulum
  Supplicaturus morti quandoquidem distaedeat
  Viuere.

PHROMIO.   Recte sane. Hinc igitur meam   60
  Exordiar telam concinnandi nuptias.
  Prima mihi Gesippo huic iniicienda tragula est.
  Huic ille semper fuit vt quisquam fuit
  Nostro amicissimus, perinde vt non vitam
  Magis amauit suam. Hiccine, noster ut   65
  Pereat, cui opitulari ipse tam facile
  Vnius adeo impendio potest virgunculae,
  Certe, si resciuerit, non sinet scio.
  Nunc ipsum vbi quaeram cogito.

[ACTUS PRIMUS. SCENA SEXTA.]

Syrus. Marsias. Chorus Mimicus. Misenus.   [*f. 126v*]

SYRUS.
  Papae, prodigium hominis sterquilinium, nebulonis. At
  Vnde quaeso edoctus peritiam tantam hac cum omnipotenti tua
  Fistula?

MARSIAS.   Mane, nondum Syre audisti omnia.

SYRUS.   Eho tu
  An nondum obsecro.

MARSIAS.   Deinde Dorivm.

SYRUS.   Dorivm.

MARSIAS.   Hypodorium.

SYRUS.
  Euax.

MARSIAS.   Lydium.

SYRUS.   Eya vero.

MARSIAS.   Phrigium.

SYRUS.   Bene.

MARSIAS.   Hypophrygium.   5

SYRUS.
  Dice.

MARSIAS.   Hypolydium.

PHORMIO. Master, where are you going now, I beseech you?

TITUS. To my couch to plead for death, since I'm tired of living.

[*Exit.*

PHORMIO. Very well.—— Now, then, I shall weave my web of arranging a wedding. My first snare must be set for Gesippus. He's always been a great friend of my master, as friendly as anyone—he hasn't loved his own life more. If he learned that my master is dying and that he could easily help him at the trifling cost of one girl, he wouldn't let him die, I'm sure of that. Now I wonder where I might find him. [*Exit.*

[I.6] *Enter Syrus, Marsias, and a Chorus of Mimes.*

SYRUS. Wonderful, you marvelous dungheap of worthlessness. But where on earth did you learn so much skill with this omnipotent pipe of yours?

MARSIAS. Wait, Syrus, you haven't heard everything yet.

SYRUS. Well, pray, will you continue or not?

MARSIAS. Next there's the Dorian.[1] [*He plays the scales.*]

SYRUS. Dorian.

MARSIAS. And Hypo-Dorian.

SYRUS. Good.

MARSIAS. The Lydian.

SYRUS. Ah, indeed.

MARSIAS. The Phrygian.

SYRUS. Fine.

MARSIAS. The Hypo-Phrygian.

SYRUS. Go on.

MARSIAS. Hypo-Lydian.

[1] Marsias plays the four modes (or scales) of Greek music (Dorian, Lydian, Phrygian, and Mixo-Lydian), each of which was associated with a particular mood, and three of the plagal scales associated with those (Hypo-Dorian, Hypo-Phrygian, and Hypo-Lydian).

SYRUS.   Ei.

MARSIAS.   Mixolydium.

SYRUS.   Et quid non?

MARSIAS.   Mira tibi Syre
   Sunt ista forsitan.

SYRUS.   Mihi? Imo diuina omnia, uixque mihi
   Induci potest, esse te vt credam hominem.

MARSIAS.   Praeter tum
   Volgares illas Orphei ac Amphyonis cantiones, quibus
   Saxa et syluas commotas memorant.

SYRUS.   Quaeso vero te   10
   Vir doctissime.

MARSIAS.   Quid vis?

SYRUS.   Caelo primoque mobili
   Opinio est mirificam quandam inesse harmoniam.

MARSIAS.   Id num cui dubium?
   Atque iccirco sidera ducunt ipsa choreas.

SYRUS.   Atque eam tua
   Nobis potest effingere fistula?

MARSIAS.   Nihil facilius.

SYRUS.
   Rogatur ut   15
   Audire liceat.

MARSIAS.   Negatur.

SYRUS.   Inclina, domine, aurem tuam.

MARSIAS.
   Non audio.

SYRUS.   Per omnipotentem tuam fistulam.

MARSIAS.   Etiamsi rogas millies.

SYRUS.   [*f. 127*]
   Cur, quaeso?

MARIAS.   Quia an id tu nescis, fatue, disciplinam
   Esse artis nostrae, plus quo possit quisque rogatus hoc minus
   Velit.

---

   15. *Rogatur ut*] the metrical position of this line following revision is unclear;
I read it as a separate line. See Textual Notes.

Syrus. Oh.

Marsias. Mixo-Lydian.

Syrus. And what not?

Marsias. I suppose this is all amazing to you, Syrus?

Syrus. To me? Yes, it's all divine, and I can scarcely be persuaded to believe that you are a man.

Marsias. Besides that, there are the popular Orphic and Amphionic songs by which the common people commemorate the moving of rocks and woods.[1]

Syrus. But let me ask you something, my most learned fellow.

Marsias. What?

Syrus. Do you think there's a miraculous harmony in the sky and the primum mobile?[2]

Marsias. Is there any doubt about it? On account of it the stars themselves dance.

Syrus. Can your pipe imitate that for us?

Marsias. There's nothing easier.

Syrus. Let's hear it.

Marsias. No.

Syrus. Bend your ear, lord.[3]

Marsias. I don't hear you.

Syrus. By your almighty pipe.

Marsias. Even if you ask a thousand times.

Syrus. Why, will you tell me?

Marsias. Because it's a rule of my art——or don't you know this, you silly fool?——that the more anyone can do, the less he wishes to do when he's asked.

---

[1] Orpheus (whose legend is analogous to that of Marsias' namesake, Marsyas) played the lyre so enchantingly that all nature stopped to listen to his music; the ἀοιδοί of Thrace, the earliest singers of Greece, are associated with his worship. Amphion's playing of the lyre caused stones to move and form a wall around Thebes.

[2] The *primum mobile* was the outermost sphere, in Ptolemaic astronomy, which actuated the movements of all the other spheres. The music of the spheres is a Pythagorean conception based on the mathematical affinity between the lyre of seven strings and the universe of seven planets. In the mystical tradition of this conception, only the spiritually pure could hear the notes that each sphere emitted and that, together, produced a divine harmony. Of course no mortal, not even Marsias, could reproduce that music.

[3] That is, listen with favor (as in Psalm 30.3).

SYRUS. Siccine ais? Imo etsi tu velles maxime, haud libuit   20
   Audire tamen. Dissimulabam.

MARSIAS.   Age age, tametsi decretum erat
   Tamen ne vertas id imperitiae ac si minime possem audies.

SYRUS.
   Siquidem saltare licet.

MARSIAS.   Ut libet.

SYRUS.   Incipe.

MARSIAS.   Ausculta.

SYRUS.   Incipe.

MARSIAS.
   Etiam stas lapis?

SYRUS.   Modulabere hodie an non?

MARSIAS.   Tu pol homo
   Videre haud compos sensuum.

SYRUS.   Quidum?

MARSIAS.   Quasi non satis   25
   Me audias modulantem!

SYRUS.   Audiam! Quid ego audiam?

MARSIAS.   Caeleste melos.

SYRUS.
   Caelestes camelos? Egone mus'cam melodiam audio?

MARSIAS.   En tibi
   Saturnum illum grauitonum inter primos obtunnienti.

SYRUS.   Perge mentirier.

MARSIAS.
   Deinde sex reliquos orbes sex diapason species pulcherrima
   Harmonia personantes, audin' tu?

SYRUS.   Eho popularis ecquis audit 30
   Vestrum? Equidem nihil audio.

MARSIAS.   Syre, subtilis oppido haec est musica.
   Deinde ad hunc cantum aures ita a puero tibi occalluerunt
     quemadmodum Nili
   Stadisenses ad Cataractas, id est, quod iam non percipis.

---

27. *mus'cam*] the contraction (without an apostrophe in MST) signals the pun
on *muscam* and *musicam.*
   28. *obtunnienti*] = *obtinnienti.*

SYRUS. You don't say so. Well then, even if you wanted very much to play it, I didn't want to hear it at all. I was only pretending.

MARSIAS. All right, even though my mind was made up, yet you shall hear it so you won't accuse me of inexperience as if I didn't know how.

SYRUS. Well, if you let me dance, go ahead.

MARSIAS. As you wish.

SYRUS. Start.

MARSIAS. Listen.   [*Marsias and the Chorus pretend to play.*]

SYRUS. Come on, start.

MARSIAS. You stand like a stone!

SYRUS. Are you going to play today or not?

MARSIAS. God, you seem incapable of hearing.

SYRUS. Why?

MARSIAS. As if you didn't hear me playing perfectly well!

SYRUS. I hear? What should I hear?

MARSIAS. Heavenly carols.

SYRUS. Heavenly camels![1] Do I hear a melody fly?[2]

MARSIAS. Listen, and tingle with the deepest tones of Saturn.[3]

SYRUS. Go on lying.

MARSIAS. Then the six remaining spheres sounding the other six parts of the octave in a most beautiful harmony. Do you hear it?

SYRUS. Oh, does any mortal hear your song? I hear nothing.

MARSIAS. Syrus, this music is very subtle, and from boyhood your ears have been as hardened to this song as the inhabitants of Stadisis are to the Cataracts of the Nile.[4] That's why you don't hear it.

---

[1] The pun is closer in Latin (*melos* = song). Cf. the pun on *Carmeli-camelos* in the draft version of *Christus Triumphans* V.1.38.

[2] Literally, a musical melody (*mus'cam* = *musicam*), but the reference to camels provokes a punning reference to a fly.

[3] Saturn, the farthest of the spheres, produced the lowest note (like the longest string on the lyre) as the moon, the nearest sphere, produced the highest.

[4] The cataracts are at the southern border of modern Egypt. Pliny tells of the Ethiopian city of Stadisis, "where the river Nile, as it thunders down the precipices, has quite deprived the inhabitants of the power of hearing" (*Natural History*, VI.35, tr. John Bostock and H. T. Riley [London, 1855], II, 99).

SYRUS.   [*f. 127v*]

   Intelligo. Sed vbi alter ille tuus cessat?

MARSIAS.   Mox aderit.   34

SYRUS.

   Atque eccum venientem. Concedamus nunc intro. Consequamini.

[ACTUS PRIMUS. SCENA SEPTIMA.]

Phormio. Gesippus.

[PHORMIO.]

   Verissimum illud hercle est, volgo quod volitat:

   Nimia properatio sibi est mora maxima.

   Quanto studiosius Gesippum quaero tanto minus

   Inuenio, nec hominis vsquam vestigium apparet quo sese

   Abduxit ut sciam. Sed vnde crepuerunt fores?   5

   Saluus sum, hominem ipsum habeo.

GESIPPUS.   Omnium rerum

   Esse satietatem aiunt. At mihi longe aliter euenit

   In mea Sempronia, cuius ego plenus numquam sum neque

   Esse possum, quin quo magis

   Intueor hoc magis perpetuo placet. Atque nunc   10

   Magnifice, ut numquam alias, postquam in vestibus video

   Oris illud iubar vt splendeat—ut liquido dixerim—

   Virginum quicquid est omnes esse carbonarias

   Aut Aegyptias si formas conferant. Excepta tamen

   Vna Pamphila, Romae olim quam vidi cum Tito meo   15

   Illi destinatam in coniugem. Exemplar adeo Naturae singulare

   Idaeae obliuiscar nunquam, quod nisi is esset

   Quem vis non fuit violare—nec vnquam velim—id in hac

   Iam designassem virgine quod Paris, ut referunt,

   In rapienda Helena.

PHORMIO.   Nae ego istud multis nominibus   20

   Audisse gaudeo.

GESIPPUS.   Quod tamen Titi mei caussa

   Numquam faciam.   [*f. 128*]

PHORMIO.   Sat habeo. Quasi modo

   Adveniens occupabo hominem. Siquis hic

14. *si formas*] ?read *si huic formas*; see Textual Notes.

Syrus. I know. But say, where is your buddy held up?
Marsias. He'll be here soon.
Syrus. And sure enough he's coming.

Enter Misenus.

Now let's go in. Follow me. [*Exeunt.*

[I.7] *Enter Phormio.*

Phormio. By Hercules, that popular saying is very, very true: the more haste, the less speed. The more eagerly I look for Gesippus, the less success I have in finding him. No trace of the man appears so I might know where he's gone. But why are the gates squeaking? I'm saved. I have the man himself.

Enter Gesippus.

Gesippus [*to himself*]. They say one can get too much of everything, but for me it has turned out quite differently with my Sempronia, because I am never tired of her and I never can be. Yes, the more I see her, the more thoroughly I like her. And now that I've seen how the day-star of her face shines—how purely, I should have said—when she was dressed more magnificently than ever before, whatever other maidens there are, if they compare their beauty to hers, are all as black as coal or as Egyptians. All but one—Pamphila, whom I saw once at Rome about to be wed to my friend Titus. Such a unique copy of Nature's Idea I shall never forget. If it had not been Titus, whom I had no will to dishonor—I would never do that—I would already have done with that girl as they say Paris did in carrying off Helen.
Phormio [*aside*]. Well! I'm glad I heard that, of all names.
Gesippus [*to himself*]. But because of my friend Titus, I would never do that.
Phormio [*aside*]. I've heard enough. I'll come up to him as if I

Vestrum, amici, quaeso sit qui Gesippum hodie
In platea hac praetereuntem.
GESIPPUS.   Men' quaerit?
PHORMIO.   Ac   25
Ipsus adest. Gesippe salue.
GESIPPUS.   Salue. Sed quid tu es
Tam tristis, tamue anhelus Phormio?
PHORMIO.   Herus meus.
GESIPPUS.
Age, enarra, Phormio.
PHORMIO.   Magno te rogat opere,
Quantum potes.
GESIPPUS.   Perge.
PHORMIO.   Priusquam supremam exhalet animam
Ad se vt venias.
GESIPPUS.   Titus meus!
PHORMIO.   Quod si non durauerit   30
Adventum tuum, claues hic suas ac summam bonorum omnium
Delegauit tibi, heredem enim nisi te ait se velle neminem.
GESIPPUS.
Deus meliora.
PHORMIO.   Nam istaec sunt pessima.
GESIPPUS.   Duc
Me ad eum ilico.
PHORMIO.   Quaeso vero, hercle.

[ACTUS PRIMUS. SCENA OCTAVA.]
Simo. Chremes.

[SIMO.]
Bene igitur ratio accepti atque numerati conuenit exceptis tantum
    quinque, meministin'
Nostrae quod reliquum est ratiunculae.
CHREMES.   Nimirum quinque
Minae.

1-2.] see Textual Notes.

were just arriving.——[*Aloud.*] Friends, I wonder if any of you here saw Gesippus going along this street.

GESIPPUS. Is he looking for me?

PHORMIO. There he is. Hello, Gesippus.

GESIPPUS. Hello. But why are you so sad and so breathless, Phormio?

PHORMIO. It's my master.

GESIPPUS. Come, tell me, Phormio.

PHORMIO. He's asking for you in particular and as soon as possible——

GESIPPUS. Go on.

PHORMIO. To come to him before he draws his last breath.

GESIPPUS. My Titus!

PHORMIO. But if he doesn't survive until you come, he's assigned you his keys here and all his possessions, for he says he wants no one but you to be his heir.

GESIPPUS. May god give him better fortunes.

PHORMIO. For these are the worst.

GESIPPUS. Take me to him immediately.

PHORMIO. By Hercules, that's exactly what I want to do.   [*Exeunt.*

[I.8]   *Enter Simo and Chremes.*

SIMO. Then our accounts are in perfect agreement, with the sole exception of the five that remain to be reckoned, you remember.

CHREMES. That's right, five minas.[1]

---

[1] A mina was 100 drachmas, about $18.00.

Simo.   Recte tenes. Quod si non pigeat tantisper hic
Te praestolari dum curro domum, haud diu cum argento
Abero.
Chremes.   Propera.
Simo.   Atque vide iam redeuntem.
Chremes.   Deo nunc maximo maximas merito   5
Ago atque habeo gratias, ita cum res mihi secundet ex
Sententia vt iam nihil sit quod rerum sim hic auidissimus amplius.
Primum hac Simonis affinitate quot simul gazas vno
Accipimus cumulo! Tum haec ei sola est. Hac spe proci
Item complusculi quam auidi ad hanc nassam inhiabant
      quotidie   10
Priores etiam me in ambienda, sed ego in potiunda potior.
Denique ego virginem habeo, vnde defuncto patre
Huc bona deuoluuntur omnia. Tum hoc quantum mihi
Solatium, quando gnati animum erga nuptias ut habet   [*f. 128v*]
Perspexerim. Tenebat etenim id me non parum, ne (quod   15
Fere fit adolescentibus) amore alicubi detentus prauo
Animum ad vxorem minus advorteret. Quod nunc tamen
Postquam sensi magis, magis timere desino. Sed eccum Simonem.
Simo.
Quinque minas quas legere volui iam dudum collectas et in
Marsupio hoc repositas faeliciter repperi et adduxi. Chreme,
      cape.   20
Chremes.
Honestus es.
Simo.   Licet numerare.
Chremes.   Imo plus in
Verba tua quam pro meis calculis.
Simo.   Laudo.
Chremes.   Sed interim
Dum eras domi Semproniam tuam vidisti? Parata ea est annon?
Simo.
Nescio. Sed ibo nunc vt siet, ac festum diem hunc dicam
Familiae vt laetos se omnes prebeant in nuptiis filiae.   25
Chremes.
Et ego sacrificum adducturus qui coniugium consecret.

SIMO. Right. And if you don't mind waiting here for a time while I run home, I'll be back with the silver before long.

CHREMES. Run along.

SIMO. Look, I'm practically on my way back already.   [*Exit.*

CHREMES. Now I'm properly grateful to the greatest god and I give him the most profound thanks, because this business works out so favorably for me and so much according to my wishes that now there's nothing further at all which I'm very eager to attain. In the first place, by this relationship with Simo how many treasures I've received in one pile. Besides, he has only this one daughter. In this hope not a few suitors have been gaping avidly at this bait every day. They outdid even me in trying, but I was better at grabbing hold. Therefore I have the girl, and when her father dies all his goods will devolve upon my house. In addition, it's a great comfort to me to have perceived my son's mind inclined toward marriage, for I was not a little worried lest, as generally happens with youths, he might be ensnared in some depraved love for someone else and be less favorably disposed toward marriage. But now that I've realized the truth better, I'm more able to stop worrying. But here's Simo.

Enter Simo.

SIMO. The five minas that I consented to get I have happily found, collected long ago and deposited in this pouch. I've brought it, Chremes; take it.

CHREMES. You're an honorable man.

SIMO. You may count it.

CHREMES. No, I have more faith in your word than in my addition.

SIMO. Well said.

CHREMES. But, by the way, while you were at home did you see your daughter Sempronia? Is she ready or not?

SIMO. I don't know, but I'll go now and see that she is. And I'll declare this a holiday for my household so they all may demonstrate their happiness at the marriage of my daughter.

CHREMES. And I'll get the priest to consecrate the marriage.

SIMO.

   Censeo.

CHREMES. Sed heus, non opus vt istac ad templum
   Transeat.

SIMO.   Imo per forum potius.

CHREMES.   Rectissime.

[ACTUS PRIMUS. SCENA NONA.]
Gesippus. Phormio.

[GESIPPUS.]

   Itan' neque cibum nec somnum per hoc triduum? Quaeso,
     quid hoc

   Miror maeroris est? Cur non accersuntur medici?

PHORMIO.   Medicum

   Praeterquam vnum morbus hic nullum habet.

GESIPPUS.   Scio deum omnium

   Malorum medicum esse ac chirurgum quoque.

PHORMIO.   Imo etiam alium.

GESIPPUS.

   Bene hercle et scis qui mederi poterit?

PHORMIO.   Tamquam te.

GESIPPUS.   Et   5

   Quid morbi est?

PHORMIO.   Tamquam tuam.

GESIPPUS.   Quin dicas igitur vt

   Sim sciens ac accersam medicos.

PHORMIO.   Non opus est medicos arcessiri, cum

   Tu solus poteris huius morbi esse Aesculapius optimus.

   In te solo Gesippe situm est

   Vt serues vitam.   [*f. 129*]

GESIPPUS.   Quasi vero dicas te aut impetrare non   10

   Posse aut meis vti beneficiis impetrando cum licet

   Non velis.

PHORMIO.   Minime, sed quia fas non est.

GESIPPUS.   Quid

   Prohibet?

PHORMIO.   Religio.

SIMO. Fine.

CHREMES. But listen, it isn't necessary for him to come this way to the temple.

SIMO. No, it's better through the forum.[1]

CHREMES. Right.   [*Exeunt.*

[I.9]   *Enter Gesippus and Phormio.*

GESIPPUS. So he's had neither food nor sleep for three days? I wonder what sort of sickness this is? Why aren't the doctors summoned?

PHORMIO. This disease has no physician but one.

GESIPPUS. Yes, God is the physician, and the surgeon as well, for all ailments.

PHORMIO. No, I mean another one.

GESIPPUS. Good, by Hercules. And do you know who can cure him?

PHORMIO. The same as you.

GESIPPUS. And what sort of disease is it?

PHORMIO. The same as yours.

GESIPPUS. Then why don't you tell me so I'll know and I can call the physicians.

PHORMIO. It's not necessary to call physicians, since you alone have the power to be the best Aesculapius for his disease. In you alone, Gesippus, is placed the means to save his life.

GESIPPUS. Indeed. As if you would say either that you couldn't obtain my good offices or that you could have them but didn't want to use them.

PHORMIO. Not at all, but because it isn't right——

GESIPPUS. What prevents you?

PHORMIO. A scrupulous conscience.

---

[1] This apparently pointless reference may have served to prevent any expectation that Chremes would later bring the priest back onstage.

GESIPPUS.   I in pessimam crucem cum tua
    Religione, furcifer.

PHORMIO.   Quia dabat hoc mihi in iure
    Iurando ne unquam referrem tibi.

GESIPPUS.   Proh scelus, quid tu   15
    Serui es? Tun' igitur patiare putidam hanc religionem tuam
    Heri obstare vitae qui vitam alit tuam, cum mederi poteris?

PHORMIO.
    Recte dicis. Itaque hercle res ipsa ferme persuadet mihi
    Periurus vt referam.

GESIPPUS.   Ne metuas, Phormio, hodie ex te
    Verum exscalpere, venefice. Quin narres.

PHORMIO.   Tametsi   20
    Iusiurandum dabam?

GESIPPUS.   Dic igitur.

PHORMIO.   Age, quod deorum modo
    Pace dictum sit dicam.

GESIPPUS.   Quid est?

PHORMIO.   Attamen non audeo.

GESIPPUS.
    Cerebrum vis tibi extundi, carnifex? Verumne possum tibi
      exsculpere hodie?

PHORMIO.   Age nunc quamvis
    Etiam inuita lingua, attamen proferam.

GESIPPUS.   Dicas libere nisi cum hero
    Simul perire velis.

PHORMIO.   Vin' ergo dici tibi quid illum   25
    Torqueat, et vnico dici verbo?

GESIPPUS.   Dic.

PHORMIO.   Amat.

GESIPPUS.   Nae
    Tu difficilem mihi gryphum praedicas. Sed quaenam illa est
    Obsecro?

PHORMIO.   Tametsi hercle efflictim interminatus est, aiebat sese
    Lubentius moriturum si tu nescires.

---

23. *vis . . . carnifex*] perhaps intended for deletion; see Textual Notes.

GESIPPUS. Go hang your conscience on a cross, you scoundrel.

PHORMIO. Because he made me swear an oath never to tell you.

GESIPPUS. Oh you villain, what kind of servant are you? Then will you let this stinking conscience of yours stand in the way of your master's life when you could heal him? He sustains your life.

PHORMIO. You're right, by Hercules, and the matter itself almost persuades me to forswear myself and tell you.

GESIPPUS. Never fear, Phormio, I can claw the truth from you today, you devil. Tell me.

PHORMIO. Even though I gave my oath?

GESIPPUS. Tell me.

PHORMIO. Well, may the gods pity me, I'll tell you.

GESIPPUS. What is it?

PHORMIO. But I don't dare.

GESIPPUS. Do you want your brains bashed out, you devil? Can't I cut the truth out of you today?

PHORMIO. All right then, though my tongue is unwilling, still I'll tell you.

GESIPPUS. Speak freely, unless you want to die along with your master.

PHORMIO. So you want to be told what's torturing him? You want to be told in just one word?

GESIPPUS. Say it.

PHORMIO. Love.

GESIPPUS. Well, you pose a tough riddle for me. But who on earth is the girl?

PHORMIO. By god, though threatened with death, he said he would more willingly die if you didn't know.

GESIPPUS.   Narra impauide.
PHORMIO.   Sempronia
   Tua.
GESIPPUS.   O Zeu, quid ego audio?
PHORMIO.   Ita est.
GESIPPUS.   Et eam vult   30
   Vxorem ducere?
PHORMIO.   Vel ducere vel mori. Nunc tui id arbitrii
   Est, Gesippe, vtrum velis vt videas. Quid ais, annon ita
   Praedixeram?
GESIPPUS.   Temporis hoc, Phormio,
   Longas deliberandi non admittit moras, neque si admitteret
   Magnopere in hac re tamen deliberandum censeo.   35
   Amicum qui in secundis rebus se profitetur, itidem in   [*f. 129v*]
      turbatis
   Par est ut praestet. Quamquam neque negare possum eam me
   Amare quoque, sed non adeo ut non amico meo facile
   Postputarim omnia etiam si vita haec effundenda sit, quae mihi
   Charior est, ut ne tanti putes esse mihi iacturam foeminae.   40
   Quod si ita res est aut in amore ita sit attonitus vt
   Absque ea moriendum sit, non sum tam ingratus, Phormio,
   Vt vnquam illius patiar salutem in meis claudier voluptatibus.
   Habeat.
PHORMIO. Deus mediusfidius tibi benefaxit, vir
   Optime.
GESIPPUS. Porro etiam hic iurabo quod potero, sed omnis scrupus 45
   Nunc est in senibus. At tuum nunc est pro hero neruos tuos
      intendere. Hoccine vt
   Potest fieri.
PHORMIO.   Siquidem de tua constaret voluntate—
GESIPPUS.
   Certe, Phormio. Age nunc.

   38. *sed*] unless Foxe intended to read MST's s_3 as *scilicet*, he neglected to change
this connective when he changed *Sane* to *Quamquam* (l. 37).
   44. *mediusfidius*] the proper position of this word is doubtful; see Textual Notes.
   46. *At*] ?read *Ad*.
   46-47.] a complicated revision makes the correct reading of these lines uncertain; see Textual Notes.

GESIPPUS. Tell me fearlessly.

PHORMIO. Your Sempronia.

GESIPPUS. Oh Zeus, what do I hear?

PHORMIO. It's true.

GESIPPUS. And he wants to marry her?

PHORMIO. Either to marry her or die. Now, Gesippus, it's up to you to decide whether you want to see him.[1] What do you say? Did I tell you how it was or not?

GESIPPUS. Phormio, the situation doesn't give us much time for deliberation, and I don't think there should be deliberation about this even if we had plenty of time. Anyone who professes to be a friend in good times should prove that he is one in difficult times as well. Though I certainly can't deny that I love her too, I don't love her so much that I would not readily put my friend ahead of everything, even if it meant losing my life, which is dearer to me than she is. So don't think the loss of a girl is of such importance to me. If he is so smitten with love that he must die without her, I am not such a scoundrel, Phormio, that I would ever allow his safety to be locked up in a prison of my joys. He must have her.

PHORMIO. God bless you, oh best of men.

GESIPPUS. Well, I'll take an oath right here that I can do it, but the whole trouble now is with the old folks. But your job now is to apply your energies on your master's behalf. How can this be done?

PHORMIO. If only you agreed to it——

GESIPPUS. Certainly, Phormio. Now do something.

[1] In the draft version, Phormio said "... whether you want to *permit* him."

PHORMIO.   Age vero gratiam.
GESIPPUS.   Imo
   Hanc rem agito siquid poteris.
PHORMIO.   De senibus dicis? Nihil
   Facilius.
GESIPPUS. Quid facturus tandem?
PHORMIO.   Dicam, et per compendium   50
   Non tam Menehmus Menehmo similis quam in uobis
   Similia sunt omnia: aetas, statura, complexio, denique
   Nisi in veste fere nil disconvenit. Ille ornatu
   Ad Semproniam ingredietur tuo, ego ero tuus
   Phormio. Vt consilium placet?
GESIPPUS.   Quid tum?
PHORMIO.   Atque iam   55
   Scio ilico posceris ad nuptias, quod si censes facere, mature
   Ad eum intus propera ac muta vestes. Alia nulla ratio est.
GESIPPUS.
   Eo. Sed heus, Phormio, libet prius sciscitari quiddam.
PHORMIO.
   Quid vis?
GESIPPUS.   Pamphilam, Fuluii filiam, Romanam vestram
   Nostin'?
PHORMIO. Nempe quae nostro.
GESIPPUS.   Ipsa an cuiquam adhuc   60
   Elocetur necne?
PHORMIO.   Nemini.
GESIPPUS.   Eo.
[PHORMIO.]
   Fabrefactus iam equus, mvro admotus est,   [*f. 130*]
   Qui si in vrbem veniat, nostrum hoc est Ilium ilicet
   Quamquam scio nimis callidum hoc praecepsque videbitur
   A me consilium. Certe in arduis rebus opus   65
   Audacia, nullum vecordiae praemium est.
   Tum haec sunt perinde omnia vt euentus habent:
   In pyrgum quae bene cadit, bene iacta est alea
   Vix iacta etiam; sin aliter, male etiam iacta optime.
   Sic consilia non ex homine sed euentis spectarier   70
   Solent: non quam bene nata sed quam bene

PHORMIO. Thanks very much.

GESIPPUS. Yes, bring this off if you can manage it somehow.

PHORMIO. You speak of the old folks? There's nothing easier.

GESIPPUS. Then what am I to do?

PHORMIO. I'll tell you. To make it brief, Menaechmus is not more like Menaechmus[1] than you two are like each other in every way: age, height, complexion—indeed, except for your clothing there's almost no difference between you. Titus will go in to Sempronia in your clothing, and I will be your Phormio. How do you like that?

GESIPPUS. What then?

PHORMIO. And now I know you're expected at the wedding immediately, but if you agree to do this, hurry inside to Titus and change clothes with him. There's no other way.

GESIPPUS. I'm going. But listen, Phormio, first I want to ask you something.

PHORMIO. What?

GESIPPUS. Do you know another Roman named Pamphila, the daughter of Fulvius?

PHORMIO. Yes indeed, she's a friend of ours.

GESIPPUS. Is she promised to anyone yet or not?

PHORMIO. No.

GESIPPUS. I'm going. [*Exit.*

PHORMIO. Now the horse is made and moved up to the wall: if it gets into the city, then and there this Troy is ours, though I know this plan of mine will seem too cunning and rash. Of course when times are tough there's a need for boldness, but there's no reward for madness. In the end these plans are all no better than their results make them: the die which falls into the dice-box favorably is cast well even if it is scarcely cast at all; but if otherwise, it is cast badly even if cast most skillfully. In the same way, plans are usually judged not from their author but from their outcome. Not how well he conceives his plans

---

[1] The Menaechmi were the twin protagonists of Plautus' *Menaechmi*, the principal source of Shakespeare's *Comedy of Errors*.

Diuinata prudentem aut amentem arguunt.
Sed sine euenire quae volunt dum ea
Potiatur modo. Dein si suboleat quid mea
Adeo, illa iam nostra erit Helena. Facile ego   75
E ruina erumpam per flammam scilicet,
Herus aliam habet ad migrandum patriam,
Gesippo tonitrua at non fulminabunt scio.
Tum illum ex orco hoc mortuum miserrimo
Rediuiuum dabimus. Quaeso quid hic incommodi est?   80
Vsquam tandem? Nam quod Gesippus sua
Auellitur? Quando haec iam altera illi charior
Est, non id illi damnum sed in lucrum deputo
Ac faenus potius maioris secerni solatii.
Quo magis hercle hoc illi gratulor, quandoquidem   85
Lubens benefaxim optimo adolescentulo.
Sed turbam videor audire intus. Praeludia
Forsan sunt ad nuptias. Viso quid agat herus.

ACTUS SECUNDUS. SCENA PRIMA.   [*f. 130v*]
Gesippus.

[GESIPPUS.]
Putabit forsitan impotentiuscule
Hoc me nunc ferre aliquis, quod Titi tam obsequens
Modo in cedenda vxore fuerim. Pol nihilo
Magis quam si nuptum daretur mihimet:
Aequa ac communis vtriusque ratio est.   5
Ita illius studeo faueoque omnino commodis,
Cui siquid bene sit, mihi ac si sit perinde
Accipio, is quasi Gesippus, ego Titus forem.
Quippe sic enim accipio mihi: qui sese
Amicos esse, non dici velint, alter alterius   10
Animum, non suum gerere, nec in suo magis quam illius
Viuere corpore debeat. Denique ita statuo
Amicitiam, non in fortunis oportere, sed in
Animo cuiusque sitam esse quicquid accidat.

---

78. *at*] ?read *ac*.
9. *Quippe, mihi*] perhaps the words were intended for deletion; see Textual Notes.

but how well he guesses—that shows a man either prudent or mad. But let their wishes come to a successful end, just long enough for Titus to get the girl. Then if my mistress gets wind of anything, she will be our Helen.[1] I will easily break out of the ruin through the flames, of course; my master has another country to go to; and I know no thunderbolts will strike Gesippus. Besides, we'll resurrect Titus from a wretched death, and what's wrong with that? Anything at all? What, because Gesippus is deprived of his girl? Since this other girl is already dearer to him, I reckon that's an advantage for him, not an injury: deprivation is rather a gain of greater comfort. All the more, by Hercules, do I wish this joy to him because I would really like to do a good turn for the nice young fellow. But I seem to hear a crowd inside. Maybe it's the prelude to the wedding. I'll go see what my master is up to. *[Exit.*

[II.1]   *Enter Gesippus.*

GESIPPUS. Maybe someone will think I've handled this too timidly because I've just been so servile to Titus in handing over my wife. Really it's nothing more than if she had married me, for Titus and I have an absolutely joint account.[2] Thus I long for his good fortune and promote that entirely. If anything is good for him, I take it to be just as good for me, as if he were Gesippus and I Titus. For I take it as my rule for those who wish to be friends and not just to be called friends, that each should bear the other's mind, not his own, and each should live in the other's body not less than in his own. In short, I conclude that friendship must reside not in the fortunes but in the minds of each, what-

---

[1] At the beginning of this speech, Phormio thought of himself as the Greek whose wooden horse would conquer Troy (Gesippus and his father); now Phormio becomes Troy who will be destroyed by Sempronia (as Helen was the occasion of Troy's ultimate ruin), if she learns of the scheme. The imagery points up the significance of the decisions that have been made and shows that Foxe thought of this as the protatic climax. This structure reflects Donatus' definition of Terentian structure, not the view common in the last half of the sixteenth century which carried the protasis through the second act (T. W. Baldwin, *Shakspere's Five-Act Structure* [Urbana, 1947], p. 233).

[2] The spiritual unity of friends was a commonplace of Neo-Platonic philosophy; see L. J. Mills, *One Soul in Bodies Twain* (Bloomington, Indiana, 1937).

Animus enim vt amicitiae custos est, ita   15
Animi rursum index est fortuna, quae
Non discutere, sed excutere amicitias   [*f. 131*]
Arguendo solet. Ita enim certus qui siet
Res cum incertae sunt certissime cernitur:
Qui persistit amicum scias; sin aliter in   20
Malis ac fortuna alternante resilit,
Hunc numquam animo coiungi facile indicium est.
Sed eccum Titum cum Phormione.

[ACTUS SECUNDUS. SCENA SECUNDA.]

Titus. Phormio. [*Gesippus.*]

[TITUS.]

"O dies festus" quin canimus triumphum, Phormio.

PHORMIO.

Arbitror.

TITUS.

O dies festus, hominis beati
Gratiis mille, mihi mille gemmis,
Mille signandus merito lapillis   5
     Candidus albis.

Ergo nunc omnes procul hinc valete,
Iteque longe procul hinc dolores.
Io triumphe, animo quieto
     Iam lubet esse.   10

O dies almus, lubet ergo nunc me,
Nunc demum exutis, positisque curis,
Cum Ioue aeternum superisque diuis
     Viuere suave.

Ecquis vnquam sub sole hoc vixit hominum cui   15
Dari magis triumphus potest
Quam mihi hodie, hodie qui paradisum ipsum deorum expugnaui

---

22. *coiungi*] = *coniungi*.
P.H. *Gesippus*] omitted in MST.

ever befalls. For the mind serves as the guardian of friendship. The index of the mind, in turn, is fortune, which is wont not to confine friendships but to refine them by putting them to the test. So, when things are uncertain, one may see most certainly who is certain. Him who perseveres you know to be a friend; but if, on the contrary, one recoils when things are bad and fortune is unsteady, it is a sure sign that that one will never be united with you in spirit. But look, Titus with Phormio.

[II.2]   *Enter Titus and Phormio.*

TITUS. Phormio, let's sing a song of triumph, "Oh Happy Day."
PHORMIO. I'm listening.
TITUS [*singing*].

>   Oh happy day of shining joy,.
>   Owed of a fortune-favored boy
>   A thousand thanks, a thousand gems,
>   A thousand white-stoned diadems![1]
>
>   Away all sorrows, far away,
>   Farewell to cares this glorious day.
>   Io[2] triumph, with delight I find
>   Restored my blissful peace of mind.
>
>   Oh life-renewing day, I cast
>   Aside my robe of woes at last
>   And joy to live eternity
>   At peace with all divinity.

What man beneath the sun has ever lived to whom a greater triumph can be given than mine today? Today I have stormed the very paradise of the gods and deprived them of all their

---

[1] It was a custom to mark fortunate dates with white stones (cf. Catullus, *Carmina* 68.138).

[2] A cry of joy, often used in hymns celebrating marriages.

Suisque omnibus orbaui faelicitatibus? Sed vbi
Gesippus nunc est, quem nimis his vlnis amplecti   [*f. 131v*]
Atque osculari gestio, ac vbi requiram cogito.   20
GESIPPUS.
  En presto, tibi ne requiras longius.
TITUS.   Gesippe mi,
  Mea commoditas, mea immortalitas, nam quibus
  Ego praeconiis caput hoc satis exornem tuum,
  Qui me creasti, qui me produxisti hodie, in caelum denique
  Collocasti hodie beneficio maximo, dum interea   25
  Propter me misere genium extenuas tuum? Nunc quid ego
  Tibi pro istis debeo, nisi ut totum me dedam tibi
  Perpetuo pro mancipio ad imperia omnia.
GESIPPUS.   Quid? Etiam
  Tu octauas gratiarum celebras, Tite? Sed dic, quaeso, de
  Apparatu isto quid fit tandem? Etiamnum quid patri   30
  Oluit?
TITUS.   Numquam aedepol homini quicquam auspicatius cuiquam
  In vita vidi succedere. Nae tu hercle Mercurium
  Pro Sosia Gesippum gessisse iam, Iouemque ipsum fabulae
  Applausorem diceres. Principio vt abs te abeo, continuo
  Ego me ad uirginem. Salutat illa advenientem, simul   35
  Et abblandule sese dare occipit, ego tum id vero
  Gaudere, illi assidere propius. Signa, consilia, caeteraque
  Occulta quae praemonueras refrico. Annulum hunc
  Demonstro tuum ac gratiam habeo. Interea dum sermones
    trahimus,
  Ad nuptias appellari illico, senes seduli adesse cum   40
  Familiis et amicis omnibus—Quid multa verba? Ducimur,
  Reducimur, sacrificamur.
GESIPPUS.   Quid tum pater interim?
TITUS.   [*f. 132*]
  Quid! Tantummodo me hilariorem solito dictitare,
  Praeterea nihil, nihil aegre ferre. Denique amici, domestici,
  Affines omnes accurrere, omnia laeta ac fausta precarier,   45

---

    36. *abblandule*] I have found no other instance of this word; presumably it is
an intensive formed from *ad* and *blandule*.

happiness. But now where's Gesippus? I long to hold him in my arms and kiss him. I wonder where to look for him.

GESIPPUS [*coming forward*]. Look, I stand before you; you need look no further.

TITUS. My Gesippus, my dearest wealth, my immortality—for with what titles could I adequately adorn your head? By your great generosity you have created me, brought me into the world today, and yet again today translated me into heaven, while at the same time, because of me, you lessen your own happiness terribly. Oh, what I owe you now for these favors if not to deliver myself utterly into your hands as a perpetual slave to your every command.

GESIPPUS. What, do you fill up octaves of thanks, Titus? But please tell me what's happening in this scheme now. Does my father suspect anything even now?

TITUS. By God, I've never in my life seen anything happen more auspiciously for any man. Really, by Hercules, you would have said that Gesippus had Mercury with him for a Sosia and Jove himself to applaud his plot.[1] As soon as I left you, I went straight to the maid, who greeted me when I approached and very sweetly began to devote her attentions to me. Rejoicing at this, I sat quite near her and recalled the tokens and plans and other secrets which you had told me about. I showed her your ring—and I thank you for it. As we were prolonging our conversation, we were summoned to the ceremony immediately. The old men were bustling around us with the whole household and all their friends, and—to make a long story short—we were led to the altar and led back, and we've made our sacrifices.

GESIPPUS. What did my father do all this while?

TITUS. What indeed! He kept repeating that I was gayer than usual and had absolutely nothing to feel bad about. Then the friends, family, and in-laws all ran in, prayed that everything would

---

[1] Sosia was a scheming slave in Terence's *Andria* and, more significantly, in Plautus' *Amphitruo*, where Mercury assumed Sosia's identity to promote Jupiter's deception of Alcmena—a bawdy parallel to the situation in Foxe's comedy. In the draft version, Foxe once called Syrus Sosias (II.7.P.H.). Note here in the Latin (l. 33) a play on words, *Gesippum gessisse*, which my translation does not capture.

Gratulari fortunam tantam ac talem coniugem. Atque
Ita habet epithasis fabulae.

GESIPPUS.   Enimvere gaudeo.

PHORMIO.

Equidem et ego triumpho.

TITUS.   Caeterum quid dehinc
Fiet ne qua fucus prodeat.

PHORMIO.   Illis eruemus oculos.

GESIPPUS.

Fuat fors pol.

TITUS.   Bene dicis. Commeamus igitur   50
Iam nunc intro, ac diem hanc carpamus hilarem.

GESIPPUS.

Praecede, Tite, tu.

PHORMIO.

Illi abiere. Nunc quid fit aut quid restat, Phormio,
Nisi ut mature te hinc in pedes conferas
Teque ab incendio vrbis euoluas quam primulum?   55
Namque hoc haud dubium est: non potest hoc silere diu
Facinus, quin alicubi flamma haec prorumpet tandem ac sua
Sese luce prodat, quod si fit, proh Statorem atque Feretrium
Iouem, quos terraemomotus in hac ciuitate dabit!
Atque illos amor, aetas, libertas, facile ruinae eximet;   60
In meos humeros vniuersa moles occumbet denique,
Cui tum effugiendi nulla copia licebit, quare id nunc prudentiae
Arbitror dum licet atque res adhuc incolumes sient:
Quae sequuntur mala ingenio antevortere, post
Vt cum veniunt—cum praeuisa veniunt—minus feriant.   65
Sed quis peregrinus ille quem ex ultima huc platea
Properantem video? Sume deus, Trebatium ego herilem
Video annon?

---

52. *Tite*] emended from *Gesippe*.
67. *Sume*] = *Summe*.

be happy and fortunate, and congratulated our good fortune and fine marriage. And that's the epitasis of this plot.[1]

GESIPPUS. Well, I'm very glad.

PHORMIO. I'm very glad about it too.

TITUS. But what will be done now so our scheme won't be exposed?

PHORMIO. We'll pluck out their eyes.

GESIPPUS. Amen.

TITUS. Good idea. Now let's go in together and enjoy this happy day.

GESIPPUS. After you, Titus.   [*Exeunt Titus and Gesippus.*

PHORMIO. They've gone. Now, Phormio, what remains to be done except to get away from here fast, slip out of the holocaust of this city as quickly as possible? There's no doubt about it, this mischief can't be hushed up long. No, this blaze is going to break out all around us and proclaim itself by its own light. If that happens, oh Jove the father and Jove the conqueror, what earthquakes it will cause in this city! Those young men will easily be delivered from ruin by love, by their youth, by their free birth; the whole burden will fall on my shoulders, and then there'll be no way for me to escape. So while I can, while things are still quiet here, I think it's prudent to anticipate with cleverness the troubles that are coming so that later, when they come—that is, when the expected happens—they'll be less painful. But who's that foreigner I see rushing this way from the other end of the street? Good god, do I see my master's servant Trebatius or not?

---

[1] Ἐπίτασις (literally, a stretching, straining) is a technical term used by Donatus and later critics for the "middle" of a play, "the increase and progress of the turbations" (Baldwin, *Five-Act Structure*, p. 34), the "most busy and troublous part of a comedy," as some Renaissance dictionaries defined it. If Titus thought of the scheme as happily completed, he should have used the term *catastrophe;* in his next speech, however, he shows that he thinks of possible future "turbations," and he may be thinking of epitasis as a *point* of beginning the turbations rather than as a section of the play.

[Actus Secundus. Scena Tertia.]
Trebatius. Phormio.   [*f. 132v*]

Scazondes.

[Trebatius.]

    Aut me fallit iter aut hae ipsae aedes sunt Titus

    Vbi apud Chremetem noster dictus est diuorsarier.

Phormio.

    Certe ipsus est.

Trebatius.   Qui vbicumque est propere mihi

    Exquirendus ac conveniendus est. Sed quid cesso

    Pultare fores ilico?

Phormio.   Quin prehendo hominem.   5

    Heus, heus, Trebati, Trebati inquam.

Trebatius.   Et nomen

    Noscitat? Hem.

Phormio.   Dico tibi, Trebati, mane.

Trebatius.   Quis

    Homo istic? Ehem, Phormionem nostrum video annon?

Phormio.

    Trebati, quid tandem huc aduentus adportat

    Tuus? Rectene domi omnia? Herus quopacto valet?   10

Trebatius.

    Valuit quidem olim, Phormio.

Phormio.   Hei mihi, quidnam istuc

    "Valuit" autem?

Trebatius.   Nempe vt mortales homines omnes

    Sumus, certaque omnes lege ad mortem nascimur.

Phormio.   Quid,

    Periit?

Trebatius.   Periit.

Phormio.   Nephanda fata.

Trebatius.   Propterea huc nunc

    Ad Titum missus cum litteris ab amicis venio, se quam   15

    Primum vt paret, proximus qui sit illius, vt gerat

    Vicem. Sed vbi is est? Duc me ad eum, Phormio.

M.H. *Scazondes*] = *Scazontes*.

[II.3]   *Enter Trebatius.*

TREBATIUS. If I'm not badly mistaken about the street, this is the
very house where our Titus is supposed to be staying with Chremes.

PHORMIO [*aside*]. It is Trebatius.

TREBATIUS. I have to find out where he is right away and go talk
to him. But I'll knock on the gates right now.

PHORMIO. [*aside*]. I'll grab the fellow.—— [*Aloud.*] Hey, Trebatius!
Trebatius, I say.

TREBATIUS. He knows my name? Well.

PHORMIO. I say, Trebatius, wait.

TREBATIUS. Who is this fellow? Well, is it really my countryman
Phormio?

PHORMIO. Trebatius, what in the world are you doing here? Is
everything all right at home? How's my master?

TREBATIUS. He was all right, Phormio.

PHORMIO. Alas, why do you say "was"?

TREBATIUS. Indeed, we men are all mortal: by an unbreakable
law we're all born to die.

PHORMIO. What, he's dead?

TREBATIUS. Yes.

PHORMIO. Oh wicked fate!

TREBATIUS. That's why I'm sent here now, with letters to Titus
from his friends to prepare himself as quickly as possible to take
over as the next in line. But where is he? Take me to him, Phormio.

PHORMIO.
  Eamus, Trebati, intro. Sed heus, tu Titum iam
  Illum qui sit non nosti.
TREBATIUS.   Nam cur ita?
PHORMIO.   Accede,
  Dum intro rem ibi omnem tibi aperiam.
TREBATIUS.   Sequor.   20

[ACTUS SECUNDUS. SCENA QUARTA.]
        Marsias. Misenus. Pythias. Midas.   [*f. 133*]

[MARSIAS.]
  Heus, alta dies, alta dies, Misene. Vah, quousque
  Somnolentiae indulseris et supinitatem tuam produxeris, bellua?
MISENUS.
  Quousque lubet. Quid tum?
MARSIAS.   Quasi domi nihil
  Sit quod agas rerum.
MISENUS.   Quasi non dudum ego
  Surrexerim.
MARSIAS.   Laudo. Quin igitur, abeamus ocyus.   5
  Diem ferme morando contriuimus.
MISENUS.
  I prae, haud diu abero.
MARSIAS.   Sequere.
PYTHIAS.   Heus, heus,
  Marsia.
MARSIAS.   Quis homo hic? Ehem, mea Pythia,
  Salue.
PYTHIAS.   Salue, mecastor, Marsia, plurimum. Sed quo
  Tu nunc, an abiturus a nobis?
MARSIAS.   Quid ni?
PYTHIAS.   Tam cito?   10
MARSIAS.
  Ita tibi uidetur forsitan.
PHORMIO.   Quaeso, Marsia, ne facias.
MARSIAS.
  Quaeso ne roges, Pythia.
PYTHIAS.   At si me ames—

PHORMIO. Let's go in, Trebatius. But listen, you don't know the Titus that he is now.

TREBATIUS. Why not?

PHORMIO. Come on. I'll tell you everything on the way.

TREBATIUS. I'm coming.   [*Exeunt.*

[II.4]   *Enter Marsias.*

MARSIAS. Hey, it's high noon, high noon, Misenus. Bah, how long will you give in to your laziness and lie flat on your back, you monster?

MISENUS [*within*]. As long as I please. What about it?

MARSIAS. As if there were nothing to do at home.

MISENUS [*within*]. As if I hadn't been up long ago.

MARSIAS. Good for you. Well then, let's go quickly. We've almost wasted the day with this dillydallying.

MISENUS [*within*]. Go ahead. I won't be far behind.

MARSIAS. Come on.

Enter Pythias.

PYTHIAS. Hey, hey, Marsias.

MARSIAS. Who's this fellow? Aha, my girl Pythias, hello.

PYTHIAS. By Castor, hello indeed, Marsias. But where are you off to now? Are you leaving us?

MARSIAS. Why not?

PYTHIAS. So quickly?

MARSIAS. Maybe it seems so to you.

PYTHIAS. Please don't, Marsias.

MARSIAS. Please don't ask me, Pythias.

PYTHIAS. But if you love me——

Marsias.   In aliis
    Amabo rebus, hic non possum obsequi.
Pythias.   Quamobrem?
Marsias.   Quam ob
    Rem tu rogas, Pythia?
Pythias.   Quia te omnes intus desiderant
    Vt choreas nuptiales agitemus festumque laetitiae hunc   15
    Consecremus diem.
Marsias.   Vah, nondum satur tu es
    Saltitando?
Pythias.   Non, mediusfidius.
Marsias.   At ego, pol, perstrependo.
Phythias.
    Credo, quia est tibi quotidianum; vix per annum hoc
    Nobis semel accidit.
Marsias.   Sed heus tibi Misenum mox
    Prodeuntem, quod si ab hoc impetrabis, nihil   20
    Detrecto.
Misenus.   Iuno Lucina fer opem.
Marsias.   Hem, num qua
    Mulier est pariens?
Misenus.   Parturiunt aedes istae, non uides,
    Marsia?
Marsias. Parturiunt aedaes nascetur ridiculus mas.
Misenus.
    Salue, sancta parens, enixa puerpera. Salue, Pythia.
Pythias.
    Abstine, sus.
Misenus.   Sustine, mus. Ecquid hic velit   25
    Pythias?   [*f. 133v*]
Marsias. Te.
Misenus.   Quia te negligit forsitan,
    Hem, Pythia, tun' me velis?
Pythias.   Ego ambos uos.
Misenus.   Qua de re?

26. *Quia*] ?read *Quid.*

MARSIAS. In other ways I'll love you; in this I can't oblige.

PYTHIAS. Why?

MARSIAS. Why do you ask, Pythias?

PYTHIAS. Because everyone wants you inside so we can kick up some nuptial dances and consecrate this holiday to merrymaking.

MARSIAS. Bah, haven't you had enough of dancing?

PYTHIAS. Heavens no.

MARSIAS. But I'm sick of all this noise.

PYTHIAS. I believe it, because to you it's an everyday thing, but for the rest of us it happens scarcely once a year.

MARSIAS. But listen, Misenus is coming out soon. If you get his agreement, I deny you nothing.

Misenus appears in a doorway.

MISENUS. Juno, queen of childbearing, help.[1]

MARSIAS. What? Where is a woman in labor?

MISENUS [*coming out the doorway*]. This house is in labor. Don't you get it, Marsias?

MARSIAS. A house in labor bears a ridiculous man.

MISENUS [*bowing to the doorway*]. Hail, holy parent, vigorous woman in labor.—— [*To Pythias.*] Hello, Pythias.

PYTHIAS. Stop, you sow.

MISENUS. Stop, you mouse.—— [*To Marsias.*] What does Pythias want here?

MARSIAS. You.

MISENUS. Well, Pythias, I suppose you want me because he neglects you?

PYTHIAS. I want both of you.

MISENUS. Why?

---

[1] See Introduction. The joke is built on the idea of a house giving birth to a man (through its door).

[Pythias.]   Paululum

   Vt demoremini diemque detis hunc nobis ad tripudia.

Misenus.

   Quid dederis?

Pythias.   Quid petieris?

Misenus.   Osculum.

Pythias.   Nae tu homo

   Suauis es, Misene.

Misenus.   Nae tu puella suauis es, mea   30

   Pythia.

Pythias. Tantisper exorare nequeo a uobis ut maneatis?

Misenus.

   Marsia, meministin' quo iter condiximus ad Cimonidis

   Nuptias?

Marsias.   Recte hercle, pene me praetierat. Pythia,

   Valebis iam. Nobis hinc abeundum.

Pythias.   Itan' stat sententia?

Marsias.

   Imo stat necessitas.

Midas.   Heus Pythia, heus, inquam, Pythia.   35

Pythias.

   Quis me vult?

Midas.   Hera inclamat te, et tu nusquam

   Audis.

Pythias.   Ain' Mida?

Misenus.   Curre. Enimuero auspicato hodie

   Piscatus hic nobis hodie euenit bonus.

Marsias.   Disperiam si viderim

   Sponsum benigniorem aut aeque dapsilem.

Midas.   Equidem aut

   Ego sponsam venustiorem.

Misenus.   Profecto sic visa est. Sed hac   40

   Abeant, nosque hinc abeamus, Marsia.

Marsias.   Assentior.

27. S.P. *Pythias* [her second speech in the line]] omitted in MST.

38. *nobis*] ?read *uobis*. But the original reading (*huc appulimus*) is first person.

39. *aeque*] emended from *aequeue*, the apparent reading of the manuscript.

39-40. S.P.] Foxe's abbreviations here are ambiguous; see Textual Notes. Earlier S.P.'s in the scene are also ambiguous, but are made clearer by the context.

PYTHIAS. To stay a little while and give us this day for dancing.

MISENUS. What will you give us?

PYTHIAS. What will you want?

MISENUS. A kiss.

PYTHIAS [*making up to Misenus*]. You're really a sweet man, Misenus.

MISENUS. You're really a sweet girl, my Pythias.

PYTHIAS. Can't I persuade you to stay for a while?

MISENUS. Marsias, do you remember, we promised to go to the wedding of Cimo's son?

MARSIAS. By Hercules, that's right. I had almost forgot.——
Pythias, good-bye now. We have to leave.

PYTHIAS. Is that your final word?

MARSIAS. But that's the final necessity.

Enter Midas.

MIDAS. Hey, Pythias. Hey, Pythias, I say.

PYTHIAS. Who wants me?

MIDAS. Your mistress is calling you, and you don't hear her at all.

PYTHIAS. Do you mean it, Midas?

MISENUS. Run along.—— I've checked the prognostications today, and this has turned out to be a prize catch for us. What do you say?

MARSIAS. May I perish if I've seen a nicer bridegroom or one so magnificent.

MIDAS. Yes, or a fairer bride.

MISENUS. Yes indeed, so she seems. But Marsias, let them go that way and we'll go this.

MARSIAS. All right. [*Exeunt severally.*

[Actus Secundus. Scena Quinta.]
Gesippus.

[Gesippus.]
Nunc quid ego in hac re consilii reperiam aut captem miser
Abducta hinc Sempronia. Ille abiit Romam. Haud potest
Hoc iam diutius occultari malum, nimisque
Vereor prius ne patri palam fiat quam ego epistolam defero.
Ita enim volo, quando ita est ut ignorari nequeat,   5
Nostro potius indicio quam ex aliis confessum iri. Quod vbi
Resciuerit, vah, quod tum reperiam illius remedium
Saeuitiae, quo non gentium mihi satius sit profugere?
Etiam nunc illius audire tragoedias videor, et tamen   [*f. 134*]
Ita res est, necesse est fieri, namque enim permagne refert   10
Ipsa in omni re explicandi ratio: fere enim res non vt
Gestae, sed vt digestae, sunt dum exponuntur iudici.
Quo nunc consultius arbitror Titi hanc syngrapham ad patrem
Perferre ocyus, linguasque sycophantycas antecapere.
Atque id nunc ago.   15

[Actus Secundus. Scena Sexta.]
Dromo.

[Dromo.]
Proh nephas, scelera, flagitia, o genus
Sacrilegum! Vixdum pol possum proloqui, ita
Totus sum confusus animi inde adeo quod modo
Mihi cum Syro ad portum uenienti nunciatum
Est. Proh diuum numen! Itan' Semproniam   5
Nobis eripi, ac in alienas terras asportarier
Herilem filiam, ac solatium vnicum
Siccine circumvenirier! Quod quidem hercule
Mihi primo incredibile fuit donec
Re mox intellecta illam hinc Romam cum Tito   10
Soluisse, Gesippum regressum ab illis domum
Persensimus. At vbi herus nunc est, cui
Haec de filia quam primum denunciem?

II.6.2. *Vixdum pol*] ?read *Vix pol.*

[II.5]   *Enter Gesippus, with a letter.*

GESIPPUS. Now what plan will I come up with in this situation?
What will I try, wretch that I am, now that Sempronia has
been taken away? He's taken her to Rome. This mischief can't
be hidden any longer, and I very much fear that my father will
find out about it before I bring him this letter. Since the situation
is such that he can't help finding out about it, I want the truth
to be known from me rather than from others. When he learns
of it, oh, what remedy will I find for his rage? It will be quite
useless for me to flee anywhere in the world. Even now I seem
to hear his tragic declamations. And yet the business is such
that there's no choice. In every circumstance, the way something
is explained is very important, because what generally matters
is not what was committed, but in what order it is transmitted
to a judge. All the more reason, I think, to bring this letter of
Titus to my father immediately and thus anticipate the tongues
of informers. And that's what I'll do now.   [*Exit.*

[II.6]   *Enter Dromo.*

DROMO. Oh abomination, wickedness, shames, oh impious race![1]
Heavens, I'm almost speechless. I'm completely dumfounded by
what I just learned when I went to the harbor with Syrus. Oh,
the will of the gods! To have Sempronia snatched from us like
this, my master's daughter carried off into foreign lands, his
only comfort outraged! By Hercules, at first I couldn't believe
it, until we soon realized for a fact that she had sailed to Rome
with Titus and that Gesippus had left them and gone home.
But now where's my master so I can tell him this news about
his daughter as soon as possible?   [*Exit.*

[1] I take this as a reference to Romans by the Greek Dromo.

[Actus Secundus. Scena Septima.]
Chremes. Gesippus. Syrus.   [*f. 134v*]

[Chremes.]
  O coelum Iouis, Neptuni maria, quid ego
  Audio? Quid ais omnium? Semproniam Tito
  Traditam, huicque ductam esse coniugem?
Gesippus.   Pater,
  Verum.
Chremes.   Tuque hinc Romam abductam vidistin',
  Syre?
Syrus. Modo ad Pyraeum, pariter etiam   5
  Vidente Dromone.
Chremes.   O Iupiter, quin ista non
  Redigent ad maniam? Et tu istarum rerum conscius,
  Carcer? Responde.
Gesippus.   Mi pater.
Chremes.   "Mi pater"!
  Os impudens ut te nihil istius "patris"
  Pudet! Et tu harum sciens rerum. Cur ergo huic   10
  Non dixti "patri"? Vt facile nunc intelligam
  Nullo alio nisi te authore incoeptum scelus
  Ac perfectum esse, qui pro lepido habes
  Coram adeo in os me deludere ludosque tibi
  Facere. Fugin' hinc?
Syrus.   Here, obsecro vero te—   15
Chremes.
  "Vero te"! Obsecro vero, Syre, te, hoc quis est
  Qui ferre queat aut perpeti? Sic os
  Obliniri, dolisque ludificarier, etiam
  In re tanta ut nusquam mallem minus!
  Nam quid hinc dicam Simoni nunc, aut fidem   20
  Apud hunc qua tuear meam, qui nisi
  Insanus essem recte egomet in hac re satis
  Vidissem mihi? Certe hercle illum quouis gentium
  Profligassem potius, haec mansisset domi.
  Atque eccum ipsum prodeuntem.   25

    7. *redigent*] ?read *redigant*.

[II.7]   *Enter Chremes, Gesippus, and Syrus.*

CHREMES. Oh, Jove's heaven and Neptune's seas, what am I hearing? What on earth are you saying? Sempronia was given to Titus and married to him?

GESIPPUS. It's true, father.

CHREMES. And Syrus, you saw her taken away to Rome?

SYRUS. No just to the Piraeus,[1] and Dromo saw it too.

CHREMES. Oh Jupiter, why doesn't this drive me mad?—— And you knew about this, you criminal? Answer me.

GESIPPUS. My father.

CHREMES. "My father"! Your impudent mouth, that isn't ashamed to say that word "father"! You even knew this! Then why didn't you tell your "father"? How easily I know now that this wickedness could not have been conceived and executed unless you were responsible for it. You think it's fun to deceive me even to my face, and to play your games.—— [*To Syrus, who is slipping away.*] Are you running away?

SYRUS. Master, I pray you in truth——

CHREMES. "In truth"! I pray you in truth, Syrus, who could endure this? Who could tolerate it? To have the wool pulled over my eyes like this, to be mocked with tricks, even in an affair so important that I can think of no worse place for it! For what will I say to Simo now? How can I save my honor in his eyes, since if I weren't insane, I should have looked after this matter properly for myself? By Hercules, I should rather have driven this fellow away, anywhere in the world, and she should have stayed at home. But look, there comes Simo now.

---

[1] Athens' seaport.

[Actus Secundus. Scena Octava.]
Simo. Chremes. [*Gesippus.*] *Syrus.*   [*f. 135*]

[Simo.]

Itane inuito me atque inscio Semproniam
Tam lepido dolo hinc abripier! Hancce quis
Quam homo viuus contumeliam vt ferat?
Sed eccum Chremetem.

Chremes.   Simo, faeliciter

Aduenis. Ad te tendebam.

Simo.   Caeterum Chreme,   5

De filia quid? Itane ut fertur cum Tito hinc?

Chremes.

Tun' igitur audistin', Simo?

Simo.   Audiui? Quid, Chreme,

Adeon' composite daedalios dolos
Vos hic astruere arbitramini vt nemo
Assequatur?

Chremes.   Mirum, igitur, ni mihi hanc   10

Authori ascribas fabulam.

Simo.   Tibi Chreme!

Minime gentium hoc filius facinus
Adolescens incoeptare ausus! Tu inscius
Istarum rerum prorsus omnium, neque tibi
Cognita fuga haec nec cogitata prius!   15
Tum filius si amasset sibi, facile eam
Auferri perferret scilicet peregrinam nunc.
Quippe accidunt haec tibi scio omnia.

Chremes.

Imo quo tu minus scis quid actum sit, Simo!
Epistolam hanc perlege.

Simo.   Scitum pol   20

Artificem, vide, postquam blanditiis in fraudem
Me pellexit polypus, mendatiis nunc elabitur
Suo se atramento offundens sepia.

P.H. *Gesippus*] omitted in MST.
17. *peregrinam*] emended from *peregrina*.
19. *quo tu*] ?read *quanto*.

[II.8]   *Enter Simo.*

SIMO [*to himself*]. Against my will and without my knowledge, Sempronia to be carried away from me by such a smart trick! How could any man living tolerate this affront? But look, there's Chremes.

CHREMES [*coming forward*]. Simo, you come just in time. I was coming to you.

SIMO. But Chremes, what about my daughter? How is she taken away with Titus?

CHREMES. Then you've heard, Simo?

SIMO. Heard! What, Chremes, do you think to fashion your Daedalean devices so skillfully that no one comprehends them?

CHREMES. In these circumstances it's no wonder you attribute the authorship of this plot to me.

SIMO. To you, Chremes! No young son in the world have dared to conceive this wickedness. You were completely ignorant of all this! You didn't know about this flight and didn't think of it beforehand! Besides, if your son had loved her for himself, of course he would easily have put up with having her carried off now to be a foreigner! Oh yes, all these things happen to you unawares!

CHREMES. But how little you know about what happened, Simo! Read this letter.

SIMO. Oh yes, look, a very clever trickster. After the polyp has lured me into his deception with his charms,[1] now the cuttlefish conceals himself in black ink and slips away with lies.

---

[1] Of the qualities which Pliny attributed to the *polypus*, the one which most struck Renaissance writers was its ability to change its colors (Pliny, IX.46, tr. Bostock and Riley, II, 418); it became an emblem for fickleness (see *O.E.D.*).

CHREMES.   Egone
    Mendatiis?
SIMO.   Namque tu, homo, quaeso, me putas
    Asinum aut quidnam esse tandem, sine naribus,   25
    Sine oculis, qui nil persentiam? Tute aut hoc
    Dissimulando infectum speras reddere?   [*f. 135v*]
    Age, responde hoc mihi.
CHREMES.   Sane si tu
    Audire non vis!
SIMO.   Principio cum primum me
    Sollicitasti de filia, numquid velle eam   30
    Te dixti tuo?
CHREMES.   Factum.
SIMO.   Numquid apud
    Te mansuram aetatem eam?
CHREMES.   Dixi.
SIMO.   Tum solus an
    Ambisti eam tu? Alios annon paranymphos item
    Plusculos nulla re te, Chreme, inferiores
    Tamen tua gratia postpositos mihi?
CHREMES.   Non nego.   35
SIMO.
    Quid ergo, dum animum induxi obsequi tibi,
    Tu nunc istam mihi captionem inicis? At
    Si eam nolles tuo, istos qui vellent sineres.
    Cur tradideris altri?
CHREMES.   Egone tradidi?
SIMO.
    Bene ergo, istaec tu verba cras fac iudici   40
    Sis vt respondeas siquidem istas ita
    Legibus habiturus sycophantias.
CHREMES.   Aliud
    Comperies. Sed me iam vicissim velim audias
    Vel verbum vnum.
SIMO.   Verbum! Quid verbum te? Nimis
    Iam diu verba nobis data sunt. Redde filiam aut   45
    Cras iuris tibi dictionem habe. Dixi.

CHREMES. I? With lies?

SIMO. I ask you, man, do you think me an ass or what? Noseless, eyeless, powerless to perceive anything? Or do you really hope, by this pretending, to make it appear that nothing has happened? Answer me that.

CHREMES. Well, if you don't want to hear——

SIMO. At the beginning, when you first approached me about my daughter, didn't you say you wanted her for your son?

CHREMES. Yes.

SIMO. And didn't you say she would stay at your house for life?

CHREMES. Yes.

SIMO. And furthermore, were you the only one to ask for her? Weren't there a number of other bridegrooms as well, in no way inferior to you, Chremes? But didn't I pass them over for your sake?

CHREMES. I don't deny that.

SIMO. Why, then, while I've been determined to gratify you, do you practise this deception on me now? If you didn't want her for your son, you could have left her for those who wanted her. Why did you give her to someone else?

CHREMES. I give her?

SIMO. Very well, then, you can be sure that you'll answer to these words before a judge tomorrow, because I'll deal with these treacheries by law.

CHREMES. You'll find out otherwise. But I do wish you would listen to me, at least one word.

SIMO. A word? What word from you? I've heard too many words for a long time now. Give me back my daughter, or tomorrow you'll have the word of the law on you. That's all I have to say.

CHREMES.   Itane saeuus es,
   Simo? Quod si ita hercle placet, pergito.
   Quandoquidem huc prouocas—
   Heus, euocate huc Gesippum mihi. Curre, Syre.
SYRUS.
   Quidem tua nunc illius faba cudetur fronte.   50
   Tute hoc intristi huic quod devorandum est innocuo.
GESIPPUS.
   Perii miser.
CHREMES.   Mastygia, viden' mihi
   Turbatas abs te quantas esse sollicitudines?
GESIPPUS.
   Obsecro, pater mi.
CHREMES.   Ne si Iupiter pro te roget,
   Carnifex. Quin apage te ex oculis ac conspectu ilico,   55
   Atque adeo dico, edico tibi, limen ne post   [*f. 136*]
   Vnquam hoc attingas diem. Abi ⟨spurium⟩.
   Syre, caput hoc abripe e ciuitate, patris
   Et patriae hostem, paricidam. Abeat.
SIMO.   Quin tu
   Abripiendus magis. Quid is commeruit?   60
CHREMES.
   Ita quidem ut ais, quin si commeritum
   Hoc meum sit, ius aeque nostrum vtrique patet?
   Quod si lubet nihil detrecto equidem. Neque
   Enim uel me conscium esse, neque tibi hoc magis
   Quam mihi molestum esse, deum testor iudicem.   65
SIMO.
   Quid! Tun' hoc mihi persuadeas, iuuenem
   Vxore ducta si amaret nisi cogente patre
   Cessurum alteri?
CHREMES.   Atqui eam Gesippus non duxerat.
SIMO.
   Quid non?

---

50. *Quidem*] ?read *Quid.*
  57. *spurium*] this reading, to be taken metaphorically as a pejorative epithet, is
a guess; see Textual Notes.

CHREMES. You're so hard, Simo, but if you want to do that, go ahead, by Hercules. Since you challenge me—— [*Shouts upstage, where Syrus and Gesippus are concealed.*]¹ Hey there, call Gesippus here to me. Run, Syrus.

SYRUS [*to Gesippus*]. Well! Now his wheat is going to be pounded on your head. You prepared this dish, and this innocent fellow must eat it.²

GESIPPUS [*aside, coming forward*]. I'm lost beyond recall.

CHREMES. You scoundrel, do you see how many worries you've stirred up for me?

GESIPPUS. I cry you mercy, father.

CHREMES. Not if Jupiter interceded for you, you villain. Out of my sight and my presence instantly! And I tell you, I order you, never after today to come near my door. Away, villain!—— Syrus, take this fellow out of the city as an enemy of his father and his country, as a parricide. Away with him!

[*Exeunt Gesippus and Syrus.*

SIMO. You deserve exile more. Why has he deserved this?

CHREMES. Indeed, just as you say, if the blame for this were mine, why shouldn't justice extend equally to both of us? And if that's what you wish, I refuse you nothing. But as god is my judge, I swear that I am not guilty and that this is no less annoying to me than to you.

SIMO. What! You would persuade me that a young man, having taken a wife, would turn her over to somebody else if he loved her—unless it were his father's idea?

CHREMES. But Gesippus didn't marry her.

SIMO. Why not?

¹ This staging is uncertain; perhaps Gesippus has left the stage after II.7 and here re-enters with him (though no new scene is marked). Note the omission of Gesippus' name from the heading of this scene.
² These proverbs mean that Chremes, in trouble with Simo for Gesippus' act, will make Gesippus suffer.

CHREMES.   Non dico ego—offucias nobis
   Ab adolescentibus factas et Phormione.   70
SIMO.
   Quis duxit igitur?
CHREMES.   Amicus Titus
   Pro Gesippo, idque tua ignorante filia.
SIMO.
   Proh diuam atque humanam fidem!
CHREMES.   Quin accipe
   Ipsius literas, vel familiam loquentem audiens
   Accede, quaeso, intro et rem cognoscito.   75
SIMO.
   Stupor huc me adigit ut quid agam nescio.
CHREMES.
   Veni, sodes.
SIMO.   Venio.

ACTUS TERTIUS. SCENA PRIMA.   [*f. 136v*]
Syrus.

[SYRUS.]
   Lachrimas mihi excussit ingenuus
   Adolescens, miseretque eius. Ah siccine
   Immerito eiectum patre ac patriis bonis
   Haeredem, filium, ut neque spem nec stabulum
   Refugii iam ullum habeat, ad summam inopiam!   5
   Quem tot bonorum hic totiusque rei haereditarium
   Fieri par fuit participem, nunc cum mendicis miser
   Squallebit in sordibus. Indignum facinus,
   O durum patrem! Ac quid commeruit, nisi
   Quod summa hominem fide ac indole decuit?   10
   Amicum ut seruaret concessit coniugem,
   Quod ego hercle rarum exemplar amicitiae
   Mirae virtutis interpretor. Ita mihi
   Deus Gesippos reperire faxit huiusmodi.
   Atque hocce nunc reponi illi pro gratitudine?   15
   Sed senes exeunt.

69. *offucias*] emended from *offusias*.
70. *factas*] emended from *factus*.

CHREMES. I can't say—tricks played on us by the young men and Phormio.

SIMO. Who married her then?

CHREMES. His friend Titus in place of Gesippus, and it happened without your daughter's knowing it.

SIMO. Oh, the faith of god and man!

CHREMES. Here, take his letter, or come inside and learn the facts from what the slaves have to say. Please.

SIMO. I'm so dumfounded I don't know what to do.

CHREMES. Come, if you please.

SIMO. I'm coming.   [*Exeunt.*

[III.1]   *Enter Syrus, weeping.*

SYRUS. That noble youth forces these tears from me; I'm sorry for him. Ah, so undeservedly a son and heir is cast away from his father and his patrimony into such extreme poverty that now he has no hope of refuge and no stall to find it in. He who should have become an heir, to share in all the wealth and everything, will now live a pauper in squalor among beggars. Shameful deed, oh severe parent! And what has he done except what was fitting for a man of the noblest disposition and the greatest loyalty? To save his friend he gave up his wife, and, by Hercules, I take that as a rare example of remarkable friendship. May God allow me to find Gesippuses of this kind. And instead of gratitude, is this his reward? But the old men are coming out.

[Actus Tertius. Scena Secunda.]
Simo. Syrus. Chremes.   *[f. 137]*

[Simo.]

Quo magis cogito, hoc minus video quod succenseam
Vel tibi iam uel mihi, Chreme, quando neque abs te neque
Contumeliae, sed amoris caussa factum reperio.
Sed eccum aduersum Syrum aduenientem tibi.

Syrus.   Factum, here,

Vt iussisti. Numquid imperas?

Chremes.   Dic, Syre, qua abiit.   5

Quid dixit tibi?

Syrus.   Ille? Nihil nisi lachrimare tantum. Mox vbi

Ad Pyraeum ventum est, nauem ut fit offendimus iam iam veli-
ficantem. Hanc conscendit, Romam vorsus, iamque viam tenere
Mediam supra sentio, quandoquidem ventus opportune dabat
Admodum.

Simo.   Duriter abs te factum nimis qui ablegasti   10

Filium, ac piget non prohibuisse pol.

Chremes.   Quid enim Simo?

Cedo facerem: non tuum damnum hoc, sed meum hoc totum
   vides.
Tua namque nobili nupta est imprimis adolescentulo,
Et qui amat illam et generi uestro prodesse poterit.
Quo tuas nunc lauto in loco, multo in beatiore satis, res sitas
   suspicor.   15
Vero ad me damnum adeo totum incumbit, qui tuam
Hodie affinitatem sperabam mihi praesidio firmo fore
Ac familiae stabiliendae, nisi is infaelix esset id
Qui probuit carcinoma meum.

Simo.   Quid tum? Num eum

Iccirco a te prorsum exiges, ac per inopiam ad   20
Latrocinia et scelus pessundabis? At meminisse oporteat
Tuum esse filium.

Chremes.   Minime, Simo, meum nolo esse mihi

Qui nolit esse obtemperans.

---

15. *lauto in loco*] ?read *loco*; see Textual Notes.

[III.2]   *Enter Simo and Chremes.*

SIMO. The more I think about it, Chremes, the less reason I see for anger either for you or for myself, since I find that the deed was done neither by you nor for insult, but for the sake of love. But look, here's Syrus coming to you.

SYRUS. Master, I've done as you ordered. Do you have any further orders?

CHREMES. Tell me where he went, Syrus. What did he say to you?

SIMO. Him? Nothing. He just cried. As soon as we got to the Piraeus, we came upon a ship on the point of sailing, as it happened. He boarded it, headed for Rome, and I think is already more than halfway there, for the wind came up very favorably.

SIMO. You acted too harshly in sending your son away, and I'm ashamed that I didn't stop you.

CHREMES. Why, Simo? Grant that I did. All the harm, you see, is mine, not yours. For your daughter is married to one of the finest young men, who loves her and could benefit your line.[1] I suspect your fortunes have been materially improved, very nicely indeed. But the harm in this weighs completely on me, since I hoped that an alliance with you today would be a great assistance to me and would fortify my family—if he hadn't been the calamity who proved it to be my cancer.

SIMO. What then? Will you for that reason thrust him from you completely and make him sink into robbery and crime because of poverty? But it would behoove you to remember that he is your son.

CHREMES. No, Simo, I don't want him to be mine who wouldn't be obedient to me.

---

[1] The earlier version is more specific in identifying Titus as a consul's son who has been called home to succeed to his father's power. See Textual Notes.

SIMO.   Age, Chreme, quamuis haec
  Mea haud minus sit querimonia, tamen id si est   *[f. 137v]*
  Quod te tantopere ulcerat, audi nunc: duas habet   25
  Frater filias; filio vtram mauis tuo elige. Affinitas,
  Dos cum sorte manent tibi ut futurae fuerant. Reduc
  Filium.
CHREMES.   Referri tibi a me gratia pro meritis non potest
  Satis, Simo.
SIMO.   Quid ais?
CHREMES.   Nihil malim equidem.
SIMO.
  Reduce igitur filium.
CHREMES.   Si censeas.
SIMO.   Maxime,   30
  At mature malis priusquam absumptus sit.
CHREMES.   Sapide
  Consulis. Sed quando tu hoc cum illo, quod si commodum est
  Hunc modo vna tecum in caena esse hic vt velit volo,
  Inter nos vt transigamus simul.
SIMO.   Faxo atque id agam
  Iam.
CHREMES.   Bene facis. Tu, Syre, ad vxorem propera, quae opus 35
  Ad caenam sunt parato ut paret.
SYRUS.   Pergo.
CHEMES.   Prouiso nunc
  Ad forum, tabellarium si quem, fors, nanciscier
  Potero, mihi qui ad filium ferat literas vt revocetur.
  Atque optime occurrit quidem, mihi qui aiebat
  Sese affuturum illic propediem: quidam hic vicinus Crito,
    frequens   40
  Qui mercatum illic Romae exerceat. Eum
  Iam exquiram primum, si domi erit, vt conueniam. Sin minus,
  Vxori relictum faciam, ad coenam, mox domum adveniens,
  Venire ad nos vt velit. Optimum ita arbitror.
  Caeterum vnum infaeliciter hercle me praeteriit interim: 45

---

40. *Crito*] the manuscript reads *Stylpho* (altered from *Albertus Discus*); Foxe
several times confused the two names.

SIMO. Come, Chremes, though my own complaint is no less than yours, if that's what's eating you so much, listen now. My brother has two daughters. Choose whichever you prefer for your son. Our alliance and the dowry with interest remain yours as they were going to be. Recall your son.

CHREMES. Simo, I can't thank you enough for your kindnesses.

SIMO. What do you say?

CHREMES. I'd like nothing better.

SIMO. Then call your son back.

CHREMES. If you think I should.

SIMO. Very much, but quickly, before he's ruined by misfortunes.

CHREMES. You give good advice. But since you recommend this course with him, if it's convenient I'd like your brother to come here to dinner, along with you, so we can work this out among ourselves.

SIMO. Fine, and I'll arrange it right now.   [*Exit.*

CHREMES. Good.——Syrus, hurry to my wife and have her prepare everything necessary for dinner.

SYRUS. I'm going.   [*Exit.*

CHREMES. Now I'll go to the forum to see if I can possibly find a courier who'll take a letter to my son for me so he can be called home. And, say, just in time it occurs to me that one of my neighbors said he's going there very soon. It's Crito, who frequently carries on business at Rome. I'll first ask if I can talk with him if he's at home; if he isn't, I'll leave a message with his wife that when he comes home soon, he should come to my house for dinner. I think that's best. But, by Hercules, one thing slipped my mind during all this, unfortunately: now that I

Simonem. Simul cogitate fratris sui adveniens
Secum ut duceret filiam, quandoquidem numquam eam memini
Adhuc videre virginem. Heus, Syre, huc redi denuo.

SYRUS.

Redeo.

CHREMES.   Vxorine ita vt imperabam?

SYRUS.   Factum.

CHREMES.   Curriculo

Transcurre ad Simonem. Dic cum veniat fratris simul   50
Adductam secum filiam ut meminerit maiusculam.
Eam videre cupio.

SYRUS.   Scilicet.

[ACTUS TERTIUS. SCENA TERTIA.]
                [*Sophrona.*]   [*f. 138*]

[SOPHRONA.]

Nae nos iniqua conditione foeminas
Omnes ad liberos esse natas arbitror:
Principio in parivndis, tum educandis, labos
Et aegritudo quanta assidet. Porro in vita denique
Siquid tum euenit praeter bonum, mulieres fere   5
Nos solae plectimur; postremo siqua est aliis
Foemina infaelicior omnium vna, ego sum infaelicissima:
Cui cum vnum fata e multis reliquere adolescentulum,
Fatis crudelior nunc patris funestauit acerbitas.
Quid tandem hic vir vult meus, miror, aut   10
Quam incoeptat dementiam, perecastor, itane
Excusso aut graui esse animo erga liberos?
Saltem non pudere hominem? Tamen non os
Vereri populi qui postquam gnatum sua
Funestauit proteruia, meque familiamque   15
Omnem coniecit in luctum. Tamen ne parum
Suam hanc ostentet ineptiam: insuper iocos
Nunc poscit etiam, conviuia agitat,

52. *Eam . . . cupio*] the reading is uncertain; see Textual Notes.
P.H. *Sophrona*] emended from *Sostrata*. Cf. III.4.P.H.
1-9.] see Textual Notes.

think about it, when Simo comes, he should bring his brother's daughter with him, since I don't remember ever having seen the girl.—— [*Shouts.*] Hey, Syrus, come back here.

SYRUS [*within*]. I'm coming.

Enter Syrus.

CHREMES. Did you tell my wife what I told you?

SYRUS. Yes.

CHREMES. Run quickly to Simo. Tell him that when he comes he should remember to bring his brother's older daughter with with him. I want to see her.

SYRUS. Of course. [*Exeunt separately.*

[III.3] *Enter Sophrona.*

SOPHRONA. Truly, I think we women were all born in our terrible situation, born for children: first in bearing them, then in raising them, how much labor and pain attends us. Besides, if anything really unpleasant happens in life, we women alone are hit with it. And if any one woman is more unfortunate than all others, I am the most unfortunate: the fates spared me only one son out of many, and now the harshness of his father, more cruel than the fates, has dishonored him. I wonder what in the world my husband means or what madness he's entering, by Castor, to feel such rigid and severe anger for his children? Has the man no shame at least? But not to fear the gossip of the people! Since he's disgraced his son with his own shamelessness, he's plunged both me and the whole house into grief! Yet it's not enough that he displays this folly: now, in addition, he even demands entertainments, plans banquets, and brings in guests

Convivas ductat, in nostris veluti
Triumphans malis. At miser interim   20
Famelicus ille algebit, esuriet satis
Qui noster horum omnium esset particeps:
Sine patria, sine patre, percitus,
Profugus aerumnis obsitus. O miserum   [*f. 138v*]
Illum, crudelem patrem! At quid commeruit?   25
Atque vt ne negem commeritum esse, tamen
Hercle si seruus aut hostis esset, quid in
Ipsum grauius animadverti potuit?
Paulum supplicii in liberos sat est etiam
Pro piaculo. Certe praecipitem quemquam patria   30
Pellere plusquam extremum est. Atque aedepol id ego
Nunc certo scio: suum si vnquam putasset filium,
Id numquam coepisset facinus, credibile est.
Alioqui qua fieret, hoc vt vnquam adeo
Ineptum ille venire in animum potuit?   35
Sed eccum hunc ipsum procedere video.

[Actus Tertius. Scena Quarta.]
Chremes. Sophrona.

[Chremes.]
Neque vir neque vxor quo veni inuentus domi. Famulis
Datum est ilico ut dicerent cum venit vt veniat
Conviua in caenam.

Sophrona.   Quos quaeso, mi uir, conviuas
Accersis hodie?

Chremes.   Quid tua hoc? Potin' tu quod nisi domi
Curare caenam? Hoc age.

Sophrona.   Accuratum est sedulo. Sed miser   5
Ille Gesippus interim!

Chremes.   Proh pergin', Proserpina, me adhuc
Accendere et animum fodicare? Nullon' pacto effecero
Praeceptis vt sis morigera, scelesta? Satin' interminatus
Sum tibi, negotium ne faxis de hac re amplius?
Quando tandem cacoethes istud tuum cornicari desinet?   10
Linguam hercle istam exectam tuam oportuit cum duxeram.

as if he were rejoicing in the midst of our troubles. Meanwhile our wretched son will go cold and hungry, starving while he should partake of all our goods—without a fatherland, without a father, abused, a fugitive overwhelmed by misfortunes. Oh, the wretched boy, the cruel father! But what has he done wrong? Or even if I don't deny that he did wrong, yet, by Hercules, if he were a slave or an enemy how could he have been punished more severely? A little punishment applied to children is adequate even for a sinful act. Surely it's more than extreme to drive anyone headlong from his homeland. By heaven I know for certain now that if ever he had thought of him as a son it's incredible that he would ever have started this wickedness. Otherwise how could it happen that this folly would ever have come into his mind? But look, I see him coming.

[III.4]   *Enter Chremes.*

CHREMES. Neither husband nor wife found at home when I went there. I've left word with his slaves that, when he gets home, they should tell him immediately to come as my guest to dinner.

SOPHRONA. Please, my husband, what guests are you inviting today?

CHREMES. What business is it of yours? Are you master of anything except looking after the dinner at home? You take care of that.

SOPHRONA. It's carefully taken care of. But meanwhile our poor Gesippus!

CHREMES. Pish, Proserpina,[1] do you go on setting me on fire and digging up my anger? Is there no way I can make you obey my orders, you whore? Haven't I warned you enough not to carry on about that any more? When will that ill temper of yours stop cawing? By Hercules, I should have cut out your tongue when I married you.

---

[1] Proserpina, wife of Pluto and queen of the underworld, was also sometimes identified with Hecate, goddess of sorcery and witchcraft and terrible figure of the night. In the draft version, Chremes here calls her merely *mulier*.

SOPHRONA.

Quaeso, mi homo, prohibebin' me amare meos?

CHREMES.   Imo

Sophrona, amor hic vester est qui nobis corrumpit filios;
Vestra haec indulgentia et pietas stulta pernicies,   [*f. 139*]
Pestis, virusque et viscus merum adolescentibus: 15
Quae cum ingenio omnes estis sculptae distortissimo,
Facile cereos ipsorum animos amussim ad vostram fingitis,
Hincque fit quod refractarios habemus liberos,
Quippe vostrum facile ad nequitiam imitantes archetypum,
Vnde facile iam scitu est non alio quam te magistra hoc strui   20
Facinus. Itaque hercle non hunc sed te eliminatam hinc
Potius oportuit. Atque adeo nisi taceas.

SOPHRONA.

Quod si hercle inducas sic animum facere, facias,
Atque etiam obtestor, Chreme, quoniam nimis me
Inuito retinere te iam diu sentio. Quamobrem quaeso aliam tibi 25
Quam lubet magis asciscas coniugem, ita demum
Mihi nec molestia nec tibi odio victura sim
Quando quidem ex me liberos tibi ferre non poteris.

CHREMES.

Mulier, si sana sis, tace modo atque abi domum.
Tibi sit edictum semel.

SOPHRONA.   Abeo.

CHREMES.   Deus bone,   30

Quanta haec esset humanae vitae faelicitas, haec si vna crux
Abesset, mulier, quod qui in vita experti quod loquor
Intelligunt. Quamquam equidem nihil est quod huic magnopere
Succenseam, quae, si icta sit desiderio filii, pietas haec est
Parentum in liberos. Quippe et meum quoque animum haud
    minus idipsum verberat,   35
Haud leniter, etiamsi dissimulare apud eam libuit
Sedulo.

22-23. originally one line in MST, and my lineation is doubtful. See Textual Notes.

SOPHRONA. I beg you, my husband, will you forbid me to love my children?

CHREMES. But Sophrona, it's this love of yours which ruins our sons. Your indulgence and foolish affection is nothing but the ruination, the bane, the poison, and the birdlime of youth. Since you women are all wrought with a most twisted nature, you readily fashion their waxen spirits after your own pattern. Hence it happens that we have obstinate children, who readily imitate your model, even to worthlessness. So it's easy to know that this wickedness was fashioned by no one but you, his teacher. By Hercules, I should have turned you out rather than him—and so I will if you don't shut up.

SOPHRONA. Well, by Hercules, if you should decide to do so, go ahead. I even beg you to do it, Chremes, since I feel that for a long time now you've kept me around very much against your will. So I ask you to take another wife whom you like more; then at last I wouldn't be overwhelmed with disgust for myself or hatred for you, because you won't be able to take my children from me for yourself.

CHREMES. Woman, if you want to stay healthy, just be quiet and go home. Take that as an order for once.

SOPHRONA. I'm going. [*Exit.*

CHREMES. Good god, how happy our life would be if this one cross, woman, were gone—as they know who are what I call experienced in life. But I really have no reason to be very angry at her. If she's tormented by concern for her son, that's the duty of parents toward their children. To be honest about it, it hammers at my heart just as hard as hers, even if by design I like to pretend in front of her.

[Actus Tertius. Scena Quinta.]

Crito. Chremes.   [*f. 139v*]

[Crito.]

     Diuinare satis quid sit negotii nequeo

     Quod Chremes modo ipsus ad me adveniens ad coenam expetit.

     Propterea prouiso scire vespere.

Chremes.   Optate mi Crito, salueas.

[Crito.]

     Et tu, Chreme optatissime. Quidnam fit rei?

Chremes.   Romam te

     Audiui profectionem parare propediem.

[Crito.]   Sospitante numine.   5

Chremes.

     Quandonam, Crito?

[Crito.]   Hodie constitueram, cras perquam diluculo

     Necessum est.

Chremes.   Optime profecto factum.

[Crito.]   Quamobrem tu istud?

Chremes.   Illic mihi

     Est, Crito, filius.

[Crito.]   Tuus!

Chremes.   Atque iam esse certo scio.

[Crito.]   Gesippus?

Chremes.

     Ad eum tua nunc opera peropus est ad

     Perferendas literas.

[Crito.]   Scilicet, sed quampridem profectus illuc aut   10

     Qua de re?

Chremes.   Longum est exordiri nunc. I mecum intro, ibi

     Et quid illo factum sit, teque quid velim facere audies.

Crito.

     Perge.

---

     1. S.P. *Crito*] omitted in MST. In later S.P.'s in this scene, Crito's speeches are assigned to Stilpho, the name Foxe originally used for this character (though he had already given that name to Crito's brother). Though he altered the name in the P.H. of this scene, he neglected to alter it in the speech prefixes and in the text at ll. 3 and 8, where I have also emended.

     7. *Necessum est*] ?read as a separate line; the words were added interlineally.

[III.5]   *Enter Crito.*

CRITO [*to himself*]. I can't figure out what's going on, that Chremes himself just came to my house and invited me to dinner. So I'm on my way this evening to find out.

CHREMES. My dear Crito, greetings.

CRITO. And you, my beloved Chremes. What's going on?

CHREMES. I've heard that you're planning a trip to Rome soon.

CRITO. God willing.

CHREMES. When, Crito?

CRITO. I decided today: I must go tomorrow, as close to dawn as possible.

CHREMES. I'm very glad it's soon.

CRITO. Why do you say that?

CHREMES. My son is there, Crito.

CRITO. Your son!

CHREMES. Now I know for sure that he is.

CRITO. Gesippus?

CHREMES. I'm in great need of your help now in carrying a letter to him.

CRITO. Of course, but how long ago did he go there, and why?

CHREMES. It's a long story to start now. Go inside with me, where you shall hear both what happened to him and what I would like you to do.

CRITO. Go ahead.   [*Exeunt.*

[Actus Tertius. Scena Sexta.]
Stylpho. Simo. Syrus. Phrygia.

Stylpho.
    Praeclarum predicas ingenium adolescentis. Atque ideo
    Eum eiecit iratus oppido?
Simo.   Oppido.
Stylpho.   Tametsi quidem
    Non commeritus, tamen profuerit illi hoc posthac ad plurima.
Simo.
    Indubie. Verum interea dum sermoni curamur,
    Relicta est nobis Phrygia.
Stylpho.   Vah tam iuuenes hos: si non oportuit, 5
    Tam festinatum.
Simo.   Quid tum vbi huc permensum sit aetatis?
Stylpho.
    Haud longe aberunt, credo. Atque eccos venire video.
Syrus.
    Stylpho, si iter foret ad concionem, haud ita festinares, credo.
    Puellam pene confecistis lassitudine.
Stylpho.   Itane, Phrygia?
Phrygia.
    Minime, pater, nisi quod me gerris suis retriuit   10
    Linguaculus hic.
Stylpho.   I, Syre, prae strue nobis viam hanc.
Syrus.
    Accipio.

[Actus Tertius. Scena Septima.]
                    Gesippus   [*f. 140*]

[Gesippus.]
    Num quisquam est sub coelo hoc vsquam natus miser
    Infaeliciori vnquam, natus ac educatus, sydere quam ego sum,
    Cui vnquam tam auersus equos sua sol iunxit ab

III.6.2. *oppido . . . Oppido*] a pun; the *-o* in the second word has a circum-
flex to distinguish it in MST.
    7. *aberunt, credo*] ?read *aberunt.*

[III.6]   *Enter Stylpho and Simo.*

STYLPHO. You're showing the outstanding character of the young
   man. And for that the angry fellow drove him out of town?
SIMO. Precisely.
STYLPHO. Though he certainly didn't deserve it, yet this will be
   very profitable to him in the future.
SIMO. No doubt. But meantime, while we're busy talking, we've
   forgotten about Phrygia.
STYLPHO. Oh these young people! If they aren't wanted, they
   come so quickly.
SIMO. How long should it have taken to get here?
STYLPHO. I think they won't be far away. And look, I see them
   coming.

                    Enter Syrus and Phrygia.

SYRUS. Stylpho, if your trip were to a meeting, I think you wouldn't
   be in such a hurry. You've almost killed the girl with fatigue.
STYLPHO. Is that so, Phrygia?
PHRYGIA. Not at all, father, except that this tongue wagger has
   worn me out with his nonsense.
STYLPHO. Syrus, go and prepare the way for us.
SYRUS. I get you.   [*Exeunt.*

[III.7]   *Enter Gesippus in rags.*

GESIPPUS. Has any poor son anywhere under the heavens ever been
   born and bred under a more unlucky star than I? Is there any to
   whom such a baleful sun has ever hitched his horses far from his

Vrbe, cui aut iustior de fortuna sua nunc esse queat querimonia—
Siuetamen fortunam istam seu fata   5
Appellem potius, siue quicquid est—qui aut omnes
Aeque calamitatum numeros absoluerit?
Nam proh caelitum terrigenumque fidem,
Quid amplius aerumnis quisquam possit his accedere?
Extorris e patria, paternis exclusus aedibus,   10
Mundi planeta octauus, sine sede, sine
Ope vagus, rerum egens omnium, tum sine
Veste nudus, sine cultu quae habui
Pro viatico—quippe perierunt omnia, cui
Porro neque rei neque spei quicquam superest, nisi in   15
Tito dumtaxat meo, ad quem durum nunc telum
Adiget me necessitas. Tum neque an idemne animus
Qui olim fuerit an cum fortuna immutatus simul
Satis scio. Caeterum quicquid est, semel experiri omnia
Quandoquidem eo Romam nunc accessimus,   20
Velit necne me internoscere,
Certum est. Quippe nunc eo res rediit vti faciam.
Sed quid pompae illuc? Numquid rex huc quispiam?
Atque hercle quem ego nunc videam? Ni me fallit facies
Ipsus est, atque certe hercle est. Cum Sempronia   25
Video. Papae, an regnum occupat? At dicam nihil.

[Actus Tertius. Scena Octava.]

Titus. Sempronia. Gesippus.   [*f. 140v*]

Titus.

Vos hinc intro abscedite. Sempronia, libet hic post epulas
Deambulare paululum, salubre est.

Sempronia.   Licet, mi vir.

Titus.

Dic nunc, meum suauium tandem, haec tibi Roma vt placeat?

Sempronia.

Ecastor pulcherrime.

Titus.   Sane, et mihi nunc multo demum placet
Impensius postquam te hic coniugem habeo, mea Sempronia. 5
Sed numquis te affectus patriae tangit interea?

own city, who could with more justice complain about his fortune (call it fortune or fate or whatever), or who has in like manner loosed all the hosts of calamities? Oh, the faith of heaven and earth, how could anyone come closer to these great misfortunes? Exiled from my fatherland, excluded from my father's house, the eighth planet of the world,[1] a wanderer without a home and without resources, destitute of everything, stripped of clothes, without the wardrobe which I had for travel—indeed everything has been lost, and neither goods nor good hope is left me unless only in my friend Titus, to whom the cruel spear of necessity now will drive me. Then I don't know for sure whether his attitude is the same as it once was or has been changed along with his fortune. Still, whatever it is, whether he wishes to recognize me or not, since I've now come as far as Rome I'm determined to try everything once. Indeed my circumstances have reached such a state now that I must do it. But what sort of procession is that? Some king coming here? By Hercules, whom should I see now? Unless I'm deceived, that's his face—and, by Hercules, it is for sure. I see him with Sempronia. Well! Is he in charge of the kingdom? But I'll say nothing.

[III.8] *Enter Titus and Sempronia, richly dressed, with attendants.*

TITUS [*to attendants*]. Leave us and go inside, all of you.——
                                                    [*Exeunt attendants.*
[*To Sempronia.*] Sempronia, I like to walk here after dinner, and it's good for us.

SEMPRONIA. As you wish, my lord.

TITUS. Tell me now, my sweet, how do you like Rome?

SEMPRONIA. My goodness, very much.

TITUS. That's good. And I like it very much more now that I have you here as my wife, my Sempronia. But still, do you feel any homesickness?

---

[1] That is, an outsider; only seven "planets" were known.

SEMPRONIA.   Aliae
   Vt sunt affectae nescio; mea haec semper cantilena fuit
   Vbique esse patriam vbi bene est, vbicumque est, ut putem.
TITUS.
   Enimvero laudo, atque immortales superis fero gratias
   Quando tandem animum tuum ita erga me esse ac volui sentio.   10
   Quo facilius nunc spero suaui ac concordi pace suauissimam
   Aetatem dehinc victuros simul.
   Prorsus enim incertus eram quo animo latura esses demum
   Personatas cum rescires nuptias, et tamen eo amor
   Armauit me: aut faciundum aut moriendum fuit.   15
SEMPRONIA.
   Quid opus istis, mi vir? Neque enim tu primus qui amasti, neque
   Ego tam tenella rerum sum quae quid fert amor nesciam.
   Quo non solum tibi aequior sum, sed mihi etiam gratulor
   Magis, quae huic nunc contigerim viro quicum concordare
   Aetatem liceat.
TITUS.   Cordate hoc, Sempronia,   20
   Nam vt praecipua in vita res est concordia, ita rursum illius
   Nullum fomentum videtur verius quam verus amor.
   Quo firmius nunc spero coniugium hoc fore nostrum si vt
   Amore primum initum est, ita animorum studium hoc et bene-
      volentiam
   Retinuerimus.
SEMPRONIA.   Ita pol volo et opto, mi domine.   25
TITUS.   [*f. 141*]
   Nunc siquid desit, Sempronia, aurum, vestes, ancillulae,
   Siue quid rerum aliud impera, insume vt voles. Omnia haec
   Tibi una mecum communia puta, mea particeps.
SEMPRONIA.
   Est gratia maxima.
GESIPPUS.   Admouebo me propius.
TITUS.   Eamus ergo intro.
   Ecce vero unquam ego ardelionibus istis purgabo oppidum?   30
   Eya vt otiosus stat veterator: fugitiuus ac circumforaneus
   Ex vultu apparet quispiam. Nimirum huiusmodi
   Planis plena sunt omnia. At ego istis ventribus remedium
   Spero inueniam propediem. Sine.

SEMPRONIA. I don't know how other women are affected, but my theme song has always been to regard my homeland as being anywhere that pleases me, wherever it is.

TITUS. You're absolutely right, and I give eternal thanks to the gods since at last I feel that you have affection for me just as I have wished. The more easily now do I hope that henceforth we will live a most sweet life together, in sweet and peaceful harmony. I was really uncertain in what spirit you would tolerate the substitute marriage when you knew about it, and yet my love so armed me that I had to do it or die.

SEMPRONIA. Why need you worry, my husband? For you aren't the first man who's been in love, and I'm not so innocent that I don't know what love does. Not only am I the more favorably disposed toward you, but I congratulate myself the more that now I have fallen to a husband with whom I may live my life in harmony.

TITUS. Wisely spoken, Sempronia, for as harmony is the principal thing in life, so in turn there seems to be no truer kindling of harmony than true love. The more constant now will our marriage be, I hope, if, as it was begun in love, we so preserve the warmth and devotion of our feelings.

SEMPRONIA. I sincerely hope and pray so, my lord.

TITUS. Now, Sempronia, if anything is wanting—money, clothing, handmaids, or anything else—just ask for it; take what you please. Consider everything here as much yours as mine, my partner.

SEMPRONIA. That is most kind.

GESIPPUS [*aside*]. I'll move closer.

TITUS. Let's go in then. [*Looking at Gesippus.*] Look at that. Will I ever rid the town of these meddlers? Look how this ancient loafer stands around! From the look of him, he appears to be some vagrant runaway slave. It's strange that every place is full of ne'er-do-wells like this. But very soon I hope to find a remedy for these—bellies. Amen. [*Exeunt Titus and Sempronia.*

[Actus Tertius. Scena Nona.]
Gesippus.

[Gesippus.]
Itan', Tite, haeccine amicis reponis officia,
In ardeliones vt vertas cum piget noscere?
O mores, o tempora, quae haec hominum perfidia
Est? Atque annon praedixi fore? Qui cum ipsi ope
Indigeant, nihil est mansuetius, post cum fortuna   5
Sufflati, agnoscunt neminem. Vah ingratitudinem!
Adeon' nullam esse in rebus humanis fidem? Proh deum
Immortalem! Atque hunc haud triuialem mihi anchoram
Existimaui adversus naufragia omnia.
Haccine caussa tam cupidus eram Romam redeundi?   10
Qui vtinam fluctibus absorptus essem funditus ut numquam
    appellerem,
Aut aliquid hic esset nunc quo honesta morte defungier
Possem. Hei mihi, quod hic habeo neminem
Qui vitam hanc mihi auferat, hisque me
Evoluat miseriis. Et quid nunc ilico   15
Cultro hoc parco perficere, quandoquidem
Extremum hoc solatium superest, vt uitam mihi
In morte queram cum vita hic mors est grauissima.
Veh mihi vt totus langueo et fathisco miser
Aerumnis sepultus prorsus, vt pedibus nequeam   20
Amplius consistere. Dulcis mors, hinc miserum abripe.

[Actus Tertius. Scena Decima.]
Chremes. Crito.   [*f. 141v*]

Chremes.
Ita quaeso te, Crito, vt facias.
Crito.   Potin' vt animo
Sis otioso, Chreme?
Chremes.   Atque ipsum si potes
Conuenias primum, sin nequeas tamen vt Tito
Tradantur hae literae facito.
Crito.   Diligentiam
Faxo videbis meam. Ecquid est aliud?

[III.9]

GESIPPUS. Is this the way you repay your friends for favors, Titus, to refer to them as meddlers when you're ashamed to acknowledge them? Oh the customs, oh the times, what is this perfidy of men? And didn't I foresee that it would be so? When men are in need themselves, nothing is more sweet-natured than they; later, when they are puffed up by fortune, they know no one. Oh ingratitude! Is there no trustworthiness in human behavior? Alas immortal god! And I thought this man no ordinary anchor for me against all shipwrecks. Was it for this that I was so eager to come to Rome? Would that I had been utterly swallowed up by the waves that I might never land, or that there were here now some means for me to die an honorable death. Alas for me that I have no one here to end my life for me and purge me of these miseries. [*He takes out a small knife.*] What, do it here and now with this little knife? This is the last comfort remaining to me, to seek life for myself in death, since life here is a death most severe. Alas for me, how utterly weak I am; wretch, how faint I become, so completely overcome by adversities that I can stand no longer. [*He sinks to the ground.*] Sweet death, carry this wretch from here. [*He falls asleep.*[1]

[III.10]   *Enter Chremes and Crito.*

CHREMES. That's what I want you to do, Crito.

CRITO. Be still, Chremes, and rest easy.

CHREMES. And if you can, speak to him first. But if you can't, at least be sure that this letter is delivered to Titus.

CRITO. I'll do my best, you'll see. Is there anything else?

---

[1] The staging here is curious. During the trial, Gesippus is said to have fallen asleep in a public way, and he has said here that he cannot stand up any longer. Presumably, then, he lies down on the stage here and is discovered, still lying in the same place, two scenes later by Martius. Meantime, however, the scene shifts to Athens for III.10. Perhaps a door at one end of the stage permanently represented Chremes' house, and another door at the other end represented Rome; if so, Chremes and Crito stayed at the Athenian end of the stage during III.10 as Gesippus lay at the other. Perhaps a third door represented the Athenian and Roman forums.

CHREMES.   Vt bene   5
  Sit tibi, nostrique memineris quod poteris.
CRITO.
  Aliud cura.
CHREMES.   Vale.
CRITO.   Et tu, Chreme
  Optime.
CHREMES.   Restat nunc mihi via carpenda ad forum,
  Vbi me Simo cum Stylphone fratre operirier
  Constituerunt ad portum vti deambulemus simul.   10
  Atque recta iam pergo illuc.

                [ACTUS TERTIUS. SCENA UNDECIMA.]
                  Martius Sicarius. [*Gesippus.*]

[MARTIUS.]
  Num quisquam hic qui me insequitur? Nemo est. Numquis hic
  Coryceus qui videt, qui me audit? Nemo est. At quem ego
  Huic properare procul video? At pecus est.
  Proh infandum ac foedum facinus! Quid egi ego
  Miser hodie, qui illum inter pugnandum   5
  Mactaui rusticum? Nunc hei mihi, quid ergo prospiciam
  Effugii mihi, quamve ineam viam potissimum
  Ad elabendum? Hac? Illac? Istac? Sed quid hoc?
  Occisus sum, quisnam hic sub lapide
  Scorpius? Quid, dormitne etiam an non? Hem,   10
  Quid cultri hoc in manibus? Mendicum quempiam
  Ebrium, satis credo. Tace, quid ego inueni nunc?
  Sicam sanguinariam hanc illi in dexteram
  Indam afabre ipsumque omni hac aspergam
  Suspitione. Nunc quid vnquam dari huic posset simile?   15
  Quod si astu rem tractauero, quin aggrediar equidem.
  Eya vero haec ita euenit res vt volui   [*f. 142*]
  Vsque edormit stipes nec persentiscit quippiam.
  O sancta Salus, quae tam acutum hoc dedisti in mentem

III.11.P.H. *Gesippus*] omitted in MST, since he does not speak in this scene.
6. *Nunc hei*] ?read *Hei;* see Textual Notes.
14-15. *ipsumque . . . Suspitione*] see Textual Notes.

CHREMES. That it go well with you, and remember me as much as you can.

CRITO. You look after other business.

CHREMES. Farewell.

CRITO. And you, my very good Chremes.   [*Exit.*

CHREMES. Now it remains for me to head for the forum, where Simo and his brother Stylpho agreed to wait for me so we might walk to the harbor together. And I'm on my way there right now.
                                                        [*Exit.*

[III.11]   *Enter Martius the cutthroat; Gesippus still lies asleep.*

MARTIUS. Is anybody here following me? Nobody. Is there any Corycean here to see me or hear me?[1] None. But who's that away over there rushing this way? It's only an animal. Oh, my terrible, wicked deed! Wretch, what have I done today? Killed that farmer in a fight! Now, woe is me, what way will I look for to escape? Which road should I take to slip away as fast as possible? [*Running about.*] This way? That way? Or that? [*He sees Gesippus.*] But I'm lost! For who is this scorpion under a rock? What, is he still sleeping or not? Aha, what's this? Some sort of knife in his hands? I think he must be some drunken beggar. Sh! What I have hit on now! I'll cleverly put my bloody dagger into his right hand and fasten all the suspicion onto him. Now what could ever be found the likes of this? But if I handle the affair cleverly, I won't become implicated in it myself. [*He exchanges knives.*] Oh, this is really turning out just as I wished, so long as he sleeps like a log and doesn't suspect anything. O holy Salus, who have made my mind so keen today, it is really true: he is

---

[1] Corycus, in Ionia, was noted for spies who kept watch on shipping in schemes of piracy. The passage anticipates *Christus Triumphans* V.4.10. There was another Corycus, in Cilicia, famous for a cave; Boccaccio's Gisippo fell asleep in a cave, but Foxe probably did not know Boccaccio's version.

Hodie, verum hercle est: ingenium non qui in pectore   20
Sed qui in manibus gerit, nec qui vbique sapit
Sed qui in loco cum sit opus sapit, vere sapit.
Ibo atque ad populum exclamabo nunc. Illius
Me assimulabo necessarium qui occisus est,
Huncque huc ducam qui comprehendant. Obsecro,   25
Populares.

[Actus Quartus. Scena Prima.]
Martius. Turba Exploratorum. Gesippus.

[Martius.]
Proh ciues vostram fidem, heccine in libera ciuitate scelera?
Siccine abierint! Subuenite. Canes emittamus venaticos
Primum.

Exploratores.   Indignum facinus!

[Martius.]   Ecce vestigia persequamur hac.
Vbinam hic homicida aut quo peruasit, miror? Singulas
Scrutemur latebras.

Explorator.   Ecce vero adeste.

Martius.   Hem, quid est?   5

Explorator.
Sanguinarium ipsum cum ferro videtisne?

Martius.   Canes
Profecto optimos. Dixin' vobis?

Explorator.   Agite, obstipemus vndique
Atque irruamus.

Martius.   Diis magnas debeo gratias.

Explorator.
Vah, sceleste, os execrandum, surge.

Martius.   Heus, sacrilege
Furcipatibulum, Stygis mastygia, tibi dico, surge.

Gesippus.   Omnipotens 10
Deus, quid est rei?

Explorator.   Constringemus manibus pedibusque
Quadrupedem.

---

1. *heccine*] = *haeccine.* ?Read *hiccine.*
7. *optimos*] MST reads *optimios.*
    obstipemus] *stipare* is common, but *obstipo* is not listed in L-S; LTL lists the
word (questionable) in M. Marcellus Empiricus (= *inculcare*).

truly wise who carries his genius not in his heart but in his hands, and who is wise not in all circumstances but in the situation where there is need of wisdom. Now I'll go and call out to the people. I'll pretend I'm a kinsman of the man who was killed, and I'll lead them here to find this fellow.—— [*Shouts.*] I beseech you, citizens. [*Exit.*

[IV.1] *Enter Martius with Cratinus and a posse with dogs;*
Gesippus still lies asleep.

MARTIUS.[1] Oh citizens, by your faith! These crimes in a free city! That the world would turn out this way! Come on. Let's send out the hunting dogs first.

A SEARCHER. Terrible crime!

MARTIUS. Look, tracks here! Let's follow them. Where's the murderer? I wonder where he's got to? Let's search every hiding-place.

A SEARCHER [*finding Gesippus*]. Look! Come here.

MARTIUS. What is it?

A SEARCHER. The bloody fellow himself, with his weapon, do you see it?

MARTIUS. Excellent dogs! Didn't I tell you?

A SEARCHER. Come, let's surround him and rush him.

MARTIUS [*aside*]. I owe many thanks to the gods.

A SEARCHER. Oh you criminal, you despicable fellow, get up.

MARTIUS. Hey, you impious gallows-rogue, scoundrel of hell, I tell you, get up.

GESIPPUS [*waking*]. God almighty, what's the matter?

A SEARCHER. Let's tie up this beast hand and foot.

---

[1] The re-entrance of a character (Martius) who has just exited at the end of the preceding act is a violation of some Renaissance critical theories.

GESIPPUS.   Obsecro, amici homines, quid ego feci?
EXPLORATOR.   Nescirier
   Tu id credis quid egeris, carnifex?
GESIPPUS.   Egone egi? Quid ego
   Egi, obsecro?
EXPLORATOR.   Dicetur mox tibi apud consules. Constringite.
   Tun' hic impune homines ciues vt mactes, bellua?
GESIPPUS.   Egone   15
   Ciues?
EXPLORATOR.   Eho, rusticum illum, dico, diuitem uiciniae hic,
   Negabin' impudens? At ferrum non negabit hoc
   Adhuc recens a uulnere.
GESIPPUS.   Supreme deus, quid hoc
   Monstri est? Nunc quid dicam aut faciam incertus sum, [*f. 142v*]
     nisi
   Tam honestam dari occasionem ad moriendum, id vero gaudeo. 20
MARTIUS.
   Lanio humani sanguinis, negabis propinquum meum
   Interfecisse, carcer?
GESIPPUS.   Scilicet.
MARTIUS.   Tum argentum
   Omne emunxisse postea?
GESIPPUS.   Factum.
MARTIUS.   Etiam confitetur. Dixin' huncce esse?
   Interrogate!
EXPLORATOR.   Tun' homicidium hoc vnquam infitiaveris, verbero?
GESIPPUS.
   Non nego.
EXPLORATOR.   Quid meritus ergo?
GESIPPUS.   Quid libet.   25
EXPLORATOR.
   Mira sane vindicta numinis quae ipsum non sinit
   Denegare hominem. Abripite, rapite, trahite ad
   Consules.
GESIPPUS.   Heu me miserum.

   16-17.] see Textual Notes.
   21. *propinquum*] ?read *rusticum illum propinquum;* see Textual Notes.

GESIPPUS. I pray you, my friends, what have I done?

A SEARCHER. You think we don't know what you've done, you villain?

GESIPPUS. What I've done! What on earth have I done?

A SEARCHER. You'll be told soon, before the consuls.—— [*To searchers.*] Tie him up.—— [*To Gesippus.*] You think you can murder citizens here and get away with it, monster?

GESIPPUS. I murder citizens?

A SEARCHER. Ha! A rich farmer of the neighborhood here, I tell you. Do you deny it, you shameless fellow? This weapon, still fresh from the wound, won't deny it.

GESIPPUS [*aside*]. God on high, what sort of portent is this? I'm uncertain what to say or do now, except to rejoice that I'm given such a guiltless opportunity to die.

MARTIUS. Butcher of human flesh, do you deny that you killed my kinsman, you criminal?

GESIPPUS. Of course.[1]

MARTIUS. And then stole all his money?

GESIPPUS. Yes.

MARTIUS. He even confesses. Didn't I tell you he was the one? Ask him.

A SEARCHER. Villain, will you deny this murder?

GESIPPUS. I don't deny it.

A SEARCHER. What do you deserve then?

GESIPPUS. Whatever you please.

A SEARCHER. Oh, the marvelous vengeance of god, which does not allow the man to deny himself. Seize him and carry him away. Drag him to the consuls.

GESIPPUS. Alas, wretched me!   [*Exeunt omnes, carrying Gesippus off.*

---

[1] Gesippus intends his answers to be equivocal, so that they may be taken as confessions.

[Actus Quartus. Scena Secunda.]
Sempronia. Phormio.

[Sempronia.]

Narrauit modo herus tuus ex te auditum, Phormio,
Pamphilam, quantum intellexi, quandam meum Gesippum hic
    amare virginem.

Phormio.

Nempe, consulis hanc Fuluii filiam.

Sempronia.   Quod ego hercule

Numquam intellexeram. Quid, hancque aiebat sibi esse compla-
    citam adeo?

Phormio.

Supra quidem mortales omnes feminas: simul cum te laudabat
    etiam,   5
Inter caeteras eam proximam. Forte enim subauscultans aderam.

Sempronia.

Cupio eam videre, Phormio.

Phormio.   Licet, hera.

Sempronia.   Deinde optimi

Adolescentis amori benefactum cupio. Tum id aequum simul
Est, vos adiutare, Phormio, cuius antea
In vestris rebus experti adeo estis operae promptitudinem.   10
Dignus est.

Phormio.   Verissimum, hera, atque hic iam dudum
Sum quandoquidem sum pollicitus illi, et faxim lubens.

Sempronia.

Merito facis. Sed estne, ut fertur, egregia?

Phormio.   Plane

Res haec est vt animi sunt amantium: qui amat,
Huic ita est quae aliis tamen eadem erit aliter. Suo   15
Quaeque lactata est vt palato placeat.

Sempronia.

Verum est, quo nunc magis te adniti velim vt summum
Amanti hoc perficias beneficium.

Phormio.   Quod queam equidem, sed seruus
Solus quid potero? Magis herum iube.

---

4. *complacitam*] emended from *complacitum*.
5. *laudabat etiam*] ?read *laudabat;* see Textual Notes.

[IV.2]   *Enter Sempronia and Phormio.*

SEMPRONIA. Phormio, your master just told me what he heard from you, that my Gesippus loves a certain girl named Pamphila. All I know about her is that she is a young girl here.

PHORMIO. Yes indeed, she's the daughter of Fulvius the consul.

SEMPRONIA. By Hercules, I didn't know that. What, did he say she was so appealing to him?

PHORMIO. Yes indeed, more than all mortal women. He even praised her the same as you, and the closest to you among all others. I happened to be there and heard him.

SEMPRONIA. I'd like to see her, Phormio.

PHORMIO. All right, mistress.

SEMPRONIA. I want to do a good turn for the love of that fine young man. And it's a good idea for you to help too, Phormio, since up to now you've proved your eagerness for work in your own enterprises. He's worthy of your help.

PHORMIO. Very true, mistress. I've been here for some time since I promised to help him, and I'd willingly do it.

SEMPRONIA. That's fine. But is she, as they say, a good catch?

PHORMIO. That's really a matter for lovers to decide for themselves: the same girl will be a prize catch to one who loves her and otherwise to others. Everybody is tempted by what pleases his own palate.

SEMPRONIA. That's true. All the more reason why I'd like you to exert yourself now to do this greatest favor for him, since he's in love.

PHORMIO. I'll do what I can, but what can I do, a mere slave? Better command my master.

SEMPRONIA.   Faciam, atque iam
  Nunc tu abi ad eam, ad me venire vt velit domum.   20
  Velle eam videre dicito, et tecum ducito.   [*f. 143*]
PHORMIO.   Fiet.
SEMPRONIA.
  Tametsi illi nulla lege obnoxia sum, tamen hoc
  Vel pro pietate illius uel officio meo debeo. Quaecumque expetit
  Semper bene huic et cupiam et faciam omnia.

[ACTUS QUARTUS. SCENA TERTIA.]
Titus et Fuluius Consules.
Martius. [*Cratinus et*] *Populus Romanus. Gesippus.*

[*Titus.*]
  Licet nunc, ciues, siquis testimonii dictionem habet
  Legibus ius vestrum persequi. Producite. Cuicumque iam
  Lubitum est impingere, licitum facimus dicere.
MARTIUS.   Etsi mihi,
  Verendi consules, natus ille qui occidit cognatus fuit
  Atque ab isto interfectum esse habeo liquidissimum, tamen   5
  Si solum ea res mihi sine testibus comperta foret,
  Numquam is forem qui hanc illi actionem intenderem.
  Nunc tot simul consciis cum manifestius id est quam ut
  Infitiari queat. Ipsum quaeso potius interrogate.
FULVIUS.   Dicite
  Testes nunc.
CRATINUS.   Non potest, iudices, testis esse certior   10
  Quam sua hominis cuiusque conscientia. Tum neque
  Quisquam immerito sceleris alligat sese qui merito
  Labis exors sit. Quamobrem non est nostris opus
  Nunc testimoniis, qui suis satis est victus testibus.
FULVIUS.
  Dicite, vidistisne cum incesserat hominem?   15
CRATINUS.
  Non, sed vestigia insectantes, dormientem cum sica hac offendimus
  Quam necdum absterserat, et quia tum ea res suspitionem

---

23. *debeo*] a doubtful reading; see Textual Notes.
P.H. *Cratinus et*] omitted in MST.

SEMPRONIA. I will. Now you go to her and have her come to me at home. Tell her I want to see her, and bring her with you.

PHORMIO. It shall be done. [*Exit.*

SEMPRONIA. Though I'm obligated to him under no law, yet I owe him this both for his good nature and from my own sense of obligation. I shall always wish him well, and everything that he desires I shall work for. [*Exit.*

[IV.3]   *Enter the consuls, Titus and Fulvius;*
Martius, Cratinus, and other Roman citizens bring in Gesippus bound.

TITUS. Now, citizens, if any of you has evidence to offer, you may seek justice from the law. Produce your evidence. Anyone who wishes to make an accusation we permit to speak.

MARTIUS. Reverend consuls, though the man who was struck down was a blood relative of mine and though I am quite certain that he was murdered by this man, yet if this thing had been discovered by me alone without corroborating witnesses, I would never be the one to bring this action against him. But now, with so many witnesses in agreement, it is so clear-cut that he cannot deny it. But please, it's better that you question him.

FULVIUS. Witnesses, you speak now.

CRATINUS. Judges, there can be no more certain witness than each man's own conscience. No man, moreover, confesses a crime without reason, no man who by rights is free of guilt. So there is no need for our testimony now, since he has been sufficiently convicted by his own witnesses.

FULVIUS. Tell me, did you see when he attacked the man?

CRATINUS. No, but we followed his tracks and found him sleeping, and this dagger with him, which he had not yet wiped. Since that aroused our suspicion, we arrested him and then bound

Dabat, manus dein vincula iniecimus et, quia nihil
Horum eluere potuit, confitentem ad vos perduximus.

TITUS.   [*f. 143v*]
Age, dicat reus nunc. Nihilne?

MARTIUS.   Tacet. Agnoscit.

TITUS.   Tun'   20
Huius es furti conscius an non? Nil respondet.

FULVIUS.   Furtum hoc
Uel diluas uel admittas necessum, iuuenis.

GESIPPUS.   Neque
Culpam neque mortem detrecto, consul.

TITUS.   Argenti dic
Quantum abstulisti?

FULVIUS.   Quid sublegisti nummorum, dicito?

GESIPPUS.
Nescio.

MARTIUS. Viginti minas.

FULVIUS.   Etiam occiso rustico?   25

GESIPPUS.
Nescio.

MARTIUS.   Non, sed caeso grauiter.

TITUS.   Quid agimus,
Fului? Vides confitentem reum.

FULVIUS.   Nempe arbitror.

TITUS.
Ecquos habes autem asseclas sceleris? Quid ais?
Mihi non respondet, tu roga.

FULVIUS.   Socii numqui sunt praeterea?

GESIPPUS.
Solus omnium ego facile miserimus.

---

30. *miserimus*] = *miserrimus*.

him. Because he couldn't explain these things, we brought him to you even as he confessed.

TITUS. Come, let the defendant speak now. [*Gesippus remains silent.*] Nothing?

MARTIUS. He stands mute. He admits it.

TITUS. Are you guilty of this robbery or not?—— [*To Fulvius.*] He doesn't answer.[1]

FULVIUS. Young man, you must either deny this robbery or confess your guilt.

GESIPPUS. Consul, I neither deny the crime nor shrink from death.

TITUS. Tell us how much money you took.   [*Gesippus remains silent.*]

FULVIUS. How much money did you steal? Tell us.

GESIPPUS. I don't know.

MARTIUS. Twenty minas.

FULVIUS. After murdering the farmer?

GESIPPUS. I don't know.

MARTIUS. No, but after gravely injuring him.[2]

TITUS. Fulvius, what do we do? You see the defendant confessing.

FULVIUS. Indeed, I think so.

TITUS. Do you have any accomplices in this crime? What do you say?—— [*To Fulvius.*] He doesn't answer me. You ask him.[3]

FULVIUS. Are there any accomplices besides you?

GESIPPUS. I'm alone, easily the most wretched of all.

---

[1] Instead of this and the following two speeches, the draft version reads as follows:
TITUS. What would you answer to this? He's silent.
FULVIUS. Young man, if you have anything to absolve you, you may speak.
GESIPPUS. He who knows everything is my judge.
FULVIUS. I know, but this answers nothing to your adversaries. They charge that you are guilty of this robbery. What do you say to this?
GESIPPUS. Excellent consul, I neither deny the crime nor shrink from death.
MARTIUS. Look, then, he confesses.
TITUS. Then you say you are guilty of attacking the farmer?

[2] This development, unique to Foxe's play, contradicts Martius' understanding in III.11 and IV.1, but prepares for the comic resolution.

[3] Instead of this speech, an earlier version reads as follows:
TITUS. Can't you absolve yourself of this crime? What do you say? He doesn't answer me. You ask him.
FULVIUS. Tell me, do you admit this robbery or not?
GESIPPUS. I don't deny it.
FULVIUS. That's it.

TITUS.   Mihi cur non respondeat   30
  Miror.
FULVIUS.   Nostine?
TITUS.   Numquam, nisi non ignota haec
  Videtur facies. Cedo, iuuenis, vbi habes patriam?
  Tu roga.
FULVIUS.   Natus tu es in iisce regionibus?
GESIPPUS.   Non.
FULVIUS.   Vbi
  Igitur?
GESIPPUS.   Athenis.
TITUS.   Hem.
FULVIUS.   Quid est?
TITUS.   Parentes?
FULVIUS.
  Parentesne viuunt tui?
GESIPPUS.   Refert id mea nihil.   35
FULVIUS.
  Quid, non parentes?
GESIPPUS.   Parentes qui aspernantur filios
  Haud esse parentes iudico.
FULVIUS.   Sortitum ergo edidisse te
  Necessum est.
GESIPPUS.   Beneficus quia in hominem eram ingratum, scilicet.
FULVIUS.
  Amicum hic habes neminem?
GESIPPUS.   Putabam equidem.
TITUS.   Satis
  Quid in hac re queam suspicari nescio.
FULVIUS.   Satis est. Vides,   40
  Tite, manifesto teneri crimine, morteque dignum.   [*f. 144*]
  Legis consulto supremam nunc pronunciemus sonti sententiam.
TITUS.
  Multa ego hic, Fului, video, quamobrem in crastinum hoc
  Proferri iudicium velim, et consultius arbitror,
  Atque rogo te etiam plurimum.
FULVIUS.   Si aequum ita censeas.   45

Titus. I wonder why he won't answer me.

Fulvius. Do you know him?

Titus. No, though his face seems familiar.——[1] [*To Gesippus.*] Tell us, young man, where is your home?—— [*To Fulvius.*] You ask him.

Fulvius. Were you born in these parts?

Gesippus. No.

Fulvius. Where then?

Gesippus. Athens.

Titus. Hm!

Fulvius. What's the matter?

Titus. What about his parents?

Fulvius. Are your parents living?

Gesippus. That doesn't concern me.

Fulvius. What, no parents?

Gesippus. I think parents who spurn their children are no parents at all.

Fulvius. Then fate must have given birth to you.

Gesippus. Of course, because I was gracious to an ungrateful man.

Fulvius. You have no friend here?

Gesippus. I thought I did.

Titus. I don't quite know what to make of this.

Fulvius. It's clear enough. You see, Titus, that he's been caught red-handed in a crime and deserves to die. I suggest that we now pronounce the supreme penalty of the law on this criminal.

Titus. Fulvius, I see much reason here for wanting to delay judgment in this case until tomorrow. I feel quite strongly about it, and I ask it of you as earnestly as possible.

Fulvius. If you think that's best.

---

[1] At this point, even more than in III.8, where Titus had previously failed to recognize Gesippus, Foxe's earlier emphasis on the identical appearance of Titus and Gesippus becomes a problem of dramatic credibility. The failure to recognize him must be explained by the drastic alteration in Gesippus' looks because of his hardships; if the play was actually staged at Magdalen, it may have involved some rather sophisticated makeup. An added factor, however, is that Titus believes the defendant guilty and does not believe Gesippus capable of committing such a crime; see IV.5.17-18.

TITUS.

Censeo. Vos interim vinctum hunc accurare in crastinum
Atque huc reductum praecipimus, ciues.

POPULUS ROMANUS.   Fiat.

[ACTUS QUARTUS. SCENA QUARTA.]
Pamphila. Phormio.

[PAMPHILA.]

Etsi hercle aegre hoc iter mihi nimisque animo aduersum siet,
Adire attamen decretum est.

PHORMIO.   Suauiter

Facis, nec dubium est quin si ires, Pamphila,
Scias vredines, acceptum id iri tibi
Quod fecit.

PAMPHILA.   Quid ni accipiam, Phormio?   5
Ducere per me liberum est quam libeat coniugem.
Amare, habere illum quid ego ut prohibeam?
Verum illud est ecastor, diis superis
Meam stabiliam fidem, viri adeo illius
Caussa, viro propterea amatori numquam vt   10
Fidam postea. Uel illum quam adamantinum
Iurarem semper mihi amatorem fore.
Mortali iuueni cuiquam quisquam vt possit
Credere?

PHORMIO.   Ah nescis quibus Athenis ille
Torrebat ignibus ad necem pene,   15
Pamphila, ut ni exprompta Gesippi sui
Adcurrisset pietas—

PAMPHILA.   Audiui, at interim
Caelebs factus ille sua pietate.

PHORMIO.   Tuque
Eadem hac pietate pariter caelebs, Pamphila.

PAMPHILA.

Scio.

PHORMIO.   Nunc quid si deus hoc quispiam voluit   20
Matrimonium vos vt caelibes iungeremini?   [*f. 144v*]

3. *ires*] MST appears to read *eris*.
15. *Torrebat*] the verb is normally transitive.

TITUS. I do.—— Meanwhile, citizens, we bid you to keep him bound until tomorrow and bring him before us then.

CITIZENS. Very well. [*Exeunt.*

[IV.4] *Enter Pamphila and Phormio.*

PAMPHILA. By Hercules, this trip is inconvenient for me and much against my will. But I've decided to go anyway.

PHORMIO. You're doing the right thing, Pamphila, and there's no doubt that, if you go, you'll understand his itches and come to accept what he did to you.

PAMPHILA. Why shouldn't I accept it, Phormio? As far as I'm concerned, he can marry anyone he pleases. How should I keep him from loving and having anything? But by heaven this I can say: because of that man and what he did, I pledge my faith to the gods on high that I shall never hereafter put my trust in another man as my lover. I would have taken an oath that he would always be as constant a lover to me as it is possible to be. How could anyone trust in any mortal youth?

PHORMIO. Ah, you don't know the fires with which he burned at Athens, almost to the death, Pamphila, so that if the ready loyalty of his friend Gesippus had not come to his aid——

PAMPHILA. I heard about it. But meanwhile that friend is made a bachelor for his loyalty.

PHORMIO. And because of that same loyalty you're likewise a bachelor, Pamphila.

PAMPHILA. I know.

PHORMIO. Now what if some god wished you two bachelors to be joined in marriage?

PAMPHILA.

  Ac quid si deus numquam te in consilia
  Admisit, Phormio?

PHORMIO.   At potest confore.

PAMPHILA.

  Non omnia euenire quae possunt, accidunt.

PHORMIO.

  Principio, quid si tua totus forma ferueat   25
  Non minus ac suae tuus quem dixi Semproniae?

PAMPHILA.

  Quid tum?

PHORMIO.   Atque hercle ita res habe.

PAMPHILA.

  Audio.

PHORMIO.   Deinde iuuenem nosti ipsum quam ingenuum,
  Doctum, spectabilem, flore ac specie
  Vndique pellicibilem, dignum qui detur satrapae.   30

PAMPHILA.

  Intelligo.

PHORMIO. Indole ac aetate florida,
  Denique prognatum bonis in vrbe bona
  Patris optimi, porro haeredem vnicum ad
  Fortunas insuper amplissimas.

PAMPHILA.   Docte quidem.

PHORMIO.

  Postremo etiam Tito tuomet (si id te mouet)   35
  Quam simillimum: perinde ac si illius esses ita
  Nihil inter'st.

PAMPHILA.   Scitus pòl fabulator.

PHORMIO.

  Age, dic igitur libera nunc fide, Pamphila,
  Si marito esses initianda, vtrum eum virum
  Malles tibi cui te maxime cordi esse sentias?   40

PAMPHILA.

  Maxime.

22. *Ac*] ?read *At*.
27. *habe*] MST may read *habet*.

PAMPHILA. And what if a god never let you in on his plans, Phormio?

PHORMIO. But it could happen.

PAMPHILA. Not everything which can happen does happen.

PHORMIO. In the first place, what if he were utterly afire because of your beauty, as much as your man was, of whom I told you, for his Sempronia?

PAMPHILA. What then?

PHORMIO. And by Hercules, take that for a fact.

PAMPHILA. I'm listening.

PHORMIO. Then again, you know how noble that young man is, how learned, how admirable, how altogether appealing for his manly vigor and appearance. He's worthy of being given to a satrap.

PAMPHILA. I know.

PHORMIO. An excellent character, the flower of youth, born to wealth in a good city and of a fine father, the only heir to an especially ample fortune.

PAMPHILA. You're very well rehearsed.

PHORMIO. Finally, he's almost identical to your friend Titus (if that moves you), so little different that it's as if you were Titus'.

PAMPHILA. Notorious liar.

PHORMIO. Come then, Pamphila, tell me now of your own free will, if you were going to be married to a husband, would you prefer to have a man to whom you felt you were most appealing?

PAMPHILA. Very much.

PHORMIO.　Recte putas, quandoquidem amor
　Vicissim amorem docet, etiam in mutis belluis.
　Iam cum te Gesippus tam efflictim deperit,
　Quo potis pacto illum tibi pensi habebis mutuo!
PAMPHILA.
　Perge comminisci.
PHORMIO.　　　　　At si dignum haud arbitrere,　　　　45
　Tamen misereat amantis, Pamphila.
PAMPHILA.　　　　　　　　Imo
　Dignum multo digniore me illum duxerim,
　Verum illud numquam crediderim, vxorem sibi
　Si vnquam induceret ducere, suam vt traduceret
　Alteri, ille vt fecit. In summa, haec vtcumque sunt,　*[f. 145]* 50
　Si sit mei adeo ut inquis expetens,
　Ipsus huc venire potest: haud te oratore est opus,
　Phormio.
PHORMIO.　Rectissime. Tum quid si hic breui
　Adesse videas?
PAMPHILA.　　Cum illo haud tecum ineam.
　Tum rationem hanc dein nosti mei haudquaquam　　55
　Iuris esse me. Parentes sunt, quorum id transigi
　Consiliis necesse est.
PHORMIO.　　　Verum ut tuum
　Non desit suffragium tamen. Exit herus.
　Mane.

[ACTUS QUARTUS. SCENA QUINTA.]
Sempronia. Titus. Phormio. Pamphila.

[SEMPRONIA.]
　Nimis incredibile est, mi vir. Non potest
　Fieri.
TITUS.　Aut ego egregie sum falsus hercle animi.
PHORMIO.
　Hera, en adductam ut iusti tibi.
SEMPRONIA.　　　　　　　　Hem, Pamphila,
　Factum ecastor comiter, suauem habeo gratiam.

41-42. *amor . . . amorem*] *Amor . . . Amorem* in MST.

PHORMIO. Good thinking, for love teaches love in return, even among dumb beasts. Since Gesippus already is desperately in love with you, how easily you will come to hold him in the like esteem.

PAMPHILA. Keep on with your pipe dreams.

PHORMIO. But if you should think him not at all worthy of you, Pamphila, yet have pity on the lover.

PAMPHILA. On the contrary, I would have thought him worthy of someone much worthier than I. But I would never have believed that, having once brought himself to take a wife, he would transfer her to someone else as he did. However that may be, to put an end to this, if he is so desirous of me as you say, he can come here himself; he doesn't need you as his spokesman, Phormio.

PHORMIO. You're absolutely right. Then what if you saw him come here shortly?

PAMPHILA. Then I would take it up with him, not with you. Besides, as you know, I am by no means my own master. My parents are in charge, and it must be done according to their plans.

PHORMIO. But so long as your own approval weren't lacking——. But wait; my master is coming out.

[IV.5]   *Enter Sempronia and Titus.*

SEMPRONIA. It's too much to believe, my lord. It can't be.

TITUS. Or else, by Hercules, I'm terribly mistaken.

PHORMIO. Mistress, look, I've brought her to you as you ordered.

SEMPRONIA. Well, Pamphila! My, this is very kind of you. I'm very

Concede iam nunc quaeso intro. Induc in   5
Aedes, Phormio. Mox ipsa adero.
PHORMIO.   Sequere sis.
PAMPHILA.
    Sequor.
SEMPRONIA.   Quamquam aedepol nescio quid ilico
    Mens iam mihi ominari coepit cum dudum hic
    Aspexeram. Sed qui scis eum esse, obsecro?
TITUS.
    Principio habitus statura conuenit.   10
    Tum ex Athenis est, nec parentes nominat,
    Hinc eiectus recens ob nescio quod facinus.
    Denique agnoscens mei, neque cum rogo
    Respondet verbum. Nec caussae quid siet,
    Qui sit, aut vnde sit satis suspicari scio,   15
    Nisi hoc scio: Gesippus vbi vbi meus est   [*f. 145v*]
    Numquam in se tantam admitteret audaciam,
    Nec cogitaret scio.
PAMPHILA.
    Quidnam fecit?
TITUS.   Quod homo improbissimus
    Vim in ciuitate hac fecit inciuiliter   20
    Liberto huic cuidam, cui cum pecunia
    Ipsam etiam irruens vitam emunxit pene miser.
SEMPRONIA.
    Hei nequitiam!
TITUS.   Vnde ingens coniectura fit
    Quisquis sit haud illum esse, et tamen quia
    Haud certum erat, iuditio subtraxi vt scirem   25
    Compertius, nuncque nec dici potest, Sempronia,
    Quantis in angustiis sum dum rem cognovero.
SEMPRONIA.
    Quid fiet igitur?
TITUS.   Quid censes nisi
    Vt Phormionem quam mox emittamus huc

---

22. *emunxit miser*] ?read *ferro emunxit;* see Textual Notes.

grateful to you. Please step inside now.—— Phormio, take her into the house.—— I'll be right with you.

PHORMIO [*to Pamphila*]. Please come with me.

PAMPHILA. I'm coming.   [*Exeunt Pamphila and Phormio.*

SEMPRONIA. Heavens, I don't know why, but my mind began to have forebodings just now, the minute I saw her here. But how on earth do you know it's he?

TITUS. In the first place, he has the same bearing and the same build. Again, he's from Athens; he won't identify his parents, and he's recently been cast out for some mischief or other. Finally, he knows me and won't answer a word when I ask him questions. I don't know what reason there might be, nor who he is, nor where he came from. But I do know this: my friend Gesippus, wherever he is, would never stoop to such shamelessness; he wouldn't think of it, I know.

PAMPHILA. What did he do?

TITUS. That wicked man has, like a barbarian, done violence in this city to one of our freedmen. The villain set upon him and almost robbed him of his very life along with his money.

SEMPRONIA. Oh villainy!

TITUS. That's why I have a strong suspicion that, whoever he is, he certainly isn't Gesippus. And yet, because I wasn't absolutely sure, I withheld sentence from him so I might know better. Now I can't even express how great are my torments, Sempronia, until I know the truth.

SEMPRONIA. What's to be done then?

TITUS. What do you think? Unless we send Phormio right away

Qui renunciet signaque expediat   30
Quam certissime ut rem esse norit omnia?
SEMPRONIA.
Nempe ita facto opus, et mature facias.
TITUS.
Heus, euocate huc Phormionem. Ecquis audiat?
PHORMIO.
Quis hic Phormionem? Here, tua vox erat?
TITUS.
Nescis tu quae gesta hic sunt forte, Phormio?   35
PHORMIO.
Num quidnam rei?
TITUS.   Gesippum potin' si vides
Meum noscere?
PHORMIO.   Vel ex unguibus,
Here, at vbi isnam est?
TITUS.   Nisi meae multum errant coniecturae,
Vinctus, cras legibus stringendus laqueo.
PHORMIO.
Tace, per immortalem deum! Ne dixeris,   40
Here, quod non potest fieri.
TITUS.   Quapropter id
Nunc est quod curriculo te transcurrere ad eum volo
Qui sit vt scias, nomen, parentes, fugam,
Ac signa diligenter renuncies singula.
Tenes quid volo?   [*f. 146*]
PHORMIO.   Singula.
TITUS.   Abi igitur faeliciter.   45
Quam totus nunc inter spem et metum animi
Perplexus pendeo quidnam ille rediens
De hac re reportet famulus. Nec scio
Vnde fit, semper in laeuam partem magis
Mens praesagit omnia. Sed quis exterus   50
Aduorsa huc platea graditur?

30. *renunciet . . . expediat*] ?read *rem renunciet* or *expediat omnia* (cancelling *omnia*
in l. 31). The line as it stands is metrically defective. *Rem*, a late addition, appears
to have been cancelled. The placement of *omnia*, very awkward in l. 31, is unclear;
syntactically it would be preferable as the last word in l. 30. See Textual Notes.
   42.] see Textual Notes.

to sort out all the evidence as clearly as possible and report back to us what he has learned about the situation?

SEMPRONIA. Yes indeed, you must do that, and quickly.

TITUS [*shouts*]. Hey, call Phormio here. Would someone listen?

Enter Phormio.

PHORMIO. Who's calling Phormio? Master, was that your voice?

TITUS. Do you by any chance know what's happened here, Phormio?

PHORMIO. There's nothing wrong, is there?

TITUS. Can you recognize my friend Gesippus if you see him?

PHORMIO. Even from his fingernails, master, but where is he?

TITUS. Unless I badly miss my guess, he's in jail and is going to be hanged tomorrow according to our laws.

PHORMIO. No! God almighty! Don't say that, master! It can't happen.

TITUS. Therefore I want you to run to him immediately. Find out who the man is—his name, his parents, the reason he ran away, and so on. Then report everything to me very carefully. Do you understand what I want?

PHORMIO. Everything.

TITUS. Then go with good luck.———   [*Exit Phormio.*
How completely perplexed I am, suspended between hope and fear of what that slave will report about this when he returns. I don't know why, but my mind keeps foreboding everything for the worse. But who's this foreigner coming along the street toward us?

[Actus Quartus. Scena Sexta.]
Crito. Sempronia. Titus.

[Crito.]
  Poli pelagique patri potentissimo
  Perpetuas ut par est primum pendo gratias
  Nostris qui tam propitium strauit mare
  Mercimoniis mihi, ut numquam quod scio
  Secundiore simul flatu et flumine   5
  Euenit nauigatio.
Sempronia.   Est ne hic Crito
  Quem video Atheniensis?
Crito.   Deinde tum
  Perlitatis rite gratiis, quod proximum
  Nunc est me paro ad negotia, ac primo ut Titum
  Conueniam de Chremetis literis.

Sempronia.   Te nominat.   10
Crito.
  Eo.
Sempronia.   Compelle prius.
Titus.   Optime vir Crito, salueas.
Crito.
  Salue, domine. Hem, Sempronia. Numnam vir hic
  Titus tuus, quaeso?
Sempronia.   Est.
Crito.   Atque ita arbitror.
Titus.
  Quiduis, Crito? Quid agitur? Gesippus ut agit?
Crito.
  Istuc huc veni ego ex te percontarier.   15
Titus.
  Vndenam?
Crito.   Quia nos reliquit multo prius,
  At huc ut aiebat se velle ad vos concesserat.
  Eho, non venit, obsecro?
Titus.   Perii.
Crito.   Quippe illum ilico
  Ex profectu tuo saeuus abegit pater.

[IV.6]   *Enter Crito.*

CRITO [*kneeling in prayer*]. First, as is proper, I pay perpetual paeans of gratitude to the all-powerful father of heavens and ocean for stretching out a sea so propitious for my business that, so far as I know, a voyage was never made under more favorable winds and waves together.

SEMPRONIA [*to Titus*]. Isn't that Crito the Athenian?

CRITO [*rising*]. Now that I've duly offered thanks, I must get down to business, and first I must find Titus about Chremes' letter.

SEMPRONIA [*to Titus*]. He said your name.

CRITO. I'll go now.

SEMPRONIA [*to Titus*]. Stop him before he leaves.

TITUS. My good man Crito, greetings.

CRITO. Greetings, my lord.—— Well, Sempronia! Is this your husband Titus?

SEMPRONIA. Yes.

CRITO. I thought so.

TITUS. What do you want, Crito? What's new? How is Gesippus?

CRITO. I came here to ask you that.

TITUS. Why me?

CRITO. Because he left us long ago, but according to what he said he would do, he came here to you. Alas, didn't he come, pray?

TITUS [*aside*]. I'm lost.

CRITO. You see, immediately after you left, his father harshly drove

Interea nemo nostrum vir quisquam virum　　　　　20
　Vidit.
Titus.　Ipsus est.
Crito.　　　　　　Atqui huc lembum quidem
　Coepisse, id certum scimus. Propterea id mihi　　　[*f. 112*]
　Huc nunc dedere aduenienti prouinciam,
　Te vt adirem literis cum his epistolaribus
　Suum sibi apud te si est ut remittas filium.　　　　25
Titus.
　Boni nos seruent superi.
Sempronia.　　　　　Hei me miseram.
Crito.　　　　　　　　　　　Quid est?
Titus.
　Et illum et nos omnes pessumdatos.
Crito.　　　　　　　　　　Quid ita?
Titus.
　Adueniens nescio quid designauit miser,
　Verum enim, Crito, in carcerem coniectus est
　Vixque heri iuditio a me ereptus in diem　　　　30
　Alt'rum. Cras denique cavssae nihil video
　Capitis quin irrefutabilem luet
　Sententiam.
Crito.　　　Sententiam! Quid ais, Tite?
Titus.
　Iamque ipsum esse illum haud ambiguum est.
　Proh caelites vestra potentia, quid huic　　　　35
　Iam exitio dari remedii poterit?
　Aut quid venire in mentem potest mihi
　Quod agam?
Crito.　　　Eho quodnam hoc nouum repentinum malum,
　Obsecro? Itane in carcerem illum, ain' tu? Quid ita?
　Quid gessit? Quid scis? Aut nescis forsitan?　　　40
Titus.
　Seruum modo amandaui Phormionem meum
　Ad eum vt iret certum qui mihi de hac re respondeat.
　Atque equidem abesse tam diu miror. Hunc quoad
　Veniat domi interim Crito expectabimus.

　36. *dari*] MST appears to read *dare*.

him out. Since then, not one of our people has seen the man.

TITUS [*aside*]. It is Gesippus.

CRITO. But he took a boat for here, we know that for sure. So, since I was just on my way here, they asked me to come to you with this letter so that, if he's with you, you'd send their son back.

TITUS. May the gods above preserve us!

SEMPRONIA. Oh woe is me!

CRITO. What is it?

TITUS. We're sunk, he and all of us.

CRITO. Why so?

TITUS. The poor devil came here planning I know not what, but now he's locked in jail, Crito. A little while ago I barely snatched him from judgment for another day, but tomorrow I see no way to keep him from paying the irrefutable sentence of death.

CRITO. Sentence! What are you saying, Titus?

TITUS. There's absolutely no doubt now that it's Gesippus. Oh, ye gods, what remedy for this disaster could be given by your power? Or what can I think of to do?

CRITO. Alas, what on earth is this new and unlooked-for trouble? You say Gesippus is in jail? Why? What did he do? How do you know? Or maybe you don't know?

TITUS. I've just sent my slave Phormio to go to him and bring me a sure answer about that. I'm surprised he's gone so long. Meanwhile, Crito, until he comes we'll wait for him at home.

CRITO.
Venio.   45

[ACTUS QUARTUS. SCENA SEPTIMA.]
Phormio.

[PHORMIO.]
 Nunc ego hac in re mirerne an maeream magis
 An doleam, aut quid dicam primum aut cogitem
 Satis nequeo dicere. Ita tot deimprouiso simul
 Hic concurrunt mala quae sensus meos
 Omnes obstupefaciunt. Proh sacra numina,   5
 Itan' Gesippum in tantum venire dedecus!
 Quod ita me deus amet bene, non tam graue [*f. 112v*]
 Quam etiam praeter omnem spem mihi ac credibile
 Accidit. Atque hunc facile, ego ut aspexeram,
 Praesensi esse, priusquam nomen mihi suum 10
 Ac signa panderet caetera. Sed quo herus abiit
 Cui hoc portem malum? Nescio nisi domum
 Se recepit forsitan.

ACTUS QUINTUS. SCENA PRIMA.
Martius.

[MARTIUS.]
 Dei iustissimi iustissimo esse iudicis
 Iuditio hoc mihi comparatum iudico.
 Nusquam cedo neque requiesco quin meum
 Velut vmbra comitetur me supplicium. Uel hac
 Nocte quam nil prorsus somni coepi genis, 5
 Horologium vsque numerans dum singulis
 Momentis occursat scelus, animum proh dolor
 Quam misere uerberans, ut mille satius
 Fuisset ceruices prebere crucibus.
 Vsque adeo intolerabile ac miserum tormentum 10
 Est conscientiae mortalibus. Cui nisi
 Homo essem hominum feriatus pessime,

 IV.7.2. *An doleam*] perhaps intended for deletion, since the phrase is awkward
and redundant; see Textual Notes.
 V.1.5. *nil*] ?read *nihil*.

CRITO. I'm coming. [*Exeunt.*

[IV.7] *Enter Phormio.*

PHORMIO. I can't say whether I should be more surprised or more sorry and doleful about this, or what to say first or even what to think. So many misfortunes crowd unexpectedly together here that they stupefy all my senses. Oh sacred gods, that Gesippus should come to such dishonor! God love me well, what has happened is as much beyond my expectation and belief as it is serious. As soon as I saw him, I readily guessed that it was he, before he revealed his name and other signs to me. But where has my master gone, to whom I must carry this bad news? I don't know, unless maybe he's gone home. [*Exit.*

[V.1] *Enter Martius.*

MARTIUS. I judge that this has been ordained for me by the most just judgment of god, a most just judge.[1] Go or stay, nowhere can I prevent my torment from following me like a shadow. How I spent this night, on my knees, not once closing my eyes in sleep, counting the hours all night long while my crime rushed into my thoughts every minute. Oh, how wretchedly did sorrow hammer at my heart, that it would have been a thousand times better to offer my neck to the gallows. So unbearably miserable is the torture of conscience in mortals. If I weren't the most worthlessly idle of men, it would never have occurred to me to

---

[1] The sources make no preparation for the villain's conversion, but Foxe was apparently aware of the dramatic problem of sudden attacks of conscience.

Numquam subiisset vni iniecisse rustico.
At nunc quam grauiter facti et piget et paenitet.
Quod si de integro incipiendi potestas foret   15
Aut laeta nunc aliquis occurrat venia,
Boni superi, quanta colerem innocentia!
At hoc iuvat interim animum: illum quod viuere
Aiunt, spemque nobis pollicentur bonam
Revalescentiae. Sed processit iam dies.   20
Miror tam abesse diu consules.

[ACTUS QUINTUS. SCENA SECUNDA.]
Pamphila. Sempronia. Fuluius. Titus.   [*f. 113*]
Gesippus. Populus Romanus.

[PAMPHILA.]
Quin has siste lachrimas, mulier, atque quod prosit potius
Modo exequamur aliquid.
SEMPRONIA.   Cupio, atque scio promeritum
Esse cui benefaxis.
PAMPHILA.   Egone? Ita deus me amet,
Iam quiduis depacisci possim, modo possem, vt illi commodem.
SEMPRONIA.
Ac si scias quam erga te semper habitum, atque ita perire nunc   5
Eum tun' pati poteris?
PAMPHILA.   Imo nemini acerbius quam mihi
Accidere hoc testor deum, aut quemquam esse qui saluum magis
Expetat.
SEMPRONIA.   Ergo, Pamphila, quid si iudicibus supplicabimus
Simul, quandoquidem solum hoc restat adminiculum vltimum
Siqua forte hoc potest impetrarier?
PAMPHILA.   Siquidem hic vsus   10
Officii sit, nunquam illi in re ulla deero.
SEMPRONIA.   Dignum te atque ei
Feceris. Atque ecce sunt praesto consules. Vtamur tempore.
FULVIUS.
Ita vt dies atque hora monet, iam nunc ad pronunciandam reo
Huic adsumus sententiam. Adeste. Meminisse vos

17. *Boni ... quanta*] ?read *Boni superi/Vitam dehinc quanta;* see Textual Notes.
18. *At*] ?read *Ac* or *Atque.*

attack any farmer, but now how terribly sorry and ashamed I
am of that deed. If I had the power to begin afresh, if some happy
chance should come to me now to start anew, ye gods on high,
how innocently I would live! But meanwhile it relieves my mind
that they say he's alive, and they hold out high hope of his
recovery. But now the day has come. I'm surprised the consuls
are absent so long.

[V.2]   *Enter Sempronia, weeping, and Pamphila.*

PAMPHILA. Well, stop crying, woman, and let's do something more
profitable.

SEMPRONIA. I want to, and I know he deserves your help.

PAMPHILA. Mine? God love me, if only I could, I'd make any deal
now to help him.

SEMPRONIA. If you know how taken he always was with you, could
you bear now to let him die this way?

PAMPHILA. No, I swear to god, that would strike no one a harder
blow than me, and there's no one more eager for his safety.

SEMPRONIA. Then what if we appeal to the judges together,
Pamphila, since that's the last and only remaining help—if by
some chance it can be done at all.

PAMPHILA. If that will do any good, I'll not fail him in any way.

SEMPRONIA. You'll have done him a service worthy of you. And
look, here are the consuls. Let's use this opportunity.

Enter Fulvius and Titus; the citizens lead in Gesippus.

FULVIUS. As the day and the hour remind us, we come together now
to pronounce sentence on this defendant. Draw near. Citizens,

Creduo, ciues, in hesterno hoc tribunali actum quid siet   15
In excutiendo crimine?

POPULUS ROMANUS.   Omnia.

FULVIUS.   Vestrum nec vllus est
Qui refellit aliquid? Quid ais tu?

GESIPPUS.   Me miserum.

FULVIUS.   Hem, quid hic,
Mulieres?

SEMPRONIA.   Suspiciendi consules ac tremendi iudices,
Mulierum siquid supplices apud uos manus valeant, per fidem
Atque clementiam obsecramus vestram supplici huic   20
Vt parcatis adolescentulo, quodque legibus modo
Districtum est id vestra resoluat modo ignoscentia.

PAMPHILA.
Vel precibus id nostris vel pietati vestrae
Vel indoli ipsius generique optimo tribuite, ut optimi
Misereat adolescentuli, patres quaeso optimi.   25

FULVIUS.
Hem, quid istuc, Tite?

TITUS.   Ego nescio.

FULVIUS.   Etiam tibi quid hic
Miror, Pamphila.

SEMPRONIA.   Patriae parentibusque Athenis summis
Summum beneficium perficite hoc, summi proceres.

FULVIUS.
Pietatem in hunc tuam et video et probo, Sempronia, neque
Equidem tam inflexilis Rhadamanthus sum siquidem res haec   30
Priua foret. Nunc cum publica est, priuato hinc affectu   [*f. 113v*]
A publico recto abduci me neque velim nec aequum censeo,
Neque Romana id seueritas si uelim patitur, nec id unquam me
    fiet
Consule. Dixi, atque ita futurum est. Quiescas, Sempronia,
Atque abi domum.

SEMPRONIA.   Hei miserae mihi.

28. *summi*] MST reads *sumi.*

I assume you remember what happened in this court yesterday during our investigation of this crime.

CITIZENS. Everything.

FULVIUS. Among you is there none to rebut anything? What say you?

GESIPPUS [*aside*]. Woe is me!

FULVIUS [*as Sempronia and Pamphila kneel before him*]. Well, ladies, what are you doing here?

SEMPRONIA. Esteemed consuls and formidable judges, if the suppliant hands of women have any influence on you, we beg you by your faith and your clemency to spare this suppliant youth. What is severe under mere laws let your mere pardon relax.

PAMPHILA. Attribute it to our entreaties or to your kindness or to the disposition and fine character of the young man himself that you have pity on this excellent youth. I beg you, worthy fathers.

FULVIUS. Well, what about this, Titus?

TITUS. I don't know.

FULVIUS. Pamphila, I wonder especially what concern this is of yours.

SEMPRONIA. Exalted leaders, do this great kindness for his country and his noble parents at Athens.

FULVIUS. Sempronia, I understand and applaud your tenderness for this man, and if indeed this were a private matter, I am not such a rigid Rhadamanthus.[1] But now, since it's public, I would not be diverted from public rectitude by private desire, nor do I think it would be fair. Even if I wanted to, Roman strictness does not permit it, and it will never happen so long as I am consul. I have spoken, and so it will be. Be quiet, Sempronia, and go home.

SEMPRONIA. Oh woe, wretched me!

---

[1] The son of Jupiter and Europa; after death he was made a judge in hell.

PAMPHILA.   Quam miseret, Gesippe, tui!   35
TITUS.

Si ita stat, Fului, tibi, vt a Romana seueritate te
Nihil abstrahat, haud tamen haec te imperat seueritas
Hominem immerito supplicio quemquam trahere. Cum is
    non commeruit,
Insontem assero: meum hoc furtum fuit, illum percussi ego
Diuitem.

FULVIUS.   Tite! Per deum immortalem, quid incoeptas monstri?   40
TITUS.

Quod verum iustumque est: meum hoc peccatum, meum
Sit supplicium. Hunc te indemnem rectum est absoluere.

MARTIUS.

Hem, quid ego audio?

FULVIUS.   Proh Capitolinum Iouem! Tuum
Hoc peccatum!

TITUS.   Nisi esset, mihi id numquam scias suerem.
FULVIUS.

Obsecro tandem, Romulidae, furtum hoc quem vos dedisse
    dicitis?   45

POPULUS ROMANUS.

Nescimus. Hunc ita cum sica hac dormientem offendimus.

FULVIUS.

Quid tu?

MARTIUS.   Itidem quod illi, consul.

TITUS.   Vel hinc scire est
Haud usquam, Fului, clarius haud istunc esse, quod in
Sopore oppresserint. Quippe in scelere qui sunt, haud facile
Somnum inire vigil sinet conscientia, tum in via sane   50
Multo minus publica. Denique ferrum suum hoc si erat,
Vagina vbinam? Cur sicam non abiecit? non abstersit simul?
Postremo si reum ipsius arguit confessio, me nihil minus vides
Confitentem: huius ego me rei reum fateor et conscium.

FULVIUS.

Dii vostram fidem, tam inauditum hoc unde accidit? Satis   55
Mirari nequeo.

GESIPPUS.   Imo ego, consul, haud ille conscius.

PAMPHILA. How I pity you, Gesippus!

[*Exeunt Sempronia and Pamphila.*

TITUS. Fulvius, if you insist that nothing will deter you from your Roman strictness, still this strictness does not demand that you drag any man off to an undeserved punishment. Since this man does not deserve it, I declare him to be innocent. I committed the robbery. I struck down that rich man.

FULVIUS. Titus! By the immortal god, what monstrousness are you attempting?

TITUS. What is true and just. The guilt was mine, mine be the punishment. It is right that you release him unharmed.

MARTIUS [*aside*]. What on earth am I hearing?

FULVIUS. Oh Capitoline Jove! The guilt is yours?

TITUS. If it weren't, you know I would never make this up.

FULVIUS. People of Rome, I beg you, who do you say committed this robbery?

A CITIZEN. We don't know, except that we found this man sleeping with this dagger.

FULVIUS [*to Martius*]. What about you?

MARTIUS. The same as they, consul.

TITUS. Well, Fulvius, from the fact that they surprised him in his sleep, nothing is more certain than that he is not guilty. A wakeful conscience will not readily let those who are guilty of crime fall asleep, certainly not in a road, much less a public way.[1] Then again, if this was his weapon, where is its sheath? Why didn't he throw the dagger away? And why didn't he clean it? Finally, if his confession proves that he is the culprit, it's no less true that I am confessing: I declare that I committed this crime; I am guilty.

FULVIUS. Ye gods, by your faith! Why has this unheard-of thing happened? I'm confounded.

GESIPPUS. But I'm guilty, consul, not he.

---

[1] See Introduction, pp. 17-18.

FULVIUS.

In ambiguo haeret mihi animus, nec quid agam scio.

TITUS.   Quid agas

Nisi hunc uti iuditio insontem expedias atque in me illud-hoc

Deriues supplicium.

GESIPPUS.   Iniquum est, consul, fieri quod commeritus is

Non sit id cuiquam supplicio vertier. Noxa est mea   [*f. 114*]

scilicet.   60

FULVIUS.

Quid tu ais, consul?

TITUS.   Enimvero mea est, est vero inquam mea,

Fului.

FULVIUS.   Idemque tu confitere, iuuenis?

GESIPPUS.   Confiteor.

FULVIUS.   Tacete. Vbi

Principio illum tum conscidisti, responde?

TITUS.   Nescio.

FULVIUS.   Vbi tu?

GESIPPUS.

In porticu angiporti cuiusdam.

POPULUS ROMANUS.   Verum est.

FULVIUS.

Senex erat an iuuenis?

GESIPPUS.   Nescio.

TITUS.   Sexagenarius.

POPULUS ROMANUS.   Scilicet.   65

FULVIUS.

Incertum haec res prorsus me consilii facit. Quin ad Senatum

rem

Recta referam, eius facturus de consilio in hac re quod dederit.

Vos vinctos retinete hos ad forum, hinc dum redeam ilico.

58. *illud-hoc*] the MST reading. I find no precedent for the compound and
am not certain what it means. ?Read *hoc.*
64. S.P. *Gesippus*] emended from *T*[*itus*].

FULVIUS. My mind is caught in uncertainty, and I don't know what to do.

TITUS. What would you do, except free this innocent man from your jurisdiction and transfer his punishment to me?

GESIPPUS. Consul, it's not fair that what someone has not deserved should be turned against him for punishment. The fault is truly mine.

FULVIUS. What do you say, consul?

TITUS. No, it's mine, I tell you. It's truly mine, Fulvius.

FULVIUS. And you confess too, young man?

GESIPPUS. I confess.

FULVIUS. Be still, both of you.—— [*To Titus.*] First, where did you attack your victim? Answer.

TITUS. I don't know.

FULVIUS [*to Gesippus*]. Where did you?

GESIPPUS. In the entrance of a certain alley.[1]

A CITIZEN. That's true.

FULVIUS. Was he old or young?

GESIPPUS. I don't know.

TITUS. Sixty years old.

A CITIZEN. That's right.

FULVIUS. This makes me utterly unsure how to decide. Well, I'll refer the matter right to the Senate and abide by their decision in this matter. Hold these men bound at the forum until I return here very shortly.   [*Exeunt all but Martius.*

[1] The draft version added, "under a fig-tree."

[Actus Quintus. Scena Tertia.]
Martius.

[Martius.]

Mirando atque stupendo meipsum pene haud penes
Sum, ita nouo ac insueto hoc attonitus miraculo
Quod mihi praeter spem ac rationem omnem obuenit.
Neque enim quid sit satis commentari queo
Nisi ex amore factum sit iuuenes quia   5
Conflagrant mutuo. Vterque altrinsecus
Se mancipat culpae vnde vterque est tamen
Alienissimus. Dii vostram fidem,
Quod hoc glutinum est, suo vt quisquam animo quam suam
Alterius habeat salutem antepositam?   10
Quid? Atque ille ego maleficae patrator rei,
Meo pro scelere horum tam immerito distrahi
Amicitiam vt sinam et tantam fidem? Mori
Tam cupidi quin sunt cum vterque est exors criminis?
Queis a me subuenirier adeo potest commode.   15
Numquam faciam, furcae etiam quingentae si mihi
Opetendae forent, quin iuuabo iuuenes
Remque omnem pandam iudici. Quod hercule
Etsi caelare queam, tamen amantium profecto miseret.
Quicquid tandem fors feret, pol, quid aedepol   20
Quam hoc feram potius, vt horum fraudi siem   [f. 114v]
Amicitiae. Itaque huius quicquid rei prius
Praetenderam, id omne refingo denuo denique
Et vltro me dedam consuli. Atque hic expectabo dum
Redeat.   25

[Actus Quintus. Scena Quarta.]
Phormio.

[Phormio.]

O Iupiter, o ciues, o me miserum, quid hoc?
Apud forum adueniens modo quod vidi miser?
Herum cum Gesippo teneri consulem.
Haeccine ciues fieri? At vnde? aut quamobrem? Nimis
O me incogitantem, qui infaelix non adfuerim.   5
Atat nunc scio: mirum ni pro illo suo

[V.3]

MARTIUS. I'm almost beside myself with wonder and amazement, stunned by such a novel and unaccustomed miracle as what's happening before my eyes, beyond all expectation and reason. I can't conceive of what this means unless it's done out of love— unless these young men burn with mutual love. Each one takes the blame for a crime of which each is completely innocent. Ye gods, by your faith, what is this bond, that each one, in his heart of hearts, places his own safety below the other's? Why? And I, the perpetrator of that vicious act, how could I allow their friendship and great loyalty to be so undeservedly shattered on account of my crime? Why are they so eager to die when each is innocent of the crime? I can so easily relieve them. Even if I were to suffer on five hundred crosses, I have no choice but to help these youths and confess everything to the judge. I could conceal it, but, by Hercules, I feel very sorry for those dear friends. By heaven, whatever fate brings in the end, I would endure anything rather than harm their friendship. And so, no matter what story I told about this before, I'll rework it all now and turn myself in to the consul. I'll wait here till he comes back.

[V.4]   *Enter Phormio.*

PHORMIO. Oh Jupiter, oh citizens, oh wretched me, what's going on? Alas, what did I see as I was coming through the forum just now? My master, the consul, held along with Gesippus. Do such things happen, citizens? But why? What's the reason? Oh thoughtless me, that I wasn't there, unfortunately. Aha! Now I know: no doubt he's made himself liable for the crime in

Noxae se huic obnoxium dedit, innoxius
Tamen qui sit. Sed an hera haec asciscit mala
Annondum etiam? Quin cesso ad eam ingredi.

[ACTUS QUINTUS. SCENA QUINTA.]
Fulvius. Titus. Gesippus. Martius. Populus Romanus.

[FULVIUS.]
Senatus rerum quoniam aliarum satagit, arbitrariam
Mihi hic agendi consulendique concessit mea
Voluntate potestatem, itidem vt in aliis hodie rebus omnibus.
Accedite. Per ego salutem te rogo, consul, quam rem agas respice
Ac muta sententiam.

TITUS.   Quin tu hoc age, Fului.

FULVIUS.   Quid hoc?   5
Quandoquidem ita uis, ita me deus amet, miseret me tui,
Miseret vtriusque.

MARTIUS.   Pace primum tua, consul optime,
Sine apud te sit loquendi copia.

FULVIUS.   Loquere.

MARTIUS.   Principio istos ego
Vtrosque hoc absoluo crimine.

FULVIUS.   Hem?

MARTIUS.   Cognatus diues
Hic quem dixi, meus numquam fuit. Hunc ego forte obuiu' his   10
Spoliaui manibus. Porro hinc profugiens, istum obiter in via
Consopitum reperi, pariter hunc in pugno quoque pugiunculum.

FULVIUS.
Pugiunculum?

MARTIUS.   Quo sese erat, quantum equidem persensi, postea
Perempturus.   [*f. 115*]

GESIPPUS.   O Iuppiter.

FULVIUS.   Perge.

MARTIUS.   Verum certum
Nescio, verum hoc tum quia opportunum satis visum est,   15
Consilium coepi ilico illi sicam hanc

---

2. *concessit mea*] I follow the earlier MST reading because the revision, *decreuit imperium,* cannot be construed with what follows.

place of his friend, even though he's innocent. But does my mistress know this bad news yet or not? I must go to her.   [*Exit.*

[V.5]   *Enter Fulvius; citizens lead in Titus and Gesippus.*

FULVIUS. Since the Senate has its hands full with other business, it has given me arbitrary power to investigate and act according to my own will, in this as in all other matters today.—— [*To Titus and Gesippus.*] Come here.—— [*To Titus.*] By your life I ask you, consul, consider what you are doing and alter your judgment.

TITUS. Just go ahead with it, Fulvius.

FULVIUS. What is this? Since you wish it so, god love me, I feel sorry for you—I feel sorry for you both.

MARTIUS [*coming forward*]. Beg pardon, eminent consul, first let me speak to you.

FULVIUS. Speak.

MARTIUS. First, I absolve both these men of this crime.

FULVIUS. What!

MARTIUS. The rich kinsman that I spoke of here was never my kinsman.[1] I met him by chance, and robbed him with my own hands. Then, as I was fleeing from here, on my way I found that fellow asleep in the road, and also this little knife in his fist——

FULVIUS. Knife?[2]

MARTIUS. With which, as far as I could judge, he was going to kill himself later.

GESIPPUS [*aside*]. Oh Jupiter!

FULVIUS. Go on.

MARTIUS. I don't know that for certain. But because this seemed such a good opportunity at the time, I conceived the idea then

---

[1] Foxe's is the only version to make it appear that the assault victim was related to the assailant.

[2] Though *pugiunculus* means, literally, a small weapon and though Gesippus' knife is apparently suitable for suicide, Fulvius' apparent surprise suggests that Foxe thought of Gesippus' knife as something less bellicose. In ll. 17 and 27 below, Martius calls it a *cultellus*, which recalls Gesippus' term for it (*culter*) in III.9.16; a *culter* is less often associated with weapons. In any case, Gesippus' knife is smaller than Martius' dagger (*sica*).

In dextram pro cultello vt insinuarem clanculum.

FULVIUS.   Hem, quid ais?

MARTIUS.

Bona fide res vt habet, consul.

FULVIUS.   Perge vero.

MARTIUS.   Quod sinu

Atque a me callide consutum est, quo tum magis omnem mihi

Excuterem suspitionem. Cognatum me confinxi rustici   20

Quo liberius hanc a me illi litem intenderem. Quod equidem

Etsi, consul, constitueram, atque etiamnum liquido possem

Facere, tamen pro tanta istorum hac amicitia

Tum commotus etiam misericordiae, numquam animum

Inducam facere.

GESIPPUS.   Boni superi.

TITUS.   Quid est, Gesippe?

FULVIUS.   Tun'   25

Haec vera memoras?

MARTIUS.   Ita me deus iuuet bene optimus,

Vel hoc argumentum dabit spectabile: culticulus hic

Illius num thecae, tum falx huic an non vaginae acquadret vt

Videas.

FULVIUS. Cedo vaginam. Vbi gladius? Euge. Monstra huc thecam

Tuam, iuuenis. O Iupiter! Conquadrant omnia.

POPULUS ROMANUS.   Scilicet.   30

FULVIUS.

Quid tu ais, adolescens?

GESIPPUS.   Enimvero vera edisseruit

Hic omnia.

TITUS.   Diis magnas habeo gratias.

FULVIUS.   Ergo in confesso liquet

Huius furtum esse. Hos resoluite.

MARTIUS.   Nempe.

FULVIUS.   Nae ego multis modis

Gaudeo, diisque plurimum habeo gratiae. Mi Tite, gratulor.

Conscende huc, collega, denuo, Tum tu liber esto, adolescens,   35

Manu absolutus libera.

17. *Hem, quid ais*] stylistically, the unrevised reading, *bona fide*, seems preferable
because of the echo in l. 18.

and there of secretly slipping this dagger into his hand in place of his little knife.

FULVIUS. What! What are you saying?

MARTIUS. I swear that's what happened, consul.

FULVIUS. Well, go on.

MARTIUS. But at the same time I cleverly devised a plan with which I could even better divert all suspicion away from myself. I pretended I was a relative of the farmer so I could more easily direct this charge away from me and onto him. Consul, though I had this all arranged and could certainly get away with it even now, yet because of the great friendship of these two I am so moved to pity that I could never bring my spirit to do it.

GESIPPUS. Gods on high!

TITUS. How is it, Gesippus?

FULVIUS. Do you swear this is true?

MARTIUS. Yes, may the best of gods help me well. But this will give you visible proof: see whether this little knife fits his sheath, and then whether the dagger fits mine.

FULVIUS [to Martius]. Give me your sheath.—— Where's the dagger? Good.—— [To Gesippus.] Young man, show me your sheath. Oh Jupiter. Everything fits perfectly.

CITIZENS. Yes indeed.

FULVIUS. What do you say, young man?

GESIPPUS. Everything he says is indeed true.

TITUS. Thank the gods.

FULVIUS. Then it's evident beyond question that he committed the theft. Release these men.

MARTIUS. By all means.

FULVIUS. Well, I'm very glad. Many thanks to the gods.—— Congratulations, my Titus. Come up here again, my colleague.—— And you, young man, be free, released with a willing hand.

GESIPPUS.   Vobis diis primum immortalibus,
   Tibi deinde, consul, immortales ut par est gratias.
FULVIUS.
   Quid iam, Tite, agimus?
MARTIUS.   Optime, nunc quaeso, quisquis es,
   Adolescens, miseri te mei vicissim misereat.
GESIPPUS.
   Supplex nunc, Tite, per genua haec et amicitiam pristinam   40
   Supplico huic ignoscas supplici, uel mea gratia hanc referas
   Gratiam: da petenti ac paenitenti veniam.
TITUS.   Aequum censeo,
   Cum nostram seruauit salutem tam comiter, nos illi   [*f. 115v*]
      suam reddere.
   Age, te quaeso, Fului, ignoscito.
FULVIUS.   Itane, Tite?
TITUS.   Quandoquidem
   Summa hodie in manu tibi potestas sita est rerum omnium.   45
FULVIUS.
   Quid tum?
TITUS.   Legittime ergo soli licet tibi si vis ignoscere.
FULVIUS.
   Si velim, at quamobrem?
TITUS.   Age, ne sis difficilis. Lachrimas
   Respice eius et paenitudinem. Deinde viginti quas sublegarat
   Minae de meo faxo restituentur, medicos praebebo de meo.
   Quid, vulnus dedit? At idem salutem hodie dedit duplicem.   50
   Dignum hoc fide sua: dignus misericordia qui misericordiam
   Praestitit. In me recipio huius nequid designet postea.
   Saltem vel mea gratia, ut solidum hoc hodie agamus gaudium,
   Age, da quaeso veniam.
GESIPPUS.   Quaeso vero, consul optime.
POPULUS ROMANUS.
   Quaesumus, consul clementissime.
FULVIUS.   Age, quandoquidem ita   55
   Uultis, fiat. Tuo hanc rem, Tite, omnem permitto arbitratui.
TITUS.
   Euge. Quoniam legittima mihi iam pro re publica quiduis hic
   57. *Euge*] ?read as a separate line.

GESIPPUS. First of all to you, immortal gods, and then to you, consul, I give eternal thanks, as I ought.

FULVIUS. What do we do now, Titus?

MARTIUS [*to Gesippus*]. Excellent youth, whoever you are, I beg you now to have pity in turn on me, a wretch.

GESIPPUS [*kneeling*]. Titus, I plead now as a suppliant, by these knees and by our former friendship, that you forgive this suppliant. For my favor grant him a favor: forgive this penitent petitioner.

TITUS. Since he saved our lives so willingly, I think it right that we return his to him. Come, Fulvius, pardon him, I beg you.

FULVIUS. You think so, Titus?

TITUS. Since total power in all matters has been placed in your hands today——

FULVIUS. What then?

TITUS. Legally you may pardon him on your own, then, if you will.

FULVIUS. If I wished to, but why should I?

TITUS. Come, don't be difficult. Look at his tears and grief. Besides, I'll see to it that the twenty minas which he stole are repaid from my resources, and I'll pay for physicians.[1] What, did he deliver a wound? Well, today he also delivered two lives. This is a sign of his reliability. He who has shown pity deserves pity. I take it as my responsibility that he will commit nothing of this sort again. If for no other reason, do this for my sake that we may have complete happiness today. Pardon him, I beg you.

GESIPPUS. I truly beg you, most worthy consul.

CITIZENS. We beg you, most gentle consul.

FULVIUS. Come, since you all wish it, so be it.—— Titus, I turn this entire matter over to your judgment.

TITUS. Good.—— Martius, since legal authority is now vested in me to decide anything here for the state, we grant you your life

---

[1] Titus' assumption of financial responsibilities and his later hiring of Martius are original with Foxe.

Statuendi est statuta authoritas, pro fide ac beneficio
Tuo vitam vicissim donatam, Marti, noxamque hanc tibi
Condonatam damus. Dimittite.

MARTIUS.   Numquam tibi a   60
Me satis referri potest gratia, consul suauissime.

TITUS.
Denique adeo te cum video paenitentem, in fidem meam
Et clientelam recipio. Meus esto. Postremo vobis tum, ciues,
Et reipublicae festum hunc insuper nuncupamus diem laetitiae.

MARTIUS.
O felicem et faustam hanc lucem!

TITUS.   Satis est.   65

[ACTUS QUINTUS. SCENA SEXTA.]
Sempronia. Pamphila. Titus. Fulvius. Martius. Gesippus. Phormio.

SEMPRONIA.
Miranda haec auribus nostris hodie quae aduolant!
Sed eccum vorsum redeuntes.

TITUS.   Heus, pallium huc mihi
Illud primarium purpureum proferte cum pileo protinus.

PAMPHILA.
Aggrediamur.

FULVIUS.   Hem, Sempronia, quid uobis nobisque hodie
Hic obtigerit, quid viro tuo, quid duobus adolescentibus   5
Audistine?

SEMPRONIA. Omnia, atque pol verum ita repertum esse gaudeo.

PHORMIO.   [*f. 116*]
Eccum, here mi.

TITUS.   Age, Gesippum primum indue, Phormio,
Hunc deinde Martium, quandoquidem propter egregiam fidem
In familiam hunc nostram recipimus.

MARTIUS.   Merito sacrum
Et adorandum caput.

TITUS.   Diis nunc primas vobis, et diei huic   10
Tum tibi, Fului, inexhaustas exhibeo gratias.

GESIPPUS.   Et ego, Tite,
Tibi mellitissime, debeo profecto immortaliter.

and pardon your crime in exchange for your act of trust and kindness.—— Release him.

MARTIUS. Most kind consul, I can never thank you enough.

TITUS. Moreover, since I see you so penitent, I take you into my trust and patronage. Be my man. In addition, and finally—— citizens, for you and for the state we declare this to be a holiday of happiness.

MARTIUS. Oh this happy and fortunate day!

TITUS. It is indeed. [*Exeunt.*

[V.6]   *Enter Sempronia and Pamphila.*

SEMPRONIA. The news that flies to our ears today is miraculous. But look, they're coming back.

Enter Titus, Fulvius, Gesippus, and Martius.

TITUS [*shouts*]. Hey, bring me my toga, my best purple one, and my felt hat—on the double.

PAMPHILA. Let's approach them.

FULVIUS. Well, Sempronia, did you hear what happened to you and to us today, to your husband, to two young men?

SEMPRONIA. Everything, and I'm very happy to find it's really true.

Enter Phormio with garments.

PHORMIO. Ho, my master!

TITUS. Come, Phormio. First get Gesippus dressed, and then Martius here, since we're taking him into our household because of his great reliability.

MARTIUS. Deservedly revered and honorable head!

TITUS. I give first thanks now to the gods and to this day, and then boundless thanks to you, Fulvius.

GESIPPUS. And I assuredly, most sweet Titus, am in eternal debt to you.

MARTIUS.   Et ego
  Vtrisque vobis, tum tibi seorsum, iuuenis candidissime,
  Non modo grates sed animam hanc acceptam etiam quam debeo,
  Refero libentissime.
SEMPRONIA.   Ita me dii omnes ament, et ego,   15
  Gesippe mi felicissime, tibi ex animo et gaudeo et gratulor.
GESIPPUS.
  Quid, Sempronia; euge, mea vero Pamphila, quam sedulam
  Mihi hodie nauastis operam in memoria habeo et habeo
  Gratiam.
TITUS.   At vnum restat, Fului.
FULVIUS.   Quid est?
TITUS.   Iuuenis hic
  Quis sit atque eius parentes nostin'?
FULVIUS.   Non.
TITUS.   Quid, Chremem   20
  Illum nobilem Atheniensem.
FULVIUS.   Hem, ephorum
  Illum scilicet mihi patrisque tui antiquum hospitem?
TITUS.
  Huius hic Gesippus est filius haeres et vnicus.
FULVIUS.
  Quid tuusne ille qui suam vltro hanc Semproniam tibi?
TITUS.
  Nimirum.
FULVIUS.   Enimvero serio iam te et fortunae tuae et   25
  Parentibus optimis, Gesippe optime, gratulor.
TITUS.   Quod si me ames,
  Pamphilam hanc, amabo, tuam quam semper sibi amauit vnice
  Vxorem illi vt despondeas.
FULVIUS.   Quid istuc, Tite?
TITUS.   Genus,
  Aetatem, amorem vides. Tum generum tibi et filiae virum
  Polliceor firmum. Age, te quaeso, Fului.
SEMPRONIA.   Quaeso hoc solidum   30
  Nobis perficias, vir optime, beneficium.
TITUS.   Quid ais?

MARTIUS. And I to both of you.—— [*To Titus.*] And to you alone, most fair young man, I willingly give not only my thanks but also my life, which I owe to you from whom I received it.

SEMPRONIA. May all the gods love me, I rejoice with you, my most fortunate Gesippus, and I congratulate you from my heart.

GESIPPUS. Well, Sempronia! And very good, my Pamphila. I remember how earnestly you two worked for me today and I thank you.

TITUS. But one thing remains, Fulvius.

FULVIUS. What?

TITUS. Do you know who this young man is and who his parents are?

FULVIUS. No.

TITUS. Why, you know Chremes, the noble Athenian.

FULVIUS. What! Of course, the famous magistrate, as I know him, and your father's old-time host.

TITUS. Gesippus here is his only son and heir.

FULVIUS. Why, was he also your friend who gave you his girl, Sempronia here?

TITUS. Certainly.

FULVIUS. Well, my good Gesippus, I truly congratulate you, both for your good fortune and for your excellent parents.

TITUS. But if you love me, I pray you, promise him your daughter, Pamphila, here in marriage. He has always loved her alone.

FULVIUS. What's this, Titus?

TITUS. You see his breeding, his youth, his love. And I promise you he'll be a stout son-in-law for you and a stout husband for your daughter. Come, Fulvius, I beg you.

SEMPRONIA. Do us this genuine kindness, I beg you, most excellent man.

TITUS. What do you say?

FULVIUS.

Siquidem gnata approbauerit illius iuditio permitto rem.

PAMPHILA.

Nempe, si tibi, mi pater, approbabitur.

FULVIUS.   Age, placet.

Fiat.

GESIPPUS.   O sancta faelicitas, merito te amo, Pamphila.

TITUS.

Quid igitur censes, Fului, nisi ut cras ineant nuptias?   35

FULVIUS.

Fiat.

TITUS.   Nunc restat nihil nisi uiginti minas pro Martio
Quas pollicitus sum vt colligam, qui istas seruauit hodie
Nobis faustitates. Atque eas domi exquiram iam et mittam rustico.
Deinde chirurgos illi prospexero insuper. Interim   [*f. 116v*]
Quaeso intus ad me omnes diuertite ut festum hunc laeticia   40
Et epulis coronemus diem. Tu, Phormio, singulos
Huc introductos facito.

PHORMIO.   Faciam. Sed vos aediculae
Nostrae spectatores singulos nequeunt capere. Deinde
Nec istis micam habemus epulae. Alioqui vos pariter
Huc introducerem. Valete et plaudite in Christo   45
Iesu qui vos in suas introducat epulas.
Amen.

FULVIUS. If my daughter approves in her judgment of him, I'll allow it.

PAMPHILA. Yes indeed, my father, if you approve.

FULVIUS. Come, I'm pleased. So be it.

GESIPPUS. Oh holy happiness. I love you very much, Pamphila.

TITUS. What do you think then, Fulvius, shall they be married tomorrow?

FULVIUS. So be it.

TITUS. Now nothing remains but for me to gather the twenty minas which I promised for Martius, who saved these festivities for us today. I'll get them at home now and send them to the farmer. Then I'll see to physicians for him. Meantime, please come into my house, all of you, to crown this joyous day with merriment and feasting.—— Phormio, you see that they're all brought in.

[*Exeunt all except Phormio.*

PHORMIO. I will.—— But look, our house can't accommodate all of you spectators. Besides, we haven't a crumb for you to eat.[1] Otherwise, I'd take you in too. Farewell, and rejoice in Christ Jesus, that he may take you in to his feast. Amen. [*Exit.*

---

[1] See Introduction, p. 8.

CHRISTUS TRIUMPHANS

Latin text and
English translation
(on facing pages)

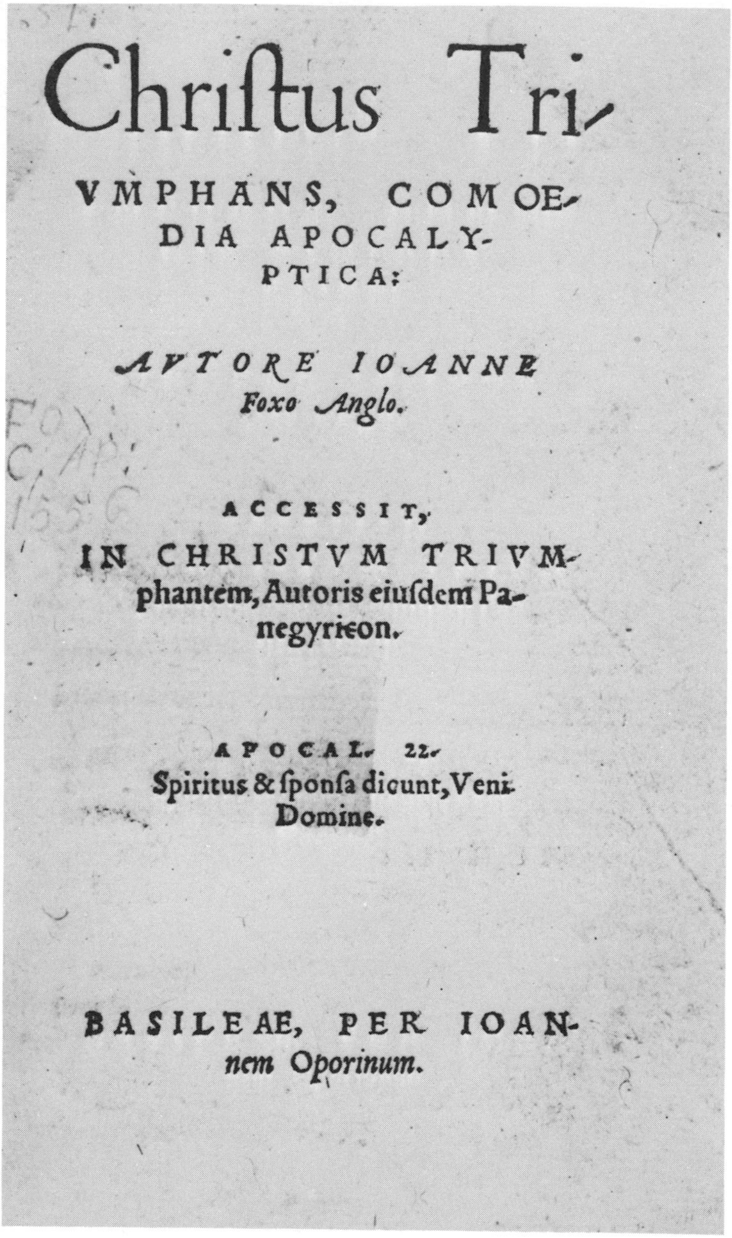

Chriſtus Tri-
VMPHANS, COMOE-
DIA APOCALY-
PTICA:

AVTORE IOANNE
Foxo Anglo.

ACCESSIT,
IN CHRISTVM TRIVM-
phantem, Autoris eiuſdem Panegyricon.

APOCAL. 22.
Spiritus & ſponſa dicunt, Veni
Domine.

BASILEAE, PER IOAN-
nem Oporinum.

Figure 2. The title page of the first edition of *Christus Triumphans* (1556). Courtesy Harvard University Library.

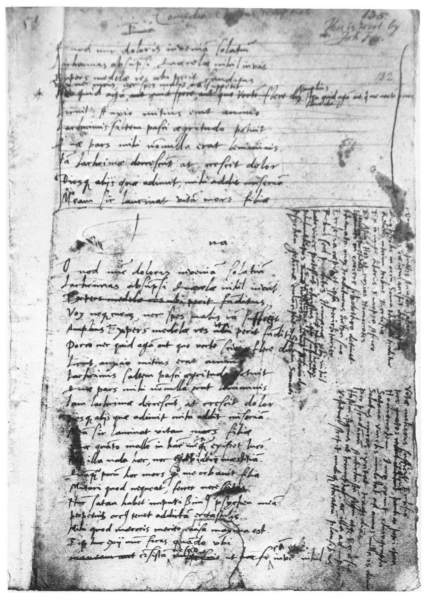

Figure 3. The Periocha and the opening lines of Act I, Scene 1, of *Christus Triumphans*, draft version (Lansdowne MS. 1045, f. 132).

[EPISTOLA NUNCUPATORIA]

Clarissimis Viris D. Bynksio, D. Aescoto, D. Kelko, cumque his uniuerso mercatorum Christianae pietati fauentium sodalitio, Ioannes Foxvs salvtem atque aeternam cum Christo societatem.

Si in nuncupandis opusculis spectari illud a uiris literatis solet, ut lucis uel ornamenti aliquid adiungant iis quibus studiorum suorum monumenta destinant, fateor longe ab eo abesse ingenii nostri foeturas, ut cuiquam splendorum afferant, ipsae potius aliorum egentes adiumentis. Sin ea uero ratio eorum est, quo promptae uoluntatis gratitudinem officiumque hoc pacto erga eos exprimant quibus se obstrictos credant, multae sunt et graues causae (uiri ornatissimi, ut spectatissimum etiam collegam uestrum D. VValtonvm eadem iungat epistola) cur, inter caeteros multos quibus multum debent bonae literae, meam erga uos obseruantiam literario hoc munusculo in primis testari debeam—uel quia seorsim

DEDICATORY EPISTLE

To the most illustrious gentlemen Messrs. Binks, Escot, and Kelke,[1] and to the whole company of merchants favoring Christian piety, John Foxe wishes health and eternal fellowship with Christ.

If in dedicating their little works literary men customarily look to add some light or ornament to those for whom they would set up monuments of their endeavors, I confess that the offspring of my genius will be far from conveying splendor to anyone; it is more the case that they themselves need the help of others. But if in fact the motive of such men is to express in this way the gratitude of a ready will and the sense of obligation to those to whom they believe themselves obliged, then, my illustrious gentlemen (and I wish this same letter could also include your distinguished colleague, Mr. Walton[2]), many and weighty are the reasons why I am obliged to give special witness of my regard for you, among many others to whom belles lettres owe so much, with this trifling literary gift—

[1] John Binks, John Escot, and (probably) John Kelke, all English exiles and merchants in Frankfurt, about whom biographical information is rather skimpy. Binks, who remained at Frankfurt even after Queen Elizabeth's accession, has not been traced in England. Escot (perhaps identified with a London Estcourt in the late sixteenth century or related to a Christopher Escot of northern England in 1559) disappears after June, 1557, when he carried a letter to John Bale in Basel. Kelke may have been a relative of a Thomas Kelke of Bristol who was imprisoned in the Tower in 1555. John Kelke was not nearly so prosperous as Binks and Escot: his property in 1557 was rated at 130 florins compared with 1,000 and 2,250 florins, respectively, for the other two in 1556. I take all this information from C. H. Garrett, *The Marian Exiles* (Cambridge, 1938), pp. 90, 151, 202. Garrett only tentatively identifies John Kelke as a merchant, but the only other Kelke in her list, Roger, lived in Basel rather than Frankfurt and is identified as a student and gentleman (who later became master of Magdalen College, Cambridge). Foxe may have thought Kelke to be wealthier than he was, or he may have named him for political balance; see Introduction, p. 28.

[2] The only Walton listed among the exiles by Garrett (p. 320) is William, whom she thinks to have been an ex-Dominican friar of Gloucester. He had fled to Frankfurt in 1554 and seceded in 1555. Garrett does not identify him as a merchant (as Foxe's Walton presumably was), but his secession would explain why Foxe could not include him among the Frankfurt merchants, especially if he was dead, as Garrett supposes.

singulari uestrae benignitati, pro non uulgaribus in me officiis, debeam non mediocriter, uel etiam magis publico literarum nomine, quibus adeo exornandis ac prouehendis mirificos uos Mecoenates praestare intelligo. Praetereo hic reliqua laudum uestrarum decora: singulare pietatis studium, pectoris cordatam prudentiam cum rara copulatam modestia, mentisque piae possessionem; et quid ego singulas uirtutum uestrarum dotes enumerando explicem quibus multo estis quam opibus faeliciores? Postulant haec non epistolarem operam, et nos breuitati studere cogunt urgentes nundinae.

Tantum de literis nunc ago, quas si uel fauore saltem uestro utcunque beneuolo dignaremini, equidem eximia id laude dignum in hominibus mercatoribus ducerem. Solebat enim hoc hominum genus quaestuariis addictum artibus, cum philologiae studiis minimum habere commercii. Nunc permutatis rerum uicibus, quos primarios potissimum Atlantas habere conueniebat, ab his fere desertae politiores literae religionisque sincerae cura nusquam magis quam apud hunc ordinem uestrum, patrocinium sibi atque asylum reperiunt. Quod quum ex aliis uobiscum, tum ex uobis sane cum primis liquere poterit, quibus satis non est honestas artes honesto fauore ac propensae uoluntatis studio, ceu benigna quadam aura fouere, nisi et impensae insuper uestrae iisdem subleuandis accedant quas quotidie in laboriosissimo hoc literarum ac linguarum cursu desudantibus subministratis, ea liberalitate ut nemo fusius, ea porro modestia et simplicitate ut uix praeter uos ipsos sciat quisquam quae tanta cum laude geritis. Etsi uero in hoc laudis genere non soli sitis, quin et alios complures tum Argentinae tum

either because I am in no small measure indebted to your exceptional benignity for the no mean kindnesses which you have severally bestowed upon me, or even more in the public name of learning, for the adornment and promotion of which I know you have shown yourselves such remarkable Maecenases.[1] I pass over here the other ornaments of your glory: the singular zeal of your piety, the judicious prudence of your hearts together with your rare modesty, and your pious minds. Why should I display them by listing the several endowments of your virtues? In those you are much more fortunate than in material riches. These things do not require my epistolary service, and the pressing market days force me to strive for brevity.[2]

I concern myself now only with learning: if you to any degree deemed this work worthy of at least your benevolent good will, I would consider that certainly enough for high praise among the merchants. That sort of men used to be taken up with the arts of profit-making and had very little commerce with studies of philology. Now that the state of things has changed, more humane letters, which had been almost deserted by these men whom it was very proper to regard as the leading Atlases,[3] and the care of sincere religion find protection and asylum for themselves nowhere more than in this class of yours. This should be clear not only from your associates but also, and indeed especially, from you yourselves. To you it is not enough to nurture distinguished arts with distinguished kindness and with the eagerness of your ready will, like some pleasant breeze, unless your cash also goes to support those same arts: you offer money daily to those sweating in the laborious pursuit of letters and languages, with such liberality that no one is more generous, but with such modesty and simplicity that scarcely anyone besides yourselves knows how praiseworthy are your acts. Although you are not, in fact, alone in this kind of laudable behavior, since you have

[1] Maecenas was the patron of Horace and Virgil and a type of literary patronage.

[2] The reference is to the Frankfurt book fair, held in April and October each year. According to the colophon, *Christus Triumphans* was published in March, 1556. J. F. Mozley notes, "All the books published by Foxe in his exile appeared in March or September, and more than once he complains ... that he must hurry over his preface or epilogue because the market is at hand and the printers are pressing" (*John Foxe and His Book* [London, 1940], p. 42).

[3] That is, they supported the world.

Francfordiae mercatores eiusdem uirtutis comites habeatis: his
tamen alius dabitur praedicandi locus et materia forsan uberior.
Haec interim uobis liberius tribuenda existimaui, partim quo
nonnulla ad uos debitae gratiae portio redeat, partim ut alii uestro
euocati exemplo non modo eximiam pietatem uestram peruideant.
sed eandem insuper in fouendis studiosorum literis studeant imitari,

Venit ergo ad uos uel, si permittitis, ad uniuersum etiam
mercatorum ordinem, *Christvs Trivmphans*. Vtinam et idem omnibus
ueniat triumphans, non in theatro, sed in nubibus; non sub aenig-
mate, sed in conspicua maiestate sui patris, cunctis conspiciendus.
Quod nec diu fortasse aberit, quanquam id nostrae certitudinis non
est quam mature affuturus sit ille. Illud liquido dixerim, eo nunc
prolapsum esse rerum humanarum σχῆμα, ut nunquam adesse
posset opportunius. Caeterum haec quae nescire nos uoluit illi
permittentes, id interim quod nostrum est agamus sedulo; ita se
quisque in eum diem ut paret ne sponsus subito irrumpens nos
supine stertentes aut impure dissolutos adoriatur. Tantoque id
maturius nobis agendum arbitror quod, expletis iam omnibus
fabulae partibus, mundi huius scena properare uidetur ad supremum
illud "Valete et plaudite"; sicque imminente rerum omnium
catastropha emensisque prorsus uaticiniis ut nil restare uideatur nisi
uox illa Apocalyptica, de coelo mox audienda, "Factvm est."
Paulus quondam ad Thessalonicenses scribens, tot abhinc seculis
sponsi aduentum expectantes, iussit ne cito animis permoueantur
quasi ille instaret dies, haud prius uenturum illum admonens quam
patefiat perditissimus ille Antichristus spiritu diuino profligandus.
At nunc si uiuerent Thessalonicenses, quanto magis aduentum
illum expectarent Domini, uelut in foribus imminentem, praesertim

several companions of the same virtue among the merchants both at Strassburg and at Frankfurt,[1] yet some other place and perhaps a more fruitful subject will be provided to celebrate them. For now, I thought this should be quite boldly dedicated to you, partly that I might render to you some portion of the esteem which I owe you; partly that I might inspire others, by your example, not only to see your great piety but especially to be eager to imitate that piety in fostering the learning of the studious.

Therefore, *Christus Triumphans* comes to you or, if you permit it, to the whole class of merchants. Would that the same Christ Triumphant might come to us all, not in the theater but in the clouds; not in allegorical representation but in the conspicuous majesty of his father, visible to all.[2] Perhaps it will not be long delayed, though how quickly he will come is not for us a matter of certitude. I would assuredly have said that the state of human affairs is now so fallen that he could never come more opportunely. But leaving to him these things which he wished us not to know, let us for now attend sedulously to that which is within our competence, so that each of us may prepare himself for that day lest the bridegroom burst in suddenly and accost us snoring on our backs or abandoned to dissoluteness. And I think we should prepare all the more quickly since it seems that all the parts of the play have been acted out and that the scene of this world is rushing to that final "Farewell, and applaud."[3] Thus, with the catastrophe of everything imminent and the prophecies completely fulfilled, nothing seems to remain except that apocalyptic voice soon to be heard from heaven, "It is finished."[4] St. Paul once, writing to the Thessalonians who were awaiting the arrival of the bridegroom so many ages ago, ordered them not to be so easily aroused in spirit as if the day were at hand; he warned them that he would not come before that hellish Antichrist should appear, to be overthrown by the holy spirit.[5] But if the Thessalonians were living now, how much more would they expect the arrival of the lord, as if he were right at the door,

[1] See Introduction, p. 29.
[2] Cf. Prologue 5 ff.
[3] The conventional conclusion of a play. *Catastrophe*, in the next sentence, is the technical term for the dramatic denouement.
[4] Apocalypse 21.6.
[5] 2 Thessalonians 2.1-3.

quum filium iniquitatis illum tam conspicue non solum reuelari sed ubique in animis pene omnium euanescentem cernerent? Et tamen perinde quasi nunquam sit adfuturus triumphalis ille Christi dies, tot nominibus promissus in arcanis literis, aut perlongo absit interuallo, tot argumentis uicinus, mirum quam altum interim mundus hic dormit securitatis lethargum. Adeo ubique crapulae, luxui, ambitioni, rapinis, latrociniis, malitiae, uirulentiae, sycophanticae, ac sordidarum rerum curis passim indulgetur a Christiano populo; charitate interim sic refrigescente in animis hominum, cum huius comite modestia, ut uix tenue eius, fere inter natura etiam coniunctos, uestigium reperias. Denique eo res rediit ut, si quis e sublimi uelut specula demissis oculis res hominum fixius conspicetur, quaquauersum nunc maturos terrae botros tempusque esse uindemiatori angelo falcem mittendi iudicet. Quocirca non abs re facturus uidebar si, inter caetera studiorum nostrorum exercitia, huiusmodi pararem aliquid, in quo propositis temporum periculis nostros aliquo pacto ad maiorem huius uitae contemptum futuraeque curam expergefacerem.

Quanquam non licuit in hoc dramate singula uitiorum genera atque crassiora uulgi flagitia more ueteris comoediae flagellare. Id enim in *Asoto* reliquisque doctissimae Germaniae comoediis, tum potissimum in concionibus quotidianis, abunde est praestitum. Nobis tantum Apocalypticam historiam prosequentibus satis erat ea duntaxat e literis sacris in theatrum transferre quae ad res potissimum ecclesiasticas pertinebant. Primum futurae immortalitatis certitudinem confirmamus, introducta animae et corporis ὑποτυπώσει,

especially since they would see the son of iniquity not only revealed so conspicuously, but everywhere in the spirits of almost everyone disappearing.

And yet, just as if that day of Christ's triumph were never coming though promised under so many names in the arcane writings, or as if it would be delayed for a very long time though according to so many proofs it is near, it is remarkable how deep is the lethargy of self-confidence in which this world sleeps the while. Christian people everywhere indulge themselves so in drunkenness, debauchery, ambition, rapine, robberies, malice, animosities, backbiting, and attention to dirty business, while charity and its companion, modesty, grow so cold in the minds of men, that you find scarcely a faint trace of charity even among those who are related by blood. Accordingly, matters are such that, if anyone looked very closely at the affairs of men, looking down, as it were, from a lofty watchtower, he would judge that the grapes of the earth are everywhere ripe and that it is time for the gathering angel to put his pruning hook to work.[1] Thus I seemed not to be doing amiss if, among the other exercises of my studies, I prepared something of this sort in which, setting forth the dangers of the times, I would arouse our people in some way to a greater contempt for this life and a greater concern for the life to come.

But I could not in this play flagellate, in the way of the Old Comedy, the several types of vices and the grosser shames of the mob. For that is abundantly performed in *Asotus* and the other comedies of the very learned Germany,[2] and especially in daily discourses. It was enough for me, following only the Apocalyptic history, to transfer as far as possible from the sacred writings into the theater those things which pertain primarily to ecclesiastical affairs. First, having introduced a representation of the soul and the body,[3]

[1] Cf. Apocalypse 14.15.

[2] *Asotus* (*ca.* 1510; pr. 1537), by the German Catholic George Macropedius, was a Christian-Terence comedy of intrigue on the prodigal-son theme. See C. H. Herford, *Studies in the Literary Relations of England and Germany in the Sixteenth Century* (Cambridge, 1886), pp. 79-88, 153.

[3] Actually, we do not meet Psyche until the fourth scene, and in the revised version we do not meet Soma at all. We hear of their situation in the second scene. Perhaps Foxe conceived of Eve and Mary as representing, respectively, soul and body. But cf. Prologue 18 and p. 229, n. 2.

aduersus Epicureos quosdam uentres, si qui de immortalitate nostra ambigant. Deinde in Nomocrate uim legis totam adumbratam dedimus, in hoc ne plus minusue ei quam par est tribuatur. Quo in genere saepe a multis grauiterque peccari uideo post Martini Lutheri tempora, ut ne frustra in libris toties uaticinatus uideatur, sese uereri dictitans ne, se extincto, uera illa iustificationis disciplina prorsus apud Christianos exolescat. Nam ut dissolutos istos nimisque laxae licentiae uoluptuarios damnat etiam prophana philosophia, ita nec hi mihi probandi uidentur qui simplices ac imbecilles conscientias legis perpetuo metu captiuas detinent, semper cum Deo secundum uirtutes suas ac uitia, submoto fere mediatore, agentes indeque caeteros omnes iudicantes, utinam et sibi non placentes quidam. Non quod legi omnem prorsus metum detrahamus, sed nec Christo rursus sua detrahenda suauitas aut minuenda gratia est; et pauidis conscientiis necessario interim consulendum. Plures fateor esse quibus uiuit adhuc Moses. At sunt rursus quibus, sub Iosua ductore militantibus, Moses ueteris militiae dux sepultus est ut eius nesciatur sepulchrum. Quanquam iidem meminerimus,

we confirm the certitude of our future immortality, in opposition
to some Epicurean stomachs—this in case anyone has any doubt
about our immortality. Next, we present the total power of the law,
represented in Nomocrates, to the end that neither more nor less
than what is fit should be allowed to it. To this sort of error I see
many people falling frequent and serious victims since the times of
Martin Luther; thus, it seems that he did not prophesy in vain when
many times in his books he repeated his fear that, when he was dead,
proper instruction in observance of the law would completely
disappear among Christians.[1] Even profane philosophy condemns
the dissolute and voluptuous for their loose licentiousness. But for
those who hold as captives their simple, foolish consciences in
perpetual fear of the law, always dealing with God according
to their virtues and their vices, almost dispelling the mediator—and
would that some who judge others after this fashion were not so
pleased with themselves—those do not seem worthy of my approval.
Not that we should completely take away all fear from the law;
but neither, in turn, should Christ's gentleness be taken from him,
or his loving grace be diminished; and necessarily, in the meantime,
there must be consideration for timid consciences.[2] I acknowledge
there are some for whom Moses still lives. But there are others,
warring under Captain Joshua, for whom Moses, the captain of
the old army, has been buried so that his sepulcher is not known.[3]

[1] I do not know what books Foxe had in mind, but cf. *Table Talk*, No. 3543A:
". . . let Satan not have his way in the church after my death. I'm very much
afraid of this. . . ." (T. G. Tappert, tr., in *Luther's Works*, ed. H. T. Lehmann,
LIV [Philadelphia, 1967], 226).

[2] Cf. Foxe's *De Christo Crucifixo Concio* (1570), translated as *A Sermon of Christ
Crucified* (London, 1570), f. 55: "Christ, & the law in a true Christen conscience
are contrary & incompatible, . . . ii thynges which can not stand together." See
also Foxe's "Notes appertayning to the matter of Election," in Theodore de
Beze, *The Treasure of Trueth* (London, n.d.), sigs. Niiii-O5v.

[3] Both Moses, whose burial is recorded in Deuteronomy 24.6, and Joshua
were regarded as types of Jesus, but Joshua was especially revered because,
among less significant parallels with Christ, he led his people into the promised
land of Canaan as Moses could not do. Joshua's name was rendered Ἰησοῦς in
the Septuagint and *Jesus* in the Vulgate, or often *Jesus Nave* through a misinter-
pretation of the Hebrew for "Joshua, son of Nun." Jerome commented that
Joshua is the type of Jesus in name as well as deed (Migne's *Patrologia Latina*,
XXII, 545). Isidor makes a distinction between Moses and Joshua similar to
that made by Foxe: "Defunctus est ergo Moyses, defuncta est lex, legalia praecepta
jam cessant, et obtinet Jesus, id est Salvator Christus Filius Dei, principatum:

numquam nisi cum honore illum sepeliendum. Atque utinam sic omnium affulgeret mentibus Christi gloria ut Mosis omnis splendor exolescat; utinam sic ubique uigeret iustitiae amor, sic omnes forent iusti, ut nulla sit illis lex posita; utinam sic omnes cum Paulo mortui ut in sese nemo, in omnibus solus uiueret Christus. Sed de his loco opportuniore.

Potissimum autem in Ecclesiae persecutionibus describendis uersatur comoediae nostrae materia, quibus infoelix ille ueterator, ex quo e coelo per Christum exturbatus est, nunquam destitit sponsam Christi fatigare. Semper enim ab initio capitalis ille accusator generis nostri fuit, nec unquam ingenitum in nos odium mutat etiamsi ministros furoris sui subinde mutet. Primos olim tumultus dedit per Pharisaeos, deinde per Caesares tyrannos et Proconsules, nunc per Episcopos et Pontifices mundum non dicendis tragoediis exagitat: id quod in primis testari hodie Anglia nostra poterit. Dominus pro pietate sua dignetur horrendos hos fluctus in serenitatem aliquando uertere, idque indubie hoc faciet maturius si nos simul cum precibus enixissime profusis uitam in melius commutatam addiderimus.

Verum ne diutius uos loquaci praefatione detineam, etiam atque etiam uos, eximii ac obseruandi domini, rogatos uelim, simul cum eiusdem sodalitatis uestrae collegis integerrimis, ut hoc qualecunque nostrae in uos obseruantiae μνημόσυνον, pro candore uestro et uobis gratum esse, simul et aliis uestra approbatione commendatum uelitis. Maiora ac nitidiora ab aliis accipietis, maiori doctrinae ubertate tinctis ingeniis. Nobis quoniam maiora in praesentia non licuit, hoc interim pauperis agelli flosculo qualicunque, hybernis his dieculis apud nos uernante, uobis uel gratificari uel certe meum

Though we should remember that he must never be buried except with honor, yet would that the glory of Christ so shine in the minds of all that all the splendor of Moses would disappear; would that the love of justice so flourish everywhere, and all men be so just, that no law would be imposed on them; would that all men would with St. Paul be dead so that no one would live in himself, and Christ alone would live in all.[1] But of these things in a place more fit.

Chiefly the matter of our comedy turns on descriptions of the persecutions of Ecclesia, with which that unhappy old devil, from the time he was driven from heaven by Christ, never stopped harassing the bride of Christ. For from the beginning he was always the chief besetter of our race, and he never changes his inborn hatred for us even if now and then he changes the ministers of his fury. Long ago he delivered his main blows through the Pharisees, then through the tyrant Caesars and the Proconsuls; now he shakes up the world with unspeakable tragedies through the bishops and the priests. Today our own England especially could testify to that: may the lord in his love deign sometime to make these horrible floods serene. And he will undoubtedly do it that much more quickly if we join to the prayers which we zealously pour forth a life changed for the better.

But let me not keep you longer with a wordy preface. My distinguished and esteemed lords, I earnestly entreat you, and also the unequalled colleagues of your company, to be kindly disposed toward this token, such as it is, of my respect for you in your splendor and to commend it to others with your approval. You will receive better and more elegant things from others whose geniuses are dyed with a greater richness of learning. As for me, since I could not at this time produce greater fruits, for the present I wanted to favor you, or in any case to attest to my devotion for you in the lord, with this little flower, such as it is, from my barren little field,

---

introducit populum in terram de quo dicit Dominus: *Beati mites, quoniam ipsi possidebunt terram* [Matthew 5.5]" (*Patrologia Latina*, LXXXIII, 371). Cf. Romans 7.4. Foxe reused part of this conception in *A Sermon of Christ Crucified* (ff. 27-28): ". . . with Moses . . . clyme vp the hyll of Nebo. . . . There may ye take a vew of this your spiritual countrey, & glorious kyngdome. . . . There shall you see our noble and triumphant Capitaine Iosue, our Sauiour Iesus . . . seuen tymes goyng about ye great City Iericho."

[1] Cf. Galatians 2.19-20.

erga uos in Domino studium testari libuit. Dominus Iesvs suam in uos pietatem in dies magis accumulet ac negotia uestra foeliciter secundet in omnibus.

In Christo multis nominibus uester
I. Foxus

De Christo Trivmphante,
in Apocalypticam Ioannis Foxi Comoediam
Laurentius Vmfredus

Non hominum palmas, peritura insignia regum,
    Nec terrenorum marcida serta ducum,
Sed mirum nullo moriturum fine triumphum
    Christi Christicolis sacra Camoena dabit:
Iusticiam fidei, coeli mysteria summa   5
    Et consecratae sancta trophaea crucis.
Christus inops, insons, uermis, contemptio plebis,
    Ludibrium Graecis, praeda reiecta suis,
Iam Deus aetheream uictor subuectus in arcem,
    Cunctis perculsis hostibus. Altus ouat.   10
Et sine praesidiis armata exarmat inermis,
    Nudus cuncta suo subiugat imperio.
Huc, huc, afflictae mentes, huc pectora fracta:
    Vobis, non aliis, noster Iesus ouat.
In cruce debellat crucis hostes, carne retundit   15
    Cuncta per infirmos stigmaticosque uiros.
In uinclis uincit, uulnus quoque uulnere curat:
    Naturae uulnus, uulnere dico crucis.
Quo praecelsa labant, sternuntur robora Basan
    Et cedri Libani, pompaque tota iacet.   20
Quo uis deuicta est Satanae, mors morte perempta est,
    Quo grassatorum fracta tyrannis erit.
Quo seruata $\psi v \chi \dot{\eta}$ rugientis ab ore leonis,
    Quo totos uiuet $\sigma \hat{\omega} \mu \alpha$ perenne dies.
Sed non Adopylus furialis ianitor Orci   25
    Nec Thanatos punget Nomocratesque ferus.

---

26. *punget*] the errata sheet in B corrects B's *pinget*.

blooming in my short winter days. May the lord Jesus heap his graciousness on you more every day, and second your affairs with good fortune in all things.

Yours in Christ in his many names

J. FOXE

On John Foxe's Apocalyptic Comedy of Christ Triumphant by Laurence Humphrey[1]

Not the honors of men, the transient trappings of kings, the withered garlands of earthly dukes, but the wondrous triumph of Christ, which will never die, the sacred Muse will give to Christians: the righteousness of faith, the most exalted mysteries of heaven, and the holy monuments of the consecrated cross. Wretched, innocent, a worm, the butt of the people, to the Greeks a laughing-stock and to his own people a rejected prize, Christ is now conveyed into the heavenly citadel, God victorious, all his enemies crushed. Exalted, he triumphs. Without troops or arms he disarms the armed; without armor he subjugates all to his authority.

Come, afflicted consciences, come, and come, shattered spirits: for you, not for others, our Jesus exults. On the cross he vanquishes the enemies of the cross: with his flesh he beats back everything for the sake of weak and dishonored men. In chains, he conquers.[2] With a wound (the wound of the cross) he cures a wound (the wound of nature). Thus exalted things give way, the oaks of Basan and the cedars of Lebanon are thrown down, and all pomp lies low. Thus is the power of Satan overcome and death is destroyed by death. Thus the tyranny of attackers will be broken. Thus the spirit is saved from the mouth of a roaring lion. Thus the body will live perpetually, through all the days. But Adopylus, the furious door-keeper of hell, will not sting, nor Thanatos or the savage Nomocrates.

---

[1] Humphrey, a demy at Magdalen College, Oxford, in 1546—after Foxe had left—was in Zurich by April, 1554, and enrolled at the University of Basel in the fall of 1555. He and Foxe became close friends, and he may have helped Foxe with the Book of Martyrs (Garrett, pp. 193-194). He later (1561) became President of Magdalen College, and almost immediately asked Foxe's permission to produce Christus Triumphans there; see Introduction, p. 34.

[2] The Latin puns on uinclis-uincit.

Quin et Psychephonos, rabiosos atque Dioctas
    Iam nostri Christi ferrea sceptra prement.
Pseudamnus furiat, sanctos spoliet Polyharpax,
    Emungat iustos diripiatque bonos.   30
Iam pastor ueniet, Pseudamnis omnibus horror,
    Agnis fictitiis nomine, reque lupis.
Tum uae Pseudamno: tibi laruam detrahet Agnus,
    Te fucata licet palliat Hypocrisis.
Vae Balamiticae quibus insidet ustio frontis,   35
    Vae tibi Romano chrismate inuncta cohors.
Roma ruet meretrix, et bestia saeua peribit,
    Mitratusque simul Gerberus ille triceps.
Occidet et Babylon sat notum et nobile scortum,
    Pornapolis Latii praesulis acropolis.   40
Quisquis coccineis hic sese uenditat ostris
    Atque cruentatis turgida turba togis
Sentiet ultorem sibi nunc instare cometam,
    Comperiet signum uindicis esse Dei.
Sed tu qui pius es, uictricia suspice signa   45
    Hancque triumphantem semper amato crucem.
Si pateris, gaude: sunt haec uexilla magistri,
    Tuque feras eadem symbola, discipulus.
Saepe Deus tentat, tentando uulnera sanat:
    Vt probet afflictat, sed probat ut reuocet.   50
Hanc spectare tibi libeat si, lector, idaeam,
    Exhibet en oculis Foxea scena tuis.

Τοῦ αὐτοῦ
[Edited by Douglas J. Stewart]

μή μάθε ῥαψωδὸν τυφλοῦ ποίημα Ὁμήρου,
    μηδὲ ματαιολόγων ψεύσματα μωρὰ βροτῶν
καίπερ ἐκεῖνα φρένας ἀφελῶν ἀπατῶσι φώτων
    ὣς δέλεαρ, κούφαις ἐλπίσι τερπόμενα,
ἀλλάγε τὴν ἱερὰν τοῦ Φόξου λάμβανε σκηνήν,   5
    σοὶ γὰρ χριστιανῷ ταῦτα θέατρα πρέπει.
ἀσπασίως δέξον σωτῆρος σταυρὸν Ἰησοῦ,

---

3. ἀπατῶσι] emended from ἀπατώοσι.

Indeed the iron sceptres of our Christ will now press down the Psychephonuses and rabid Diocteses. Let Pseudamnus rage; let Polyharpax rob the holy, cheat the just, and plunder the good. Now a shepherd will come, the terror of all Pseudamnuses—lambs in name but false, and wolves in deed. Then woe to Pseudamnus: the Lamb will remove your spectre, though painted hypocrisy cloak you.[1] Woe to those in whom burns a Balaamite's nature,[2] and woe to you, the throng anointed with the oil of Rome. Rome the harlot will fall, and the savage beast will perish, and with it the triple-mitred Cerberus. The famous and infamous Babylon will also fall, citadel of Pornapolis the leader of Latium. Whoever prostitutes himself here to the scarlet and purple robes, and that proud crowd in blood-red cloaks,[3] will now feel an avenging comet threaten and will learn that it is a sign of the punishing God. But you who are faithful, look up to signs of victory and always love this triumphant cross. If you suffer, rejoice: these are the ensigns of your teacher, and you, the pupil, must bear these standards. Often God puts to the test, and by testing he heals wounds: he afflicts to test, but he tests that he may redeem.

Reader, if you would like to see this idea, behold, Foxe's stage presents it to your eyes.

By the Same
[Translated by Douglas J. Stewart]

Read not the bardic poem of the blind Homer, nor the foolish lies of babbling mortals even though these things deceive the wits of simple men like bait, thrilling with empty hopes.[4] Rather, take up the sacred play of Foxe, for this kind of play is more worthy of you as a Christian. Accept gratefully the cross of Jesus the savior,

---

[1] See V.1.18.

[2] See Numbers 22-24.

[3] So I interpret a difficult passage; apparently it refers to cardinals and those who allow themselves to be misled by cardinals.

[4] Professor Stewart points out that ll. 4 and 11 are paraphrased from Solon, Frag. 1, 36-37.

σταυρὸν τριστίμιον, σταυρὸν ἀλεξίκακον.
δεῦτ' οὖν ὦ πτωχοὶ χερσίν τε ποσίν τε τρέχοντες,
πτωχὸς ἀνὴρ Φόξος πλοῦτον ἔδωκε μέγαν.   10
δεῦρ' ὅστις πενθεῖς πάθεσ' ἀργαλέοισι πιασθεὶς
οὐ σῶν εὑρήσεις φάρμακον ἄλλο κακῶν.
δεῦρ' ἄγε προς μοῦνον ἰατρὸν ταχέως φύγε Χριστὸν,
ᾧ δεῖξον νοσερᾶς τραύματα δεινὰ ψυχῆς.

De Infirmo Christo et Scandalo Crucis: Ad Ioannem Foxum
Idem

Tu quidem ueros celebras triumphos,
Sic tibi et sanctis merito uidetur;
Sed caro oblatrat renuitque sensus,
    Obstrepit orbis.

Nam quis est splendor rutilans ouantum?   5
Laureae fasces, iubilum, decorue,
Quae tua enarrat lepido cothurno
    Musa triumphans?

Pauperem Christum uideas misellum,
Exulem, terris dubiis uagantem,   10
Saepe combustum, simul atque caeco
    Carcere clausum.

Quae fuit quondam benedicta uitis,
Quam sua dextra pater ille patrum
Fixit, et sanctis manibus rigauit   15
    Dulcis Iesvs.

Foxe, nunc eheu maledicta uitis,
Nobiles botri pedibus teruntur
Impiis, sacras sacer Antichristus
    Diripit uuas.   20

En aper spumans fera foeda syluae,
Hanc sorex uastat, spoliat, racemat:
Diruta est sepes, prope dissipata est
    Vinea culta.

22. *sorex*] this is the reading of the Harvard copy of B; the British Museum copy reads *sorec*, and the errata sheet "corrects" it by printing the same word. Perhaps Foxe intended some accusative to be construed with *Hanc*, such as *forem*.

the cross thrice-precious, the cross that fends off evil. Approach, ye poor, running on hands and feet.[1] A poor man, Foxe, has given you great riches. Approach, whoever suffers and is burdened by terrible woes. You will find no other remedy for your ills. Flee here to Christ your only physician, and to him show the terrible wounds of your soul.

On the Infirm Christ and the Scandal of the Cross: To John Foxe by Laurence Humphrey

You celebrate true triumphs indeed, as it seems—and deservedly so—to you and to the saintly. But mere flesh rails and common sense denies and the world shouts "Nay." What is this glowing brightness of people rejoicing? The bundles of laurel, the wild shouting, the splendid trappings which your triumphant muse chronicles in a happy buskin?[2] See poor Christ wretched, an exile wandering in dangerous lands, often burned and as often shut up in a dark dungeon. England,[3] once a blessed vine, which the father of fathers planted with his right hand and which sweet Jesus watered with his holy hands, is now, alas, a cursed vine, O Foxe: our famous grapes are trodden down by impious feet; the unholy Antichrist plunders our holy grapes. Lo the frothing boar, horrible beast of the forest, and the shrew-mouse ruin and strip and glean this arbor.[4] The hedgerow is destroyed, the tilled vineyard nearly ruined. The

---

[1] Professor Stewart notes, "an appropriation of a standard Homeric formula, here somewhat grotesquely; cf. *Iliad* 20.360-361." The intended sense is probably of crawling. Foxe uses the figure in Latin at *Titus et Gesippus* I.1.56.

[2] The buskin was the boot used in tragedy.

[3] The word is supplied from a marginal note ("Anglia") in B.

[4] The passage may be corrupt: the verbs should be plural, *Hanc* has no referent, and *sorex* seems a curious word to link with *aper*. See the note to the Latin text.

Abfugit cultor, fugiunt columbae   25
Territae pennis aquilae uorantis:
Non sub umbroso timidus recumbet
    Palmite turtur.

Squallor et luctus lachrymaeque regnant:
Saccus et sordes, cinis atque puluis,   30
Lazarus pauper dominantur isto
    Foxe triumpho.

Ergo mittantur citharae sonantes,
Lugubrem mecum tetricam Camoenam
Euoca: dulci posita Thalia,   35
    Triste canamus.

Iam piis uotis Dominum precemur,
Visat ut uitem uacuam, iacentem,
Satanae fibras resecante uerbi
    Falce reuellat.   40

Quo bonos fructus ferat atque lectos,
Floreat radix, bona terra crescat,
Gemmet, et passim sua longa fuse
    Brachia spargat.

Quo magis serpat, patulasque fundat   45
Iam comas, omnes adopacet oras
Pampinis, tandem quasi pressa palma
    Laeta resurgat.

Christe o pastor, Deus Israelis,
Visita uitem suibus patentem,   50
Pelle labruscas, madefac sacrato
    Germina rore.

Agne, Pseudamnos procul hinc fugato,
Et tuum regnum sinito uenire,
Virginem sponsam male sordidatam   55
    Respice sponse.

tiller takes to flight; doves flee, frightened by the feathers of the devouring eagle; no timid turtledove rests beneath the shady vine-branch. Mourning and grieving and weeping prevail: sackcloth and dirty garments, ashes and dust, and poor Lazarus are supreme in this triumph, Foxe. Then away with your noisy lutes. Call up with me a sad and doleful Muse. Put sweet Thalia aside and let us sing something sad.[1] Now with pious prayers let us pray to the lord to look after our barren and fallen vine, to tear out the roots of Satan with the pruning hook of his word. So may the vine bear good and choice fruits, may its root flourish, may fertile soil increase, may it put forth buds and spread its branches far and wide. So may it extend itself and now pour forth its far-flung tendrils and shade all the boundaries with its foliage and, like a bent palm tree, rise up again healthy at last. O Christ our shepherd, God of Israel, visit the vine which is exposed to the swine, drive away the wild vines, and water the seeds with your sacred dew. O lamb, drive the Pseudamnuses far from here and let your kingdom come. O bridegroom, look upon your virgin bride in wretched shabbiness.

[1] Thalia was the muse of comedy.

Ad Lavrentivm I. Foxus De Uinea

Plectra squallentis gemebunda lyrae,
Dulce Laurenti decus, et querelas
Mitte: non laetis quadrat haec Thalia
    Dorica rebus.

Vineam Christus nimium feraci   5
Ebriam luxu tumidamque fastu
Corripit flagris, petulantis uuae
    Stemphyla tundens.

Vina quum uellet, dedit haec labruscas,
Carduas, squillam, asphodelos, lupinum: 10
Ocio effrenis, nimiumque pleno
    Perdita cornu.

Hinc apros, ursos, tygrides, leones
Et lupos istos, sata culta uasto
Ore qui uastant, meruere nostrae   15
    Crimina uitae.

Hinc fugit cultor, trepidant columbae,
Vnguibus uncis aquila furente,
Voce dum tristis gemit impedita,
    Turtur ab ulmo.   20

Scilicet Christi manus haec amica est.
Dum putat uites, uitiis medetur.
Caedit, ut seruet. Meritis minora
    Flagra feramus.

Ergo uel plagis meliora discas.   25
Stupra, uim, fraudes, φυλοχρημοσύθην,
Turgidi inflatos animi tumultus,
    Ocia, nugas,

John Foxe to Laurence: Of the Vineyard

Away with the doleful plectrum of your mourning lyre, sweet honored Laurence, away your contentiousness: this Dorian Thalia[1] is not fit for happy affairs. With his scourges Christ smites a vineyard drunk in excessive lushness[2] and swelling with pride; he crushes the fruit of a wanton vine.[3] When he would wish for grapes, this vineyard, grown wild from idleness and ruined by a horn too full, yielded wild vines, thistles, onions, asphodels, and lupine. Thus, the sins of our life have deserved these boars, bears, tigers, lions, and wolves which devastate our planted crops with their vast mouths. Hence the tiller flees, the doves tremble as the eagle ravages with his crooked claws, and the sad turtledove keens in a choked voice from the elm. Of course, this hand of Christ is friendly: as he prunes the vines, he cures of vices; he cuts to save. Let us bear scourges which are less than we deserve. Then, England,[4] from these very toils learn better things. Abandon corruptions, o Briton, and

---

[1] Thalia would not sing in the Dorian (majestic) mode.
[2] The Latin word has a double meaning, luxuriant growth and debauchery.
[3] Literally, the pressed olives (στέμφυλα) of the grape.
[4] Supplied from a marginal note ("Anglia") in B.

Impotens mundi studium, rapinas,
Odium, caedes, κακότηθ' ἄπασαν   30
Mutuas rixas, rabiemque linguae
    Linque Britanne.

Efferat si te nimium secunda
Aura, te rursus grauior reducat:
Vinea ut fias Domino, Britanne,   35
    Grata colono.

Haud diu uindex tamen haec paternae
Spero, Laurenti, manat ira uirgae:
Altera, post hanc, fore spero, carpas
    Messe racemos.   40

FINIS.

violence, frauds, greed, the heightened passions of a proud spirit, idleness, jesting, fruitless zeal for worldly gain, rapines, hatred, murders, all manner of wickedness, mutual bickerings, and angry language. If too strong a following wind carry you away, let a stronger one bring you back, o Briton, that you may become a vineyard pleasing to your husbandman the Lord. But, Laurence, I hope the vengeful anger of our father's rod will not wait long. I hope, after this harvest, you will gather grapes in a second harvest.

[Prologus]

Eua

Maria

Satan

Psychephonus ⎫

Thanatus   ⎬ lictores

Adopylus, seruus

Nomocrates, tyrannus

Anabasius, nuncius

Christus

Psyche, anima humana

Raphael, angelus

Petrus, apostolus

Saulus, qui et Paulus

Archiereus, pontifex

Nomologus, sacerdos

Polyharpax, scriba

Dioctes, persecutor

Pseudamnus, Antichristus

Pornapolis, meretrix Babylon

Ecclesia, mater

Africus ⎫

Europus ⎬ adolescentes

Hierologus, concionator

Chorus quinque uirginum

[Populus]

[Chorus]

[Muti]

[Desmophylax]

[Dromo]

[Zenodorus]

[Colax]

[Parthene]

---

[1] *Soma*] this character does not appear in the revised version of B; in the manuscript, his counterpart is an important character for a time and is called Sarcobius (from σάρξ, flesh, humanity, and βίος, life). Soma (σῶμα) means body.

Satan] also referred to at times by the classical names Dis and Pluto. In Act V, he assumes the name Lucifer.

Psychephonus] soul-murder (ψυχή and φόνος); Bienvenu interpreted his allegorical significance as standing for sin, the "sergent du diable." In Act V, he assumes the name Hypocrisis, wearing a Franciscan habit.

Thanatus] death (θάνατος). In Act V, he assumes the name Martyromastix, i.e., scourge of martyrs (μάρτυρ and μάστιξ).

Adopylus] Bienvenu called him a doorkeeper, equivalent of Cerberus, apparently deriving the name from πύλη, door. Laurence Humphrey, who presumably knew, agreed; see his poem "De Christo Triumphante," 25, above. Foxe may also have had in mind the verb ἀδοπῶ, to sacrifice. In Act V, he is called Catholicus, a reference to the papal title of Spanish kings. In the manuscript version, Adopylus does not appear and his speeches are divided among other characters, including one variously called Theorgilus, angry God (θεός and ὀργίλος) and Theomenes, wrath of God (θεός and μηνία).

Nomocrates] power of the law (νόμος and κράτος); i.e., the Old Testament law. In the manuscript version (III.1-2) he is called Dicologus, probably not advocate (δικολόγος), but letter of the law (δίκη and λόγος).

Anabasius] an ascent (ἀνάβασις), because he is a messenger up from hell.

Psyche] soul (ψυχή).

Archiereus] high priest (ἀρχή and ἱερεύς). See p. 255, n. 1.

Nomologus] regard for [or word of] law (νόμος and λόγος). See p. 255, n. 1.

Polyharpax] robber of much or many (πολύς and ἅρπαξ); Bienvenu glossed the name as equivalent to "pince-maille" (pinchpenny).

Dioctes] persecutor (διωκτής). In Act IV, he assumes the name Symmachus;

DRAMATIS PERSONAE

PROLOGUE

EVE, *mother of Soma and Psyche*

MARY, *mother of Christ*

SATAN

PSYCHEPHONUS *and* THANATUS, *attendants on Satan*

ADOPYLUS, *servant of Satan*

NOMOCRATES, *a tyrant*

ANABASIUS, *a messenger from hell*

CHRIST

PSYCHE, *the human spirit*

RAPHAEL, *angel of God*

PETER, *the apostle*

SAUL, *later the apostle* Paul

ARCHIEREUS, *the high priest*

NOMOLOGUS, *a priest*

POLYHARPAX, *a scribe, servant of Archiereus*

DIOCTES, *a persecutor*

PSEUDAMNUS, *the Antichrist, the pope*

PORNAPOLIS, *the whore of Babylon, mistress of Dioctes*

ECCLESIA, *the church, wife of Soma and mother of Europus, Africus, and Asia*

AFRICUS *and* EUROPUS, *youths, sons of Ecclesia*

HIEROLOGUS, *a preacher*

CHORUS *of five virgins attendant on Ecclesia*

CITIZENS

CHORUS *of priests, Vatican officials, and attendants*

Mute Characters

DESMOPHYLAX, *a jailor*

DROMO, ZENODORUS, *and* COLAX, *servants of Nomocrates*

PARTHENE, *a virgin, handmaid of Ecclesia*

---

see p. 305, n. 1. In the manuscript he is called Cosmetor, leader (κοσμήτωρ), and Machonomus, strife of the law (μάχη and νόμος). In the draft version, Abadon has all speeches after Act III which B assigns to Dioctes; the name of Abadon, who does not appear in B, is taken from Apocalypse 9.11 and means destruction in Hebrew (= Apollyon in Greek and Exterminans in Latin).

Pseudamnus] false lamb (ψεῦδος and ἀμνός). In IV.6.34, he is referred to as Eudamnus.

Pornapolis] whore city (πόρνη and πόλις), that is, Rome. In the draft version, she is the mistress of Abadon; see the note on Dioctes.

Asia] she does not appear in the play, but is referred to several times. From a Christian viewpoint, Asia suffered worse hardships than Europe and had less hope of earthly improvement.

Africus] in IV.7.8, he is called Afer.

Europus] sometimes called Europaeus; in the manuscript at V.1 he is called Europlethius.

Citizens, Attendants] the attendants include, for instance, the characters summoned by Psychephonus at IV.8.58-60 who are referred to in a subsequent speech prefix as "Chorus." Presumably all such roles were performed by the chorus of five virgins which concludes the play, though their costume would be different.

Desmophylax] jailer (δεσμοφύλαξ). The character is referred to once (III.2.10), and the word may refer to his function, not to his name.

Dromo] cf. the Dramatis Personae of *Titus et Gesippus*.

Zenodorus] perhaps gift of Zeus (Ζήν and δῶρον), or of a foreigner (ξένος), or hireling of my right hand (ξένος and δόρυ).

Colax] flatterer (κόλαξ).

Parthene] virgin (παρθένος).

227

CHRISTVS TRIVMPHANS, [*f. 132; p. 1*]
Comoedia Apocalyptica.
Autore Ioanne Foxo Anglo

PROLOGVS

Salutem uobis, fructumque ex laboribus. [*f. 155v*]
Sibi uicissim a uobis silentium rogat
Poeta nouus, spectatores noui, nouam
Rem dum spectandam profert in proscenium.
Christum quippe triumphantem inferimus. Vtinam   5
Hunc coelitus liceat potius in nubibus
Triumphantem suspicere. Forsan nec diu
Id erit ludi quum iacebunt scenici.
Quippe oculis tum ipsi cuncta contuebimur,
Re quum ipsa mittit nunc quae promittit Deus.   10
Rerum interim per transennam simulachra
Spectare haud pigeat, tantum quae praeludimus.
Res tota sacra est totaque Apocalyptica:
Audita quae multis, nunquam at uisa est prius.
Sacro ergo indulgete silentio, sacris   15
Vt in templis suescitis. Oculos enim sacros
Perinde ac aures esse, qui minus decet? [*p. 2*]
Ecclesiae primum hic qualemcunque faciem
Dabimus, Satanae et tumultuantis furias.
Expressum Antichristum cum Babylonica   20
Cernetis meretricula, quas turbas dabit.
Aderit et Nomocrates, suo qui chirographo
Infestat omnia. Sed in omnibus tamen

CHRIST TRIUMPHANT
An Apocalyptic Comedy
by John Foxe of England

PROLOGUE

Good health to you, and fruit from your labors. Our new poet, in his turn, asks for himself silence of you, new spectators, while he brings onto the stage something new for you to see: to be precise, we bring you Christ Triumphant. Would rather that we could see him coming from heaven, in triumph in the clouds. Perhaps it will not be long before stage representations will lie neglected; then indeed we will see all with our own eyes, when God sends in actual fact what he now only promises. For now, do not be ashamed to view through a netting the images of things, which is all we play. Our matter is totally sacred and totally apocalyptic, what has been heard of by many but never seen before.[1] Therefore indulge us with sacred silence, as you are wont to do in holy churches. For why is it less fitting for the eyes than for the ears to be trained on sacred objects.

Here we will present first, after a fashion, the figure of Ecclesia[2] and the passions of the raging Satan. You will see the Antichrist portrayed, with his Babylonian whore, and the troubles he will cause. Nomocrates too will be here to upset everything with his

---

[1] This is not strictly so: see Herford, pp. 124-125n. But Herford also says that *Christus Triumphans* does not "stand in direct line with anything that had preceded it." See Introduction, p. 38. In the manuscript version, Foxe distinguished between things seen and *read* and was more explicit in describing the source of the "History" as "sacred letters." Such claims to originality were conventional: cf. Milton's statement that *Paradise Lost* treats "Things unattempted yet in Prose or Rhyme" (I.16).

[2] Or, the idea of Ecclesia; the first draft read *Idaeam* for *faciem*. If *primum* is used temporally, the statement is not literally true, for we do not see Ecclesia until III.1. Perhaps Eve and Mary represent the universal church; but the Dedicatory Epistle suggested that they represent soul and body (see p. 209, n. 3); cf. p. 243, n. 2.

Triumphat Christus, scena quod spectabitur.
Fauete igitur linguis, ferteque silentium.   25
Nos pro silentio linguas locabimus.
Nasus ualeat omnis, densque sycophanticus,
Nigrae et loliginis succus, quicquid nigrumque
Est, tristis Aristarchus, mordaxque Memmius.
Musae haud canunt nostrae nisi cum Gratiis.   30
Nos Roscii haud omnes sumus mimi, at neque
Vos Momi spero. Hac spe saltamus fabulam.
Placere actores omnibus;
Prodesse poeta, nocere studet nemini.
Idemque a uobis sibi reposcit mutuum,   35
Vobis et ipse plausurus canentibus.
Comoedia si prolixa sit, at ingens erat
Et multiplex materia. Habet hiatus et
Lamas, fateor, at tam pugnantia nectere
Natura haud rerum patitur. Ast bonis placent   40
Etiam mediocria, malis ne eximia quidem.
Habetis ergo officium Prologi. Rei
Habete nunc summam, summo compendio.   [*p. 3*]
Breue argumentum inquam haud breuis comoediae.

---

27. *sycophanticae*] transliterated from the Greek συκοφαντικός. Plautus uses a
substantive *sycophantia* in the sense deceitfulness (L-S).

writ.[1] But in everything Christ triumphs nevertheless, as will be seen on our stage.

Be kind with your tongues, then, and give us your silence, and we will replace your silence with our words. Let every keen nose be away, and every sharp tooth;[2] farewell to the ink of the black cuttlefish and everything black, to sad Aristarchus[3] and mordant Memmius.[4] Our Muses do not sing at all except with the Graces.[5] We mimes are not all Rosciuses,[6] but neither, I hope, are you Momuses.[7] In this hope we dramatize our fable. The actors want to please everyone, the poet to profit everyone and harm no one.[8] It is really a loan which he asks of you, and when you are doing the playing, he will applaud you. If the comedy be long, its matter was large and complex. It has gaps and bogs, I confess, but the nature of things does not allow such warring elements to be connected. Still, even the mediocre pleases those of good will, and not even something extraordinary pleases those of ill will.

There you have the office of Prologue. Now here is a summary of the matter in very brief form: I shall speak a brief argument of a comedy which is not brief at all.[9]

---

[1] That is, Mosaic law. The word *chirographo* was perhaps taken from the Vulgate, Colossians 2.14: "[Christ blotted out] the handwriting of ordinances that was against us . . . , nailing it to his cross." In the "Panegyricon" appended to B, Foxe twice quotes this verse in Latin (pp. 101, 118).

[2] Cf. Horace, *Satires* I.4.100.

[3] An Alexandrian critic who attacked Homer's poetry and questioned its authenticity. In the manuscript version, Foxe used the name Druso—perhaps Claudius Drusus Nero (cf. Horace, *Carmina* IV.4.18); in DuCange, *drusus* is given with a meaning *contumax*.

[4] Gaius Memmius, to whom Lucretius dedicated *De Rerum Natura*. Sallust admired him (*Jugurthine Wars* 27 and 30), but Cicero, who thought him intellectually shallow, accused him of often prosecuting but seldom defending people (*Brutus* 136, 247). He seems to have been a querulous sort; see Cicero's *Familiar Epistles* 13.1.

[5] There is a pun on the common noun for kindness.

[6] Q. Roscius Gallus was a celebrated Roman actor whose name was proverbial. Cicero defended him in one of his orations.

[7] God of censure, mockery, and laughter, the personification of faultfinding. In Hesiod he appears among the children of Night (*Theogony* 214).

[8] The Horatian doctrine of *utile et dulce* which underlies most Renaissance criticism.

[9] Terence's plays average just over a thousand lines; *Eunuchus*, the longest, has just under 1,100. Plautus' plays are somewhat longer, averaging about 1,200 lines, with *Miles Gloriosus* the longest at 1,437. *Christus Triumphans*, like *Titus et Gesippus*, contains about 1,500 lines.

PERIOCHA

Dvos Euae gnatos accusante Satana,   [*f. 132*]
Nomocrates coelitus accepit chirographum
Quo Psyche in Orcum, Soma Thanato traditur,
Relictis interim tribus Ecclesia
Ex coniuge liberis, Europaeo, Africo,   5
Et Asia. Hos et noxios Nomocrates
Prehendens, in carcere Sciolethro detinet,
Thanato mox traditurus lictori suo.
Ecclesia coepit et ipsa periclitarier.
Rebus sed perditis, humanae ubi nihil   10
Vires potessunt, Christus adest Philanthropos
Nimisque miseros adiutat Adamidas.
   Psychen Gehennae emancipat, spem Somati
Vitae melioris sufficit, Ecclesiae
Tres gnatos exoluit, Pauli ac Petri opera.   15
Nomocratem iure exuit chirographi.
Satanam uinclis mulctat ad annos mille. Is demum
Solutus miras excitat tragoedias
Per Pseudamnum Antichristum, Agni atque Ecclesiae
Hostem. Agnus at triumphat, ac illa ad nuptias   20
Vestitur. Strepit undique theatrum plausibus.

ACTVS I. SCENA I.   [*p. 5*]
Trimetri Iambici.
Eva.

[Eva.]
   Qvod nunc doloris inueniam solatium?
   Lachrymas absumpsi; querelae nihil iuuant.
   Vox neque curis nec spes malis iam sufficit.
   Expers medelae, res ita perit funditus.
   Porro nec quid agam aut quo uortem scio. Flere dum   5
   Licuit, anxio mitius erat animo:
   Lachrimis saltem pasci aegritudo potuit,
   Quae pars mihi nonnulla erat leniminis.
   Iam lachrimae decrescunt, at crescit dolor.
   Diesque aliis quae adimit mihi addit miseriam.   10

ARGUMENT

When Satan brings charges against the two children of Eve, Nomocrates receives from heaven a writ under which Psyche is put into Orcus[1] and Soma[2] is turned over to Thanatus. Soma leaves three children by his wife Ecclesia: Europus, Africus, and Asia. Seizing these also as criminals, Nomocrates holds them in the prison Sciolethrum,[3] intending to turn them over to Thanatus, his lictor. Even Ecclesia herself begins to be threatened. But when all is lost and human powers are of no avail, Christ comes, the philanthropist, and helps the wretched children of Adam. He frees Psyche from Gehenna. He provides Soma with hope of a better life. With the aid of Paul and Peter, he frees the three children of Ecclesia. He strips from Nomocrates the authority of his writ. He sentences Satan to chains for a thousand years. Freed at last, Satan incites wondrous tragedies through Pseudamnus, the Antichrist, enemy of the lamb and of Ecclesia. But the lamb triumphs, and she is dressed for her wedding. On all sides the theater resounds with applause.

[I.1]   *Enter Eve.*

EVE. What solace now can I find for my sorrow? I have used up my tears, and complaints are useless. Words are inadequate for my cares, and hope for my ills. Destitute of a remedy, my situation is utterly lost. I don't know what more to do or where to turn. While I could weep, my troubled spirit was easier: at least my grief could be nourished with tears, and that was a sort of balm for me. Now that my tears grow fewer, my pain grows greater, and the day, which relieves others' misery, only adds to mine.

[1] The classical underworld.
[2] See the notes to the Dramatis Personae.
[3] See the note to the Latin text at III.1.13.

Meam sic lancinat uitam mors filiae,
Quae quanto mallem in hanc non exisset lucem:
Neque illa mala haec, nec ego uiderem moestitiam.
Quanquam parum hoc, mors quod me orbauit filia:
Mutari quod nequeat, ferret necessitas.   15
Nunc Satan habet impurissimus Psychen meam,
Perpetuis Orcus tenet addictam ergastulis,
Mihi quod moeroris merito causa maxima est.
Eoque huc exii nunc foras quando ubi
Consistam nescio, ut eam etsi iuuem nihil,   20
At me gemitu interim lachrimisque expleam   [*f. 132v*]
Gnatae causa, quae dum usque in suppliciis erit,
De me haud unquam supplicium sumere desinam.   [*p. 6*]
Aequum est: mali quae mater fuerim et particeps.
Sed quid mali hoc, mulier quod oppleta lachrimis   25
Vorsus tendit uiam? Sisto me, ut quid ferat
Boni maliue sciam.

ACTUS I. SCENA II.
Trimetri.
Maria. Eua.

[MARIA.]
Mvlier an usquam uictitat altera malis
Onustior, uita aut cui uita sit minus?
At quid meus meruit Iesus tam sonticum,
In quem tanta rabie pontificum exarserit
Lymphata immanitas?
EVA.   Hem, de quo haec filio   5
Agitat?
MARIA.   At ille iam suis functus abiit
Doloribus, mihi dolores crescunt magis.
EVA.
Quid huic turbatum fit, maneam an interrogem?
MARIA.
Vocem quis hic astans intercipit? Ehei,
Dum capto solitudinem, in turbam incidi.   10
EVA.
Quem filium, mulier, aut filiam innuis?

Thus does my daughter's death mangle my life. I would much prefer that she had never come into this world: then she would not have seen her misfortunes, nor I this sadness. But it isn't enough that death has deprived me of my daughter Psyche: what could not be altered, necessity would endure. Now, that infamous Satan has her; Orcus holds her enslaved in perpetual bondage: that by rights is the greatest reason for my sadness. So now, since I don't know where to stay, I've come out here. Even if I can't help my daughter, at least I may glut myself with lamentation and tears on her behalf. So long as she is in torments, I will never stop inflicting her torment on myself. It is only right, since I was the mother of evil and a partner in it. But what's the trouble here, that a tearful woman is coming this way? I'll stand here to find out what good or ill she's bringing.

[I.2]   *Enter Mary.*

MARY. Lives there another woman anywhere more laden with misfortunes? Or a life to whom life is less meaningful? But why has my Jesus deserved such harm, that the maddened savagery of the priests should have been kindled against him in such fury?

EVE [*aside*]. Well, who's the son she's brooding about?

MARY. But he has endured his agonies now and is gone, while my agonies grow the more.

EVE [*aside*]. Should I wait, or ask her why she's so upset?

MARY [*seeing Eve*]. Who's standing here eavesdropping? Alas, I search for solitude and I've stumbled into a crowd.

EVE. Woman, what son or daughter do you mean? And why are

Quidue os saliua distillans composita?
Ludis forsan tu me. At misereri magis,
Non irridere miserorum casus decet.

MARIA.

Vox noua, sed uultus, ut reor, Euam arguit,   15
Antiquam auiam.

EVA   Eua sum, ipsa omnium unica
Aduorsitatum auia, satrix, nutrix, parens:
Maledicta, recto si me nomine dixeris,
Haud alio posthac me titulo appellites.   [*p. 7*]

MARIA.

Falsos omitte questus. Infoelicitas   20
Quid sit, praeter me, experta nulla est foemina.

EVA.

Loquuntur quam stulte multi quae nesciunt!

MARIA.

Miseram satis utramque scio, et quid si Deus
Nos ideo coniunxit pariter, coniuncta uti
Miseria magis sibi foret solatio?   25
Saepe malorum, in malis, comes est dimidium.

EVA.   [*f. 133*]

In aliis spes est, mihi nec Salus opem ferat.

MARIA.

Qui nam? Istuc quod tibi tam graue est scire ardeo
Si fas efferri sit, Eua parens, quae tegis.

EVA.

Hei mihi!

MARIA.   Quicquid sit, aperire utrique meliu'st.   30

EVA.

Hei mihi, hei gnatae uicem!

MARIA   At te comprime qua queas
Ratione si sapis.

EVA.   Sine uero.

MARIA.   Tamet-
si neque mihi minus istuc male est, age
Vice agamus mutua. Vlcus quod tuum est uti
Retegas, tu scies meum.

you driveling continuously? Maybe you're mocking me. It's more proper to pity the misfortunes of the wretched than to ridicule them.

MARY. Your voice is young, but your face, I think, proves you to be Eve, my old grandmother.

EVE. I am Eve herself, the only grandmother of all adversities—and their begetter, nurse, and parent. Cursed, if you would call me by my right name; hereafter call me by no other title.

MARY. Enough of these false complaints! No woman but me has tested what misfortune is.

EVE. How stupidly many speak what they do not know!

MARY. I know we are both wretched enough. Then what if God has brought us together so that our misery might be likewise joined, with greater comfort for itself? In misfortunes, to have a companion is often to halve the misfortunes.

EVE. In others there is hope, but Salus[1] can bring no assistance to me.

MARY. Why? I long to know what's so troublesome to you, Mother Eve, if you're free to tell me what you're concealing.

EVE. Woe is me!

MARY. Whatever it is, it's better to open up to each other.

EVE. Woe is me, and woe for the sake of my daughter.

MARY. But if you are wise, compose yourself with what reason you can muster.

EVE. Do stop.

MARY. Come, though it's no less irksome for me, we'll proceed in turn. You shall know what my sore spot is if you'll reveal yours.

[1] See *Titus et Gesippus* p. 75, n. 1.

Eva.   Age, age, tamet-   35
si quidnam istuc proderit?
Maria.   Etiam pergis?
Eva.   Age, iam
    Scies.
Maria.   Leuius te premet aliis quod exprimis.
Eva.

Gnatam dedit olim summi patris mihi
Benignitas, suam ad ipsius imaginem,
Psychae cui nomen addidi quod animae   [*p. 8*] 40
Haud secus ac in loco mihi erat propriae.
Quid multis? Hanc, cum fratre una pubescere
Dum coepit, mox abrupto aetatis stamine,
Haerentem abripuit mors ingrata amplexibus.
Maria.

Morbon' aut casu alio periit?
Eva.   Pomi scilicet ·   45
Infoelix dum praegusto morsum, pessimus
Acherontico serpens quod aconito imbuit.
Maria.

Miseram mihi tuam, gnataeque uicem praedicas.
Eva.

Imo nihil etiam in hac re miserum.
Maria.   Hem, quid est?

Ah comprime tam longa haec precor suspiria.   50
Quem tandem luctus mulier habebit modum?
Eva.

Vix dum supremam moribunda edidit uocem,
Mox Stygiis Satan aduolat e faucibus,
Luridus, ater, atrox, piceus, proferens
Scriptam e decretis nescio quam syngrapham,   55
Qua Psychen, iure meam, uendicat sibi.
Denique ui correptam, me inuita, filiam
Perpetuos in barathrum ad cruciatus detulit.
Maria.

Quid ais?
Eva.   In perpetuos secum carceres
Satan meam auulsit Psychen, mea uiscera: 60

EVE. All right, but what good it would do——

MARY. Are you still carrying on?

EVE. All right, you shall know it now.

MARY. What you express to others will oppress you less.

EVE. The kindness of the father on high once gave me a daughter, the very image of himself,[1] to whom I gave the name Psyche, because she held for me nothing less than the place of my own soul. Why prolong it? Just when she and her brother began to mature, her thread of life was broken and unpleasant Death snatched her away as she clung to my embraces.

MARY. Did she die of a disease or of some other mishap?

EVE. An apple, to be specific.[2] Unhappily, when I tasted a bite of it, a terrible serpent had imbued it with a hellish poison.

MARY. You're describing your own mishap as well as your daughter's.

EVE. No, there's nothing so terrible even in this.

MARY. Well, what is? [*Eve almost breaks down.*] Oh, restrain those deep sighs, I pray you. What end of grief will woman finally have?

EVE. Scarcely before my dying daughter had uttered her last word, suddenly that ghastly, gloomy, black, and pitchy Satan flew up from the Stygian jaws, producing some sort of writ taken from the laws, by which he claimed Psyche for himself though she's mine by right. Then, over my objection he seized my daughter by force and delivered her into the abyss for perpetual tortures.

MARY. What!

EVE. Into perpetual imprisonment with himself Satan snatched away my Psyche, the fruit of my womb. There he made her a

---

[1] Genesis 1.26.

[2] Genesis 3.6; the apple, of course, is from a much later tradition.

Ibi perpetuis sine ope misera in maeroribus,
Mancipium daemonis agit arbitrio.   [*p. 9*]

MARIA.
Sed quid frater adolescens interim? Illene
Viuit?

EVA.   Soma nempe? Nescio. Nomocrates
Et hunc tyrannus captiuum abduxit suo ac   65
Lictori Thanato in seruitutem tradidit,
Relictis ex Ecclesia tribus domi
Vxore paruulis, Asia, Europo, Africo.

MARIA.   [*f. 133v*]
Miseret me nimis utriusque. At nulla interim
Auxilii lux affulget?

EVA.   Nisi quae omnibus.   70

MARIA.
Quaenam illa?

EVA.   Laeso doloris remedium est
Inimici dolor.

MARIA.   Quid id uerbi uelit?

EVA.
Futurum olim quia audieram, coelitus
Serpenti ut huic teratur tartareum caput.

MARIA.
Vndenam amabo id?

EVA.   Mulieris aiebat ex   75
Semine.

MARIA.   Quam uellem!

EVA.   At quis nunc filius hic tuus,
Quem caesum lachrimas? Ecce quae me uis, ipsa te
Non cohibes.

MARIA.   Iesum dico, meum unigenitum,
Idem quem dedit olim mihi Deus uirgini.

EVA.
Quid, uirgini?

MARIA.   Prorsus uiri sine commercio   80
Cuiusquam, Gabriele paranympho, ac conscio
Iosepho meo.

EVA.   Eho, nae haec tu mira nuncias.

slave under the control of a demon, in eternal sorrows without the slightest chance of assistance.

MARY. But what about her young brother meanwhile? Is he alive?

EVE. Soma, you mean. I don't know. The tyrant Nomocrates carried him off as a captive too and delivered him into servitude to his lictor, Thanatus. Asia, Europus, and Africus—his three little children by his wife Ecclesia—are left at home.

MARY. I'm very sorry for them both. But isn't there any ray of help shining?

EVE. None but that which shines for everyone.

MARY. What's that?

EVE. For the afflicted, an enemy's pain is a remedy of one's own pain.

MARY. What does that mean?

EVE. It will come to pass from heaven, as I once heard, that the hellish head of this serpent will be trodden down.

MARY. How, pray tell?

EVE. From the seed of a woman, it was said.[1]

MARY. How I'd like to be that woman!

EVE. But now who's this son of yours whose death you bewail? Look, don't you hold back what you want me to tell.

MARY. I call him Jesus, my only-begotten son. Like your daughter, God gave him to me some time ago, though I was a virgin.

EVE. What! A virgin?

MARY. Yes, without knowledge of any man. Gabriel was my bridesman, and my husband Joseph knew about it.[2]

EVE. Well! You really report miracles.

[1] A note in B cites Genesis 3.[15].

[2] The draft version, calling Gabriel an intermediary, was closer to the account in Luke I.26.

MARIA.

At mira magis si quae per uitam gesserit
Omnia scias. Sed ne te multis differam: [*p. 10*]
Virtutis ut semper comes it inuidia,   85
Diu celatum bene indicantes odium
In hunc gentis primores iniiciunt manus,
Dehinc ad supplicium infamis rapiunt crucis.
Iamque ex eo secundus hic agitur dies
Quod nec somnum neque cibum capio: pumex   90
Vt non siet, quam ego lachrimando, exuccior.

EVA.

Quodnam ob facinus hanc tantam ausi tyrannidem?

MARIA.

Verum uis dicam?

EVA.   Maxime.

MARIA.   Equidem neque
Causam nec crimen scio. Hei uero maxime Deus,
Quid hic tumultuatum e sublimi audio?   95

EVA.

Et ego.

MARIA.   Coelum nisi ipsum ruat, id quid siet
Miror.

EVA.   Quin expectemus paululum: noui
Aliquid hic monstri coelum opinor parturit.
Magne Deus, fugiamus curriculo. Satan
Ipse est, bilem quantam spirans! Nos ne pariter   100
Vnco praecipitet suo.

ACTUS I. SCENA III.   [*f. 134*]
Eivsdem Rationis.
Satan. Psychephonus. Adopylus.

[SATAN.]

Hoho, quo nunc decidi?
Aut ubi sum, aut quo uertam primum? Nunquam minus
Mei compos in uita prorsus fuerim, ita   [*p. 11*]
Pugnando, cadendo, bile atque insania
Exagitor, neque quid consilii ineam scio.   5

---

88. *infamis*] the MSC reading, *infame,* is possible but metrically inferior.

MARY. But there are more miracles if you knew all that he did in his life. To be brief, though, envy always travels as the companion of virtue. The leaders of our people, revealing openly their long-concealed hatred, set hands on him and dragged him to the punishment of an infamous cross. That was two days ago now,[1] and I've neither slept nor eaten. A pumice stone could not be more dry than I am from weeping.

EVE. For what crime did they dare such terrible tyranny?

MARY. Do you really want me to tell you?

EVE. Very much.

MARY. In fact, I know of no reason, no crime. [*Thunder sounds.*] Great God! Woe indeed! What's this tumult from heaven that I hear?

EVE. I hear it too.

MARY. I wonder what it is, unless the sky itself is falling.

EVE. Let's not stay here an instant. I think the sky is giving birth to some new monstrosity here. Great God, let's run quickly! It's Satan himself, breathing bilious rage. Don't let him drag us down with him on his hook.[2]   [*Exeunt.*

[I.3]   *Enter Satan.*[3]

SATAN. Oh, oh, where have I fallen now? Where am I? Where should I turn first? Never in my life have I been less in possession of myself, I'm so upset by fighting and falling, by anger and madness. I don't know what sort of plan to undertake. I'm turned

[1] It is (more symbolically than actually) the day before Easter.

[2] Perhaps echoing the "hook that was fastened to the neck of condemned criminals, and by which they were dragged to the Tiber" (L-S).

[3] The scene is based on Apocalypse 12.9, but Foxe has distorted the usually accepted chronology by dramatizing the fall of Satan after we have been told of the fall of man and the crucifixion of Christ. This arrangement of the three "falls," together with the implicit allusion to Easter in I.2.89, emphasizes the titular theme; it suggests, moreover, that the telescoping of time in this play is a purposeful artifice: the play does not violate the unity of time if time does not exist in the normal earthly sense. Alternatively, perhaps we should regard the two previous scenes, with characters who (in the revised version of B) do not reappear in the play, as prologue.

Extorris e coelo eliminor, ubi
Loci nihil est reliquum. Hei malum, heu Michael!
Age, fruere quantum libet uictoria,
At non tua tamen, o bone, neque tuis
Parta uirtutibus. Deus si te iuuet   10
Aliquis, quid mirum adeo? Quod si monomachia
Mihi cum iis uelitandum esset angelis
Archangelisque, cherubicae ac seraphicae
Vna licet omnes accedant decuriae, hic
Aut si darentur praesto, ut his ego manibus,   15
Vnguibus ac calcibus raperem, rumperem, agerem,
Discerperem, ruerem, prosternerem,
Excerebrarem, elumbarem, funderem,
Truderem, tunderem, exossarem, denique
Insultarem, pellerem, pulsarem, caederem.   20
Duces primum ipsos torribus inuaderem,
Reliquos dentibus degluberem, postmodum
Coruis darem. Quosdam furcis infigerem,
Exemplis quosque se dignis disperderem.
Oh Psychephonum ac Adopylum uideo.
PSYCHEPHONUS.   Ditis   25
    Hic uocem audire uisus sum an non?
SATAN.   ὦ πόποι,
    Nunccine tandem?   [*p. 12*]
PSYCHEPHONUS.   Quid tandem?
SATAN.   Equidem his si unguibus
    Vos nunc dilaniem, credo id merito fieri.
ADOPYLUS.
    Quid autem?
SATAN.   Stygicolae, mastigiae, perfugae.
PSYCHEPHONUS.
    Qui dum?
SATAN.   Post caedem in auxilium acceditis.   30

26. *Hic uocem audire*] emended from *Audire hic uocem audire* (B) and *Audire hic
uocem* (MSC).
    29. *Stygicolae*] I find no other instance of this compound.

out of heaven. An exile. There's no place left. Oh the misfortune! Oh Michael! Go to, how pleased you are to enjoy your victory! But it isn't your victory, my good fellow, and it wasn't begot by your powers. If some god helps you out, what's so miraculous? But if I'd been able to fight it out alone with those angels and archangels, even if all the divisions of cherubs and seraphs joined in, or if they were suddenly presented to me here, how I'd tear into them with these hands, nails, and feet! I'd smash them and dash them and bash them and gash them and mash them and crash them and hash them and thrash them and gnash them and lash them and slash them; I'd rush them and push them and crush them and squash them.[1] First I'd light into the leaders themselves with firebrands. I'd flay the rest with my teeth and then give them to the crows. I'd nail some to crosses and do them in with punishments worthy of them. Oh, I see Psychephonus and Adopylus.

Enter Psychephonus and Adopylus.

PSYCHEPHONUS. Did I seem to hear the voice of Dis here or not?
SATAN. Oh fie! Here at last?
PSYCHEPHONUS. Why "at last"?
SATAN. Indeed! If I tore you apart with my nails, I think you'd deserve it.
ADOPYLUS. But why?
SATAN. Styx-dwellers, scoundrels, deserters!
PSYCHEPHONUS. Why?
SATAN. After the slaughter's over, you come to help.

---

[1] I have tried to render the tone rather than the precise lexical sense of the passage.

PSYCHEPHONUS.

Quas hic caedes memorat?

SATAN. Eho, caput mihi an

Non totum hoc fissile ac apocopatum cernitis?

PSYCHEPHONUS.

Equidem nihil cerno.

SATAN. At at ego sentio.

ADOPYLUS. Here,

Capitis exors qui sit sentire qui potest?

SATAN.

Dico actam hanc rem esse funditus.

PSYCHEPHONUS. Quid id cedo?   35

SATAN.

Coelo eiecti, forum ac ius omne amisimus.

PSYCHEPHONUS.   [*f. 134v*]

Quid ita?

SATAN.   Michael dum duello me adoritur,

Antiquus hostis, ita luctando diu a meis

Actum est sedulo, uerum quid multis? Inualuit

Demum ille, nos excludimur—uos belluae   40

Dum stertitis.

PSYCHEPHONUS. Bona uerba.

SATAN.   Sed age, sua

Coelicolae trophaea erigant municipes:

Nos tertiam tamen stellarum ducimus

Partem. Postremo in terris, si coelo haud licet,

Inuitis astris etiam ipsis, regnabimus   45

Arbitrio legeque nostra uti uolumus.   [*p. 13*]

Mirari nec satis queo quis tam potens

Michaelis hyperaspistes is fuit

Qui tantum in coelo stratagema hoc dedit.

Verum quid nunc primum exequar? Sequimini   50

Huc intro, Furiae, quid Psyche iam gerat

Reliquique uisam. His duplicata tormina

Faxo haec dum ira est recens. At at, euax quid hic

Reperio? Nullus sum: numen sentio.

32. *apocopatum*] a participial form, apparently without precedent, from the substantive *apocope*.

PSYCHEPHONUS [*to audience*]. What slaughters is he talking about?

SATAN. Oh, don't you see my head all split and cut off?

PSYCHEPHONUS. Really, I see nothing.

SATAN. Oh! I feel it.

ADOPYLUS. Master, if one doesn't have a head, how can one feel it?

SATAN. I tell you it happened—completely.

PSYCHEPHONUS. What happened?

SATAN. We were thrown out of heaven. We lost the field and all our power.

PSYCHEPHONUS. How?

SATAN. While Michael, my old enemy, engaged me in battle, my followers managed through long and vigorous striving to—but why drag it out? He prevailed at last, and we're expelled—while you beasts were snoring.

PSYCHEPHONUS. Sweet words.

SATAN. But let the heavenly burghers set up their victory monuments. We still led off a third of the stars.[1] Even if the stars themselves are against us, at last we'll reign on earth if not in heaven—our judgments, our law, whatever we wish. I can't help wondering who that mighty defender of Michael was who was such a great general in the sky. But now, what to do first? Follow me inside, Furies, to see what Psyche and the others are doing now. I'll make their guts hurt double while my anger is fresh. [*They start through a door, but are thrown back.*] Oh, oh, what do I find here? I'm undone. I feel a divine presence. Who's

---

[1] A note in B cites Apocalypse 12.[4].

Quis tam audax e meis populator atriis,   55
Etiam Psychen meam ductat? Domi ac foris
Videns nolensque mulctor.

ACTUS I. SCENA IIII.
Tetrametri Acatalectici.
Christus Rediuiuus. Psyche. Satan. Psychephonus.
Thanatus. [Adopylus.] Raphael Angelus.

[CHRISTUS.]
Exi ergo mea
Mecum Psyche.

PSYCHE.   Tua uero, quicquid sum, mi Iesu, maximo
Merito tuo.

SATAN.   Ringor.

PSYCHE.   O sanctitas.

PSYCHEPHONUS.   Rumpor.

PSYCHE.   O pietas.

THANATUS.
Occidor.

CHRISTUS. Ero mors tua o mors, morsus inferne tuus.

ADOPYLUS.   Irrideor.

SATAN.
Quid agimus?

PSYCHE.   An unquam cuiquam tot, tam insperata,   [*p. 14*]
tam noua,   5

Tam miranda ac stupenda ostendi? Miserae quantum hoc nunc
mihi,

Praeterque supraque spem omnem, obiicitur gaudium? O
foelicitas.

SATAN.
O infoelicitas.

ADOPYLUS.   Papae numen spirat quantum!

PSYCHE.   Ergo mi
Iesu, astrata genibus tuis, mea uita, mi parens, Deus

---

55. *atriis*] silently emended by L from *atreis*, the reading of B and MSC.
P. H. *Adopylus*] not in B or MSC; see Textual Notes.
3. *sanctitas*] parallel with *pietas* in this line and probably authorial, but possibly
a misreading of MSC's *faustitas*.

such a daring plunderer as even to lead my Psyche out of my halls?[1]
At home and abroad, as I'm forced to admit, I'm abused.

[I.4] *Enter Christ resurrected, leading in Psyche, and Thanatus.*

CHRIST. Come out with me then, my dear Psyche.

PSYCHE. I am yours indeed: whatever I am, my Jesus, is by your
  great desert.

SATAN [*aside*]. Grrr!

PSYCHE. Oh holiness.

PSYCHEPHONUS [*aside*]. I'm shattered.

PSYCHE. Oh piety.

THANATUS [*aside*]. I'm slain.

CHRIST. I will be your death, oh Death, and your sting, oh hell.[2]

ADOPYLUS [*aside*]. I'm mocked.

SATAN. [*aside*]. What to do?

PSYCHE. Has anyone ever been shown so many unhoped-for
  miracles, such stupendous news? How great is this joy now
  thrust upon me in my wretchedness, joy above and beyond my
  every expectation! Oh happiness!

SATAN. [*aside*]. Oh unhappiness!

ADOPYLUS [*aside*]. Strange how much majesty he breathes!

PSYCHE. Therefore, my dear Jesus, I prostrate myself at your knees,
  my life, my father, my God. My redeemer and only salvation,

---

[1] Symbolically, of course, the reference is to spiritual redemption, but Foxe
seems to have had in mind the old tradition of the harrowing of hell. Bienvenu,
however, denied that Foxe had this papist idea seriously in mind and called the
passage an example of poetic license.

[2] A note in B refers to Oseae 13.[14]. Foxe needed no contemporary inspiration
to use this passage (or its echo in 1 Corinthians 15.55, which Foxe used in III.5),
but the letter "Ad Pivm Lectorem" prefaced to Nicolaus Bartolomaeus' *Christus
Xylonicus* in the 1540 Basel anthology of *Comoediae ac Tragoediae Aliquot ex Novo et
Vetere Testamento Desumptae* also cites it. Cf. p. 283, n. 1.

Meus. Redemptor ac salus unica, mea iam non sum, ita   10
Tuis istis me totam factis facis tuam.

CHRISTUS.   Filius in hoc
Apparuit Dei, opera ut dissipet diaboli.

THANATUS.   Hei malum.

SATAN.
Mirando, stupendo, insaniendo non sum apud me.

CHRISTUS.   En accipe
Nunc immortalitatis Psyche tibi in palmis palmarium hoc. [*f. 135*]
Quid trepidas, animula mea?

PSYCHE.   Eccum illum, a dextris imminet
       meus   15
       Satan.

SATAN.   Oh, uisus sum.

CHRISTUS.   Hostem libro hoc percellito.

SATAN.   Hei mactor miser.

CHRISTUS.
Dico tibi, chirographum redde huc sceleste obligatorium.

SATAN.
Nam qua lege illud cedo?

CHRISTUS.   Insontem qua me mactastis, Satan.   [*p. 15*]
Meministin' factum?

SATAN.   Vah, funditus prorsusque conteror.

CHRISTUS.
Cape nunc, Psyche, ut affigatur cruci.

SATAN.   Proh nunc intelligo: 20
Hinc uis Michaelis illa, et coelo et terris spolior.

CHRISTUS.   Data est
Omnis mihi potestas in coelo et terra. Heus heus, Raphael,
Clauem hanc abyssi sume cum capistro. Age, mysanthropum hunc
Mastigiam faxis alligatum in tartara.

THANATUS.   Scitum est fugere in loco.

RAPHAEL.
Factum mi princeps accurabitur.

CHRISTUS.   Annos per mille, impetum   25
Ne quem det, firmetur, locumque signes signaculo meo.

by your deeds you make me so completely your own that I no longer belong to myself.

CHRIST. In this has appeared the son of God to scatter the works of the devil.

THANATUS [*aside*]. Oh terrible!

SATAN [*aside*]. I'm so astonished and stupefied and out of my senses that I'm beside myself.

CHRIST. Well now, Psyche, take into your hands this prize of immortality. My little soul, why do you tremble?

PSYCHE. Look there, my enemy Satan threatens us from the right.

SATAN [*aside*]. Oh, I've been seen.

CHRIST. Smite the enemy with this book.[1] [*Taking the book, she beats Satan.*]

SATAN. Oh, I'm slain horribly.

CHRIST. You scoundrel, I tell you, return that binding writ to me.[2]

SATAN. Under what law?

CHRIST. Because you sacrificed me, an innocent, Satan. Do you remember doing that?

SATAN. Oh, I'm completely bruised, from the bottom up.

CHRIST [*giving Psyche Satan's writ*]. Psyche, now take it so it can be nailed to a cross.

SATAN. Oh, now I recognize you: Michael's power came from you, and I'm deprived of both heaven and earth.

CHRIST. All power in heaven and earth is given to me.[3]—— Ahoy, Raphael.

Enter Raphael.

Take this key to the abyss and this chain. Go tie up this misanthropic rogue in hell.

THANATUS [*aside to Adopylus and Psychephonus*]. In this situation it's a good idea to run.   [*Exeunt Thanatus, Psychephonus, and Adopylus.*

RAPHAEL. It shall be attended to, my prince.

CHRIST. Let him be chained for a thousand years,[4] that he may mount no attack. Mark the place with my seal.——

[*Raphael leads Satan out.*

[1] In the draft version, ". . . with this cross."
[2] A note in B refers to Colossians 2.[14].
[3] A note in B cites Matthew 28.[18].
[4] A note in B refers to Apocalypse 20.[1-3].

Euge ad discipulos nunc accede mecum, Psyche, una huius ut
Fiant simul euangelii participes. Mox ad patrem
Feremur in paradisum pariter, fratrem ubi Soma tuum
Laeta expectabis interim.   30

ACTUS II. SCENA I.
Senarii.
Raphael.

[RAPHAEL.]
    Captiuus nunc summi imperio principis,
    Annos ad mille, magnus firmatur Satan:
    Queisque alios strinxit, stringitur ipse uinculis.   [*p. 16*]
    Post rursus e latebris laxandus paululum,
    Quo secum in errorem pessundet plurimos   5
    Orbemque seducat latum, quo tempore
    Ecclesia tristibus est agitanda casibus.
    Interea Pornapolis, mutuata daemonis
    Tyrannide, late instabit, uicariam
    Vicem administrans illius quam fortiter.   10
    Tumultus illa in orbe non paruos dabit,
    Suo cum Diocte, quanquam nisi corpora
    Nihil laedet ille aliud mortalium. Interim
    Psychae equidem nostrae nostrisque in coelo omnibus
    Res sic in tuto collocatas gratulor,   15
    Quo nomine Agno perpetuae sint gratiae,
    Sanguine qui tantum peperit hoc palmarium.
    Iam quantis hoc Mariam nostram gaudiis
    Ac Euam praecipue ipsam perfundet cogito
    Vbi haec quae gesta sunt ita esse audiuerint.   [*f. 135v*]   20
    Sed perfectis iam rebus, ad herum me reuortier
    Tempus monet, ubi nihil hic cur maneam aliud est.

Good. Now, Psyche, go with me to my disciples that they may share this good news one and all. Soon we'll be taken together to my father in paradise, where for the time being you will happily await your brother Soma.[1]   [*Exeunt.*

[II.1]   *Enter Raphael.*

RAPHAEL. The mighty Satan now is held captive for a thousand years by order of the highest prince, bound in the very chains with which he bound others.[2] After a little while he's to be released again from the shades, to sink many into error with himself and to lead the wide world astray. At that time Ecclesia must be tormented with grievous misfortunes. Meanwhile, Pornapolis, assuming the demon's tyranny and with great vigor administering his office in his stead, will push his menace far and wide.[3] She'll visit no small disorders on the world, helped by her friend Dioctes, though he will harm nothing in mortals except their bodies. For now, I rejoice for our Psyche and for all our people in heaven that their cases are so safely disposed. For that reason let eternal thanks be given to the lamb, who obtained this great prize with his blood. I can imagine how great are the joys this will inspire in our Mary and especially in Eve when they hear of the things which have happened. But now that my business is finished, it's time to return to my master, since there's no other reason for me to stay here.[4]   [*Exit.*

---

[1] The theological reference is to the immediate spiritual redemption, to be followed at the Last Judgment by the resurrection of the body.

[2] A note in B cites Apocalypse 20.[3, 7-8].

[3] A note in B cites Apocalypse 13.[1-2]. Foxe follows one of several venerable traditions in interpreting the first beast as Rome (whore city), presumably because its seven heads represented the seven hills of Rome, its ten horns the ten persecutions by the Caesars.

[4] After this scene in the manuscript version appears a scene showing Eve and Mary, who are introduced after Raphael notes their approach:

EVE. Now I see that nothing could happen to men which is so much beyond hope and belief that the power of God does not outstrip it.

MARY. I must look for Eve, wherever she is, so I may tell her the news of my daughter.

EVE. Stop, Mary. I know everything.

ACTUS II. SCENA II.   [*f.136*]
Tetrametri Acatalectici
Archiereus. Nomologus. Saulus. Polyharpax Scriba.

[ARCHIEREUS.]
    Ain uero, Nomologe, adhuc reperiantur qui in nomine hoc
    Praedicare perstitant?

NOMOLOGUS.   Nimium.

ARCHIEREUS.   Imperium nec uererier   [*p. 17*]
    Nostrum, nec minis neque exemplis porro terrerier?

NOMOLOGUS.
    Certissime.

2. *perstitant*] B and MSC agree on this unprecedented reading, probably a coined intensive of *persto*.

2-3. *uererier . . . terrerier*] my translation misses the quadruple rhyme.

[II.2]   *Enter Archiereus and Nomologus.*[1]

ARCHIEREUS. Nomologus, do you mean people are still found who
  persist in preaching in his name?
NOMOLOGUS. Too true.
ARCHIEREUS. Don't they respect our authority? Haven't threats or
  punishments been used to frighten them?
NOMOLOGUS. Of course.

MARY. You know my news?
EVE. Yes. I heard it, saw it, believe it, the thing which transports me beyond all
  human joys. I'm dreaming unless I see what I desire to see, for I see you,
  Psyche, now reborn from the depths.
MARY. God love me, I'm happy.
EVE. Oh, what power of words can be given me great enough, father on high,
  to celebrate your divinity sufficiently and as I would like? Oh charity! What
  piety this is! And that you undertake so much labor for my sake, my Jesus,
  and because of my Psyche! Besides, you promise the right of your kingdom to
  my son Sarcobius.
MARY. Eve, didn't I often tell you that my mind foresaw something great from
  this boy?
EVE. I remember. And the more I think about God, the more I wonder at his
  prudence. Salvation vanished because of a woman; now it is restored again
  because of a woman. In me nature begot death; in you grace comes to life,
  that the salvation of everyone would be due to grace, not to nature. In me
  the most just God exposed the worth of sin and showed his anger; in you, in
  turn, he opened the arms of his pity.
MARY. I don't know about other women, but I know I have never deserved
  anything worthy of this son except that it seemed good to God to confer on
  men who are not at all great the great kindnesses which they had not expected.
EVE. You speak very truly. And now I think I have lived long enough, and it is
  a pleasure to leave since I've now seen with my own eyes these things which
  have happened to my children and to me and to my offspring.
MARY. But now it's time to hurry to Mt. Horeb with the apostles and also the
  other disciples, Eve. My son promised to have some sort of business there in
  a little while, and said we must not be late. [?A reference to the Ascension on
  Mt. Olivet; Acts 1.9.]
EVE. Let's go.
MARY. But quickly, my dear, for look, the chief priest is almost here—the wolf in
  the fable, as they say.

[1] From the note beside l. 1 in B citing Acts 4.[1-2], we can identify Archiereus,
the chief priest, as Annas. Nomologus is probably a Sadducee: note his social
pride in condemning the low-caste Christians (ll. 7-11), consistent with the
aristocratic Sadduces; and compare the meaning of his name. In the draft version
of this scene, Nomologus' speeches are assigned to Machonomus (= Dioctes),
and some of Archiereus' to Thanatus.

ARCHIEREUS. Monstri simile. At unde haec tibi certa? Qui sciam?
NOMOLOGUS.

Vidi, audiui, interfui. Denique semper, nescio   5
Quo successu, haec gliscit secta magis, ita ut rem ipsam Dei
Dicas uoluntate geri, horum usque adeo crescit indies
Numerus.

ARCHIEREUS.   Hi quinam sint audire gestio.
NOMOLOGUS.   Quos credis, nisi

Ex ima fece: fracti ciceris emptores, telonii,
Agasones, sutores, iisque consimiles, ex triuiis   10
Ac compitis circumforanei.

ARCHIEREUS.   Hui! Plebs uidelicet

Abiecta atque execrabilis, Deum qui nesciunt.

NOMOLOGUS.   Sane.
ARCHIEREUS.

Et quid tandem hi neotorculi adferunt?

NOMOLOGUS.   Christum se credere

Rediuiuum ac uidisse: huius se testes oculatos asserunt.

ARCHIEREUS.

Profecto, quantum suspicor, celere nisi malo huic remedium   15
Reperimus, plus mortuus incommodi quam olim uiuus dabit.

NOMOLOGUS.

Haud dubium est.

ARCHIEREUS.   Tum hoc, nunc aliud persentio.
NOMOLOGUS.   Quidnam? [*p. 18*]
ARCHIEREUS.   Hinc nobis fames

Illa, omniumque penuria rerum, hinc coeli intemperies,
Pestes, podagrae, porrigines, alias praeter uitae grauedines,
Quae haud aliunde quam ex secta hac pullulant.

NOMOLOGUS.   Veri nimis   20

Simile.

ARCHIEREUS.   Itaque quid nunc agam in hac re cogito, nec etiam
satis adhuc
Certum scio.

---

13. *neotorculi*] I find no other instance of this compound; *torculum*, literally a wine press, was sometimes used for a printing press. Foxe may have intended a pun on *neotericus*, new, which LTL glosses, "Scriptores neoterici, quibus antiqui opponuntur."
17.] as in MSC; B prints as two verses, broken after *persentio*.

ARCHIEREUS. Monstrous. But how may I know these things which you're so sure about?

NOMOLOGUS. I saw them, I heard them, I was there. Besides, I don't know how, but this sect keeps growing bigger: their number increases so much every day that you would say it's happening by the will of God.[1]

ARCHIEREUS. I want to know who these people are.

NOMOLOGUS. Who do you think? The dregs of humanity: sellers of broken chickpea, customs men, ostlers, cobblers, people like that, vagrants from the wrong side of town.[2]

ARCHIEREUS. Whew! The mean and detestable mob, of course, people who don't know God.

NOMOLOGUS. Quite right.

ARCHIEREUS. And what, pray, are these new presses publishing?[3]

NOMOLOGUS. That they believe in Christ resurrected, that they've seen him; they claim they were eyewitnesses.

ARCHIEREUS. Well, I strongly suspect that unless we find a remedy quickly for this ailment, he'll cause us more trouble dead than he did alive.

NOMOLOGUS. There's no doubt about it.

ARCHIEREUS. Then there's this other strong feeling that I have.

NOMOLOGUS. What's that?

ARCHIEREUS. This is the source of our famine, the scarcity of everything, the bad weather, the plagues, gouts, dandruffs,[4] not to mention the other ailments in our lives, which sprout forth from no other cause than from this sect.

NOMOLOGUS. Too true.

ARCHIEREUS. So I wonder what I should do now in this matter; I'm still not sure.

[1] Cf. Acts 4.4. With the opening words of this speech cf. below, p. 416, l. [6.
[2] Cf. Acts. 4.13.
[3] See note to Latin text.
[4] In the draft version, "wars."

NOMOLOGUS.   Quid agas, nisi τῶν χειρῶν, quod aiunt, νόμῳ?
   Haereticos proteras probe ferro, flamma, elementisque omnibus.
   Dignitatem in primis procures uestram sarta tectaque ut
   Siet. In omnes synagogas mittendi cereales, qui haereses,   25
   Blasphemias, schismata uolgi fortiter instrepitent auribus.
   Molliores qui sient sacerdotiis, offa uelut
   Vncta, facile quo uelis prolicies. Cui ego palmarium
   Tribuo. Reliquos ui, qua potest, pugnabitis. Sin, uti fit,
   Se habent clam, omni sub lapide scorpius sese tegat   *[f. 136v]*
     aliquis   30
   Ne cui quid sit tutum undique. Verum illud discipli-
     nae erit: *[p. 19]*
   Nisi ex concilio nihil hos aduersus mouerier. Ita
   Honestior erit, honeste fucatur quae, crudelitas.
ARCHIEREUS.
   Scite mones, etsi neque prorsus immemorem.
NOMOLOGUS.   Credo. Quid enim
   Tam affabre dici possit uigilantia quin praeeat tua?   35
SAULUS.
   Pontificem platea modo hac praeteriisse dictitant,
   Atque praesto eccum.
ARCHIEREUS.   Quid Saulus adueniens apportitat?
SAULUS.
   Summam consummato salutem pontifici.
ARCHIEREUS.   Expecto quid
   Rerum nuncias.
SAULUS.   Nae nos ignauiae omnes merito
   Incusandi sumus, hos qui pingues pexosque haud reprimimus   40
   Piscatorculos, hominem qui hunc nunquam populi cessitant
   Ingerere auribus ac Mosen fasque omne inuertere. Quod adeo
   Haud fit nostra nisi ex incuria, dum nemo horum obuiam it
   Audaciae. Quod si me ad hanc prouinciam idoneum satis
   Statuitis organum, age, literis inautorate me   45

---

25. *cereales*] DuCange lists the word in the sense messenger, servant.
26. *instrepitent*] normally an intransitive verb.
45. *inautorate*] DuCange lists the word as equivalent of *cooptare*.

NOMOLOGUS. What would you do except, as they say, use the law
of force? Wear down these heretics properly, with iron and flame
and all the elements.[1] Your first care should be for your authority,
that your house will be in good repair. Send your servants into
all the synagogues to drum into the ears of the mob their heresies,
blasphemies, and schisms. The more pliant among them you'll
easily entice to your will with priesthoods, an anointed morsel,
so to speak: I think that's the best course. The rest you'll oppose
with as much force as you can. But if, as they usually do, they hold
to their ways in secret, let a scorpion be concealed under every
stone so there'll be no safety anywhere for any of them. But it
will truly be the way of policy to take no action against them
except by the authority of the council. In that way your cruelty
will be more respectable because it's painted to look respectable.
ARCHIEREUS. Wise advice, but you're not advising a completely
ignorant man.
NOMOLOGUS. I believe that, for what could be said so cleverly that
your vigilance would not anticipate it?

Enter Saul.[2]

SAUL. Everyone says the priest has just passed this way. Look, there
he is.
ARCHIEREUS. Saul is coming. What does he have on his mind?
SAUL. The best of health to you, most exalted priest.
ARCHIEREUS. I'm waiting for your report of things.
SAUL. We all really deserve to be called cowards for not suppressing
these doltish, wool-headed fishermen who keep hammering that
man into the ears of the people and upsetting Moses and the
whole divine law. This surely wouldn't happen except for our
neglect in that no one is hindering their audacity. But if you
appoint me to this business as your proper instrument——, well,

---

[1] In the draft version, all four elements (fire, earth, air, and water) are represented (with "cross" standing for air).
[2] A note in B refers to Acts 9.[1-2].

Vestris in hos ut liceat quid uelim quidque ualeam,   [*p. 20*]
   paululum
Experirier.

ARCHIEREUS.   Quid ages cedo?

SAULUS.   Egone? Quod dignum sit in
   Maleficos, quodque omnes, quum sit factum, dicetis probe.

NOMOLOGUS.
   Probe dicis.

ARCHIEREUS.   At enim, si populus interim quid?

SAULUS.   At enim
   Experiundo scies.

ARCHIEREUS.   Verum age, quo te mitti primum postulas?   50

SAULUS.
   Damascum me zelus uocat impotens: plurimum ibi assuescere
   Audio.

ARCHIEREUS.   Dic, zelus unde hic tantus te incessit, cedo?

SAULUS.   Nescio,
   Nisi quia iamdudum in hos insigne aliquid edere flagrat
   Animus, et spero profore.

ARCHIEREUS.   Mirum Nomologe, nobis nisi
   Quoquo modo usui siet hic adolescens.

NOMOLOGUS.   Idem et ego arbitror.   55

ARCHIEREUS.
   Age, sino quod uelis.

SAULUS.   At quo maturius, hoc consultius.
   Principiis occurrendum ilico, ne sero post, ac cum uelis,
   Non liceat.

ARCHIEREUS. Heus heus, Polyharpax.

POLYHARPAX.   Quis euocator hic? Here,
   Tu quid uis?   [*p. 21*]

ARCHIEREUS.   Saulo huic quamprimum ut concinnentur literae
   A nobis mandatoriae. Faxis uide.

POLYHARPAX.   Videbitur.   60

ARCHIEREUS.
   Appenso sigillo insuper e plumbo ceraque duplici.
   Audin'? Ad Damascenos.

46. *hos*] emended, following MSC and Le, from B's *nos*.

authorize me with credentials from you to try a little something against them, whatever I wish and whatever I can.

ARCHIEREUS. Pray what will you do?

SAUL. I? What should be done to criminals. And when it's done, you'll all say it was done well.

NOMOLOGUS. That's the way to talk.

ARCHIEREUS. Yes, but what if the people, however——

SAUL. Yes, but you'll know by trying it.

ARCHIEREUS. Well, tell me, where do you ask to be sent first?

SAUL. An uncontrollable desire pulls me to Damascus, where I hear they're especially strong.

ARCHIEREUS. Please tell me why this great zeal has seized you.

SAUL. I don't know, except that for a long time my mind has burned with a desire to do something notable against these people, and I hope it will do some good.

ARCHIEREUS. Nomologus, I wouldn't be surprised if this young fellow were useful to us in some way.

NOMOLOGUS. I agree.

ARCHIEREUS. Well, I grant your request.

SAUL. But the faster the better. We must strike now, while it's still early, lest later on, when you might wish to do something, it not be possible.

ARCHIEREUS [*shouts*]. Hey there, Polyharpax.

Enter the scribe Polyharpax.

POLYHARPAX. Who's calling here? Master, what do you wish?

ARCHIEREUS. Our commission to Saul here must be prepared as quickly as possible. See to it.

POLYHARPAX. It shall be seen to.

ARCHIEREUS. With a seal of lead and double wax affixed on top, do you hear? To the Damascenes.

POLYHARPAX.   Fiet.
ARCHIEREUS.   At accurate.
POLYHARPAX.   Fiet.
ARCHIEREUS.   Et
   Mature.
POLYHARPAX.   Quin factum puta.
ARCHIEREUS.   Restat nunc Herodes mihi,
   Ita ut decreui, conueniendus, Petrum, quem in neruo habet, uti
   Nobis producat ad necem. Os ita aliis oppilabimus.   65
   Hoc principio nunc exequar. Ades, Nomologe, mecum una.

ACTUS II. SCENA III.   [*f. 137*]
Senarii.
Petrus.

[PETRUS.]
   Qvid hoc rei est? Quae platea est? Aut ubi sum? Vbi
   Is qui perduxit huc? Aut dormis forsitan,
   Petre, aut uigilas. Mortuus an uiuus haec
   Video? Aut ludit me imago noctis aliqua?
   At quantum me sentio, experrectus sum probe.   5
   Collustro ac circumspecto clare singula.
   An non uicus hic est piscinam secus, sacrum
   Spectans templum uorsus? Ehem, euge manum scilicet
   Domini agnosco Iesv, qui me ferreo
   Herodis emancipauit ab ergastulo   [*p. 22*]   10
   Viaeque ductorem praemisit angelum,
   Qui, primum disiecta catena duplici
   Repansisque ultro e ferro foribus, uiam
   Per medias placide patefecit custodias.
   Nuncque a me quo repente euasit nescio   15
   Bonus ille hodoeporus meus, nisi id scio: libere
   Quo nunc animo libitum est ut ire liceat.
   Ac cum ad me nunc redeo magis, est hic meus   [*f. 137v*]

   7. *piscinam*] normally meaning a fish-pond or swimming pool, here probably meaning a fishmarket.
   16. *hodoeporus*] transliterated from the Greek ὁδοιπόρος, used by Homer for a comrade. Jerome used *hodoeporicon* for an itinerary (L–S). Bienvenu translates Foxe's word as "sauuegarde."

POLYHARPAX. It will be done.

ARCHIEREUS. But carefully.

POLYHARPAX. It will be done.

ARCHIEREUS. And quickly.

POLYHARPAX. Consider it done.   [*Exeunt Polyharpax and Saul.*

ARCHIEREUS. Now, as I've decided, it remains for me to meet with Herod so he'll turn Peter over to us for execution. He has him in prison now. That way we'll stop up the mouths of the others. I'll take care of this right now. Nomologus, come with me.[1]

[*Exeunt.*

[II.3]   *Enter Peter.*[2]

PETER. What's happening? What street is this? Where am I? Where's the person who brought me here? Peter, are you asleep or awake? Am I seeing this dead or alive? Is some apparition of the night playing a trick on me? But as far as I can tell, I'm very much awake. As I look around me, I recognize everything. Isn't this the street beside the fishmarket, looking toward the holy temple?[3] Aha, of course! I recognize the hand of the Lord Jesus. He freed me from Herod's iron prison and sent an angel to lead the way. The angel broke the double chain, then threw open the iron gates, and quietly made a path through the middle of the guards. How my good guide has slipped away from me so suddenly I don't know, but I do know how much of a pleasure it is to my spirit to be able to move freely. And now that I'm regaining

---

[1] In the manuscript draft, Thanatus goes to consult with priests, and we see next a short scene in which Sarcobius (= Soma), a leading figure in that version, laments that, because of the madness of the priests, one may not venture safely out of doors; he is then invited by Rhodus (named for Rhoda in Acts 12.13) to come to Mark's house and pray for the imprisoned Peter.

[2] A note in B cites Acts 5, but the scene is actually based on Acts 12.

[3] Foxe may have had a particular setting in mind here, as he did later in V.2. 20-31. From the thirteenth century on, Basel had a fish market, along a canal called Der Birsig, near the Rhine. If this was the market which Foxe had in mind, he could have been looking east toward the Münster or west toward St. Peter's. See a representation of fourteenth-century Basel in the endpapers of *Basel in Vierzehnten Jahrhundert* (Basel, 1836), in which the fish market is No. 39.

Marcus uicinus quidam. Ibi proximum est ubi
Memet recipiam, ut hanc illi primulum   20
Laetitiam obiiciam. Post id, mox ad alios
Itemque ad alios me fratres transferam,
Vt omnes tam stupenda haec prodigia Dei
Spectent illiusque praedicent potentiam.

ACTUS II. SCENA IIII.
Trimetri Iambici.
Anabasius.

[ANABASIUS.]

Adsum, Anabasius e profundis manibus,
Ad Pornapolim meretricem illam Babel
Cum missititiis a Plutone literis:
Obuinctus ipse cum sit, haec uicem suo
Cum Diocte imperii legatam ut obeat   5
Donec, Tartareo exolutus carcere,
Annorum post chiliada emergat denuo;
Simul ut renunciem, in Iesum hunc uirus suas
Ac uires omnes euomat, aut, si nihil   [*p. 23*]
In hunc modo restat mortalis quod manus   10
Valeat, in suos saltem conuertat impetum.
In hoc omnem explicet uim neruosque exerat:
Huius amicos nactus quoscunque fuerit,
Spoliet, instet, terra marique persequens—
Quo iure, quaque iniuria, refert nihil.   15
Iniuria parua est hostem qua uindices.
Haec scilicet in mandatis ut dedit herus.
Nunc peragam ordine quo iussit omnia.

ACTUS II. SCENA V.
Tetrametri Acatalectici, cum Catalecticis.
Polyharpax. Saulus. [*Populus.*]

[POLYHARPAX.]

Confectae sunt literae herus cui iussit adolescentulo: ubi uolet,

---

3. *missititiis*] MSC has the correct form, *missitiis;* Foxe probably altered the word in revision, coining an intensive form for the sake of the metrics.

4. *Obuinctus*] *vincio* is common, but I have not found other uses of *obvincio*.

II.5.P.H. *Populus*] omitted in B and MSC.

my senses, my friend Mark lives somewhere near here. There's his neighborhood. I'll go there to give this happy news to him first. After that, I'll go right away, first to some of the brethren and then to others, so that everyone may behold these stupendous miracles of God and celebrate his power.

[II.4]   *Enter Anabasius.*

ANABASIUS. I am Anabasius from the deepest shades,[1] come to the famous whore of Babylon, Pornapolis, with letters sent by Pluto. Since he's enchained, she and her lover Dioctes are to assume his seat of rule in his stead until he is released from his prison in Tartar and emerges again after a thousand years. Also I must direct her to spit out venom and exert all her energies against that fellow Jesus; or, if nothing remains to be done against him because his mortal power is so strong,[2] to turn her attack upon his followers at least. She should unfurl all her power in this task, use all her might. When she lights on any of his friends, she should plunder them and chase after them, pursue them by land and sea, with what justice or injustice it matters not: injustice is trivial if you take vengeance on an enemy with it. This, of course, is in the commission which my master has given. Now I must carry out everything in the way he commanded.   [*Exit.*

[II.5]   *Enter Polyharpax.*[3]

POLYHARPAX. The letter's finished for the young fellow my master ordered it for. It's ready when he wants it. I'm surprised he isn't

---

[1] A note in B cites Acts 13, but this must be an error for Apocalypse 13. In the earliest version, Pluto's letters are to Abadon, who is to be Pluto's (i.e., Satan's) viceroy.

[2] Foxe may have meant ". . . because his human hand waves good-bye," i.e., he has left the earth; cf. Prologue 27.

[3] Bienvenu omitted this comic scene from his translation.

Praesto sunt. Ac miror non comparere. At in ipsa ellum obuiam
Prospicio fabula, oculi nisi prospiciunt parum.
SAULUS.   Ehem, tun' hic,
Polyharpax, tam cito?
POLYHARPAX.   Iamdudum aetatem.
SAULUS.   Aduenienti quid obiter
Remorae obiectum ni esset, praeuortissem.
POLYHARPAX.   Atque ego non dico
nunc,   5
Domi interim dispendia, mora ex hac, quanta suffero
Hic te dum expecto commorans.   *[p. 24; f. 138]*
SAULUS.   Credo. Attamen de schedulis
Quid? Transactan' res est?
POLYHARPAX.   Prorsus pol, ac diligenter.
SAULUS.   Amo
Te. Cedo Polyharpax ergo ubi sunt, ut dissoluar hinc?
POLYHARPAX.
Non secus hercle pro germano, Saule, ac si agendum esset meo. 10
SAULUS.
Credo, habeoque gratiam. At ubi interim syngrapha?
POLYHARPAX.   At si scias
Quantum in ea re mihi sudatum sit! Praeter id, quod bis eadem
Rescribenda fuerant.
SAULUS.   Vsuuenire solet, scio. At pridem
Me expectant comites.
POLYHARPAX.   Iam quod aliis saepe accidit, aliis
Qui instrumenta conficiunt quemadmodum qui in uestibus,   15
Causas per se bonas, male tractando, reddunt non bonas:
Alii incuria, quidam studio, multi etiam inscitia,
Vel pretereundo quae maxime opus, saepe uel addendo quae
Nihil iuuant. Quorum hic nihil fit, ut hic ne dicam insuper.
SAULUS.
Dico, Polyharpax, iam haud uacat auscultare pluribus.   *[p. 25]*
Proin   20
Ita, herus ut iussit, me absolutum facito.

---

2. *At in*] ?read *Ac in*, as in MSC.

here. But look, even as I'm talking, I see him coming, unless my eyes are bad.

Enter Saul.

SAUL. Well, are you here so quickly, Polyharpax?

POLYHARPAX. Ages ago.

SAUL. If I hadn't been delayed on the way, I would have been here before you.

POLYPHARPAX. And I won't go into the great amount of time I'm losing at home because of this delay while I'm standing around waiting for you.

SAUL. I believe it. But what about my commission? Is it finished?

POLYHARPAX. Completely and carefully.

SAUL. I love you. Pray, then, where is it, Polyharpax, so I can get on my way?

POLYHARPAX. By Hercules, Saul, just as if I had had to do it for my own brother.

SAUL. I believe it, and I'm grateful. But now where's the document?

POLYHARPAX. But if you knew how much I've sweated on this thing! Besides, these things had to be written twice.

SAUL. That's usually necessary, I know. But my companions have been waiting for me a long time.

POLYHARPAX. What often happens when some fellows prepare documents for others is that by handling badly causes which in themselves are good, they render them not so good, after the manner of tailors: some through inattention, some through overeagerness, many even through ignorance, either by skipping what is most important or often by adding what doesn't do any good. To say no more about it, none of these things happened in the present case.

SAUL. I tell you, Polyharpax, I don't have time to listen to you any longer, so let me get going, as your master ordered.

POLYHARPAX.   Propudium ut nihil
  Intelligit.
SAULUS.   Quidnam?
POLYHARPAX.   Si nescis, dicam. Nummulis erant
  Perungendi aliquot lassati articuli.
SAULUS.   Haud recte forsitan,
  Polyharpax, me tenes. Theologus sum, pigmenta nescio.
POLYHARPAX.   Age,
  Satis pernosti quid uelim. Quid opus uerbis?
SAULUS.   Tametsi ea   25
  Ad me res nihil attinet nec quicquam inde prorsus mihi
  Praeter laborem metitur, tamen ut ne producas longius,
  Cape modo.
POLYHARPAX.   Quid hoc?
SAULUS.   Drachma. Satis pro re nostra hocque
    labore imputo.
POLYHARPAX.
  Ha, ha, hae.
SAULUS.   Quid rides?
POLYHARPAX.   Suauem hominem ac scitum.
SAULUS.   Nam quid ita?
POLYHARPAX.
  Quasi hactenus in ciuitate haud usquam uixeris, ut uita quae   30
  Fert hominum nescias.
SAULUS.   Sic uita cuiquam haec est quisque ut uelit
  Esse homini. Qui recte sciunt uti haud a uita ipsi, at ab his
  Vita regitur. Verum ne longum faciam, potius plura quam
  Secter, hem didrachmum: cedo literas.   [*p. 26*]
POLYHARPAX.   Imo harum tibi
  Redemptio quinque solidum est, si emptas uelis.
SAULUS.   Ah iniquus 35
  Nimium, Polyharpax, ne sis.
POLYHARPAX.   Nunc pecuniam an scripta potius
  Penes me utrum horum uelis, id tecum supputa.
SAULUS.   Vah, dic mihi.
POLYHARPAX.
  Quid?
SAULUS.   An te nil pudet?

POLYHARPAX [*to the audience*]. It's shameful how little he knows.

SAUL. Why?

POLYHARPAX. If you don't know, I'll tell you. My weary fingers should have been greased with a little money.

SAUL. Polyharpax, perhaps you have the wrong idea about me. I'm a theologian; I know nothing of these material things.

POLYHARPAX. Come, you know well enough what I want. What need is there of words?

SAUL. This sort of thing doesn't concern me, and nothing at all matters to me except my work. But still, so you won't carry this on any longer, just take this. [*He gives him money.*]

POLYHARPAX. What's this?

SAUL. A drachma.[1] I think it's enough for our deal and for this work.

POLYHARPAX. Ha, ha, ha.

SAUL. Why are you laughing?

POLYHARPAX. You're a smooth and clever fellow.

SAUL. Why so?

POLYHARPAX. As if you'd never lived in any city till now and so didn't know what life requires of men.

SAUL. Life is such as each man wishes it to be. Those who know how to spend it properly are not ruled by life: life is ruled by them. But so I can pursue more important matters rather than continue this, here's a double drachma. Give me the letter, please.

POLYHARPAX. No, if you want it, the price of this letter is five solidi,[2] to you.

SAUL. Oh, Polyharpax, don't be so wicked.

POLYHARPAX. Decide for yourself now which of these you want to remain with me—either the money or the letter.

SAUL. Oh! Tell me something.

POLYHARPAX. What?

SAUL. Does nothing shame you?

---

[1] See p. 69, n. 1.

[2] The solidus was a Roman gold coin in the time of the emperors, worth about twenty-five denarii (over $4.00) at first, but later devalued by about half.

POLYHARPAX.   Videlicet, turpe facinus, hui,
Si quod meum est iustum quodque omnes factitant lexque tribuit,
Abs te id exigam. Papae!

SAULUS.   Crede modo, praeter quos petis   40
Vix duo supersunt nummuli ad apparatum itinerarium.
Saltem ut miserescat te mei, Harpax.   [*f. 138v*]

POLYHARPAX.   Vt lubet. Pecuniam ut
Inuitus insumas num ego insto? Ius meum quod postulo,
Id opinor cuique licet. Quod si tibi graue est, recte. Damni adhuc
Nihil est: quod suum est uterque id retineat sibi. Quid tibi   45
Vis amplius?

SAULUS.   Os durum ac aridum.

POLYHARPAX.   Etiam maledicta congeris?
Caue sis, quod si iterum faxis, geminabitur, crede,   [*p. 27*]
    precium.

SAULUS.
Κακὸν οἶτον ὀλμαί.

POLYHARPAX.   Quid mussitas autem?

SAULUS.   Hoc dico, mihi
Vnum ut respondeas.

POLYHARPAX.   Age.

SAULUS.   Herus an non iussit literas
Has te mihi?

POLYHARPAX.   Iussit.

SAULUS.   An non stipem pendit seruitutis   50
Tibi?

POLYHARPAX.   Recte.

SAULUS.   Mihi hinc an ullus ususfruct'st?

POLYHARPAX.   Nescio.

SAULUS.
Huic nonne obsequium debes uictum unde accipis?

POLYHARPAX.   Pulchre.

SAULUS.   Nihil
Proficio. At nimium ego ineptus, perdenda quum pecunia
Sit, tempus qui perdo simul tot circumsitus negotiis.
Age, ne parum Polyharpax sis, pecuniam hanc rape. Cedo huc   55
Diplomata.

POLYHARPAX. It's easy to see my base wickedness, oh yes, if I demand from you what is mine by right, what all men practise, and what the law allows. Wonderful!

SAUL. Just believe this: besides what you're demanding, I have scarcely two bits[1] left for provisions for my trip. At least show me mercy, Harpy.

POLYHARPAX. As you wish. Do I urge you to spend your money when you don't want to? What I demand is mine by rights, and that, I think, is everybody's privilege. But if it's hard for you, so be it. There's still nothing lost: let each of us keep what's his. What more do you wish for yourself?

SAUL. Hard and miserly words.

POLYHARPAX. Do you throw insults too? Take care, because if you do it again, believe me, the price will be doubled.

SAUL [muttering]. May you die an evil death.[2]

POLYHARPAX. What are you muttering now?

SAUL. I'm saying that I'd like you to answer me one thing.

POLYHARPAX. Go on.

SAUL. Did your master order you to give me this letter or not?

POLYHARPAX. He did.

SAUL. Doen't he pay you for your service?

POLYHARPAX. Yes indeed.

SAUL. Then don't I have the right of usufruct?

POLYHARPAX. I don't know.

SAUL. Don't you owe obedience to him from whom you receive your support?

POLYHARPAX. Bravo!

SAUL. I'm not getting anywhere. But, since the money must be lost, I'm being very stupid to lose time also, tied up in such haggling. All right, Polyharpax, so you won't be dissatisfied, take this money. Let's have the documents, please. [Giving him money.]

---

[1] Literally, two sesterces. A sesterce was worth one-fourth of a denarius, or less than a nickel.

[2] Saul mutters in Greek, and Polyharpax does not hear or cannot understand.

POLYHARPAX.   Recte conuenit ratio. Cape nunc abique quo
  Velis.
SAULUS.   Et tu quo dignus es, in malam miseram multam crucem.
POLYHARPAX.
  Ain', scelus?
SAULUS.   Dignum hercule sordibus tuis.
POLYHARPAX.   Praestiterat hoc,
  Si uiuo, non factum conuicium pontificis scribae.
SAULUS.   Imo scrobae
  Magis.
POLYHARPAX.   Lacessis, Cerbere!
SAULUS.   Ain', canis?   [*p. 28*]
POLYHARPAX.   Hem bacchatus si sies   60
  Satis, cape nunc.
SAULUS.   En foeneratum tibi.
POLYHARPAX.   Siccine?
SAULUS.   Perfortiter.
POLYHARPAX.
  Vae carnibus hodie tuis.
POPULUS.   Adeste, ciues, irruite,
  Obruite fustibus. Iam si deferbuit satis calor,
  Abite modo.
POLYHARPAX. At ego pol si uiuo—
POPULUS.   Abite inquam.

ACTUS III. SCENA I.   [*f. 139*]
Iambici Trimetri.
Ecclesia.

[ECCLESIA.]
  Vterque nunc mater paterque pariter
  Clausere diem, quod etsi mihi aliquandiu
  Magis erat, nunc minus est tamen cruciabile,
  In uitam quando resurgent postliminio,
  Christus sicuti ac scripturae mihi praenunciant.   5

---

59. *scrobae*] apparently a coinage intended to echo *scribae* cacophonously.
It probably plays on *scrofa*, sow (cf. *scrofula*), and *scrobis*, ditch (cf. *scroba* in
DuCange); note also *scobis*, sawdust.

POLYHARPAX [*handing over the commission*]. That's good thinking. Take it now and go where you please.

SAUL. And you go where you deserve, onto a great, terrible, wretched cross.

POLYHARPAX. What's that, you scoundrel?

SAUL. That's what your rottenness deserves, by Hercules.

POLYHARPAX. As I live, you'd have been better off not to abuse the scribe of the chief priest.

SAUL. More scrub than scribe.[1]

POLYHARPAX. You provoke me, Cerberus!

SAUL. What's that, dog?

POLYHARPAX. Oh! If you've ranted enough, take that now. [*Striking Saul.*]

SAUL [*striking back*]. There, you're repaid.

POLYHARPAX. Is this the way things are?

SAUL. Indeed it is.

POLYHARPAX. Woe for your skin today.

Enter citizens.

A CITIZEN. Come, citizens, rush them. Beat them with your cudgels.—— Now, if you've cooled off enough, get out.

POLYHARPAX. But by Pollux, as I live——

CITIZENS. Get out, I say. [*Exeunt separately.*

[III.1] *Enter Ecclesia.*

ECCLESIA. Now both my father and my mother have ended their days.[2] That was quite painful to me for a while, but now it is less so, since they will rise again to life by the right of postliminium,[3] as Christ and the Scriptures assure me. Then I have another source

---

[1] See the note to the Latin text.

[2] Adam and Eve, actually Ecclesia's father-in-law and mother-in-law, as Psyche, below, is her sister-in-law. The speech was originally written, in the manuscript version, for Sarcobius, Eve's son and Psyche's blood brother; his tormentor in the following scene was Dicologus.

[3] The "right to return home and resume one's former rank and privileges" (L-S).

Tum id aliud est mihi quod principium gaudii est:
Psyche quod soror ex Orco iam pace fruitur,
Quam Christus coelicolis indigetauit meus.
Nunc sola sum Ecclesia relicta cum tribus
Gnatis, Asia, Africo, et Europaeo. Sed et   10
His nunc misera spolior, quos Nomocrates
Tyrannus implacabilis in carcerem
Abduxit Sciolethron sordidissimum,
Serpentibus, anguibus ac foetore obsitum.
Quod ni esset, superesset aliqua spes solatii.   [*p. 29*] 15
Nunc sine notis amicisque omnibus, inops
Ac orba, terraeque peripsema, deseror—
Vnicus adhuc, ni quod superest sponsus mihi
Christus, nostrae semper baculus familiae.
Sed quam infoeliciter huc processi hodie! Venit   20
Nomocrates, meus lictor. Quid agam?

ACTUS III. SCENA II.
Trochaici
Nomocrates. Ecclesia. [Desmophylax. Dromo.]

[NOMOCRATES.]
Me nisi argumenta fallunt omnia, foeminam modo
Inuenire quam uolui repperi.
ECCLESIA.   Me certe ipsam petit.
NOMOCRATES.
Edico mulier tibi, tun' Ecclesia es, Adamitica
Stirpe sata, ac Euae peccatricis posthuma proles?
ECCLESIA.   Licet
Haud me clam est quidnam struunt, tamen culpae quae nullius 5
Scio me consciam, age, fors quicquid feret, quid metuam
Innocens?
NOMOCRATES.   Quin mihi respondes?
ECCLESIA.   Neque parentum neque me
Nominis pudet.   [*f. 139v*]

13. *Sciolethron*] I find no precedent for this word. Bienvenu renders it "prison tenebreuse," presumably deriving it from the Greek σκιά, shadow, and λήθη, hell (from the name of its river of forgetfulness).
P. H. *Desmophylax. Dromo.*] omitted in B and MSC.

of joy: my sister Psyche now enjoys peace outside Orcus, since my dear Christ has proclaimed her to be among the dwellers in heaven. Now I am left, Ecclesia alone, with my three children, Asia, Africus, and Europus, but unhappily I am deprived even of them now, for Nomocrates, an implacable tyrant, has carried them off into that ghastly prison Sciolethron,[1] beset with serpents, snakes, and stench. Except for this, there would remain some hope of comfort. Now I am deserted, without all friends and acquaintances, poor and bereft, the scum of the earth, except that the bridegroom still remains for me: Christ, always the support of my family. But how unfortunate that I came here today! Nomocrates, my lictor, is coming. What should I do?

[III.2]   *Enter Nomocrates, attended by Desmophylax and Dromo.*

NOMOCRATES. Unless all signs deceive me, I've found just the woman I wanted to find.

ECCLESIA [*aside*]. Sure enough, he's looking for me.

NOMOCRATES. I say to you, woman, aren't you Ecclesia, sprung from Adam's line and last descendant of the sinner Eve?

ECCLESIA [*aside*]. It's no secret from me what they're scheming. But since I know that I'm not guilty of any fault, why, whatever chance brings, what shall I fear, being innocent?

NOMOCRATES. Why don't you answer me?

ECCLESIA. I'm not ashamed of either my parents or my name.

---

[1] The prison is apparently in the shadow (or the shades) of hell; see note to the Latin text. In the early draft, the children were in the prison of desperation, beset with toads, snakes, and stench.

NOMOCRATES.   Scin' ergo ius in omnes esse mihi
  Qui peccant, meam ut in hos potestatem exequar arbi- [*p. 30*]
    trariam?
  Quamobrem agedum, Desmophylax, actutum abripite   10
  Ac Thanato lictori in seruitutem tradite perpetuam
  Ita ut officii nostri ratio postulat.
ECCLESIA.   Itane in
  Seruitutem uero liberam?
NOMOCRATES.   Qui peccat seruus est
  Peccati.
ECCLESIA.   Sit. At ego quid egi innocens?
NOMOCRATES.   Mulier, nihil in
  Te iniustum a nobis fiet: id primum tibi praedictum ut siet.   15
ECCLESIA.
  Bene. Quid admisi igitur uobis fas explanare arbitror.
NOMOCRATES.
  Quasi cum Psyche sorore una pomi haud esses particeps,
  Cuius tum omnes cogitatus in malum accliues sient.
  Denique quid recens patraris Syneidesis ancillula
  Indicio fecit tua. Sed quid uerbis, mihi uendita   20
  Sub peccato quum sis? Idque si nescis, abi curriculo
  Dromo ad Psychephonum. Huc chirographum ocyus remittat, huic
  Satanaeque quod permiseram. Atque eccum, exire uideo.

ACTUS III. SCENA III.   [*p. 31*]
Iambici Acatalectici.
Psychephonus. Nomocrates. Thanatus Lictor. Adopylus. Ecclesia.

[PSYCHEPHONUS.]
  Hac illac circumcurso, nusquam quietum sistendi locum
  Inuenio, ita metus omnes mihi sensus expectorat, neque
  Fugae finem aut consilii principium reperio.
NOMOCRATES.   Quid mali haec
  Fert turbatio?
PSYCHEPHONUS. Ehem Nomocrates, hei malum!
NOMOCRATES.   Qui dum, Psychephone?
  Effare obsecro.
PSYCHEPHONUS.   Velimus nolimus, perimus.

NOMOCRATES. Don't you know, then, that I hold authority over all who sin and I can use my discretionary power against them?—— Then come, Desmophylax,[1] arrest her on the spot and deliver her into perpetual slavery to my lictor, Thanatus, just as the duty of my office demands.

ECCLESIA. Do you thus deliver a truly free woman into slavery?

NOMOCRATES. Whoever sins is a slave of sin.[2]

ECCLESIA. Amen. But what have I done? I'm innocent.

NOMOCRATES. Woman, you will suffer no injustice from us. Understand that from the outset.

ECCLESIA. Very well. Then I think it proper for you to explain what wrong I have committed.

NOMOCRATES. As if you didn't share in the apple along with your sister Psyche, with the result that all your thoughts are predisposed to evil.[3] Your handmaid Syneidesis,[4] moreover, has proved what you've done lately. But why talk about it, since you are sold to me under sin?[5] And if you don't know that,—— Dromo, run quickly to Psychephonus and have him send me immediately the writ which I entrusted to him and Satan. But look, I see him coming.

[III.3]   *Enter Psychephonus, the lictor Thanatus, and Adopylus.*[6]

PSYCHEPHONUS. I run hither and yon, and nowhere do I find a quiet place to rest, because fear dispells all my senses and I find no end of flight and no beginning of a plan.

NOMOCRATES. What sort of trouble does this excitement signal?

PSYCHEPHONUS. Oh Nomocrates! Ah, trouble!

NOMOCRATES. How so, Psychephonus? Out with it, I beseech you.

PSYCHEPHONUS. Like it or lump it, we're licked.

---

[1] See the note to the Dramatis Personae.

[2] A note in B cites John 8.[34].

[3] A note in B cites Genesis 6.[12-13].

[4] The name means conscience (συνείδησις).

[5] A note in B cites Romans 8.[14]. In that chapter, Paul distinguishes between the law of God and the "law of sin that is in my members" and that leads to death; this latter is the power of the law of Nomocrates.

[6] Adopylus does not appear in this scene in the draft; his speeches are divided between Psychephonus and Thanatus. A mute character, Dromo, is listed in the P.H. in manuscript.

NOMOCRATES.   Nam quid ita?   5
PSYCHEPHONUS.
    Acta haec res est.
NOMOCRATES.   Dicturusne es?
PSYCHEPHONUS.   Sepulti inquam sumus.
NOMOCRATES.   Rei
    Quid obtigit?
THANATUS.   Psychephone, explorata omnia faxis uide. Haud
    Ausim ingredi.
NOMOCRATES.   Miror quid sit.
THANATUS.   Nomocrates, quid iam fiet?
NOMOCRATES.
    Quid ergo?
THANATUS.   Nos omnes pessundedit.
ADOPYLUS.   Occidit.
NOMOCRATES.   Quis?
ADOPYLUS.   Stirpitus.
NOMOCRATES.
    Quis istic?
THANATUS.   Ego quem occideram.
NOMOCRATES.   Qui tandem?
THANATUS.   Christus.
NOMOCRATES.   Xylonicus 10
    Ille? Hem, quem ligno pridem egomet addixeram mortalitus?
THANATUS.   At
    Resurrexit.
NOMOCRATES.   Resurrexit?
PSYCHEPHONUS.   Resurrexit.
NOMOCRATES.   Quid audio?
ADOPYLUS.   [*p. 32; f. 140*]
    Plutonias porro insuper.
NOMOCRATES.   Hem quid insuper?

7-9. *Psychephone . . . Nos*] I follow MSC; see Textual Notes.
10.] as in MSC; B prints as two verses, the first ending *occideram*.
    Xylonicus] see p. 279, n. 1.
11. *mortalitus*] I have found no other uses of this adverbial form.

NOMOCRATES. Why so?

PSYCHEPHONUS. Our business is done for.

NOMOCRATES. Aren't you going to tell me?

PSYCHEPHONUS. I tell you, we're buried.

NOMOCRATES. What's happened?

THANATUS. Psychephonus, see that you make everything clear. I wouldn't dare start.

NOMOCRATES. I wonder what it is.

THANATUS. Nomocrates, what will happen now?

NOMOCRATES. What, then?

THANATUS. He's sunk us all.

ADOPYLUS. He's murdered us.

NOMOCRATES. Who?

ADOPYLUS. Root and branch.

NOMOCRATES. Who?

THANATUS. The one I had killed.

NOMOCRATES. Who, I ask you?

THANATUS. Christ.

NOMOCRATES. That fellow on the cross?[1] What, the man I myself sentenced to die on the cross some time ago?

THANATUS. But he's risen.[2]

NOMOCRATES. Risen?

PSYCHEPHONUS. Risen.

NOMOCRATES. What am I hearing?

ADOPYLUS. Yes, and besides that, Pluto's——

NOMOCRATES. Oh, what more?

---

[1] C. H. Herford (p. 139n.) points out that the word *xylonicus* was probably coined by Nicholas Bartholomaeus for his play *Christus Xylonicus*. The 1531 edition of that play contains a critique by Emericus Troianus, who explains the title as follows (f. iv^v): "Indixit autem operi titulum, *Christvs Xylonicus*, quod is de suis in signo hostibus triumphum egerit, suaque morte, mortem superauerit." In the 1542 anthology of *Comoediae ac Tragoediae Aliquot ex Novo et Vetere Testamento Desumptae* (Basel, 1540), a letter "Ad Pivm Lectorem" explains the term more precisely: "Ideo uero auctor Xilonico titulum fecit, quod Christus ἐν ξύλῳ, id est, in ligno potitus sit νίκη, id est, uictoria" (p. 451). Foxe must have used the word ironically, however, for Nomocrates would not have intended the exultant implications which Bartholomaeus had in mind.

[2] A note in B cites Matthew, Mark, Luke, and John, without specific reference.

ADOPYLUS.   Arces opesque omnes populatus.

NOMOCRATES.   Quid narras?

THANATUS.   Plagiarius Psychen   14
Vi abreptam auexit secum.

NOMOCRATES.   Nusquam sum certa haec si nuncias.

PSYCHEPHONUS.
Certissima.

THANATUS.   Diabolum ipsum mulctauit uinculis.

NOMOCRATES.   Quid ais?

THANATUS.
Antigraphen tuam e manibus illi irruens extorsit ilico.

NOMOCRATES.
Chirographum meum, Psychephone?

PSYCHEPHONUS.   Sic est.

NOMOCRATES.   Interii miser.

ECCLESIA.
Sancta Salus, quid ego spei hic uideo?

ADOPYLUS.   Nos profligat e medio   19
Nutu hinc mirabili.

NOMOCRATES.   At de chirographo quid tum? Perge, Thanate.

THANATUS.
Id ubi mox arripit in crucem, ostentat ilico discerptum ac Psychae
Traditum.

NOMOCRATES.   Hei occidens occidi, meomet ego gladio.

ECCLESIA.
Quantos hic mihi suo triumphos portat nuncio?

NOMOCRATES.   Quis hic
Miror Pancratistes tantus, tantum qui nobis facinus hoc?

THANATUS.
Nescio, nisi quia uestis colluxit scripturarum undique   25
Corollulis distincta mire.   [*p. 33*]

13-14. *opes-/que omnes*] I follow MSC; B reads *opesque/Omnes*.

17. *antigraphen*] transliterated from Greek ἀντιγραφή, a defendant's plea or a
plaintiff's indictment. TLL cites *antigraphus* (copy-clerk) and *antigraphon* (tran-
script) as late Latin words.

19. *Nos*] the MSC reading; B reads *Hos*.

26. *Corollulis*] *corolla* is a Plautine word, but I have found no precedent for
the diminutive form.

ADOPYLUS. He's devastated all of Pluto's citadels and power.

NOMOCRATES. What are you telling me?

THANATUS. The thief snatched Psyche by force and carried her away with him.

NOMOCRATES. If what you tell me is true, I'm done for.

PSYCHEPHONUS. It's very true.

THANATUS. He sentenced the devil himself to chains.

NOMOCRATES. What!

THANATUS. He set upon him and wrenched your indictment right out of his hands.

NOMOCRATES. My writ, Psychephonus?

PSYCHEPHONUS. Yes.

NOMOCRATES. Woe is me, I'm dead.

ECCLESIA [*aside*]. Holy Salus, do I see some hope here?

ADOPYLUS. He smashed us, whish, with a miraculous nod.

NOMOCRATES. But about the writ, what then? Go on, Thanatus.

THANATUS. That he grabbed quickly, tore it up, displayed it on a cross, and gave it to Psyche.

NOMOCRATES. Oh, I'm dead, killed by my own weapon.

ECCLESIA [*aside*]. How great are the joys he brings me with this message!

NOMOCRATES. I wonder who this great athlete[1] is who commits such outrage on us?

THANATUS. I don't know, except that his clothing shone, marvelously decorated all over with garlands of scriptures.

---

[1] *Pancratiastes* (the correct form) refers to a combatant in the *pancratium,* a wrestling and boxing event. Cf. *agonista* in the "Panegyricon" (p. 101).

NOMOCRATES.   Quid aiebant?
THANATUS.   Omnia
  Haud poteram: unum legi.
NOMOCRATES.   Quid?
THANATUS.   "Mors absorpta est in uictoriam."
NOMOCRATES.
  Quid tu, Psychephone?
PSYCHEPHONUS.   "Nos post triduum uiuificabit denuo."
NOMOCRATES.
  Certe Messias est. Mirum ni ipse est saluus et ego peream.
ADOPYLUS.
  Tum Petro praeterea clauem tradidisse nunc eum   30
  Fama est.
NOMOCRATES.   Clauem, quam?
ADOPYLUS.   Carceris pol maledictionis tuae,
  Qua Ecclesiae huius liberos manu expediat libera.
NOMOCRATES.
  Cadauer sum.
ADOPYLUS.   Illucque abiisse eum ad illos nunc certo suspicor.
NOMOCRATES.   [*f. 140v*]
  Deficio doloribus. Ah tollite amabo me.
PSYCHEPHONUS.   At at, Nepenthes huc
  Actutum aliquis. Labascit herus in syncopen.
THANATUS.   Nomocrates,   35
  Vah, siccine ut animum despondeas? Redi ad te inquam. Redi,
  Nomocrates. Hinc auferamus intro: ferte manus, curam ut hanc
  Dormiscat paululum.
ECCLESIA.   Quae haec rerum metabole'st? Luctu ille, ego
  Gaudio ita pene exanimata sum, ut me uix capiam satis. [*p. 34*]
  Proh summe Iesv, solus qui miseris amicus es. At enim   40
  Qui tragici hi satrapae, tam magnifice qui incedunt obuiam?
  Interim ego nimis cesso haec natis simul impartire gaudia.

NOMOCRATES. What did they say?

THANATUS. I couldn't see everything. I read one.

NOMOCRATES. What did it say?

THANATUS. "Death is swallowed up in victory."[1]

NOMOCRATES. What about you, Psychephonus?

PSYCHEPHONUS. "He will restore us to life after three days."[2]

NOMOCRATES. He's the Messiah for sure. No doubt about it, he's saved and I'm lost.

ADOPYLUS. Besides that, there's a rumor that he has now given Peter a key.[3]

NOMOCRATES. A key? What key?

ADOPYLUS. The key to the prison of your curse, with which he has a free hand to release the children of Ecclesia here.

NOMOCRATES. I'm a corpse.

ADOPYLUS. I imagine he's certainly gone there for them by now.

NOMOCRATES [*starting to fall*]. I'm weak from grief. Ah, please hold me up.

PSYCHEPHONUS [*supporting Nomocrates*]. Oh! Quickly, nepenthe here, someone. The master is about to faint.

THANATUS. Ah Nomocrates, that you would lose your courage this way! Come to your senses, I say; come, Nomocrates.—— [*To Psychephonus.*] Let's take him inside. You take his hands. Let him sleep off this trouble for a while.   [*They carry Nomocrates off.*

ECCLESIA. What a switch this is! He's overcome with grief, I almost as much with joy. I can scarcely contain myself. Oh great Jesus, you alone are a friend to the wretched. But who are these grand satraps coming this way in such magnificence? Well, I'll go share these joys with my children.   [*Exit.*

---

[1] A note in B cites Osea 13.[?14], but the verse is actually in 1 Corinthians 15.54. Cf. p. 249, n. 2.

[2] Cf. Mark 9.30.

[3] A note in B cites John 19, but the correct reference is probably Matthew 16.19; cf. John 20.23.

ACTUS III. SCENA IIII.
Senarii.
Dioctes. Anabasius. Pornapolis Meretrix.

[DIOCTES.]

Mvndi huius magnipotens dux ac deus Satan,
Huc me e uasto pelagi emittens gurgite,
Rei herciscundae praefecit principem,
Missis huc literis mihi signatoriis
Quas Anabasius ex Orco ascendens pertulit,   5
Cum diademate decuplo ac regni fascibus,
Mihi simul ac Pornapoli amasiae meae:
Quo iure quicquid est sub Olympo uspiam
Imperii uendico super linguas et tribus.
Regem in terris Deus ut hic ungit suum,   10
Itidem Plutonia iam surgant regna uolumus.

ANABASIUS.

Heus, Pornapolis, tuque Dioctes, cui maxime haec
Loquor, priusquam incipias, sic primum putes,
Tu quam capessis haud rem esse leuem. Deo   [*p. 35*]
Durum repugnare est, tibi quin duras dabit.   15
Quo magis opera opus est praesenti nunc tua.
Quippe hanc ita pugnam tibi paratam censeo,
Non nisi permagna quae emenda audacia est.
Fortunam fortitudo facit.

DIOCTES.   Sine modo,

Anabasi, inquam. Mundus hic duos simul   20
Minime soles sustinet uno in Zodiaco.   [*f. 141*]
Certum est, aut me Christum hunc aut me illum persequi,
Vtrique quoniam haud una regnabimus.
Sed quid regem nos illum pertimescimus,
Miserum atque reiiculum, pauperemque scilicet,   25
Qui aliud nihil iniurias quam pati potest?

ANABASIUS.

At enim pati hoc quo euadet uereor denique.

---

9. *et*] B has an ampersand; perhaps we should read *ac*, following MSC.
15. *duras*] we might expect the neuter *dura*, but both B and MSC have the feminine form.

[III.4] *Enter Dioctes, Anabasius, and Pornapolis the whore.*[1]

DIOCTES. The mighty leader and god of this world, Satan, sent me here out of the vast whirlpool of his sea and, in these letters with seals which Anabasius carried up from Orcus together with a tenfold diadem and the fasces of rule,[2] has made me his executor in overseeing his affairs—me along with my mistress, Pornapolis. On this authority I claim all rule under Olympus over all tongues and tribes everywhere. As God anoints his king here on earth, so we wish for the ascendancy of the Plutonian kingdoms now.

ANABASIUS. Listen, Pornapolis, and you too, Dioctes, to whom especially I speak: before you begin, you should consider first that what you are eager to do is by no means easy. It's hard to fight against God; he'll certainly give you hard times. All the more is there a need now of your resolute effort. Indeed I think such a battle is prepared for you that it is not to be won except with very great boldness. Fortitude makes your fortune.[3]

DIOCTES. Stop that now, Anabasius, I say. This world will scarcely endure two suns together in one zodiac. It's certain that either this Christ will drive me out, or I him, since we won't both reign together. But why do we fear that miserable and worthless king, actually a pauper who can do nothing except endure injuries?

ANABASIUS. But I fear he'll endure that by which in the end he'll escape.

---

[1] In the draft version, only Abadon and Anabasius are present in this scene, and Dioctes does not appear hereafter. See note to Dioctes in the Dramatis Personae.

[2] A note in B refers to Apocalypse 13.[1]. The fasces were a symbol of power in ancient Rome.

[3] Cf. the proverbial "Fortune favors the bold."

Dioctes.

Vah, qui me ad audaciam instruis, ipse deficis?

Anabasius.

Fateor.

Dioctes.   Iam opus mihi est Theseos asciscere huc,
Expromptae saeuitiae, gladiatorie   30
Hos qui proterant Christicolas. Prope ac habere me
Spero ad sententiam. Heus Nero, euocetur huc
Domitianus, Traianus, Verus, Aurelius,
Maximinus, Decius, Valerianus, Dio-
cletianus, Constantius. His ego decem   35
Decem legabo diademata ducibus,   [*p. 36*]
Christum hunc aduersus operam uti nauent fortiter.

Pornapolis.

Imo intus ut conueniamus satius est
Praeceptisque instruemus accuratius.
Anabasi, adsis et ope et consilio simul.   40

DIOCTES. Bah, you who urge me to be bold are fainting away yourself.

ANABASIUS. I admit it.

DIOCTES. Now I need to get some Theseuses here, men of ready fierceness, to crush these Christians with the strength of a gladiator. I hope I have some near for my purpose.—— [*Shouts.*] Hey, summon Nero here, and Domitian, Trajan, Verus, Aurelius, Maximinus, Decius, Valerianus, Diocletian, and Constantius.[1]—— For these ten rulers I will commission ten diadems that they may work vigorously against this Christ.

PORNAPOLIS. But it's better that we meet inside and instruct them quite carefully in our methods.—— Anabasius, you come too, with your help and counsel. [*Exeunt.*

---

[1] Verus is presumably Septimius Severus, though Septimius' reign was earlier than that of Marcus Aurelius (one of whose names was Verus). The inclusion of Constantine's father, Constantius, is puzzling, for in the *Acts and Monuments* Foxe called him "very excellent, civil, meek, gentle, liberal," and "a maintainer and a supporter of the Christians" (ed. Stephen R. Cattley, I [London, 1841], 237). Most other historians agree with that judgment. Perhaps Foxe here confused Constantine's father with his son, Constantius II, whom Hilarius attacked as an evil persecutor (*Patrologia Latina*, X, 574 ff.). More likely, he included Constantius simply to set up the reversal of fortune which Anabasius describes as happening upon Constantine's succession (IV.2). The tradition of delineating ten persecutions by Roman emperors was instigated by a desire to reconcile history with Apocalypse and goes back to the fifth century: to Sulpicius Severus, according to Gibbon (*Decline and Fall of the Roman Empire*, ed. J. B. Bury [New York, 1914], II, 115); or to Augustine's friend Paulus Orosius, according to F. L. Cross (ed., *Oxford Dictionary of the Christian Church* [London, 1958], p. 1047). But the lists often disagree with each other. Orosius (as summarized in Cross) and Sulpicius (*Patrologia Latina*, XX, 147) both include Nero, Domitian, Trajan, Marcus Aurelius, Septimius Severus (Sulpicius calls him simply Severus), Decius, Valerianus, Aurelian, and Diocletian. Of these, Foxe omits only Aurelian in the present list, but he includes him in the *Acts and Monuments*, which presents a list identical to Orosius' except that it attributes the eighth persecution to Aemilian, Paternus, and Galerius (257-259 A.D.) instead of Valerian (260 A.D.). Orosius includes Maximinus Thrax (probably Foxe's Maximinus, but see IV.1.8 and p. 299, n. 2), whereas Sulpicius calls his reign a period of general peace and substitutes Hadrian; Sulpicius links Maximian with Diocletian for the tenth persecution.

ACTUS III. SCENA V.
Eivsdem rationis.
Ecclesia. Paulus conuersus.

[ECCLESIA.]

Qvid ais, Paule? Petrus liberos meos
De carcere inquis eductos abduxit domum?

PAULUS.

Certe inquam, Asiam, Africum, et Europaeum.

ECCLESIA.   Ipseque
Ipsa in re adfuisse te refers?

PAULUS.   Simul
Et testis, actor, et nuncius utque redeas   5
Ad se domum. Tuum misere aduentum expetunt.

ECCLESIA.

Mi Paule, ne frustra nunc me in spem coniicias.

PAULUS.

Vah, duran' adeo te esse fide?

ECCLESIA.   Haud creduas.
Ast chirographum quum habet Dei Nomocrates—

PAULUS.

Quid tum?

ECCLESIA.   Qui id pote fieri est?

PAULUS.   At ego te metu   10
Nunc omni eximo. Quem tu tantopere pauitas
Tyrannum, iure hunc obligatorio exuit   [*f. 141v*]
Christus, Ecclesia, noster.   [*p. 37*]

ECCLESIA.   Ain' uero?

PAULUS.   Dei
In nos inscriptum digitis chirographum
Erasit, comminuit, e medio sustulit.   15

ECCLESIA.

Vnde id, a Deo quod factum est, infectum ut siet?

PAULUS.

Ego dicam tibi. Legem qui sanxerit,
Hanc idem rursus ut abrumpat in manu est.
Nec semper eundem esse, si res non sinit,
Licet. Olim ut legibus nobiscum ageret Deus,   20
Iustum tempusque ferebat. Nunc non Deus,

[III.5]   *Enter Ecclesia*[1] *and Paul converted.*

ECCLESIA. What's that, Paul? You say Peter has freed my children from prison and taken them home?

PAUL. That's what I said—Asia, Africus, and Europus.

ECCLESIA. And you say you were there at the same time?

PAUL. As a witness and a participant, and also a messenger to you to go to them at home, where they are awaiting your arrival with difficulty.

ECCLESIA. My dear Paul, now don't send me into a vain hope.

PAUL. Ah, will you be so distrustful?

ECCLESIA. Don't believe that. But since Nomocrates has God's writ——

PAUL. What about it?

ECCLESIA. How is it possible that that could happen?

PAUL. But I'll free you now of all your fear. As for this tyrant whom you fear so much, Ecclesia, our Christ has stripped him of his binding authority.

ECCLESIA. What! Really?

PAUL. With his own fingers he erased the scripture of God which had been written against us; he tore it up and did away with it.

ECCLESIA. How is it that what was made by God can be unmade?

PAUL. I'll tell you. In his hands who sanctioned the law it rests in turn to destroy it. He need not always be the same if the circumstances don't permit it. Once justice and the times demanded that God deal with us by laws. Now not God, but the times

---

[1] Originally, Sarcobius (with appropriate changes in the text); see Textual Notes.

Ipsa at uero mutantur tempora. Causa dum
Manebat apud iudicem integra, uiguit
Tantisper iusta in nos uindicta numinis,
Nos quae peccati merito traduxit reos.   25
Nunc causa longe haec aliter mutata euenit.

ECCLESIA.

   Qui cedo?

PAULUS.   Legis quaecunque a Deo poena haec erat
Nostris statuta erratibus, per iustitiam
Remitti haud potuit. Transferri potuit. Vbi
Satis iuri datum est, ius quid agat amplius?   30
Nostra agebatur causa: hanc totam in se transtulit
Christus, qui mortuus unus est pro omnibus,
Mors unde occisa his est qui Christo uiuimus.

ECCLESIA.

   Quo pacto, Paule, uice omnium unus mortuus?

PAULUS.

   Qui minus unus quam olim peccauit pro omnibus   [*p. 38*]   35
Tuus, Ecclesia, pater?

ECCLESIA.   Audio. Sed unus hic
Restat scrupus.

PAULUS.   Aquilam in filice metuis.

ECCLESIAM.

   Mors quia perinde manet, idem omnium exitus.

PAULUS.

   Res parua mors est, uis at mortis maxuma
Animam quae pessundat. Ea ubi adempta sit,   40
Illa facile contemnitur. Quae aeterna non
Est non mors dicenda est, sopor at temporarius,
Post quem lux excipit certissima. Iacet
Corpus, at id noctium paucarum est, laetior
Nos dum euocat dies. Interea luce iam   [*f. 142*]   45
Psyche fruitur aeterna, nostri pars.

ECCLESIA.   Scio.

PAULUS.

   Iam qui Psychen e barathro, idem et Soma tuum
Restituet ipsum, ut ne quid dubites.

ECCLESIA.   Scilicet.

themselves are truly changed. So long as our case remained before a judge, undecided, just so long did God's just punishment remain in effect against us, deservedly proving us guilty of sin. Now the situation has turned out to be drastically altered.

ECCLESIA. How, pray tell?

PAUL. Whatever penalty of the law had been decreed by God for our transgressions could not in justice be remitted, but it could be transferred.[1] When the law has been satisfied, what more should the law do? Our case was disposed of: Christ transferred the whole case onto himself; he is one dead man in exchange for us all. Hence it is that death has been killed for those of us who live in Christ.

ECCLESIA. How is it, Paul, that one may be dead in place of all?

PAUL. How is it less than that, once, one man—your father, Ecclesia —sinned for all?

ECCLESIA. I understand, but this one doubt remains.

PAUL. You're afraid of an eagle on a fern.[2]

ECCLESIA. Because death remains as before, still the end of everybody.

PAUL. Death is a small thing, but the strength of the death which destroys the soul is very great. When that has been removed, death is easily scorned. What is not eternal should be called not death, but a temporary sleep, after which a most sure daylight ensues. The body lies in disuse, but that is a matter of a few nights until a happier day calls us forth. Meantime Psyche, a part of us, already enjoys eternal daylight.

ECCLESIA. I know.

PAUL. He who has already released Psyche from the abyss will likewise restore your Soma himself, have no doubt.[3]

ECCLESIA. Of course.

---

[1] A note in B cites 2 Corinthians 5.[?14, 21]. Cf. 1 Corinthians 15.21-22.

[2] A nonexistent danger, since a fern would not support an eagle; cf. IV.8.32. I find no precedent for the proverb. There may be a play on *silice* (crag).

[3] A note in B refers to 1 Corinthians 15.[35-55]. In the draft, Paul uses the common nouns *soul* and *bodies* instead of *Psyche* and *Soma*.

Paulus.

  Non quae modo sunt, rerum est spectandus exitus:
  Futura sunt, uerba fere quae spondent Dei.   50
  Christo ut post mortem euenit resurrectio,
  Cum illo et nobis hoc ponendum domicilium est.
  Nitidius quo redintegretur denuo,
  Sementis e terra ut nitidior pullulat.

Ecclesia.

  Equidem plus uideo spei, animo quam queam   55
  Concipere. Ibo ac scripturis cum animum conferam.

Paulus.

  Sapis.

Ecclesia.   Adsis quaeso nunc, Paule, intro ut eadem haec,
  Mihi quae dixti, dicas itidem liberis.   [*p. 39*]

Paulus.

  Paratus sum, omnibus ut prosim, debitor.

ACTUS III. SCENA VI.
Eadem cum Superioribus.
Psychephonus.

[Psychephonus.]

  Enimuero quae conueniunt quaeque adsolent
  Signa esse ad mortem huic esse omnia uideo
  Hero meo Nomocrati, postquam iam neque
  Medicinae, somni, neque cibi retentio est.
  Nec panacea ulla, nec scammonium, θεῶν   5
  Neque χείρ, omnes porro neque therapeutici
  Nec empiritici pilum medelae conferunt.
  Certe et quod dicendum hic siet mihi non placet.
  Atqui illud miror interim, ex his neminem
  Satis hoc morbi cognoscere genus quod siet.   10
  At eo omnes congruunt commutandum sibi
  Coelum esse, hinc in Babyloniam maxime ut migret,
  Quod eum sibi aerem esse autumant aptissimum

---

    6. *therapeutici*] transliterated from the Greek θεραπευτική, the title of a work by Galen.

    7. *empiritici*] the substantive *empiri* occurs, but I have found no other instance of an adjectival form.

PAUL. We must consider not only those things which are, but the end of things, those things yet to come which the words of God promise soon. As the resurrection came to Christ after his death, so with him we must put aside this dwelling that it may be restored in greater splendor, just as seeds sprout from the earth in greater splendor.

ECCLESIA. Truly I see more to hope for than I can grasp with my mind. I'll go and reconcile my thoughts with the scriptures.

PAUL. You are wise.

ECCLESIA. Please come inside with me now, Paul, to tell my children these same things which you've told me.

PAUL. I'm prepared, as a debtor, to be of service to everybody.[1]

[*Exeunt.*

[III.6] *Enter Psychephonus.*

PSYCHEPHONUS. Truly I see in my master Nomocrates all the things which are associated with death and which usually are signs of death.[2] For he doesn't hold down medicine or food now and he doesn't sleep. No panacea or scammony, no skill of the gods, not even all the therapeutic or empiric practitioners bring the slightest remedy.[3] I'm certainly not pleased that this must be said. But I'm amazed that out of all these no one recognizes what sort of disease it is. Yet all agree that he should have a change of climate —that he should move away from here, especially to Babylonia, because they say that air is best for him which is impure and which

---

[1] A note in B cites Romans 1.[14].

[2] The description of Nomocrates' illness perhaps owes something to Lactantius' account of Galerius' fatal disease (*Patrologia Latina* VII, 246) or to some similar account. Foxe himself describes Galerius' disease in *Acts and Monuments* (ed. Cattley), I, 239.

[3] The empirics were an important Alexandrian school of physicians, dating from the third century B.C., who rejected the study of anatomy and based their practice of medicine entirely on experience (observation, history, and judgment by analogy), on the actual phenomena of disease rather than its causes. The term *therapeutic* presumably refers to Galen's treatise, which concentrates on causes by its emphasis on the humors and the pneumata.

Feculentus qui sit, turbidum ac quiddam magis
Spirans. Quod equidem neque consilium improbo,   15
Nam qui hic ius omne amisit, clauibus ac bonis
Cunctis exutus, quid quaeso hic agat amplius?
Sed quis homo hic circunspectans uenit? Atque ut modo [*f. 142v*]
Contemplatus sum, nuncius Ditis est, simul
Antiquae et notitiae et militiae a puero particeps.   20

ACTUS III. SCENA VII.   [*p. 40*]
Quadrata Anapaestica Catalectica.
Anabasius. Psychephonus.

[ANABASIUS.]

Etsi ad languorem cursando fatisco miser, mihi tamen esse
Deputo in hac re quoscunque labores capio leues, sacrilegis
Dum malefaciam modo.
PSYCHEPHONUS.   Quae hic malefacta fabricat? Heus Anabasi.
ANABASIUS.

Quis Anabasium hic?
PSYCHEPHONUS.   Veteres non respicis amicitias?
ANABASIUS.   Ohe mi
Psychephone.
PSYCHEPHONUS. Quid hic, aut quem circunspicis?
ANABASIUS.   Hic Christicolae, si 5
Qui sint, cornicibus ut sacrificem.
PSYCHEPHONUS.   Quamobrem istos?
ANABASIUS.   Tun' adhuc
Christum illum nescis, Psychephone, perrupit qui Acheronta,
tuamque
Secum traduxit Psychen?
PSYCHEPHONUS.   Quid ni?
ANABASIUS.   Cosmetora ipsum Satanam
Gordiis uti strinxit nodis?
PSYCHEPHONUS.   Scio.
ANABASIUS.   Gentem esse porro relictam
Hinc nobis infestam omnibus?
PSYCHEPHONUS.   Oppido gens procax nimium. Atque 10
Si quid modo apud nos edidere scias.

8. *Cosmetora*] transliterated from the Greek κοσμήτωρ, the commander of an
army; Foxe uses the word again at IV.4.96.

blows somewhat more turbidly. I don't think that's a bad idea at all, for, since he's lost all his authority here and is stripped of all his keys and his goods, what more could he do here? But who's this fellow coming along and looking all around? Just as I thought, he's Pluto's messenger, from his youth an adherent of both our old cause and our ancient campaign.

[III.7]   *Enter Anabasius.*

ANABASIUS [*aside*]. Although I'm growing so terribly tired I could faint from this running around, yet I consider insignificant any hardships which I undergo in this effort if only I can work some mischief on the impious.

PSYCHEPHONUS [*aside*]. What mischief is he up to?—— Hey, Anabasius.

ANABASIUS. Who said "Anabasius" here?

PSYCHEPHONUS. Don't you care about old friendships?

ANABASIUS. Hey there, my friend Psychephonus.

PSYCHEPHONUS. What are you doing here? Whom are you looking for?

ANABASIUS. Christians, if there are any here, so I can sacrifice them to the crows.

PSYCHEPHONUS. Why them?

ANABASIUS. Don't you know yet about that fellow Christ, Psychephonus, who ripped up hell and carried your Psyche away with him?

PSYCHEPHONUS. Why wouldn't I?

ANABASIUS. And how he tied up our leader, Satan himself, in Gordian knots?

PSYCHEPHONUS. I know.

ANABASIUS. And that the people who are left are very hostile to us all since then?

PSYCHEPHONUS. The people are very insolent indeed. And if you only knew what they've done among us!

ANABASIUS.   Quid?
PSYCHEPHONUS.   Herus Nomocrates.
ANABASIUS.
   Quid is?
PSYCHEPHONUS.   Ecclesiae tres liberos noxae modo reos in   [*p. 41*]
   Custodiam subigit maledictionis.
ANABASIUS.   Eho purulento hoc
   In carcere?
PSYCHEPHONUS.   Videlicet Africum, Europaeum, et tertiam opinor
   Asiam.
ANABASIUS.   Perge.
PSYCHEPHONUS.   Hos Petrus, cum Paulo nescio quo aliisque,   15
   Effractis compedibus iniussu heri emisit manu.
ANABASIUS.   Amabo
   Qua sutela illud?
PSYCHEPHONUS.   Clauis cuiusdam machina.
ANABASIUS.   Quid herus? Non-
   ne repetundarum cum illis postulans, hos eripuit?
PSYCHEPHONUS.   Quid
   Faceret? Non una illa clauis est: ubique clauigeri sunt,
   Christiani quot sunt. Quin nec Tartara iam tuta audio. Sed uos 20
   Qua in re molestant iam? Cedo.
ANABASIUS.   Minis ac terroribus ubique
   Obturbant omnia: Christum rediturum ac regnum praedicant quod
   Regna minuat haec omnemque potentiam auferat. Satanae ipsi
   Interitum ominantur ac aeterna uincula.
PSYCHEPHONUS.   Praeter etiamnum
   Nunc quae patitur?
ANABASIUS.   Tricae sunt, praeut quae porten-   [*p. 42*]
      dunt alia.
PSYCHEPHONUS.   Quaenam?   25
ANABASIUS.   [*f. 143*]
   Stagnum ignis sulphureum.
PSYCHEPHONUS.   Papae!
ANABASIUS.   Vtcunque modo uincimus ipsi,
   Victoriam post promittunt sibi. Quodque magis miror apud me,
   Nusquam ille Furias mandat suas Satan, ubi, siquando
   Volet potentiam ostendere, ubique quin obstant diruuntque

ANABASIUS. What?

PSYCHEPHONUS. My master Nomocrates——

ANABASIUS. What did he do?

PSYCHEPHONUS. He threw the three children of that dreadful Ecclesia—common criminals—into prison under his curse.[1]

ANABASIUS. Whew, in this festering prison?

PSYCHEPHONUS. Yes. Africus, Europus, and a third one—Asia, I think.

ANABASIUS. Go on.

PSYCHEPHONUS. Peter, with somebody named Paul and others, broke their chains and set them free without the authorization of the master.

ANABASIUS. What device did they do that with, will you tell me?

PSYCHEPHONUS. The device of a certain key.

ANABASIUS. What about the master? Didn't he seize them and demand restitution of those with them?

PSYCHEPHONUS. What could he do? That key isn't the only one: there are key carriers everywhere, as many as there are Christians. Why, I hear that even Tartarus isn't safe now. But tell me now, how are they annoying you?

ANABASIUS. They're upsetting everything everywhere with threats and terrors. They predict that Christ and his kingdom will return to threaten these kingdoms and sweep away all their power.[2] For Satan himself they prophesy death and eternal chains.

PSYCHEPHONUS. Even beyond what he's suffering now?

ANABASIUS. These are trivial compared with the other things they predict.

PSYCHEPHONUS. What?

ANABASIUS. A sulphurous pool of fire.

PSYCHEPHONUS. Wow!

ANABASIUS. However much we suppress them, they promise victory for themselves in the end. And what's more amazing to me is that Satan doesn't order his furies into action. Now, if ever, he'll wish to show his power, since these people are standing up against him

---

[1] In a draft version, Dicologus (= Nomocrates) is said to have imprisoned Ecclesia and her three children "not in the cave of Trophonius but in the Labyrinth of desperation." (The oracle of Trophonius in Lebadea inspired gloom in its clients.)

[2] A note in B refers to Daniel 2.[44].

Quod struimus, inuito etiam Adopylo ipso, quem iam nihil
    timent.   30
Quo obnixius hos nunc sudores suffero nostro
Pro Diocte, hos ut obtorto collo ad cruces rapiam. Atque
Vide pene quod exierat.
PSYCHEPHONUS.   Quid?
ANABASIUS.   Psychephone, uti sies
Praesto. Solutus dum aduenit, iubet Satan sibi tua
Opera opus ad quaedam magnopere fore ut moneam, uenienti   35
Ne quid sis in mora. Manubias sperat recuperare se.
Sed cesso iter coeptum pertendere?
PSYCHEPHONUS.   Quonam?
ANABASIUS.   Mecum igitur si
Venias, in uia dixero.

ACTUS IIII. SCENA I.   [*p. 43; f. 143v*]
Trimetri.
Dioctes.

[DIOCTES.]

Trecentos plus minus annos iam supputo
Inde adeo quod cum Christianis hostibus
Confligimus. Quos si non omnes, maximam
Opinor partem fregimus. Protriuimus
Virtute rara ac ui meorum Caesarum   5
Decem, quos ut par est effere nequeo,
Sua sunt sic functi Sparta. Ast unus tamen
Impense Maximinus, qui aere legibus
Insculptis etiam—nulla ne aboleat dies—
Perquam pol scitum hoc commentum addidit: omnia   10
Vberius prouenire, quin et gratius
Ire dies, Christiano effuso sanguine.
Etsi uersa coeli repente temperie
Eam facile uanitatem coarguit Deus,
Verum utcunque haec sunt, factum tamen ab eo est   15
Sedulo. Sed ut horum ferme iam expletae uices

---

8. *Maximinus*] emended, following MSC, from B's *maximus*.

and destroying what we build even in spite of Adopylus himself, whom they fear not at all. That's why I'm keeping up my efforts on behalf of our Dioctes[1] all the more vigorously, so I can wring their necks and nail them to crosses. But look what almost slipped my mind.

PSYCHEPHONUS. What?

ANABASIUS. Be ready, Psychephonus. By Satan's order I must advise you that, when he is freed and returns, he'll have great need of your services for certain matters; when he comes, you must not be delayed, for he hopes to recover his booty. But I must continue the trip I've undertaken.

PSYCHEPHONUS. Where?

ANABASIUS. If you come with me, I'll tell you on the way. [*Exeunt.*

[IV.1]   *Enter Dioctes.*

DIOCTES. By my reckoning, it's been three hundred years now, more or less, that we've been fighting against our Christian enemies. I think we've shattered most if not all of them. We've worn them down with the rare vigor and power of my ten Caesars. They've administered their Sparta[2] so well that I can't celebrate them as they deserve. But one especially, Maximinus,[3] who even added to the laws engraved in bronze this very clever decree—let no day wipe it out—that everything would prosper more abundantly and even the day would pass more pleasantly if the blood of Christians were poured out. Though God easily disproved that deception by this sudden change from temperate weather, yet, be that as it may, he carried out his plan vigorously.[4] But as the terms of these Caesars are now almost up, it rests with me to set

[1] In the earliest draft, his efforts are on behalf of Nero, Trajan, and Decius; in subsequent scenes, Abadon has all of Dioctes' speeches.

[2] Named, no doubt, for its rigorous administration.

[3] From the account which follows, this is clearly not Maximinus Thrax (235-238 A.D.), usually included in lists of the ten persecuting emperors (see p. 287, n. 1), but Maximin Daia, a Caesar in the Eastern Empire in the time of Constantine (305-313 A.D.).

[4] Foxe probably read of this incident in Eusebius' *Ecclesiastical History*, IX.7 (*Patrologia Graeca*, XX, 810-815; see the translation by R. J. Deferrari, The Fathers of the Church, XXXIX [New York, 1955], 217-218). The decree (a

Sunt, alios restat nunc monarchas sufficiam,
Etsi mihi in hac re tamen Anabasi opus
Consilio est communicato prius. Adeoque
O fors, eccum ipsum de quo agebam uideo.   20

ACTUS IIII. SCENA II.
Octonarii, unus Senarius.
Anabasius. Dioctes.

[Aɴᴀʙᴀꜱɪᴜꜱ.]

  Nae ego nunc nimis uideo, contra stimulum ut calces   [*p. 44*]
    quam nihil iuuat.

Dɪᴏᴄᴛᴇꜱ.

  Quae haec oratio est?

Aɴᴀʙᴀꜱɪᴜꜱ.   Quis hic loquitur? Hem.

Dɪᴏᴄᴛᴇꜱ.   Nunquid fers,
    Anabasi?

Aɴᴀʙᴀꜱɪᴜꜱ.

  Quin tu hinc fugis, here, quoquo ac quantum queas?

Dɪᴏᴄᴛᴇꜱ.   Egone?

Aɴᴀʙᴀꜱɪᴜꜱ.   Fuge,
    Inquam.

Dɪᴏᴄᴛᴇꜱ.   Quid ergo est?

Aɴᴀʙᴀꜱɪᴜꜱ.   Percontari mitte, quodque res monet
  Agas magis. Rerum mundum omnium, quantum ad fugam est opus,
  Para.

Dɪᴏᴄᴛᴇꜱ.   Ad fugam? Quamobrem?

Aɴᴀʙᴀꜱɪᴜꜱ.   Etiam pergis? Nempe huc
    rediit res: pedum   6
  Opus officio est.

Dɪᴏᴄᴛᴇꜱ.   Qui cedo?

Aɴᴀʙᴀꜱɪᴜꜱ.   Constantium
  Noras illum?

Dɪᴏᴄᴛᴇꜱ.   Rem modo qui publicam gerit scilicet.

Aɴᴀʙᴀꜱɪᴜꜱ.   Imo
  Qui gessit potius.

Dɪᴏᴄᴛᴇꜱ.   Quid eo autem?

Aɴᴀʙᴀꜱɪᴜꜱ.   Is mortem obiit.

Dɪᴏᴄᴛᴇꜱ.   Obiit?

up other monarchs, though in this I need to consult the counsel of Anabasius before I proceed. And lo and behold, as it happens, the very person I was talking about.

[IV.2]   *Enter Anabasius.*

ANABASIUS [*aside*]. Well, I now see too well how little it avails to kick against the spur.

DIOCTES. What sort of talk is this?

ANABASIUS. Who's speaking here? Well.

DIOCTES. What do you say, Anabasius?

ANABASIUS. You'd better fly from here, master, anywhere at all and as fast as you can.

DIOCTES. I?

ANABASIUS. Fly, I say.

DIOCTES. Why?

ANABASIUS. Stop asking questions. Instead, do what the situation demands. Prepare to dispose of everything, so great is the need for flight.

DIOCTES. For flight? Why?

ANABASIUS. Do you still persist? I tell you, the matter has come to this: you have to use your feet.

DIOCTES. Tell me why.

ANABASIUS. Do you know that Constantius?

DIOCTES. Certainly, he rules the country now.

ANABASIUS. No, rather he did rule it.

DIOCTES. What do you mean?

ANABASIUS. He died.

DIOCTES. Died?

---

rescript, or answer to an appeal from Maximin's subjects), which was indeed cut into bronze tablets and publicly exposed about the Eastern Empire in 312 A.D., is quoted in full by Eusebius. Foxe has distorted its substance somewhat. The rescript blames "those who belonged to the accursed folly" of Christianity for former unpleasantness, but boasts that now the weather is temperate and the crops flourishing because the Roman gods are being venerated. It does not actually advocate killing Christians, however; it urges the subjects to drive them out of their cities. In IX.8, Eusebius describes the wars and famine which then hit the Empire and which he interprets as God's disproof of the rescript.

ANABASIUS.   Eius in
  Munus Constantino suffecto filio.   [*f. 144*]
DIOCTES.   Quid tum?
ANABASIUS.   Quid tum?   10
  Is Christo nunc amicus, nobis inimicus'st acerrimus
  Factus.
DIOCTES.   Factum auertat Satan.
ANABASIUS.   Porro bellum in nos nunc struit
  Quam mox, ni cedimus, Dioctes.
DIOCTES.   Quid illunc illuc abstulit
  A nobis tam cito?   [*p. 45*]
ANABASIUS.   Enimuero incommode sane in arma dum
  Proficiscens indormit, e coelo crux in oculis fulgurat   15
  In hostes praeferens uictoriam. Omen arripit ilico ac
  Pugnam occipit. Denique eo res rediit: rediit uictor is
  Christi auspiciis et opera. Hactenus habent principia. Nunc
  Quid reliquum sit tu supputa.
DIOCTES.   Tun' haec pro certo?
ANABASIUS.   Certissima.   19
DIOCTES.
  Quo nunc abis?
ANABASIUS.   Ad Plutoniam basilicam, hero haec quae gesta sunt
  Vt retegam.
DIOCTES.   At me quid fiet?
ANABASIUS.   Eho conclamata in re, consilium
  Ne captes.
DIOCTES.   Siccine ergo a uobis me frustrarier?
ANABASIUS.   Age
  Modo, futurorum spe praesentia sustine, Dioctes, ipse dum
  Solutus emergat Satan—haud diu erit—qui Theseam hic manum
  Apporrigat. Interim, ut scena est, ita personam geras. Vt in   25
  Comoediis haud eadem omnino drammata exeunt si haud sinit
  Fabula, ita mundum hunc tecum choragium esse   [*p. 46*]
    quoddam cogita,
  Vbi non quid uelis, at quod imponitur, induendum est.

17. *occipit*] I follow MSC; B reads *accipit*.

25. *apporriget*] *porrigo*, but not *apporrigo*, is a standard word. But Ovid uses *apporrectus*, as if from *apporrigo* (LTL).

ANABASIUS. His son Constantine has been placed into his office.[1]

DIOCTES. So what?

ANABASIUS. So what! He's become a friend to Christ now and our harshest enemy.

DIOCTES. Satan forbid!

ANABASIUS. Indeed, Dioctes, unless we surrender, he's now planning war on us as soon as possible.

DIOCTES. What pulled him away from us so quickly to this?

ANABASIUS. Well, as he was marching to battle under very unfavorable circumstances, he went to sleep and before his eyes a cross shone from heaven predicting victory over his enemies. He took it as his sign then and there and went into battle. The affair turned out like this: he returned a victor under the standards of Christ and with his assistance.[2] There you have the start of it; now you guess the rest.

DIOCTES. Do you know this for a fact?

ANABASIUS. Absolutely.

DIOCTES. Where are you going now?

ANABASIUS. To the cathedral of hell to report to my master what's happened here.

DIOCTES. But what about me?

ANABASIUS. Listen, when the battle cry sounds, don't stop for counsel.

DIOCTES. Oh, that I could be so disappointed in you!

ANABASIUS. Come now, Dioctes, in hope of the future endure the present, until Satan himself emerges free. It won't be long before he offers his Thesean hand here. Meantime, play your part after the manner of the stage. As in comedies, plays don't end altogether the same if the story doesn't permit it,[3] so think of this world as a sort of drama school, where you must play the role not as you wish but as it's assigned to you.

---

[1] See p. 287, n. 1. Constantius died in 306 A.D., but Constantine did not succeed immediately.

[2] This account is derived, ultimately, from Eusebius' life of Constantine, I.28-31 (*Patrologia Graeca*, X, 943-947). The sign was the chi-rho symbol of Christ; the battle was presumably against Constantine's Eastern rival Maxentius.

[3] T. W. Baldwin translates "characters never go out completely till the play is finished" and interprets as a reflection of the principle of the empty stage (*Five-Act Structure*, p. 356); but I take *drammata* to mean plays, not characters.

DIOCTES.   Ita mones?
ANABASIUS.

Nam quid uis aliud? Quem non ducunt fata, trahunt denique.
DIOCTES.

Fateor.
ANABASIUS.   Si sapis. Ecquid uis?
DIOCTES.   Nunc quod restat, Latium aliquod 30
    Vbi lateam quaerendum est. En autem, quem hinc parturiunt
        fores?
    Spectatores, si quis quaerat, ego non adfui.

ACTUS IIII. SCENA III.   [*f. 144v*]
Trimetri.
Ecclesia.

[ECCLESIA.]
    Qvanquam mihi tot undique circumstrepunt cruces,
    Cui praeter uitam nihil superest, haec si tamen
    Dicenda est uita, inuita quam circumfero.
    Vnum hoc animo penitus persuasi mihi:
    Vita haec nihil unquam feret tam felleum   5
    Quod non ferendo patiar Christi uel mei
    Causa: in nostram tam amicus est familiam.
    Viro qui Somati primum ac parentibus
    Spem resurrectionis spondet mortuis.
    Tum qui me praeterea miserosque liberos   10
    Gehennali hoc exoluerit ergastulo.
    Quo magis haec leuia, corpus quae feriunt, fero,
    Quae etsi pungunt, punctus tamen id tempori' est,   [*p. 47*]
    Illa aeternum durant. Caeterum ut ut haec sient,
    Nae illud mihi magni instar solatii est. Dies   15
    Quos coelestis pater dedit Alcedonios,

---

13. *tempori' est*] I follow MSC; B reads *tempori,est* (in all copies which I have seen).

DIOCTES. Is that your advice?

ANABASIUS. Well, what else would you want? Those whom the fates don't lead, they finally drag.

DIOCTES. I admit that.

ANABASIUS. You will if you're wise. Do you want anything else?

DIOCTES. Now it remains for me to seek some Latium to hide in.[1] But look, whom are these gates bringing forth?—— Audience, if anyone asks, I haven't been here. [*Exeunt.*

[IV.3] *Enter Ecclesia.*

ECCLESIA. So many tormentors clamor all around me, and I have nothing left except life, if indeed this is to be called life which I bear so unwillingly.[2] Yet I am utterly persuaded of one thing: this life could never bring anything so full of gall that I could not endure it by suffering for the sake of my Christ. He's such a friend to our family. In the first place, he promises a hope of resurrection for my dead, my husband Soma and my parents; besides that, he freed me and my wretched children from this hellish prison. The more trifling, then, do I hold these things which beset my body: though they sting, yet their sting is only of a moment, while those gifts last forever. Besides, however these things may be, these halcyon days which the heavenly father has granted are a source

[1] Latium, the district containing Rome and hence the center of the popes; cf. above, Humphrey's "De Christo Triumphante", l. 40. My translation misses a pun in the Latin (*Latium—lateam*).

[2] The draft manuscript also assigns this scene to Ecclesia and refers to her husband as Soma, not Sarcobius; see Textual Notes. The first eleven lines in the manuscript version read as follows: "My husband Soma now is dead, and I, Ecclesia, am left alone, a woman with three children. Besides, I hear Asia is in danger from the Turks. What woman's spirit would these things not drive out whose spirit is not a stock? That one woman should be battered by so many blows of fortune! First in the death of a husband whom persecution took from me. Next there's this other matter of the calamities of my daughter: it's not clear whether she's still alive. Meantime—but let me not rehearse the great poverty that now besets me. On account of Christ my goods are so ravaged and I am so thoroughly weakened, I am between the Symplegades, a widow, deprived, barren, ejected from home and country, beset by cares and the hatred of men. Nothing remains to me but life—if this is to be called life which I bear so unwillingly. Though so many crosses din about me on all sides, I am completely persuaded of this one thing: this life will never bring anything so full of gall that I will not bear by tolerating it, since my dear Christ has freed me from this hellish prison."

Vbi pulso tandem Diocte, mihi liceat
A persecutionibus feriarier:
Ex quo primum Constantinus Britannicus
Republica potitus est, pace iam diu   20
Fruimur, nisi quod omnia foedat rabies
Turcica. Tum nescio quid nobis scripturae adhuc   [*f. 145*]
Praesagiunt post annos mille grauius,
Solutus cum e capistro redierit Satan.
Atque hem, quid ego hinc audire procul uideor apud   25
Antipodas, strepitus quos subterraneos?
Hei mihi, uereor quid monstri abitur. Nam non leue
Id esse, tellus quod tremiscens subsilit,
Nimis dubito. Ac ni me annus fallit et animus,
Adest iam tempus, bellua cum promittitur   30
Apocalyptica: nec longe abesse potest, ubi
Vbi sit. Tum quas hic turbas adueniens dabit
Haud obscurum est. Nec an is iam siet satis
Scio. Nisi id quicquid fuerit, haud est animus hic
Haerere diutius, ne quod nolim uideam.   35

ACTUS IIII. SCENA IIII.   [*p. 48*]
Trimetri.
Satan Solutus. Anabasius. Dioctes. Psychephonus. Pseudamnus.

[SATAN.]
Salutem atque benedictionem Acheronticam,
Quotquot sitis. At quid hoc? Proh portas inferi.
Itan' nemo gratatum huc prouolat? Semel
Nec ex uinclis salutat reducem? Populus hic
Friget. Vide absentia quid facit! At ubinam   5
Dioctes saltem ac Psychephonus?
ANABASIUS.   Iam aderunt, scio.
SATAN.
Profecto quantum uideo, multo haec res secus
Atque ego augurabar euenit. Proin ut tempora,
Ita mutanda consilia sunt. Atque eia
Quam dextro Mercurio succedunt omnia   10
Ad unguem ilico. Vah, quanti est sapere miseris.

27. *leue*] I follow MSC; B reads *bene*.

of great comfort to me, for Dioctes has finally been banished and I'm granted a respite from persecutions. Since Constantine the Briton first ruled the country, we've enjoyed peace for a long time. Only the Turkish madness mars everything.[1] Besides that, the scriptures still portend some heavier burden for us after a thousand years, when Satan comes back freed from his bonds. And listen, don't I hear something far off near the Antipodes, some subterranean noises? Woe is me, I fear something ominous is afoot. I suspect only too strongly it's nothing trivial, because the earth is trembling and leaping up, and unless the year and my feelings deceive me, the time is now at hand when the Apocalyptic beast is prophesied. Wherever he is, he can't be far off. What troubles he'll cause when he comes is not at all difficult to imagine. I don't know whether this is he now, but if not, whatever it is, I don't intend to stay here any longer, lest I see what I don't want to see.
[*Exit.*

[IV.4] *Enter Satan, freed, and Anabasius.*[2]

SATAN. Greetings, and blessings from hell, all of you. But what's this? Look, I've come through the gates. Does no one rush forth to wish me joy? Or greet me just once as I return from my chains? The people here are cold-hearted. See what absence does. But where, at least, are Dioctes and Psychephonus?

ANABASIUS. I'm sure they're already on their way.

SATAN. Really, as far as I can see, this has turned out quite differently from what I predicted. Well, my plans must be changed to suit the times, and ah, how all things work out for a clever Mercury,[3] right down to the fingernail. Yes, it's worth a great deal to be wise during misfortunes.

---

[1] The Turks at this time controlled all of southeastern Europe and were much feared through the remainder of the continent.

[2] Satan is thus *freed* after the end of the ten persecutions; in the *Acts and Monuments*, Foxe said that Satan was *tied up* at that time (ed. Cattley, I, 304). A note in B cites Apocalypse 19 (? = 20.7-8, in which Satan returns to raise Gog and Magog).

[3] Among other things, Mercury was god of dexterity, because he was so clever.

ANABASIUS.

Quid incoepturus cedo?

SATAN.   Quod ubi rescieris,

Daedalias dixeris superare machinas.

Scilicet equo hoc nostra facile fient Pergama,

Ne dubita.

ANABASIUS.   Resipisco.

DIOCTES.   Audire modo uocem   15

Visus sum Zebub.

SATAN.   Diocten ac Psychephenum

Video.

DIOCTES.   Equidem te, here, restitutum gratulor.

PSYCHEPHONUS.   [*p. 49; f. 145v*]

Nos quibus hic labyrinthis tenemur nescis.

SATAN.   At

Theseo uos filo expediam commodum.

Id qua efficiam probe prouisa est methodus.   20

DIOCTES.

Audistin' ergo?

SATAN.   A principio omnia. Sed mane

Huc dum euoco quem uolo. Heus, Pseudamne, Pseudamne

Inquam. Men' nemo hic audit? Heus, ex tertio

Inferno Pseudamnum exire impero.

PSEUDAMNUS.   Quis malum

Nobis exorcista hic? At princeps ipsus est.   25

SATAN.

Ehodum ad me, vosque adeste pariter, ut quae agam

Mysteria ministri sitis ac testes mihi.

Primum initiis ex quantulis in copias

Quantas creuit nomen Christiadum cernitis,

Christi praesidio, eius dum insistunt legibus: 30

Quippe hinc tantum his robur, nobisque infirmitas.

Iam id unicum superest consilium denique:

Quod ui haud licet conficiamus ut astutia.

Sampsoni huic erademus per meretriculam

---

14. *nostra*] I follow MSC and N; B reads *nostro*.

ANABASIUS. Tell me, what are you going to try?

SATAN. When you find out, you'll say it surpasses the devices of Daedalus. Indeed, with this horse Troy will easily be ours, never doubt it.[1]

ANABASIUS. My spirits are improving.

Enter Dioctes and Psychephonus.

DIOCTES [*to Psychephonus*]. I thought I just heard Zebub's voice.[2]

SATAN. I see Dioctes and Psychephonus.

DIOCTES. Master, congratulations! You've been restored.

PSYCHEPHONUS. You don't know the labyrinths we're trapped in here.

SATAN. But I'll free you in due time with a Thesean thread.[3] My technique for doing it is well provided for.

DIOCTES. Have you heard then?

SATAN. Everything, from the beginning. But wait while I call someone here that I want.—— [*Shouts.*] Hey, Pseudamnus. Pseudamnus, I say. Doesn't anyone here listen to me? Hey, Pseudamnus, I order you to come out of the third hell.[4]

Enter Pseudamnus.

PSEUDAMNUS. Which of you devils has spirited me here? But it's the prince himself.

SATAN. Come here to me.—— [*To Dioctes and Psychephonus.*] And you come too to be my ministers and witnesses when I perform my mysteries.[5] First, you see how the tribe of Christians has grown from such tiny beginnings into huge numbers. They're under the protection of Christ so long as they follow his laws: hence their great strength and our weakness. Because of that, we're left now with only one plan: to accomplish by cleverness what we can't accomplish by force. We'll shave the head of this Samson

[1] Cf. *Titus et Gesippus* I.9.62-63.

[2] The nickname (Hebrew for fly) is less respectful than Beel (= lord) would be; for a similar irony, cf. p. 279, n. 1.

[3] Cf. *Titus et Gesippus* I.4.22-23.

[4] Cf. the three-part division of Dante's Inferno, the lowest part being for the souls of the fraudulent; there, in the eighth circle, are found several popes (Canto XIX) and, at the very bottom, Satan himself (Canto XXXIV); see the plan in Canto XI.

[5] A note in B cites 2 Thessalonians 2.[7].

Caput. Saepe etenim machinis facilius   35
Tolluntur pondera. Ita hic astu nobis opu'st.
Etenim Deum aduersus reniti inscitia est.
Is dum sufficit opem, operam no' omnem ludimus.
Sin pote fieri est, a Christo ut diuaricent suo,   [*p. 50*]
Dehinc uictis facile leges imponimus.   40
Praeterea haud ulla restat remedii anchora.

ANABASIUS.

Sed id qua efficiamus uereor.

SATAN.   Nihil est. Sine.

ANABASIUS.

Itane ais?

SATAN.   Principio id tute, Anabasi, in animum
Reuoca: Christum olim ipsum in solitudine
Tentamine quo adorsus sum, simili in hos modo   45
Agendum stropha. Mundi illicibiles opes
Deliciasque ingeram; uitae lubentias
Omnigenas, ceu Circaea pocula, subiiciam
Probe; mille addam ueneficiis praelitos
Honores, dynastias, titulos celebres: 50
Voluptatis nulla aberit esca. Quicquid in
Mundo celsum est, tentigine aut ulla lenocinans,
Incutiam, ueneno ut qui aspergant saccharum.   [*f. 146*]
Ita ui quos nequeo, frangam mollitie. Siquidem
Natura haec rerum est: mala quos conciliant uiros,   55
Eosdem dissoluit luxuries. Porro ad haec
Munia nemo est Pseudamno uno expromptior:
Vsque adeo mirus est simulandi artifex
Agnum ut, quum uideas, esse ex uultu iudices.
Quae causa est hunc cur ad me accitum, uosque nunc   60
Attendere uelim quae dissero. Pseudamne, tu
Principio in Babylona te auferes, ubi
Cum gazula hac pecuniaria atrium haud   [*p. 51*]
Eneruiter obsidebis pontificium,

---

38. *no' omnem*] I follow MSC; B, presumably mistaking the apostrophe for a
nasal macron, reads *non omnem*. The MSC contraction stands for *nos omnem*.

50. *dynastias*] transliterated from the Greek word δυναστεία, power.

53. *saccharum*] = *saccharon*. I follow MSC; B has *saccarum*.

with the help of a whore.[1] As great weights often are lifted quite easily with engines, so we need a device here, because it's folly to stand up to a god. So long as he supports them with his power, we squander all our effort, but if we can work it so they're scattered from their Christ, then we'll easily impose our laws on a conquered people. Except for that, there's no other chance of improvement.

ANABASIUS. But how we can accomplish that I'm afraid——

SATAN. There's nothing to it, believe me.

ANABASIUS. Is that so?

SATAN. First call to mind, Anabasius, that I once took on Christ himself in the desert with temptation;[2] I have only to work on these people with the same weapon. I'll press upon them all the seductive wealth and delights of the world; I'll offer them all manner of life's pleasures, the Circean cup as it were;[3] to those elixirs I'll add a thousand painted glories, worldly empires, and distinguished titles. No allurement of pleasure will be wanting. I'll inspire them with whatever is lofty in the world, or whatever entices with lechery, like those who sprinkle poison over sugar. So those whom I can't break with force, I'll break with softness. For this is truly the nature of things: men who are won by vices are melted by luxury. Now, no one is better equipped for these tasks than this fellow, Pseudamnus: he's such a master of deception that, from his appearance when you see him, you'd declare him to be a lamb. That's why I summoned him to me, and now I'd like you to listen to what I tell him.—— Pseudamnus, go first to Babylon. You'll lay strong siege to the college of high priests[4] there with this purse of gold, so that when the see becomes vacant,

---

[1] Judges 16.
[2] Matthew 4.1-10.
[3] Cf. *Titus et Gesippus* I.4.3-4.
[4] That is, the College of Cardinals.

Vt cum sedes uacet, ex asse hanc facias tuam.   65
Quid non uenale muneribus? Aurum ubi rubet,
Nihil expugnatu difficile est. Demum ubi ad
Rerum fastigia penetraris, haud leuem
Pontificem te geras cautio est: Christi unicum
Videri te uicarium plausibile fuat.   70

PSEUDAMNUS.
  Audio.
SATAN.   Imo aude potius.
PSEUDAMNUS.   Si queam assequi.
SATAN.
  Vah, scripturae non desunt fulcra qui ingenium
  Habet. Scis quid Petri ille locus suggerit:
  Acumen cui est, quiduis quocunque pertrahit.
  In coelo ut is, ita in terris ad te unum omnia   75
  Traxeris. Hunc denique referre undique addecet.
  Leges faxis, martyrum scriptas sanguine,
  Queis orbem ceu naribus arbitrio agas tuo.
  Quoniamque suos habet ille, tibi adiunges quoque
  Symmistas lateri. Tum Ecclesia nec deerit   80
  Tibi facticia, sponsam itidem is ut habet suam,
  Sed exquisitis quae exornetur uestibus
  Prorsusque regio strepitu diffluat.
  Dabis et hunc fornicationis cyathum
  Quo reges meretricio inebriet toxico.   85
  Luxu imbues ac deliciis omnia,
  Quo fiet hos ut pessundes ad inertiam.   [*f. 146v*]
  Virtutem enim uoluptas uiros dedocet.   [*p. 52*]
  Sin refractarius tibi quis obaudiat
  Calcitro, haud mora quin elementis uindices   90
  Omnibus.
PSEUDAMNUS.   Id agnus opinor non fecit Dei.
SATAN.
  Porro ausculta insuper, auremque utranque arrige.
  In rebus publicis priuatisque omnium,

65. *hanc*] the MSC reading, *hac*, is tempting, but is in the wrong gender.
72. *fulcra*] the normal sense is bedposts (L-S), but LTL gives a broader sense
(= *fulcimenta*), props.
82. *exornetur*] I follow MSC to improve the scansion; B reads *ornetur*.

by this money you'll make it yours. What can't be bought with bribes? When your gold is true-colored, nothing is hard to overcome. When you've finally achieved the height of power, you must be careful to conduct yourself as no ordinary pontiff. Let it be plausible that you seem to be the only vicar of Christ.

PSEUDAMNUS. I understand.

SATAN. Stand up to it instead.

PSEUDAMNUS. If I could carry it off!

SATAN. Come now, supports of scripture aren't lacking if one has the right temperament. You know what that position of Peter offers: whoever is sharp enough can pull anything wherever he wishes. On earth you will do as the one in heaven does, get everything for yourself alone. It behooves you, then, to reproduce him in every way. You'll make laws, written in the blood of martyrs, with which you may rule the world according to your will, by the nose as it were. And since he has his priests, you'll also attach priests to your side. Again, as he has his bride, you won't be without a false Ecclesia; but let her be decked out in exquisite clothes and completely abandoned to the clamor of royalty. You'll also give her this cup of fornication with which to intoxicate kings with the poison of harlotry.[1] You'll infect everything with lechery and pleasures. So it will happen that you'll sink these people into ignorance—for pleasure unteaches men virtue. But if some grumbler should obey you reluctantly, make no delay, but punish him with all your resources.

PSEUDAMNUS. That, I think, the lamb of God didn't do.

SATAN.[2] Now listen to something else; perk up both ears. You should involve yourself in the public and private affairs of all

[1] Apocalypse 17.4.
[2] The early draft essentially omitted this speech and the three following speeches.

Praecipue in comitiis suffragiisque ordinum,
Illic tute, Pseudamne, immisceas. Ubi   95
Cosmetor si quis sit creandus laicis,
Ita cum illis ius electionis partias,
Falx ut tua sit omni in messe posita.
Hoho, ut hoc mihi consilio placeo? Principes
Hoc pacto reddes facile ad genua supplices.   100
Tum confirmationem ex te ut petant uide:
Qui placeant modo; qui minus, hos pro libidine
Submoueas. Si quid in te sentis uspiam
Mouerier, ipsos inter se principes
Committere scitum est. Bellum aut Turcis inferant: 105
Victoria qua tendit, tu tendito; uicta pars
Supplex inuita aderit, tibi quod erit utile.
Sic ipse utrinque inibis gratiam. Fidem
Seruare te, nisi res mouet, haud monuerim:
Cum regibus raro, cum haereticis nuspiam.   110
PSEUDAMNUS.
    Fiscum at si pecunia destituat interim?
SATAN.
    Parata uia est: in Turcas expeditio
Agitur, ad eam rem aere opus et neruis bellicis.   [*p. 53*]
Rem quum omnes dederint, uerba tu dabis omnibus.
Postremo tria sunt in uita mortalium: 115
Cibi, crimina, connubia, audin'? Clauem qui habet
Messem suo hinc uentri peramplam fecerit.
Abi nunc Pegaseo quantum queas gradu
In Babylonem, Pseudamne: in magnis mora haud iuuat.
DIOCTES.
    Recte sane, siquidem is nunc agit animam   120
Capitolinus flamen, necdum an obiit scio.
SATAN.
    Sed cautio una est quae restat porro priusquam
Incipias pithecismos tuos quo pallies
Melius: Nomocratem quoquo modo tibi
Asciscas sentio. Id enim ad sanctimoniae   125

123. *pithecismos*] transliterated from the Greek πιθηκισμός.
     pallies] the verb *pallio* is rare (LTL).

ranks, Pseudamnus, especially in conventions and elections. If some leader is to be chosen by the laity, you must share the right of election with them so that your sickle is found in every harvest.[1] Ho ho, how pleased I am with this plan! In this way you'll easily bring princes before your knees as suppliants. Then see to it that they seek confirmation from you: if they please you, fine; if not, remove them at your whim. If you sense that something is being plotted against you somewhere, it's a good idea to set the princes against each other. Or have them start a war on the Turks. Where the victory is inclining, you incline the same way. The side that's beaten will come to you as an unwilling suppliant, and that will be profitable for you. Thus you'll come into favor with both sides. I wouldn't advise you to remain loyal unless the occasion warrants it: rarely to kings, never to heretics.

PSEUDAMNUS. But if sometime the treasury should lack money?

SATAN. A way is ready: an expedition is undertaken against the Turks. For that there's a need of money and the resources of war. When they've all given of their substance, you'll give all of them words. Finally, there are three main factors in the life of mortals: sustenance, sins, and sex.[2] You understand? Whoever has the key will reap with it a splendid harvest for his own stomach. Now go to Babylon, Pseudamnus, as fast as possible, with the speed of Pegasus. In great affairs delay doesn't help at all.

DIOCTES. Excellent, for the priest of the Capitoline is now breathing his last.[3] I don't know whether he's dead yet or not.

SATAN. But before you begin, there's still one piece of advice remaining: the better to cover up your monkeying around, I think you should take Nomocrates as your associate in some capacity. That will convey a reputation for holiness, since he's

---

[1] A draft version compared Aesop's lion sharing its spoil.
[2] Literally, food, crimes, and marriages.
[3] That is, the pope in Rome, one of whose hills was the Capitoline.

Opinionem refert, quando is adeo
Integer habetur uir ac moribus piis.
Congredere una, Dioctes, imperium tibi is
A Constantino ut ereptum redintegret.
Psychephone, tu uola praeceps Nomocratem   130
Quaesitum, ubi ubi sit, huicque addictum uide.
Tu, Anabasi, auri hanc uim accipe qua monilia,
Corollas, lineas Atrabum seu Laodiceas,
Coccum atque purpurissum, pallasque insuper
Auro hyacinthoque florulentas, byssinas,   [*p. 54*]   135
Virgatas, undulatas, holosericas
Conquiras, queis Pornam polias, meretriculam
Babyloniam illam, nostin'?

ANABASIUS.   Intelligo.
SATAN.   Atque eam
Ad Pseudamnum aduehas, uestitam munditer.
ANABASIUS.   [*f. 147*]
Nunquid aliud?
SATAN.   Nisi ut matures.
ANABASIUS.   Ladas   140
Non ipse pernicius nec lubentius.
SATAN.

Postquam his distribui operas, mihi nec ocii est
Locus. Ad Turcas me feram primiter, eos
Vt exstimulem in Palaestinos ac Rhodos,
Moxque in Byzantium, inde et in Vngariam ac   145
Gentes conterminas. Confecto hoc classico,
Recta me praecipitabo Babyloniam, meos
Visurus denuo. Sed quid cesso bellua?
Satanam modo stertere non sinunt haec tempora.

---

131. *addictum*] ?read *adductum*, the MSC reading.
133. *Atrabum*] properly, *Atrebatum.*
        seu] I follow MSC; B reads *ceu*. But cf. V.4.10 Textual Notes. Foxe uses
ceu in *Titus and Gesippus* I.4.27.
137. *Pornam polias*] note the pun on *Pornapolis.*

held to be such an upstanding man of pious ways.—— Dioctes, you go with him too so he can restore to you the rule which was seized by Constantine.——[1]   [*Exeunt Pseudamnus and Dioctes.* Psychephonus, fly quickly. Find Nomocrates, wherever he is, and see that he joins Pseudamnus' cause.—— [*Exit Psychephonus.* Anabasius, you take this sum of gold to buy necklaces, crowns, cloth of Arras or Laodicea,[2] scarlet and purple, robes flowered in gold and hyacinth, made of striped and patterned cottons, and all-silk. With these things adorn Porna, the Babylonian whore. Do you know her?

ANABASIUS. Yes.

SATAN. When she's elegantly dressed, take her to Pseudamnus.

ANABASIUS. Nothing else?

SATAN. Nothing, except that you hurry.

ANABASIUS. Ladas[3] himself wouldn't go faster, or more willingly.
    [*Exit.*

SATAN. Now that I've distributed jobs to them, there's no time for me to be at leisure. First I'll go to the Turks to stir them up against Palestine and Rhodes, then against Byzantium, and finally against Hungary and the adjoining countries.[4] Once I've sounded that battle signal, I'll rush straight to Babylonia to see my people again. But why delay, brute? These times just don't allow Satan to snore.   [*Exit.*

---

[1] In the draft version, Constantine is not referred to and Dioctes is told to change his name.

[2] Artois, with its capital Arras, was famed for its clothing and tapestries from ancient times. Laodicea ad Lycum was famous for its beautiful soft wool. Laodice was also a "stock name for women of high rank, meaning 'princess' " (*Oxford Classical Dictionary*). In Apocalypse III.15, Laodiceans were called "lukewarm" in their religious sensibilities. The draft version adds a request for hides from Zebulun (a tribe of Israel if I interpret *Zebellinis* correctly) and from Madaura (in Numidia).

[3] A very fast runner of Laconia, referred to by Catullus and Juvenal.

[4] The Turks captured Jerusalem, along with the rest of Syria, from the Egyptian Mamelukes in 1516 (it had been in Moslem control for centuries); Rhodes from the Order of St. George in 1522; Constantinople (= Byzantium) from the Roman Emperor in 1453; and Budapest, also from the Holy Roman Emperor, in 1526.

ACTUS IIII. SCENA V.
Catalectici Trochaici.
Ecclesia. Africus. Europus.

[ECCLESIA.]

Mvndi canescentis iam occasus monet, gnati, bene ut
Subducta ratione sitis ad constantiam. Scitis
Tempora enim haud abesse longe Paulus quae praenunciat,   [*p. 55*]
Filius ubi perditionis reuelandus sit. Et Asiae
Tum sororis sortem cernitis, quae capitua, heu dolor,   5
Sub Turca seruit quam misere. In uobis restat unicum
Firmamentum mihi: quo magis, uestri causa, anxia
Sum, necubi solutus in malum malus trudat Satan.

EVROPUS.

Vulgo fama, mater, est, oriturum Antichristum esse, at hunc
Esse ego Mahometum reor Asiaticum qui nostram adeo   10
Diuexat familiam.

ECCLESIA.   Est, at non unus est ille tamen.

Antichristi tot sunt Christus quot habet hostes. Caeterum
Confessi isti, qui cauerier potessunt magis,   [*f. 147v*]
Minus incommodant. Qui praetexunt officio fraudem, ab iis
Demum Uertumnis cauendum, gnati, granditer moneo.   15

EVROPUS.

Adcurabimus sedulo.

ECCLESIA.   Eo ad nepotes reliquos

Visura quid agant. Vos, uti tempus est, cum lubet reuortite. [*p. 56*]

AFRICUS.

Animo haud excidet unquam, Christo nomen quantum: omnes
     sumus
Peccatorculi, at nos enixissime quos Nomocratis
Ex dira cauea adeo eripuit misericorditer.   20
Sed quis egreditur, irrumpens tam immaniter?

[IV.5]   *Enter Ecclesia, Africus, and Europus.*

ECCLESIA. The decline of this aging world now warns you, my sons, to have your accounts in good order as to your steadfastness, for you know that the time is not far off when Paul predicts that the son of perdition must be revealed. Besides, you see the fate of your sister Asia, who is so wretchedly enslaved under the Turk—oh the sorrow! In you remains my only support. All the more anxious am I for your sake lest that evil Satan, now on the loose, push you into misfortune.

EUROPUS. Mother, the rumor among the people is that the Antichrist is about to arise, but I think he's the Asian Mohammed, who's so troubling our family.

ECCLESIA. He is, but he isn't *the* one. There are as many Antichrists as there are enemies of Christ. But these confessed ones are less troublesome since we can take better precautions against them. The ones who conceal fraud under obedient service—I warn you, my sons, to be very much on your guard against those Vertumnuses.[1]

EUROPUS. We'll be very careful.

ECCLESIA. I'm going to my other kinfolk to see what they're doing. You come back when you wish and when there's time.   [*Exit.*

AFRICUS. I'll never forget how great is our debt to Christ. We're all sinners, but especially we whom he snatched so mercifully from the dreadful pit of Nomocrates. But who's coming out in such a wild rush?

---

[1] Vertumnus was the god of the seasons and a symbol of mutability; cf. Horace, *Satires* II.7.14. Cooper's *Thesaurus*, however, called him a god "supposed of the Painims to haue the gouernaunce of mens mindes, or, after some, of bying and sellyng."

ACTUS IIII. SCENA VI.
Dioctes. Africus. Europus.

[DIOCTES.]

Proh Ditis pol ingens numen. Quid hic satis
Exultem gestiens? Nunquam qui laetius
In uita uiderim quicquam succedere,
Nec uirgula magis diuina. Vix adhuc
In basilicam irruimus, moribundus miser   5
Expirat praesul. Arripit ex tempore
Occasionem noster ilico. Vah illius
Quid ego pingam hypocrisim!

AFRICUS.   Hem, quae haec est fabula?

DIOCTES.

Primum quam uero uultu sanctimoniam
Simulans scelus lumina conuertit omnium!   10
Virtutis si uidisse' exemplar diceres
Nomocratem secum semper habere in ulnulis,
Mox donariis proceres sensim facere suos,
Dehinc in plebis quoque gratiam subrepere.
Demum ubi suauem lucri uidet odorem omnibus,   15
Coepit tentare animos iamque cominus
Cruciferas admouere machinas. Proh fidem,   [p. 57]
Quid non expugnant auri tormenta sacra? Quid
Verbis opus? Comitia adsunt. Praeda nos
Penes est facta. Denique quod ego pol   20
Hercle meros triumpho panegyricos.   [f. 148]

EVROPUS.

Quos hic triumphos praedicat?

AFRICUS.   Rogita.

DIOCTES.   Quisnam homo
Loquitur? Hem, num nam plus satis, quod dixeram?
Prior hos occupo. Amici, quid uobis hic statio est?
Pannosa quaeso quae penuria haec, uiri   25
Qui haud estis improbi?

---

17. cruciferas] DuCange lists the neuter noun crucifer, a type of money, and the
masculine noun cruciferi, an order of monks; Prudentius used crucifer as an epithet
for Christ (L-S). I find no precedent for an adjectival form.

[IV.6]   *Enter Dioctes, running happily.*

DIOCTES [*to audience*]. Oh the great majesty of Dis! I want to leap
for joy, but how could I rejoice enough? Never in my life have
I seen anything turn out more happily. There's no wand more
divine[1] Scarcely had we run into the basilica when the wretched
dying pontiff breathed his last. Right then, on the spur of the
moment, our leader seized the occasion. Oh, how could I paint
his hypocrisy?

AFRICUS [*aside to Europus*]. Well, what's this story?

DIOCTES [*to audience*]. First how the rascal turned everyone's head,
pretending holiness with a straight face. You would have called
him a model of virtue if you'd seen him keeping Nomocrates
always with him at his elbow, next gradually winning those
princes over with gifts, then stealing into the good graces of the
people as well. Finally, when he saw that the smell of lucre was
sweet to everybody, he began to test their characters and to move
up his cross-bearing devices.[2] By my faith! What won't the awe-
some engines of gold overcome? In short, the conclave began;
the spoils are ours. And that, by Hercules, is why I'm celebrating
these triumphs.

EUROPUS [*aside to Africus*]. What triumphs is he talking about?

AFRICUS [*aside to Europus*]. Ask him.

DIOCTES [*aside*]. Who's speaking? Well, did I say more than I
should have? I'd better speak to these fellows first.—— My
friends, what's your station here? Pray, what's this tattered
poverty? You certainly aren't mean men.

---

[1] Sc. than Pseudamnus'. There may be a play on words: Cicero uses *virgula
divina* for a divining rod (L-S). Cf. *Titus et Gesippus* I.5.34.

[2] Coins with crosses on them (DuCange). See the note to the Latin text.

EVROPUS.   Probitatem quam opes
  Tuemur citius. Sed quid id sit quod modo
  Tecum uenisti mussitans? Episcopum
  Fuisse opinor mortuum.
DIOCTES.   Sic est.
EVROPUS.   Et in
  Vicem eius adoptatus nostin' quinam siet?   30
DIOCTES.
  Papae, uir in uita optimus, seruus Dei, ac
  Pietas ipsa.
EVROPUS.   Et nomen potin' edicere?
DIOCTES.
  Pseudamnus.
EVROPUS.   Pseudamnus? Quid istuc nominis?
DIOCTES.
  Quid dixi? Eudamnus inquam, agnus ut agnoteros
  Nusquam sit: ipsum esse ut dicas agnum Dei.   35
AFRICUS.
  Equidem laetor facto.
DIOCTES.   Atque ut scire liceat,
  Vide modo: iam primum ubi renitendo diu   [*p. 58*]
  Inuitu' haud potuit suffragiis quin cederet,
  Continuo ille: Abi, inquit, Symmache mihi
  (Id etenim nomen erat), quantum queas foras,   40
  Indigetem si quem Christi reperias indigum
  In nostras quem recipiam fortunulas.
  Meum, praeter uirtutem, esse haud quicquam uolo:
  Caetera aliorum. Itaque in uos incidisse nunc
  Laetor. Mecum modo haud pigeat congredi.   45

31. *Papae*] is there a pun on *papa*, pope?

33. *Quid . . . nominis*] B repeats the S.P. *Europus* here. Perhaps Foxe intended
to assign the words to *Africus* and wrote the wrong name by mistake. More
likely, he accidentally wrote the S.P. in the wrong place and neglected to cancel
it in correction. I follow MSC.

34. *agnoteros*] this coinage is a multilevelled pun: *agnus* (lamb), and ἁγνός
(holy), with a Greek comparative suffix. Cf. also the Greek verb ἀγνοέω, to be
ignorant, and the Latin verb *agnosco*.

EUROPUS. We're quicker to look after our probity than our wealth. But what were you muttering just now as you came in—that the bishop is dead, I think it was?

DIOCTES. That's right.

EUROPUS. And do you know who's been chosen in his place?

DIOCTES. Yes indeed, a man of a very just life, a servant of God, piety itself.

EUROPUS. And can you tell us his name?

DIOCTES. Pseudamnus.

EUROPUS. Pseudamnus? What sort of a name is that?

DIOCTES. What did I say? I should say Eudamnus,[1] for nowhere is there a lamb more lamblike.[2] So you'd say he's the lamb of God himself.

AFRICUS. I'm very happy about that.

DIOCTES. To know what he is, just consider this. When, after a long period of resistance, he couldn't prevent them from voting him in against his will, he said without hesitation, "Go out as quickly as possible, my dear Symmachus" (for that was my name),[3] "and see if you can find any needy saint of Christ to whom I may give my trifling earthly goods. I wish nothing for myself but virtue; let others have the rest." So I'm happy I came upon you now; don't be reluctant to come with me.

---

[1] Dioctes means it to be taken as a compound of εὖ, good, and ἀμνός, lamb. Could Foxe have meant an ironic pun on δαμνάω, a variant of δαμάω, to overpower?

[2] See the note to the Latin text.

[3] Either Foxe or Dioctes used *was* when *is* would have been more deceptive. *Symmachus* is a Greek word for an ally, but Foxe may have been alluding to Quintus Aurelius Symmachus, who in the 380's A.D. championed the pagan gods against the Christian emperors and provoked replies from Ambrose and Prudentius.

Evropus.

  Est gratia, Symmache, merito quae tibi
  Debetur ex animo.
Dioctes.   Sed mane. Herus huc
  Ipse incedit foras. Concedite paululum.

ACTUS IIII. SCENA VII.   [*f. 148v*]
Iambici Acatalectici, Unus Senarius.
Pseudamnus. Psychephonus. Dioctes. Europus. Africus.

[Pseudamnus.]

  Qvid ais, Psychephone? Satin modo in collegas dapsilis
  Visus sum?
Psychephonus.   Perquam, Pseudamne.
Pseudamnus.   Et quid nunc futurum illis reris,
  Postquam tot latifundiis a me ditati diffluant?
Psychephonus.

  Insignes fortunae, uenti uelut ingentes, insignia
  Naufragia faciunt.   [*p. 59*]
Pseudamnus.   Ita spero.
Dioctes.   Here, salue. Bonos si tu hos satis   5
  Noris, dignos queis benefaxis putes.
Pseudamnus.   Ingenuos cum uideo,
  Vultus arguit. Eho, qui dicimini?
Europus.   Gemini ex iisdem sati
  Parentibus, ego Europus, is Afer dicitur.
Pseudamnus.   Age, mei sitis:
  Vna domus, communis familia sit.
Africus.   Bene sit, quum pius es.
Pseudamnus.

  Pietatem afflictam praeterire est impium.   10
  Porro cum fortuna, a me nomina accipietis simul.
  Tu, Europe, pauonia hac plumigata cum coronula

---

  1. *collegas*] the classical sense is colleagues, but DuCange lists the word in the sense here meant.
  8. *Afer*] elsewhere in this scene (S.H. and l. 13) Foxe changed the name to *Africus;* either he overlooked this one, or he felt he needed a dissyllable.
  10.] identified in MSC and B as the senarius listed in the M.H.
  12. *pauonia*] a variant of the normal *pavonina* (LTL).
     plumigata] I find no precedent for this verbal form.

EUROPUS. That's a kindness, Symmachus, for which we must be indebted to you from the heart.

DIOCTES. But wait, my master himself is coming out here. Wait a moment.

[IV.7]   *Enter Pseudamnus and Psychephonus.*

PSEUDAMNUS. What do you say, Psychephonus? Have I seemed generous enough toward the members of the college?

PSYCHEPHONUS. Extremely so, Pseudamnus.

PSEUDAMNUS. And how do you think it'll be with them after they abandon themselves to all those country estates I've enriched them with?

PSYCHEPHONUS. Great fortunes, like great winds, cause great wrecks.

PSEUDAMNUS. I hope so.

DIOCTES [*leading Europus and Africus forward*]. Hello, master. If you knew these good men well, you'd think them worthy of your kindness to them.

PSEUDAMNUS. I can tell from their faces that they're upstanding men. Hello, how are you called?

EUROPUS. We're brothers born of the same parents. I'm Europus, and he's called Africus.

PSEUDAMNUS. Come, be mine. Let's be one household, one common family.

AFRICUS. Very good, since you are a holy man.

PSEUDAMNUS. It's wicked to neglect afflicted piety. Along with your prosperity you'll receive titles from me. Europus, you take this peacock-plumed crown; you shall be Defender of the Faith.[1]

---

[1] For this time, Europus becomes identified with the English monarch, preparing for the last-act emphasis on the suffering of the English church. In 1521, Henry VIII's long-standing wish for a papal title like that of Continental monarchs was gratified when Pope Leo X awarded him the title "Defender of the Faith." English monarchs still bear the title, though the faith defended is different. The award was a recognition for Henry's "golden book," as Leo called it, the *Assertio Septem Sacramentorum Contra M. Lutherum*. Henry's seal after 1532 shows a plumed helm (though not necessarily with a peacock's plumes) and the title "Def. Fidei," and both symbols continued into later realms. See J. Harvey Bloom, *English Seals* (London, 1906), and J. M. Brown, "Henry VIII's Book, . . . and the Royal Title of 'Defender of the Faith,' " *Transactions of the Royal Historical Society*, VIII (1880), 242-261.

Fidei Defensor esto. Tu uero cum rhomphaea, Africe,
Hac, Christianissimus appellator. Iam ite hac uos intro. Age,
Dioctes atriensis, inquam, introductos ad me face   15
Apothecas ad penuarias: famescunt forsitan
Inedia. Abite. Bene procedit. At ubi Porna tam diu
Restitat, aduentum quo minus adproperat? Salta,   [*f. 149*]
   Psychephone, in
Cubiculum. Eia, prius si memorassem, aduentassiet.

ACTUS IIII. SCENA VIII.   [*p. 60*]
Eivsdem rationis.
Pornapolis Meretrix Babylon. Pseudamnus. Psychephonus.
Ecclesia. [*Chorus*].

[PORNAPOLIS.]
  Vos hinc reuortite, abite. Proh summum tonantem, quantum in hac
  Nunc forma ac magnificentia est quod gestiam!
PSEUDAMNUS.   Quos huc mea
  Fert plausus Pornula!
PORNAPOLIS.   Pseudamno χαίρειν.
PSEUDAMNUS.   Suauiolum meum,
  Quidnam istuc gestiens adeo quod aduenis?
PORNAPOLIS.   Quod nix tibi
  Credibile sit, si narrem.
PSEUDAMNUS.   Quidnam?
PORNAPOLIS.   Quanto in pretio ac honore sim, 5
  Vbicunque sim, omnibus.
PSEUDAMNUS.   Narra quaeso.
PORNAPOLIS.   Quippe dum me effero
  E foribus ad te ueniens, summam per plateam affectare uiam
  Visum est. Hic ubi primum conspicua sum, concurrunt ceu ad
    deum
  Vndique. Forum ac uias omnes obstipari multitudine.

P.H. *Chorus*] omitted in MSC and B.

3. *suauiolum*] the classical sense, in Catullus, is a little kiss (L-S); here it is used metaphorically as a term of endearment. Bienvenu translates the word "mignonne iolie."

9. *obstipari*] a Plautine word, "To stoppe chinkes" (Cooper). Cf. the standard *stipare*, "to crowd together" (L-S).

And you, Africus, take this weapon; you shall be called Most
Christian.[1] Now go inside.—— Dioctes, I say, my steward, come,
take them in to the larder; they may be hungry from fasting.
Go on.   [*Exeunt Dioctes, Africus, and Europus.*
It's going well.[2] But where is Porna loitering so long? Why
doesn't she hurry?—— Psychephonus, run to her chamber.——
                             [*Exit Psychephonus.*
Oh, if I'd told him earlier, she'd have been here by now.

[IV.8]   *Enter Pornapolis the whore of Babylon, and Psychephonus.*

PORNAPOLIS [*as to people offstage*]. Turn back, you people. Go away.——
   Oh thunderer on high, how delightful this form and splendor is!
PSEUDAMNUS. What a racket my Pornula brings here!
PORNAPOLIS. Pseudamnus, hello.
PSEUDAMNUS. My sweet, why do you come so happily?
PORNAPOLIS. You'd scarcely believe it if I told you.
PSEUDAMNUS. What?
PORNAPOLIS. What esteem and honor I'm held in by everybody,
   wherever I go.
PSEUDAMNUS. Please tell me about it.
PORNAPOLIS. As I was leaving my gates to come to you, it seemed
   a good idea to take the main street.[3] As soon as I was seen there,
   people crowded all around me as if I were a god. The forum and

---

[1] Africus is here associated with France. The papal title "Roi-Très-Chrétien"
(Most Christian) was bestowed on Pepin the Short and confirmed on the twelfth-
century Capetins (M. Martin, *Le Roi de France ou les grandes journées qui ont fait la
monarchie* [Paris, 1963], p. 110). (In *Acts and Monuments*, Foxe named Charlemagne
as the first recipient of the title; ed. Pratt, I, 374.) The seals of many French
kings show a figure holding a staff of justice and a sceptre; the staff could be
taken as a spear (*rhomphaea*), and so Foxe apparently took it.

[2] At this point, the draft version included the following colloquy:

But where is Nomocrates, to whom I would restore the authority of the prison?
PSYCHEPHONUS. Don't do that, master.
PSEUDAMNUS. Why not?
PSYCHEPHONUS. Lest you get beaten by your own beast.
PSEUDAMNUS. Quiet. Isn't scripture a sufficient key when we wish?
PSYCHEPHONUS. But I'm afraid the key which is useful isn't true.
PSEUDAMNUS. I think what matters is not what's true, but what the people think
   is true. Do you get me?
PSYCHEPHONUS. Very good.

[3] A note in B refers to Apocalypse 17. Foxe altered a number of details.

Mirari. Sciscitarier a meis quae sim. Ecclesiam,   [*f. 149v*]
  inquiunt,   10
Omnipotentis Dei, Agni sponsam, ueritatis columen.   [*p. 61*]
Procumbere omnes ilico, adorare opido. Quin et pedum
Porro osculari uestigia. Mox tres fiunt reges obuiam.
Iis propino cyathum fornicarium huncce. Vinum ubi
Concaluit, uultus primum labascere omnium. Simul   15
Inter se consusurrari inuicem. Inde ut submoueam rogant
Famulos. Semoui. Soli ubi sumus, occipiunt, forma quae
Mea, aetasque sua—amoris pariter quam impotens telum siet.
Quorsum inquam haec? Vin' scire? Admodum? Arcanum at id
  esse: etsi pudeat haud,
Posse haud fateri tamen. Aurem do: "Faciem quo magis,"
  inquiunt,   20
"Spectamus hanc, minus hoc ferre quimus." Quid tum? "Vnius ut
Concedas noctis copiam." Quod ni impetrent, nullos fore.
Suadent, orant, obsecrant, suspirant. Hic ego uultum, oculos,
Ac gestus hominum attendo satis, lustroque singula.
Vbi serio agere uideo, coepi detrectare primulum,   [*p. 62*]   25
Sueuimus ut meretriculae cupidos cum cupimus magis esse qui
Nos ambiunt. Demum ignescere ubi cerno, magis memet dare
His familiarius. Postremo, quid uerbis opus? Annui,   [*f. 150*]
Pignus coepi, cras ut redirent iussi—siquidem diem tibi ut
Dixi hunc, Pseudamne, datura sum.
PSEUDAMNUS.   Vah, ut dulci te osculo capio,   30
  Mea lux.
PORNAPOLIS.   At unus restat nodus.
PSEUDAMNUS.   In scirpo fors.
PORNAPOLIS.   Ecclesia haec
  Quae latitat, nos ne prodat tandem.
PSEUDAMNUS.   Aquilam ex filice metuis.
  Sine, hos ego gryphos depuluerabo facile. Tu interim

---

14. *fornicarium*] this adjectival form is late; DuCange explains it "ex forni-
catione natus, spurius."

33. *depulverabo*] the verb *depulvero* is unprecedented, but Plautus uses the word
depulverans as an equivalent to *abstergens* (LTL).

all the streets were blocked by the mob. They stood in wonderment. They asked my people who I was. They said I was the Ecclesia of almighty God, bride of the lamb, supporter of truth. Then and there they all fell down and adored me exceedingly. Why, they even kissed the tracks of my feet. Soon three kings came to meet me. I toasted them with this cup of fornication. When the wine grew warm in us, first everyone's expression began to slacken, and they began to whisper back and forth to each other. Then they asked me to send my servants away. I did so, and when we were alone, they began: what my beauty and their prime— well, how uncontrollable the shaft of love would be on either account. Why should I tell you these things? You want to know? All right, but you must keep it secret; I'm not at all ashamed, but it can't be told. I listened to them. They said, "The more we look at your face, the less we can bear up." What to do then? "Do grant us the riches of one night." Unless they got it, they said, they'd be lost. They urged, begged, implored, sighed. I paid close attention to the men's faces, their eyes and gestures; I watched everything they did. When I saw that they were serious about it, I began to be a little coy, as we courtesans usually do when we want to make our eager clients more eager. Finally, when I saw that they were on fire, I began to appear more friendly to them. At last, to be brief about it, I consented, I took their pledges, and I told them to return tomorrow. I'm going to give this day to you as I promised, Pseudamnus.

PSEUDAMNUS [*kissing her*]. Oh, with what a sweet kiss I hold you, my light.

PORNAPOLIS. But one knot remains.

PSEUDAMNUS. In a bulrush, perhaps.[1]

PORNAPOLIS. This Ecclesia who's hiding out, lest she expose us in the end.

PSEUDAMNUS. You're afraid of an eagle from a fern. Don't you worry, I'll easily pulverize these griffins.[2] Meantime, Porna,

---

[1] Proverbial expression from Plautus and Terence: to look for nonexistent difficulties.

[2] Legendary animals, part lion and part eagle; hence, imaginary problems.

Telam pergas, Porna, hanc porro pertexere. Reges temeto tuo
Temulentos faxis, nobis ut se obstringant suaque omnia. Nihil   35
Cuiquam legitimum sit nostro ni initiato charactere
Prius. At quae illinc mulier eminet pexa ac uultu turbido?

ECCLESIA.

Horresco misera id quid sit Byzantii quod aiunt: uae hodie
Ecclesiam inuasse Dei, e coelo auditum clare. At filii   [*p. 63*]
Vbinam hic sint quos cupiam?

PSEUDAMNUS.   Haec quidnam portitat? Heus
    mulier, sodes,   40
Quae sis?

ECCLESIA.   Ecclesiae equidem nomen fero.

PSEUDAMNUS.   Proh anathema.

PORNAPOLIS.   Audin' hanc?

PSYCHEPHONUS.
    Haeretica.

PSEUDAMNUS.   Tun'te Ecclesiam esse?

ECCLESIA.   Negabon' esse, quae
    Siem?

PSYCHEPHONUS.   Schismatica.

PORNAPOLIS.   Miseret me. Canis quis te mulier
    Commorsit rabiens?

PSYCHEPHONUS.   Lymphatica.

ECCLESIA.   Quidnam tibi hic mecum rei'st?

PORNAPOLIS.
    Mihi loquitur.

PSYCHEPHONUS.   Vuycleuista.

PSEUDAMNUS.   Apage sis cum sordibus   45
    Hinc. Tun' Ecclesia ut sies?

PSYCHEPHONUS.   Anabaptistica.

ECCLESIA.   Anabaptista non
    Sum. Ecclesia sum orthodoxa.

---

37. *pexa*] Foxe several times uses this word in a sense the opposite of the literal meaning, well-combed, new. He apparently had in mind the Plautine sense, beaten, or, when he referred to Ecclesia's clothes, shaggy—though from age, not in the Horatian sense of woolly from being new, having the nap still on (L-S).

39. *inuasse*] both the sense and a false start in MSC (*ingress-*) show that this is the correct reading; it is found in the Harvard copy of B (MSC is unclear), but other copies of B which I have seen read *iuuasse*.

you go right on weaving your web. Make the kings drunk with your wine[1] so they'll bind themselves and all their prerogatives to us, and nothing will be lawful for anyone except it first have our mark on it. But who's that tattered woman coming out over there with a troubled expression?

Enter Ecclesia.[2]

ECCLESIA [*aside*]. I'm terribly afraid of what the Byzantines are saying—alas, that they have today attacked God's church; I heard it clearly from heaven. But where could my sons be, whom I would long to have here?

PSEUDAMNUS. What's she brooding about?—— Hey, woman, if you please, who are you?

ECCLESIA. I bear the name Ecclesia.

PSEUDAMNUS. Oh, anathema!

PORNAPOLIS. Do you hear her?

PSYCHEPHONUS. Heretic!

PSEUDAMNUS. You claim to be Ecclesia?

ECCLESIA. Shall I deny who I am?

PSYCHEPHONUS. Schismatic!

PORNAPOLIS. I pity you. What mad dog has bitten you, woman?

PSYCHEPHONUS. Madwoman!

ECCLESIA. What have you to do with me?

PORNAPOLIS. She's talking to me.

PSYCHEPHONUS. Wycliffite![3]

PSEUDAMNUS. Away from here with your mourning garments. You claim to be Ecclesia?

PSYCHEPHONUS. Anabaptist![4]

ECCLESIA. I am not an Anabaptist; I am orthodox Ecclesia.

---

[1] A note in B cites Apocalypse 18.[3]; cf. 17.2.

[2] C. H. Herford (p. 145) assumed that Ecclesia is on stage from the beginning of the scene and compares the scene in *Pammachius* in which "Parrhesia listens to the diabolical plans of Pammachius and his ally Porphyrius." He may be right, for Foxe does not indicate a new scene at this point as he often does when a character enters. But in l. 37 Pseudamnus speaks of her as coming out (*eminet*).

[3] A Lollard, follower of John Wyclif, fourteenth-century reformer and first English translator of the Bible.

[4] A follower of a radical Protestant sect founded at Zurich in 1514.

PSEUDAMNUS.   Proh polum arcticum atque antarc-
ticum.
ECCLESIA.   [*f. 150v*]
Quid clamitas?
PSEUDAMNUS.   Quae si pergas, nae ego te dabo ubi neque polum
Videas arcticum aut antarcticum.
ECCLESIA.   Quid uis tibi?
PSEUDAMNUS.   Dico te
Ecclesiam non esse. Te esse dicito.
PORNAPOLIS.   Ecclesiam ego   50
Me esse inquam, sponsam Christi.
ECCLESIA.   Tune?
PORNAPOLIS.   Tu negas?
PSEUDAMNUS.   Ita senties.
ECCLESIA.   [*p. 64*]
Ecclesiamne te?
PORNAPOLIS.   Aio.
ECCLESIA.   Asiae, Africi, ac Europi matrem
Esse, ego quae siem?
PORNAPOLIS.   Quid agimus?
PSEUDAMNUS.   Hem, haeccine fieri schismata?
PSYCHEPHONUS.
Origenista.
PSEUDAMNUS.   Mulier, dico ego tibi, praestiterat hos non fieri
Fucos.
ECCLESIA.   Eho, redigitis me ut quae sim nesciam.
PSEUDAMNUS.   Imo quae sies   55
Scimus satis.
ECCLESIA.   Quaenam?
PSYCHEPHONUS.   Paupercula de Lugduno quaepiam.

---

52. *Ecclesiamne*] I follow MSC and N; B reads *Ecclesia'ne.*

PSEUDAMNUS. By the north and south poles!

ECCLESIA. What are you bawling at me?

PSEUDAMNUS. If you keep this up, why, I'll fix you so you won't see either pole, north or south.

ECCLESIA. What is it to you?

PSEUDAMNUS. I tell you, you are not Ecclesia.—— [*To Pornapolis.*] Tell her you are.

PORNAPOLIS. I tell you I am Ecclesia, the bride of Christ.

ECCLESIA. You?

PORNAPOLIS. Do you deny it?

PSEUDAMNUS. You'll feel it.

ECCLESIA. You? Ecclesia?

PORNAPOLIS. That's what I say.

ECCLESIA. And the mother of Asia, Africus, and Europus, as I am?

PORNAPOLIS [*to Pseudamnus*]. What do we do?

PSEUDAMNUS. Well, are we to have schisms?

PSYCHEPHONUS. Origenist![1]

PSEUDAMNUS. Woman, I tell you, you'd better not carry on these pretenses.

ECCLESIA. Oh, you make me not know who I am.

PSEUDAMNUS. But we know quite well who you are.

ECCLESIA. Who?

PSYCHEPHONUS. Some poor woman of Lyons.[2]

---

[1] A follower of Origen, who earned the wrath of his own and some other bishops in the third century. Bienvenu translated the word as "Lutherienne."

[2] The Waldenses, founded in the late twelfth century, were known as the Poor of Lyons. Frequently persecuted (and later memorialized by Milton in Sonnet XVIII), they were having an especially difficult time in the 1550's.

[PSEUDAMNUS.]

Nam Ecclesiam, qui te uidet, an quisquam putet? Ac iam audies.
Heus, symmistae, decretistae, canonistae, cosmosophoi
Codicillares, holoporphyri, uos ptochopluti ordines,
Copistae, sigilliferi,   60
Adeste. Haeccine nobis Ecclesia est an non?

CHORUS.   Est.

PSEUDAMNUS.   Iam uides.

ECCLESIA.

Stat firma Dei electio, habens signaculum hoc: scit ille qui
Sunt eius.

PORNAPOLIS.   Quid ait?

PSEUDAMNUS.   Quid ais?

PSYCHEPHONUS.   Here, prorsus uero insanit haec
Corybantica.

PSEUDAMNUS.   Sic uidetur. Heus, tenete inquam repagulis
Lunaticam hanc atque ad Bethlemitas insanam abducite,   [p. 65]
Meque hinc sequimini.   66

ACTUS V. SCENA I.   [f. 151]
Senarii.
Satan. Psychephonus. Thanatus Lictor. Adopylus.
Europus. Hierologus.

[SATAN.]

Compositis nunc Asiae rebus, rursus in
Europam me reducem recta transfero,
Pseudamnus quid agat ut sciam: si bene,

---

57. S.P. *Pseudamnus*] I follow MSC; B continues the speech to Psychephonus, but he seems incapable of uttering anything but imprecations.

58. *symmistae*] an ecclesiastical Latin word, taken from Greek συμμύστης (L-S).
decretistae] DuCange lists the word for one who studies papal decrees.
canonistae] I have not found the word elsewhere, even in DuCange.
cosmosophoi] I have not found this compound in either Greek or Latin; the elements, of course, are Greek κόσμος, world, and σοφός, wise.

59. *ptochopluti*] based on the Greek compound πτωχοπλούσιος, a doubtful word for pretending poverty (from πτωχός and πλοῦτος). It refers here to friars.

60. *Copistae, sigilliferi*] DuCange lists both nonclassical words, for copyists and seal-keepers. Both words were omitted from the draft version of the play.

63. *ais*] I follow MSC; B has *ait*, probably echoing *ait* in Pornapolis' speech.

[PSEUDAMNUS]. Would anyone who sees you think you're Ecclesia? And now you shall hear. —— [*Shouts.*] Hey, all you priests, decretists, canonists, official cosmosophists, cardinals, you orders of monks, copyists, and scribes,[1] come out here.

Enter Chorus.

[*Pointing to Pornapolis.*] Is this our Ecclesia or not?
CHORUS. Yes.
PSEUDAMNUS [*to Ecclesia*]. Now you see.
ECCLESIA. The election of God remains fixed with this sign, that he knows who his people are.
PORNAPOLIS. What does she say?
PSEUDAMNUS. What do you say?[2]
PSYCHEPHONUS. Master, this Corybantic is truly and utterly mad.[3]
PSEUDAMNUS. So she seems.—— [*To Chorus.*] Hey, keep this lunatic behind bars, I say. Take the madwoman off to Bedlam.[4]——

[*Chorus leads Ecclesia off.*
[*To Psychephonus and Pornapolis.*] Follow me this way.   [*Exeunt.*

[V.1]   *Enter Satan, carrying several costumes.*

SATAN. Now that matters in Asia are under control, I come right back to Europe to find out what Pseudamnus is doing. If he's

---

[1] Vatican functionaries, satirically characterized. See the notes to the Latin text.

[2] In the draft version, Pseudamnus here asks if Ecclesia does not believe the church to be Catholic and she says yes; but when Pseudamnus asks next if she does not believe Pornapolis to be Catholic, she says no. Cf. Foxe's "De Regno Clauium Disputatio adversus perturbatas conscientias" (Lansdowne MS. 388, ff. 105-110v); which attacks the view that the pope is the successor of Peter.

[3] The Corybantes were Phrygian priests of Cybele whose religious rites included frenzied orgiastic dances.

[4] The London hospital for the insane, officially St. Mary of Bethlehem.

Vt laudem; sin minus, ut succenturier.
Sed sta hic dico, Satan, pedetentim tamen   5
Vt agas. In Asia minime modo sumus.
Vt locus, ita cum loco mutanda consilia.
Illic ui, hic astu rem tractabimus affabre.
Primum habitus hic, cum nomine, ponendus est:
Vesteque, quam ueste tego, tegam me, tectius   10
Vt fallam. Sed ubi reliqui? Proh Furias,
Mihi quos in hac re adesse opus est. Psychephone,
Thanate, Adopyle, ubi ubi estis? Adesse momento impero.
At quae mora haec, momento quum Satan imperat?

PSYCHEPHONUS.
    Quid uis?

SATAN.   Ornamenta haec capite.

ADOPYLUS.   Quid tum?

SATAN.   Meoque   15
Exemplo facite. Iam ego Satan haud sum, lucis at
Me uos dicetis angelum. Tu, Psychephone,
Hypocrisis esto hoc sub Francisci pallio.   [*p. 66*]
Tu, Thanate, Martyromastix re et nomine sies:
Quemcunque nactus sis Christi uere pium,   20
Huic quid agas ex nomine officium ut teneas.
Tibi Catholici nomen, Adopyle, imponimus.
Pseudamnum adite nunc. Inde per urbes, agros,
Pagosque omnes uos diffundite. Itidem fici ut
In oculis insident, uos per omnia   25
Spargite. Sed quos aduentare hic uideo? Agite
Orationi ut seruiatis. Faxitis probe.
Dominus uobiscum.

PSYCHEPHONUS.   Et cum spiritu tuo.

SATAN.
    Oremus.

19. *Tu*] ?read *Tum*, the apparent reading in MSC.

doing well, I'll commend him; if not, I'll replace him. But wait a minute, Satan; you must go slow. We aren't in Asia now. As the place changes, so must plans be changed along with it. There we proceeded by force, but here we'll manage our business cleverly and by guile. First I have to put aside this garb along with my name: to cloak more effectively how I conceal myself in a cloak, I'll conceal myself in a cloak. But where are the others? By the Furies, I need them near me in this business.——— [*Shouts.*] Psychephonus, Thanatus, Adopylus! Where are you? I command you to come instantly. But why this delay when Satan commands something instantly?

Enter Psychephonus, Thanatus, and Adopylus.

PSYCHEPHONUS. What do you wish?

SATAN [*giving them costumes*]. Take these costumes.

ADOPYLUS. What then?

SATAN. Do as I do. [*He puts on a costume.*] Now I'm not Satan, but you'll say I'm the Angel of Light.[1] Psychephonus, you be Hypocrisis under this cloak of Francis.[2]——— Then, Thanatus, you be Martyromastix in deed and name:[3] if you meet any follower of Christ who is truly loyal, do anything to him in my name to hold onto your office.——— Adopylus, we bestow upon you the title Catholic.[4]——— [*They put on costumes.*] All of you go to Pseudamnus now. Then disperse yourselves through all cities, fields, and provinces. Scatter yourselves everywhere, like the fig trees which are constantly before our eyes. But who are these people I see coming here? Come, be occupied in prayer; do it properly. *Dominus vobiscum.*

PSYCHEPHONUS. *Et cum spiritu tuo.*

SATAN. *Oremus.*

---

[1] That is, Lucifer.

[2] Hypocrisy (ὑπόκρισις); literally, a reply, or playing a part on stage. The Franciscans were perhaps the most vilified of the four orders of monks.

[3] Scourge of martyrs.

[4] Adopylus and this sentence are missing from the draft version. Adopylus now becomes identified with the King of Spain, who would of course be thought of as Philip II. Alexander VI had conferred the title "The Catholic" on King Ferdinand in 1494, during the Pope's struggle with France, after the conquest of Granada and a series of victories over Charles VIII. (*The History of Comines Englished by Thomas Danett*, VIII.17, Tudor Translations [London, 1897], p. 350).

EUROPUS.   Incredibile dictu, Hierologe,
   Et monstri simile, Pseudamnum te dicere   30
   Antichristum esse?
HIEROLOGUS.   Non ficus est ficus magis.
EUROPUS.
   Qui scis?
HIEROLOGUS.   Res, tempus, uita, doctrina arguunt
   Et locus ipse.
SATAN.   Pessundor.
EUROPUS.   Et Pornapolim hanc
   Meretriculam esse Babel Apocalypticam,
   Ain' tu?   [*f. 151v*]
HIEROLOGUS.   Sic re comperies.
THANATUS.   Irritor.
EUROPUS.   Et   35
   Ecclesiam te gnesiam matrem scire ubi
   Sit, meque ubi sit adducere?
HIEROLOGUS.   Certe, Europe mi.
PSYCHEPHONUS.
   Quin irruimus?
EUROPUS.   Duc me ad eam amabo.   [*p. 67*]
SATAN.   Haeresis,
   Haeresis, o ciues.
PSYCHEPHONUS.   Scandalum, blasphemia,
   Abominatio desolationis in   40
   Loco sancto stans. Succurrite.
HIEROLOGUS.   Quidnam rei hoc?
SATAN.
   Tun' esse Pseudamnum pseudopontificem,
   Sacrilege?
PSYCHEPHONUS.   Dathon, Abyron.

---

36. *gnesiam*] transliterated from the Greek γνήσιος, literally meaning legitimate.
40-41.] it is tempting to assign these lines to Thanatus, as the manuscript does.

Enter Europus and Hierologus.

EUROPUS [*to Hierologus*]. That's incredible, Hierologus, it's monstrous! You say Pseudamnus is the Antichrist?[1]

HIEROLOGUS [*to Europus*]. A fig tree is not more a fig tree.

EUROPUS [*to Hierologus*]. How do you know?

HIEROLOGUS [*to Europus*]. The circumstances, the timing, his life, his doctrine, and even his office prove it.

SATAN [*aside*]. I'm sunk.

EUROPUS [*to Hierologus*]. And you say Pornapolis is the Apocalyptic whore of Babylon?[2]

HIEROLOGUS [*to Europus*]. So in fact you will learn.

THANATUS [*aside*]. I'm exasperated.

EUROPUS [*to Hierologus*]. And you know where Ecclesia, my true mother, is and will take me there?

HIEROLOGUS [*to Europus*]. Certainly, my dear Europus.

PSYCHEPHONUS [*to Satan*]. Let's get them.[3]

EUROPUS [*to Hierologus*]. Please take me to her.

[*He starts to leave with Hierologus.*

SATAN [*rushing forward and shouting*]. Heresy, heresy! Oh citizens!

PSYCHEPHONUS. Scandal, blasphemy, abomination of desolation standing in a holy place! Help!

HIEROLOGUS. What on earth is this?

SATAN. You desecrator, do you say that Pseudamnus is a false pontiff?

PSYCHEPHONUS. Dathon and Abiron!

---

[1] A note in B cites Apocalypse 19.[?19-20, the defeat of the beast]; the final turning point in the play is here signalled by Hierologus' disclosure. Continental readers would probably have identified Hierologus with Martin Luther, like Theophilus in Kirchmayer's *Pammachius;* but see p. 345, n. 2.

[2] The draft version refers here to "Pornapolis, whom they call Catholic."

[3] At this point, the draft version contains the following exchange:

SATAN. But let me sing: "In the beginning was the Word, and the Word was with God." [John I.1]

HIEROLOGUS. What's this speech?

SATAN. "The peace of God here."

PSYCHEPHONUS. "And of St. Francis." [cf. l. 67]

THANATUS. "And of St. Carmel."

EUROPUS. What camels do I see here? [cf. the pun in *Titus et Gesippus* I.7.6-7].

SATAN. "We are here from Greenwich, servants of God and sons of blessed Francis" [see Introduction, p. 33, n. 7].

THANATUS.   Chore, Doel.
HIEROLOGUS.
 Vtinam non sit.
EUROPUS.   Quae haec hominum intemperies?
SATAN.   Quid, et
 Pornapolim prostibulum esse meretricium?   45
HIEROLOGUS.
 Si non sit, se factis declaret aliam.
SATAN.
 Proh fulmen et sulphur superum.
PSYCHEPHONUS.   Proh polos
 Mundi atque uiam lacteam.
THANATUS.   Quid agimus?
HIEROLOGUS.
 Europe, procul ab his cauendum censeo.
EUROPUS.
 Eamus.
SATAN. Nos ad Pseudamnum dum currimus,   50
 Tu hic, Hypocrisis, obserua interim quo is abeat.
PSYCHEPHONUS.
 Profecto haec si sic abeant, Satanae ac suis
 Id tantum restat ut scribam epitaphium.
 Animusque ea in re haud scio quid pracsagit mali.
 Primum haec ita diu' esse haud pote est: tantos fucos 55
 Ac flagitia fieri in urbe haud sinet Deus,
 Eiusque lenitas haec tanta uereor
 Quorsum tandem euaserit. Insuper horoscopum
 Ascendi nuper: cum Saturno ubi Iupiter
 Coniunctus in Arietis decimo, quid nescio *[p. 68]* 60
 Laeuum minatur, in aspectu tetragono
 Signum occupante Marte foemineum. Atenim
 Strepitum audire uideor aduentantium: *[f. 152]*
 Quisque ut fert fabula, ita scenae inseruiat.
 Kyrieleeson, Christeleeson, Kyrieleeson. Pater noster. Aue Maria,
  etc.   65
 Et uiscera beatae uirginis. Et uulnera quinque
 Sancti Francisci, etc.

  63. *audire*] the manuscript reading, *haurire*, is appealing.

THANATUS. Korah and Doel![1]

HIEROLOGUS. Would that he weren't!

EUROPUS. What is this madness of these men?

SATAN. What, and you say Pornapolis is a sluttish prostitute?

HIEROLOGUS. If she weren't, she'd prove herself otherwise by her deeds.

SATAN. By the lightning and sulphur of heaven!

PSYCHEPHONUS. By the poles of the universe and the Milky Way!

THANATUS. What should we do?

HIEROLOGUS. Europus, I think we should keep far away from these fellows.

EUROPUS. Let's go.   [*Exeunt Hierologus and Europus.*

SATAN. Hypocrisis, while we run to Pseudamnus, you stay here and watch where that fellow goes.   [*Exeunt Satan and Thanatus.*

PSYCHEPHONUS. Well, if the affair is going this way, there's nothing left for me but to write an epitaph for Satan and his followers. I feel in my soul that this will come to some sort of grief. In the first place, it isn't possible that things can go on long this way: God won't allow such disgraceful deceptions to occur in the city, and I fear where his great gentleness will lead. Besides, I've recently cast my horoscope, and Jupiter, in conjunction with Saturn in the tenth house of Aries, is threatening some misfortune, since Mars is in a feminine sign in a square aspect.[2] But I seem to hear the sound of people coming. Each must play his part on the stage as the plot requires. [*He prays.*] *Kyrie eleison, Christe eleison, kyrie eleison. Pater noster, Ave Maria,* etc. And the fruit of the blessed Virgin's womb. And the five wounds of St. Francis, etc.[3]

---

[1] Dathon, Abyron, and Korah were enemies of Moses (Numbers 16). Doel (the spelling of B and the manuscript) must be Doeg the Edomite, who killed eighty-five priests on Saul's order (1 Samuel 22.9-22); Bienvenu reads *Doeg*.

[2] Foxe did not believe in astrology. Cf. his statement that John Cheke was "a little too much addicted to the curious practising of this star-divinity, which we call astrology" (*Acts and Monuments*, ed. Pratt, VIII, 257). And see my article "John Foxe on Astrology," *ELR*, I (1971), 210-225.

[3] Psychephonus, as a Franciscan monk, pretends to be reciting his breviary. The five wounds of St. Francis are the stigmata. In the original manuscript version, Psychephonus begins by reciting from John I.1.

ACTUS V. SCENA II.
Trochaici Tetrametri Catalectici.
Pseudamnus. Satan Palliatus. Psychephonus Hypocrita.

[Pseudamnus.]

    Haecne fieri flagitia? Vbi scelus illic nunc siet

    Monstrari uolo. Ecquis hic est?

Satan.   Hypocrisis.

Psychephonus.   Papam uti, et

    Card'nalium senatum conseruare digneris:

    Te rogamus, audi nos. Vt lineos, laneos episcopos—

Satan.

    Satis est. Respice inquam, Hypocrisis.

Psychephonus.   Quisnam homo intercipit?   5

    Proh pietatis culmen, Pseudamne! Vide, precibus extra me

    In purgatorium usque rapi sum uisus, atque audin' quae ibi

    Vidi fieri? Deus mala auertat.   [*p. 69*]

Pseudamnus.   Quid est?

Psychephonus.   Scotus

    Et Thomas quam immaniter se caedebant facibus:

    Moxque ingens, tota in culina umbrarum, questus obortus est.   10

Pseudamnus.

    Qui nam?

Psychephonus.   Missae quia tantopere ubique frigeant,

    Illi eo calent impensius, iam nec sperare exitum.

    Haec ubi specto, ecce haereticorum ilico psammocotiae

    Myriades, infinita undarum ui, scintillitus

    Totam abolent Aethnam purgatoriam.

Satan.   Ominosa haec mihi   15

    Perparum placent.

Pseudamnus.   Sed ubi ille haereticus interim?

---

    3. *Card'nalium*] B and later editions read *Cardualium;* MSC, which does not have an apostrophe, is unclear.

    4. *audi nos*] I supply these words from MSC; B reads *&c.*

    13. *psammocotiae*] transliterated from the Greek ψαμμακόσιοι.

    14. *Myriades*] a Greek word, found in medieval Latin (TLL).

       scintillitus] I find no other instance of this adverbial form.

[V.2]   *Enter Pseudamnus, Satan in his cloak, and attendants.*

PSEUDAMNUS. Did these disgraceful things happen?[1] I want to know where that scoundrel is now. But who's this?

SATAN. Hypocrisis.

PSYCHEPHONUS [*praying*]. Deign to preserve the pope and the college of cardinals; hear us, we implore you. As flax and wool, our bishops——[2]

SATAN. That's enough, Hypocrisis. Look here, I tell you.

PSYCHEPHONUS. Who interrupts me? Oh, Pseudamnus, the model of piety! Look, as I was praying, I seemed to be transported outside myself and into purgatory. And listen to what I saw happen there. May God avert misfortunes!

PSEUDAMNUS. What is it?

PSYCHEPHONUS. Scotus and Thomas[3] were beating themselves savagely with firebrands, and soon a great lamentation arose in that whole kitchen of shades.

PSEUDAMNUS. Why?

PSYCHEPHONUS. Because everybody is cooling off so much on masses now, those spirits are burning that much more intensely, and now they have no hope of escape. While I was watching, myriads of heretics as numberless as the sands of the shore extinguished that whole fiery Aetna of purgatory as if with the infinite force of waves.

SATAN. I don't like these omens very much.

PSEUDAMNUS. But where's that heretic meanwhile?

---

[1] A note in B refers to Apocalypse 19.

[2] "Te rogamus audi nos" is a refrain in certain Catholic liturgies; I have not found the other parts of this prayer, and Foxe may have made them up.

[3] Duns Scotus and Thomas Aquinas, the great (and conflicting) scholastic philosophers of the thirteenth century, were especially scorned by sixteenth-century reformers. A draft version had them engaged in a *diro duello*, and Foxe may have intended *se* (l. 9) to be read "each other."

PSYCHEPHONUS.   Papae,
  Interim tun' haereticum esse dicis iusque concilii
  Violas? Haud faxis nephas.
PSEUDAMNUS.   Haereticum dico, hac qui modo.
PSYCHEPHONUS.
  Vah intelligo, Hierologum nempe illum, hac qui se abduxit recens
  Cum Europo una per plateam dextram. Collegium   20
  Vbi sit nostin'? Ultra ponticulum. Ego pone insequor immaniter.
  Vbi persensit, obliquat uiam in uicum alium, item in alium,
  Ad phanum donec uentum sit. Hic quia instare me uidet   [*p. 70*]
  Nec desistere, uiam uorat pedibus quantum ualet.   [*f. 152v*]
  Denique cursu uicit carnifex. At ubi sit prope   25
  Tamen hariolor. Ad forum cum acceditis escarium,
  Quadriuium illic est, transuersis plateis sese in angulos
  Rectos scindens. Hic relicta dextra, ad laeuam uergite
  Vicus qua decliuis, recta ad portam uos praecipitat,
  Versus utramque ursam. Illic secus portam, adeoque uel in   30
  Ipsa porta potius, carcer Bocardo est. Ibi est. Capin'?

PSYCHEPHONUS. Indeed! Do you declare Meanwhile[1] to be a heretic and violate the authority of the council? Don't commit that wrong.

PSEUDAMNUS. I say the heretic who was just here.

PSYCHEPHONUS. Oh, I know him: it was Hierologus who just left here with Europus. They went down this street on our right. Do you know where the college is, beyond the little bridge? I chased after him fiercely. When he realized that, he changed directions, first into one street, then into another, until he got to the church. He didn't stop there, because he saw that I was still following; he ate up the road with his feet as fast as he could. The scoundrel finally outran me. But I can pretty well guess where he is. As you approach the Cornmarket, you come to Carfax, where the intersecting streets go off at right angles. Ignore the right and turn left, where a street leads down a hill and brings you quickly right to the city gate, toward the two Bears. There, beside the gate—or rather right in the gate—is the prison, Bocardo.[2] He's there. Do you follow me?

[1] If this is the correct interpretation (and *interim* makes little sense except as a proper name), Psychephonus is ridiculed for stupidity.

[2] Foxe clearly had Oxford in mind: the prison, Bocardo, was located in the North Gate in Oxford (hence the orientation by the two Bears, Ursa Major and Ursa Minor, located in the northern sky). Latimer and Ridley and Cranmer were imprisoned there from March 1554 (before that they had been in the Tower of London), and Cranmer was still there as Foxe wrote (he was executed on March 21, 1556). Latimer and Ridley were executed on October 16, 1555, and Hierologus probably represents one or both of them; in the next scene, we hear that Theosebes has joined Hierologus, and he probably represents the other bishop: apparently both Hierologus and Theosebes are killed.

Another recognizable feature of Oxford is the Cornmarket leading downhill from an intersection (Carfax, in Oxford, is a corruption of *quatervois*, which is derived from *quadrivium*) to the North Gate (though the downhill gradient is very slight). Other features are harder to identify, and I cannot be as certain of Psychephonus' bearings as the manuscript prompter in the Harvard copy of B, who transposed Foxe's "left" and "right" in l. 28. Several Oxford bridges have been called "little" at one time or another. Anthony Wood identified the hermits of Pettypont as being located at Magdalen Bridge (in the east), which has never been very small (*Survey of the Antiquities of the City of Oxford* [*1661-6*], ed. Andrew Clark, Oxford Historical Society, XV [Oxford, 1889], 411); but he also identified Little Bridge with Quaking Bridge, which in 1498 was said to be the western bridge (Wood, p. 433; see Herbert Hurst, *Oxford Topography*, Oxford Historical Society, XXXIX [Oxford, 1899], and for old maps, see XXXVIII [Oxford, 1899]). Even Grandpont, in the south, was called a "little Bridge" (Hutten's *Antiquities of Oxford* [1632], quoted by Hurst, p. 32)! From a perspective inside

PSEUDAMNUS.

Agite actutum uos, inquam, ut fortes decet satellites
Martyromastigae, inquisitores, articulifices,
Artolatrae, gymnopodes, dicaspoli, decretarii, incendarii.
Vbi ubi est, inuentum hunc Hierologum facite. Atque auditis? ad
Diocten abducite. Eum quid opus sit facto, instruam probe.   36
Sed Pornapolim uideo. Vos abite.

ACTUS V. SCENA III.   [*p. 71*]
Iambici Trimetri.
Pornapolis. Pseudamnus. Anabasius. [Zenodorus. Dromo. Colax.]

[PORNAPOLIS.]

An usquam os audiri tam proiectum aut impudens
Pornapolim dicere meretriculam ut audeat?
Nec hiscat tellus? Coelum aut rubet fulmine?
Sed Pseudamnum, ubi sit, conuentum nimis expeto.

PSEUDAMNUS.

Pornapolis, audistin' igitur?

PORNAPOLIS.   Audisse rogitas   5
Publica iam fabula quum simus omnibus?
Scripturas iam omnes lectitant: latomi, fabri,
Figuli, et qui non? Uulgique faex (mihi quod male est)
Iam coepit sapere. Quin et mores insuper
Nostros ad Euangelii trutinam exigunt.   10

PSEUDAMNUS.

Plus prope in hac re mali uideo quam remedii.

---

33. *martyromastigae*] apparently a coinage. The standard form of the second element is *mastigiae*.

    articulifices] apparently a coinage, but from standard elements, *articulus* and *-fex* (from *facio*).

34. *Artolatrae*] apparently a coinage from the Greek words ἄρτος, a loaf of wheat-bread, and λατρεία, worship. The allusion is to transubstantiation.

    gymnopodes] transliterated from the Greek γυμνοπόδης, barefoot, and referring to discalced orders of monks. In the draft version, they are called *pulpifices*, i.e., flesh-making (?fat ?transubstantiating), after earlier being called *Sarbonarii* (?of Sorbonne).

    dicaspoli] transliterated from the Greek δικασπόλος, law-giver, judge.

    decretarius] LTL lists this word for judicial.

P.H. *Zenodorus . . . Colax*] omitted in MSC and B.

PSEUDAMNUS. Go quickly, I tell you, as brave helpers should. My martyr-scourges, my inquisitors, my indictment-makers, my bread-worshippers, my discalced followers, my judges, my decretists, my incendiaries,[1] be sure to find this Hierologus wherever he is. Then take him to Dioctes, do you hear? I'll instruct him thoroughly about what to do. But I see Pornapolis. Go.   [*Exeunt all but Pseudamnus.*

[V.3]   *Enter Pornapolis and attendants.*

PORNAPOLIS [*aside*]. Was ever a speech heard so forward or impudent? To dare to say Pornapolis is a whore![2] Doesn't the earth gape open, the sky glow with thunderbolts? But where's Pseudamnus? I'm eager to talk to him.

PSEUDAMNUS. Pornapolis, have you heard then?

PORNAPOLIS. You ask if I've heard, when we're already a common story on everybody's lips. They're all diligently reading scriptures—stonecutters, smiths, potters, everybody. And, what I think is bad, the dregs of the people are starting to be wise now. What's more, they're even weighing our traditions in the scales of the gospel.[3]

PSEUDAMNUS. In this I see more sickness near than I see remedy.

---

the city, no colleges were beyond any river bridges. St. John's Hospital was outside the East Gate, and in 1331 was said to be by the Little Bridge (Hurst, p. 206); and Blackfriars south of town was beyond Grandpont, and also beyond a small bridge (Trill Mill Bow) over Trill Mill Stream (Hurst, pp. 40-41). Or perhaps Foxe had in mind a footbridge over a stream—such as the little bridge (near Magdalen?) on which Master Harley hung his cloak during the dawn stroll which Foxe laughed about in a surviving poem (Lansdowne MS. 388, f. 59). Similarly, the church mentioned in Psychephonus' description could be any of several.

[1] See the notes to the Latin text. The incendiaries painfully recall the burnings of Mary's reign.

[2] The draft version added a line calling Pseudamnus the Apocalyptic beast.

[3] Pornapolis expresses the Catholic position concerning two issues under dispute with reformers: the reading of Scriptures by laymen, and the relative weight of traditions and Scriptures.

PORNAPOLIS.

Iam hos nec uincla, unguli, eculei, enses, tormina,
Flammae nec ultrices, nec quicquam territat.

PSEUDAMNUS.

Consilii quid capiam cogito. Zenodore, abi
Hac cum rosa aurea ad Dynasten blanditer.   *[f. 153]*   15
Tu ensem aurea tectum uagina ad Dynamicum   *[p. 72]*
Perfer. Dromo, tuum est linolaneum hoc pallium ad
Nesophilum uti feras. Principes uolo primulum
Adamantino mihi ut stringantur foedere.

17. *linolaneum*] perhaps a coinage, though the elements of the compound are of course standard words.

PORNAPOLIS. Now these people aren't frightened by chains, rings, racks, swords, torments, punishing flames, or anything else.

PSEUDAMNUS. I wonder what course to follow.—— Zenodore,[1] go and soften up Dynastes with this golden rose.[2]—— You, take this sword in a golden sheath to Dynamicus.[3]—— Dromo, your job is to take this linsey-woolsey pallium to Nesophilus.[4]—— First I'd like these princes bound to me in an ironclad league;

---

[1] See the notes to the Dramatis Personae. This passage, with its topical allusions, was added to the manuscript version after being omitted in the earliest draft.

[2] Dynastes (δυνάστης) means ruler, here specifically Mary Tudor. The golden rose is a papal honor, blessed on Laetare Sunday and presented to royal figures whom the pope thinks deserving. In Foxe's time it was a single golden rose; since the late sixteenth century, it has been a golden plant with varying number of blossoms (*The Catholic Encyclopedia* [New York, 1913], VI, 629-630). Pope Julius III sent a golden rose to Mary, by his nuncio Antonio Agostini, on January 27, 1555 (*Calendar of State Papers* [*Spanish*], XIII, 137; Gaetano Moroni Romano, *Dizionario di Erudizione Storico-Ecclesiastica*, LIX [Venice, 1853], 131; G. C. Young, *Ornaments and Gifts Consecrated by the Roman Pontiffs. The Golden Rose, the Cap and Sword, Presented to Sovereigns of England and Scotland* [London, (1860)], pp. 32-33).

[3] Dynamicus (δυναμικός), powerful, refers to Philip II, Mary's husband. The sword in a golden sheath is another papal gift, blessed on Christmas Eve and presented with the words "statuimus te Principem Catholicum." At the same time as the presentation of the golden rose to Mary, Julius III sent a sword (and cap) to Philip (Moroni, *Dizionario*, LXX [Venice, 1851], 50).

[4] The pallium is the symbol of office given to archbishops. It is made of wool, not linsey-woolsey; by Old Testament law, wool and linen could not be woven together (Deuteronomy 22.11). One thinks immediately of Cardinal Wolsey and of Skelton's attack on him in "Why Come Ye Not to Courte?" 125-128: "We shall have a *tot quot* / From the Pope of Rome, / To weue all in one lome / A webbe of lylse wulse." Foxe may have known of this poem, but his immediate object, as Bienvenu noted, was Cardinal Pole, Cranmer's successor as Archbishop of Canterbury. Pole did not receive the pallium until March 22, 1556, after Cranmer's execution, but he had taken over the administration of the archbishopric on December 11, 1555, when Cranmer was officially deprived, and his appointment as archbishop was a foregone conclusion. Nesophilus (νῆσος and φίλος) means island-lover, and a complex pun is involved. In the apocalyptic books, islands are equated with deserts as places separated from God (e.g., Isaiah 13.22, 34.14, Ezekiel 27.35, Apocalypse 6.14, 16.20); Alcuin interpreted Apocalypse 6.14 as follows: "Per insulas vero minoris justitiae homines accipimus adhuc in tribulationibus fluctuantes" (*Patrologia Latina*, C, 1127). Pole's life shows him to have been the opposite of an island-lover, for he had spent years in exile and had resisted as dangerous many invitations to return home; he had finally returned to the island as papal legate in November, 1554, after Mary's accession. Foxe may have had another level of meaning in mind, Pole's cardinalate: νῆσος was a purple garment, like the Roman praetexta.

Est disciplinae hoc. Quid aliud uolui? Colax,   20
Tu ad Diocten propera annulo cum hoc gemmeo.
Ausculta in aurem. Intellextin? Eadem tibi
Quae dixi, illi ut dicas face. Virum ut se hic gerat.

ANABASIUS.

Alas, mihi si quis nunc adaptet Daedalus,
Pseudamno damna haec ut feram quam primulum.   25
Atque eccum. Euge Pornapolis, utriusque me
Miseret.

PORNAPOLIS.   Quidnam mali, Anabasi, est?

ANABASIUS.   Quod si uelim,
Effari nequeam.

PSEUDAMNUS.   Primum mihi id unum expedi:
De Hierologo quid?

ANABASIUS.   Vinctus est, ac Theosebes
Cum eo una. At quid tum? Tu tamen nihilominus   30
Vorsuram soluis.

PSEUDAMNUS.   Quid ita?

ANABASIUS.   Mundus quia, diu
Iam oculis captus, uidere coepit. Naribus
Diutius nec duci, homines literae ac
Linguae passim perpoliunt. Fuco nihil
Proficitur. Imperio undique tuo oppeditur: 35
Claues uilescere, bullas concacarier.
Fulmen ubique ac diadema triplex temnier.   [*p. 73*]
Christum ipsum uiuere. Corpus monstrum esse duo quod
Alit capita. Pompam, luxum, libidinem,
Saeuitiam, doctrinam, ueneficia, scelera,   40
Fucos, fumos, uitaeque strepitum tragicae,
Facile qui sis arguere: Antichristum esse te
Denique constanter credier.

PSEUDAMNUS.   [*f. 153v*]
Quid ais?

ANABASIUS.   Te Antichristum, Pseudamne, esseque
Pornapolim hanc, pellicem Babyloniam die   45
Magis lucescere.

43.] both B and MSC have notes identifying the meter of this line as dimeter.

that's good tactics. What else did I want?—— Colax,[1] you run
to Dioctes with this jeweled ring.[2] I'll whisper in your ear.
[*He whispers.*] Do you understand? Be sure to tell him what I told
you.—— [*To Pornapolis.*] I hope Colax proves manly.

Enter Anabasius.

ANABASIUS [*aside*]. Alas, if some Daedalus would fix it for me now
to suffer these misfortunes in place of Pseudamnus as soon as
possible! There he is.—— Oh Pornapolis, I pity you both.

PORNAPOLIS. What's wrong, Anabasius?

ANABASIUS. I couldn't tell you if I wanted to.

PSEUDAMNUS. First tell me one thing: what about Hierologus?

ANABASIUS. He's in chains, and Theosebes[3] with him. But so what?
You've jumped from the frying pan into the fire.

PSEUDAMNUS. Why so?

ANABASIUS. Because the world, long blinded, is now beginning to see.
Men won't be led by the nose much longer. Everywhere they're
being refined by letters and languages. Nothing is achieved by
deception. Everywhere they're farting at your orders and shitting
on your bulls. Your keys are worthless, and your thunder and
triple crown[4] are universally scorned, for they say Christ himself
lives and that a body which sustains two heads is a monstrosity.
They say your pomp, extravagance, lust, savagery, doctrine,
poisonings, crimes, trickeries and trumperies, and the tumult
of their tragic life easily prove who you are: they firmly believe
that you are the Antichrist.

PSEUDAMNUS. What?

ANABASIUS. That you are the Antichrist, Pseudamnus. And they
say it's clearer than day that Pornapolis here is the Babylonian
whore.

---

[1] Flatterer. Menander and Plautus wrote comedies so titled.

[2] Probably a reference to the jewelled ring which is a symbol of papal office.
There had been two changes in the papacy in 1555: Julius III had died in April,
and his successor, Marcellus II, in May; Paul IV had then been elected.

[3] God-fearing (θεοσεβής); see p. 345, n. 2.

[4] Symbols of the papacy.

PSEUDAMNUS.   Men' Antichristum, cedo?

ANABASIUS.

 Bestia quem signat scilicet Apocalyptica.

PSEUDAMNUS.

 Mundus mirum ut delirat senio: bestia

 Turcam haec monstrat Mahometicum.

ANABASIUS.   Id et responderam. At

 Contra illi (ut sunt acutuli) "Phy," inquiunt,   50

 "Fieri haud pote est." Quidum? "Primum scriptura quod

 Sedem hanc obtenebratum iri praenunciat"—fateor

 Id vobis euenisse, haud Turcis: certum est modo

 Res quum splendescunt Turcicae indies magis.

 Dein neque negari possit quin uulnere   55

 Vno haec sit capitali plectenda bestia,

 Quae, recuperato ictu, sanescet denuo.   *[p. 74]*

 Id quod nimis in triagonesa est gente liquidum:

 Negatam quae prius, nunc iterum firmat fidem,

 Nesophili nostri opera. Eoque secunda habent   60

 Illum pro bestia, idem quam uates nunciat.

PORNAPOLIS.

 Me miseram.

PSEUDAMNUS. Qui putant?

ANABASIUS.   Vitae ac uoci quia

 Inanimem bestiae reddidit imaginem

 Suis phrenapatiis, agni dum cornua

 Fingit lupus, tygride quauis immanior.   65

 Remque ita habere, ipsa res (inquiunt) arguit.

 Haud haec in Turcas, uos nisi Turcae sitis,

 Congruere. Tum Europaeus ne nos deserat

 Insuper, ut affectum uideo, metus est.

PORNAPOLIS.

 Pseudamne, ni me fulcitis, labasco.

PSEUDAMNUS.   Vah,   70

 Leui perculsa nuncio tam muliebriter?

---

 53. *vobis*] I follow MSC; B reads *nobis*.

 58. *triagonesa*] a coinage from Greek τρι-, three, and ἀγών, struggle; I know no precedent for the adjectival suffix *-esa* (could it be from *edo, esus?*).

 64. *phrenapatiis*] transliterated from the Greek φρεναπάτης, soul-deceiver.

PSEUDAMNUS. Me the Antichrist, was that?

ANABASIUS. The very one that the Apocalyptic beast symbolizes.

PSEUDAMNUS. It's astonishing how the world is going mad in its old age. That beast symbolizes the Mohammedan Turk.

ANABASIUS. I answered that too. But they say in response——how clever they are!——"Fie, it cannot be." Why? First because scripture foretells that its power will be overshadowed, and I confess that that has happened to you, not to the Turks, since it's certain that the Turks' interests grow brighter every day. Then again, it couldn't be denied that the beast is to be struck with one deadly wound and that, recovering from the blow, he'll regain his strength,[1] and that's too clearly true with the thrice-suffering people,[2] who now reassert the faith which, through the effort of our Nesophilus, they formerly denied; so they take him for the second beast which the prophet also foretold.

PORNAPOLIS [aside]. I feel awful.

PSEUDAMNUS. How do they figure?

ANABASIUS. Because in their mad fancies he restores to life and speech the lifeless image of the beast;[3] and a wolf, fiercer than any tiger, feigns the horns of a lamb. And they say the fact proves itself: these things don't fit the Turks at all, unless you are the Turks. In addition, there's the fear that Europus will abandon us, as I see him inclined to do.

PORNAPOLIS. Pseudamnus, if you don't hold me up, I'm ready to fall.

PSEUDAMNUS. Bah! So womanish to be overwhelmed by trivial news?

---

[1] See Apocalypse 13.3.

[2] The English; the earliest draft located them "on an island." Bienvenu translated the phrase "la gent Britannique."

[3] See Apocalypse 13.15.

Pornapolis.

Non, sed nescio quid morbi me subito impetit.
Oborta primum uertigo mihi synciput
Exturbat. Cor molari ueluti lapide
Premitur. Pes nec officio fungitur.   75
Proin me hinc abducite, et medicos, quantum potest,   [*f. 154*]
Adducite.
Pseudamnus.   Anabasi, tu hinc ad laeuam occupa.
Ego me hic praebebo ad dextram.   [*p. 75*]
Pornapolis.   Vix sum pedum
Compos.

ACTUS V. SCENA IIII.
Scazontes Iambici.
Africus. Europus. Ecclesia.

[Africus.]

Fratrem matremque Ecclesiam tota iam urbe
Lassesco quaerens, quos diu nunc non uisos
Videre gestio. Eoque maturius huc me,
Ex Africa ueniens castrisque relictis,
Retuli tantas in Europa postquam audiui   5
Turbas salui ne sint ut uideam. Ita ut esse
Accipio et laetor. Sed quid hic susurratum
Extra fores audio? Pontificius si quis
Venit, uenisse me uideri in hoc nolim
Articulo.
Evropus.   Num quis Corycaeus seu Melampygus   10
Hic est? Nemo est. Quid? Nullus auritus Midas
Vsquam, uel sub lapide dentatus dormiscens
Scorpio? Nihil est, mater, pericli: in portu adsis
Licet.
Africus.   Fratrem germanum, quem uolo, Europum
Video.
Evropus.   Quod seclum hoc! Quae peruersitas! Tectis   15
Nulli tutum ut sit prorepere sacerdotum ob
Vaesaniam!

79. *Compos*] as in MSC; B prints the word as part of l. 78.
10. *Melampygus*] transliterated from Greek μελαμπῦγος; see note opposite.

PORNAPOLIS. No, but all of a sudden some sort of sickness is coming over me. A new dizziness whirls my brain. My heart is squeezed as if by a millstone. My feet won't function. So take me away from here and bring doctors as soon as possible. Take me in.

PSEUDAMNUS. Anabasius, hold her on the left. I'll take the right side.

PORNAPOLIS. I can scarcely walk. [*They help Pornapolis off.*

[V.4]   *Enter Africus.*

AFRICUS.[1] I'm growing weary of searching through the whole city for my brother and my mother, Ecclesia, whom I long to see since I haven't seen them for a long time now. I left my camp in Africa and came here all the more quickly after I heard of so many tumults in Europe that I could see they might not be safe. I trust that they are, and I'm glad. But what's the buzzing I hear outside the gates here? If some pope's man is coming, I wouldn't want it known that I've come at just this moment. [*He hides.*

Enter Europus.

EUROPUS [*aside, looking around*]. Is there any Corycean spy here,[2] or any black-bottomed Hercules?[3] No one. What, no long-eared Midas anywhere,[4] no sharp-toothed scorpion sleeping under a rock?——[*Calling.*] Mother, there's no danger. You may enter in safety.

AFRICUS [*aside*]. I see Europus, the twin brother that I'm wishing for.

EUROPUS [*aside*]. What an age this is! What perversity, that because of the madness of the priests no one can creep out of doors safely.

---

[1] A note in B cites Apocalypse 17, but I find no parallel. (?Perhaps Chapter 18, which tells of the fall of the whore.)

[2] See p. 147, n. 1, and p. 419.

[3] Black nates, especially associated with Hercules, were thought by the Greeks to be a sign of virility and strength. But Europus must think of it as a pejorative term, since he is clearly thinking of possibly dangerous enemies. Note too that Satan hopes for another pagan demigod, Theseus, to help him.

[4] Midas was given ass' ears by Apollo for favoring Pan in a music contest.

Ecclesia.   Quod ego nunc profugium quaeram
Misera? Aut quo uertam amplius? Adeo cuncta   *[p. 76]*
Periclis plena, iamque ipsum nec desertum
Tutum sit a serpentibus?

Africus.   Mea mater,   20
Salue.

Ecclesia.   Quid, mi gnate, Africe mi, uenistin? Iam
Miseriarum me merito omnium coepit
Obliuio, te ubi recipio reducem.

Evropus.   Equidem saluum
Atque ualidum, germane mi, restitutum te
Nobis gaudeo.

Ecclesia.   Quando uenisti?

Africus.   Modo mater.   25

Ecclesia.
Mirari te scio satis tam depexam me
Ac stygmaticam adeo undique conspici. Sed nil
Horum pudet me, Christi quae causa sponsi
Suffero.   *[f. 154v]*

Africus.   Me miserum, ut te affectam domum offendo
Rediens!

Ecclesia.   Sic, nate, mihi ut nec in carne solidum   30
Nec in terris tutum quicquam siet. Porro
Vidua ac egens bonis omnibus ac patria exul
Mutilor, cui ad ultimam nihil amplius possit
Miseriam accedere.

Africus.   Proh nephas, quisnam tanti
Sceleris autor sacrilegus? Quam mox monstrari   35
Hominem gestio.

[Evropus.]   Pseudamnus, Christi atque bonorum
Hostis omnium.   *[p. 77]*

Africus.   Vah, eaque reor causa extrusit
Me in militiam hinc.

17. *profugium*] LTL lists the form as equivalent to the standard *perfugium*.
26. *depexam*] cf. IV.8.37n. above.
27. *stygmaticam*] the standard form would be *stigmosam* (LTL).
36. S.P.] B reads *Ec[clesia]*; MSC is ambiguous. See Textual Notes.
37. *omnium*] the MSC reading, *hominum*, is tempting and could have been misread as *omnium*.

Enter Ecclesia, scarred.

ECCLESIA. What refuge should I seek now, wretch that I am? Where else can I turn, since every place is full of dangers and not even the desert is free of serpents?

AFRICUS [*coming forward*]. My dear mother, hello.

ECCLESIA. What! My son! My Africus! Have you come? Now I have reason to begin to forget all my miseries, for I welcome you back.

EUROPUS. Indeed, my brother, I rejoice that you are restored to us safe and well.

ECCLESIA. When did you come?

AFRICUS. Just now, mother.

ECCLESIA. I know you're quite surprised to see me so battered and scarred all over. But none of this is my shame, since I endure it for the sake of my bridegroom, Christ.

AFRICUS. Woe is me that I return to find you afflicted at home.

ECCLESIA. So much so, my son, that there is nothing solid in my flesh[1] and nothing safe for me anywhere in the world. Besides, I'm a widow, bereft of all my goods, and an exile cut off from my country.[2] To that last misery no greater for me could be added.

AFRICUS. Oh wickedness! What scofflaw is the author of such a wrong? I want to see that man immediately.

ECCLESIA. Pseudamnus, an enemy of Christ and of all good men.

AFRICUS. Oh, it was for that reason, I guess, that he hustled me away from here into military action.

---

[1] Cf. the famous crux in *Hamlet* I.2.129.
[2] Cf. *Titus et Gesippus* III.7.10 ff.

Europus.   Est artis pontificiae istuc,
   Si quem fors indolis uideant erectae
   Aut metuant principem, bello occupant, ipsi   40
   Impune in aurem ut dormiant.
Africus.   At ego somnum hic
   Excutiam mastygiae probe. I mecum, frater,
   Cerebrum ni Cerbero extundam cani ilico. Dein
   Scripto milite, atria arcesque inuasero, ac Europam
   Hydra exonerabo actutum Acherontica, ne quid   45
   Boni amplius mali hinc metuant. In aurem quin
   Ipsis dormire liceat.
Ecclesia.   Haud ita decet, nec
   Patiar uim unquam fieri.
Africus.   Cur non?
Ecclesia.   Quia enim dabo
   Consilium rectius et melius. Vis omnis
   Facessat: minas in patientiam, uires in   50
   Preces uertemus. Telum oratione una
   Nullum potentius: machina ipsum haec perrumpit
   Coelum. Illorum inferre est, nostrum ferre iniusta:
   Sors quippe haec sanctorum, et uictoria est. Christi
   Nisi aduentu, haec extingui bellua haud quita est: 55
   Illi ergo trophaeum hoc permittemus integrum.
   Nam ad me quidem quod attinet, sic inducor:
   Quae fero, Christi causa quum fero, lubens ferre.   [*p. 78*]
   Maiora ille: illo maiores haud sumus. Illius
   Sunt stigmata: suam is causam pro arbitratu   60
   Vindicet. Etsi diu iam pertulerim, haud is
   Diu tamen aberit, spero, malis qui imponet
   Finem. Nos interim, tempus uti diei est,
   Iunctis instemus precibus. At unde crepuerunt
   Fores?
Africus.   Quid uirgines lychnophorae captant   65
   Praetensis huc quae facibus affectant miror.

---

38. *pontificiae*] the standard adjective is *pontificalis* (LTL).
65. *lychnophorae*] transliterated from Greek λυχνοφόρος.

EUROPUS. It's a papal art. If they happen to see any leader of noble temperament or if they're afraid, they keep him busy in war so they may sleep on their ears in safety.

AFRICUS. But I'll shake up the scoundrel's sleep well enough now. Go with me, brother. If I don't beat the brains out of that dog Cerberus! Then I'll raise an army, invade his courts and citadels, and relieve Europe quickly from that hellish Hydra,[1] so that from now on good men need fear no further evil and those fellows won't be able to sleep on their ears.

ECCLESIA. That's not right at all. I'll never allow force to be used.

AFRICUS. Why not?

ECCLESIA. Because I'll give you a plan which is both better and more proper. All violence must end. We'll change threats into patience, force into prayers. No weapon is more powerful than a single prayer: this is an engine which breaks through heaven itself. Their way is to inflict injustices, ours to endure them: this indeed is the lot of saints and their victory. Except by the coming of Christ, this beast cannot be destroyed.[2] So we'll let him have this trophy untouched, because as far as I'm concerned I'm resolved to endure willingly whatever I endure since I endure it for the sake of Christ. He bore greater ills, and we are not greater than he. The stigmas are his; let him vindicate his cause as he will. Though I have suffered for a long time now, yet I hope he who will bring an end to troubles will not be absent long. Meantime, let's entreat him with our joint prayers, since it is the proper time of day. But why are the doors creaking?

AFRICUS. I wonder what these lamp-carrying virgins want? They're coming toward us holding torches in front of them.

---

[1] Africus alludes to two of Hercules' labors.

[2] A note in B refers to Apocalypse 13-14, and just below another note cites 2 Thessalonians 2. Both passages prepare for the second coming of Christ; the former passage chronicles the rise of the beasts of the sea and the earth, and the vision of the lamb and the virgins. Foxe's five virgins (not the 144,000 of Apocalypse) enter just below.

ECCLESIA.

Comitissae sunt meae: meum scio sponsum
Ad nuptias expectant quoad ueniat.

ACTUS V. SCENA V.   [*f. 155*]
Scazontes Iambici.
Chorus Quinque Virginum. Ecclesia. Europus. Africus.

[CHORUS I.]

Nox etsi sera perquam sit et intempesta,
Adeoque gallus iam auditus tertius, certum est
Vigilando haud defatigari tamen sponsus
Dum uenit ad nuptias.

CHORUS 2.   Itaque cantu noctis

Nos aliquo trudamus taedium. At ipsam sponsam   5
Video. Hera, salue.

ECCLESIA.   Saluete. Merito uos

Laudo amoque, saluti sic quae inuigilatis
Mundus dum altum dormit perditionis somnum.

CHORUS 3.   [*p. 79*]

Alios nescio. Nos quod facimus, facere nostrae
Id esse curae ducimus. Sed miseram me,   10
Quid id rei est, hera, corpus undique quod liuet
Vibicibus?

ECCLESIA.   Stigmata haec, si nescitis, gemmae

Meae sunt unionesque unicae, sponsi
Quae causa circumfero.

AFRICUS.   Mihi imperare ultra

Nequeo, quin debeam homini scelesto scelus,   15
Nostrae qui tantum hoc familiae inflixit nephas.
Eamus inquam, Europe frater.

ECCLESIA.   Etiam tu

Pergis?

EVROPUS.   Sine mater.

ECCLESIA.   Non sino inquam. Matrem si

Me habetis, matri obtemperetis: facite ipsa
Vos quae uelim facere.

---

67. *comitissae*] DuCange lists the word in a different sense, the wife of a comrade.

ECCLESIA. They're my bridesmaids. I know they're keeping watch for my bridegroom until he comes for the wedding.

[V.5]   *Enter chorus of five virgins.*

CHORUS 1. Though the night be very late and stormy, and the third cock has already been heard, yet I am determined not to be exhausted from my vigil until the bridegroom comes for the wedding.

CHORUS 2. So let us drive away weariness with a song of night. But I see the bride herself.—— Hail, mistress.

ECCLESIA. Hail. Deservedly do I praise and love you, who thus keep watch over my safety while the world sleeps the deep sleep of perdition.

CHORUS 3. I do not understand the others. We do what we consider it our duty to do. But mercy me, mistress, why is your body red all over with stripes?

ECCLESIA. These stigmas, if you don't know, are my jewels, my only pearls, which I wear for the sake of my bridegroom.

AFRICUS. I can't contain myself any longer from the mischief that I owe to the mischievous scoundrel who inflicted such infamy on our family.—— Europus, my brother, I say let's go.

ECCLESIA. Do you still go on?

EUROPUS. Let us, mother.

ECCLESIA. I won't let you, I say. If you acknowledge me as your mother, obey your mother. Do what I want you to do.

AFRICUS.   Age, quae uelis manda.   20
   Manemus.
ECCLESIA.   Primum ergo preces hic omnes mecum
   Capessite, uotaque iungamus simul.
CHORUS 4.   Recte
   Monemur. Dic ergo hera primum Ecclesia, nosque
   Vocem uoto sequemur tacito tuam.
ECCLESIA.
   Miseriis et lachrymis oppleti, ad te, chare   25
   Iesv, palmas protendimus, tua ut dextra
   Opem ferat diuinam, humana nos quando
   Prorsus destituunt praesidia. Satis iam
   Satis abfuisti longa nimis secula, nos dum
   Miserae interim peculii tui ouiculae ubique   [*p. 80*]   30
   Caedimur, exurimur, rapimur ferro, flamma,
   Ac fluctibus. Elementum nullum in nostram non
   Stragem stringitur. Adeoque res redit, nusquam
   Loci ut quicquam tuis sit reliquum in desertis
   Etiam ultimis, Dioctes sic cuncta ubique   35
   Penetrat, rabiesque Pseudamnica. Age, et quem tandem
   Miseriae pones modum? Mundus quondam,
   Christe, abs te uictus quam diu sese impune
   Poena in nostra efferet? At te flectat miseranda
   Rerum facies. Flectant Ecclesiae sponsae   40
   In hoc corpore stigmata. Sponse, uoluptas, rumpe,
   Age, coelos ut tuos ruamus in amplexus.
   Cito, ueni cito, Domine, caro ne forsan salua
   Nulla maneat. At quae noua lux et odoris mira
   Fragrantia repente adspirat sensibus? Ipsa   45
   Tum terra uidetur concuti.
                        (Hic ex editiori theatri loco, repansis
                        cortinis ostendunt se uelut e coelo
                        sedilia et libri positi, simulque orna-
                        menta demittuntur quibus Ecclesia
                        induitur, praeparata ad nuptias.)
CHORUS 5.   Ergo, sorores,
   Actutum lampades paratae ut sint quaeque
   Videat: sponsus iam imminet foribus. Sedes

AFRICUS. Come, command what you wish; we're staying.

ECCLESIA. First, then, all of you here pray with me. Let's unite our prayers.

CHORUS 4. We are properly advised. Lead us, then, mistress Ecclesia, and we will follow your words with our silent prayer.

ECCLESIA [*praying*]. Filled with miseries and tears, we stretch forth our hands to you, dear Jesus, that your right hand may bring divine assistance, for human resources fail us completely. Far, far too many ages have you been away while we, the wretched little sheep of your own flock, are everywhere butchered by the iron, consumed by the flame, and carried off by the waves: not an element but is committed to our slaughter. We reach the point that no place at all is left for your people, not even in the wildest deserts: Dioctes and the madness of Pseudamnus reach into all affairs everywhere. Come, and set some end to our misery at last. How long, oh Christ, will the world, long ago conquered by you, exalt itself in our suffering? Let the pitiful sight of our condition move you; let these stigmas on the body of your bride Ecclesia move you. My bridegroom, my beloved, come, break through the heavens, that we may rush into your embraces. Quickly, come quickly, lord, lest perchance no flesh remain unharmed. But what new light, what wondrous fragrance of perfume suddenly breathes upon my senses?[1] And now the very earth seems to tremble. [*Here from the upper part of the theater, when the curtains open, are shown as if from heaven thrones with books placed upon them. At the same time garments are lowered in which Ecclesia is dressed and prepared for the wedding.*]

CHORUS 5. Quickly then, sisters, let each one see that her torches are ready. The bridegroom is now near the door. See, the thrones

---

[1] A note in B cites Apocalypse 21, the account of the new heaven and the new earth; no reference is made there to fragrances, and Foxe's note presumably points to what follows in this scene rather than to this sentence.

Videte positas et apertos libros, Vestes
Porro delapsas sponsa queis sese exornet   50
Ad nuptias.
Ecclesia.   Mira uero, praeter supraque
     Spem, oculis ego quae uideo.
Africus.   Magne Deus, magna haec
     Miracula quid uolunt miror. Tum etiam libros   [*p. 81*]
     Satis apertos quos uideo, quid ferant horreo.
Evropus.
     Atqui quum attentius lego quid in dextro sit   55
     Volumine aureis insculptum literis,
     Nunquid uides?
Africus.   Recte nunc uideo in hanc nempe
     Sententiam: "Hierusalem uidi nouam, coelo
     Descendentem, a Deo paratam uti sponsam
     Viro ornatam suo. Datumque illi est ut se   60
     Cooperiat byssino puro atque splendido, etc."
Evropus.
     Haec ita sunt modo, diuina quae sunt, humana
     Vt omnia uincant gaudia.
Africus.   Gaudio ita sum ut qui
     Sim ubique sim nesciam.
Chorus i.   O nos foelices, sponsus
     Postquam aduentat, spectatus tam diu ad nuptias.   65
     Sed interim sponsam cessamus ornare
     Bombycina hac palla. Ast pexis eam pannis
     Discingamus prius. Age, ubi instita iam illa
     Bibapha? Peplum porro addamus cum syrma
     Hyacinthia. Tu, Parthene, crepidas has   70
     Pedibus et calopodia subiice. Cedo autem
     Periscelidas illic quae secus calyptram ad

56.] a note in MSC identifies the meter of the line as "Senar. iamb.".

69. *Bibapha*] a Greek word, βαφή, dipping in dye, with a Latin prefix, *bi-*.

70. *hyacinthia*] the standard form is *hyacinthus; Hyacinthia* is the name of a Spartan festival (L-S).

71. *calopodia*] a Greek word, diminutive of καλάπους; but in Greek it means a shoemaker's last, not the shoes themselves. (καλόπους means having beautiful feet.) DuCange lists *calopodium* as a Latin word.

72. *Periscelidas*] the normal form would be *periscelides*.

are in place, and the books are opened, and garments are lowered in which the bride may deck herself for the wedding.

ECCLESIA. Wondrous indeed and far beyond my hope are the things I see.

AFRICUS. Oh great God, I marvel at what these great miracles mean. And the books which I see open, I shudder at what they contain.

EUROPUS. While I concentrate on what is written in the golden letters of the right-hand volume, do you see anything?[1]

AFRICUS. I see clearly now, even to this sentence: "I saw the new Jerusalem descending from heaven, prepared by God as a bride adorned for her husband. And to her it was granted that she be arrayed in linen shining and pure," etc.[2]

EUROPUS. Only these divine joys are sufficient to surpass all human joys.

AFRICUS. I'm so happy I don't know who or where I am.

CHORUS 1. Oh we joyous people, for the bridegroom, so long awaited, is coming for the wedding. But now let's deck the bride in this silken robe.[3] First we'll free her from these shaggy garments. Come now, where's that double-dyed flounce? Next we'll add the mantle with a train of hyacinth. Parthene,[4] put these sandals and shoes on her feet. Now the leg bands, please; they're lying

---

[1] A note in B cites Apocalypse 20.[12].
[2] A note in B cites Apocalypse 21.[2].
[3] The manuscript version ends at this point.
[4] Virgin.

Manum adiacent. Deinde hoc flammeum collo
Circundemus et torquem cum murenulis ex   [*p. 82*]
Auro quadruplicem. Sancta Salus, diuinitus cuncta   75
Vt quadrant corpori! Restat deinceps nunc
Calantica capiti quam concinnemus cum
Diademate. Quid nunc aliud est? Chirothecas
Et riculam hanc in manus cape. Proh gemmarum
Quantus et emblematum fulgor! Dicas ipsam   80
Inesse claritatem Dei. Hera, dic sodes,
Nouo in hoc tibi nunc ut places synthemate?
ECCLESIA.   Sponso
Postquam placeo, mihi nunc demum placeo.
CHORUS.   Quanta
Vero Hierologum et Theoseben uinctos perfundent
Foelicitate, haec ita ubi esse audierint!
EVROPUS.   Perquam   85
Itaque mox haec ut resciscant censeo.
ECCLESIA.   Nunc quid
Hic restat amplius?
CHORUS.   Nisi uti uentantes
Epithalamio aliquo nunc excipiamus
Has nuptias.
AFRICUS.   Assentior.

EPITHALAMIVM.

Sponse, memor nostri, rumpant tua numina nubes,   90
    Daque tuis redeat, te redeunte, quies.
Longa satis, seruator, abes nunc secula terris,
    Nos tua dum gemimus gens laniata lupis.
Mundus ut in nostram praeceps insanit et ardet
    Perniciem, tutum nil sinit esse tuis.   95
Vndique desertos fera nos sic fata fatigant,
    Nullaque non nostro sanguine terra rubet.

---

77. *Calantica*] in the best classical manuscripts, the standard form is *calautica*.
78. *Chirothecas*] a combination of two Greek words, χείρ, hand, and θήκη, repository. DuCange lists it as a Latin word.
82. *synthemate*] transliterated from a Greek word, σύνθεμα, sum or assembly.
87. *uentantes*] *vento* is a nonce-word, found in Varro (L-S).

there right next to her hat. Then we'll wind this red bridal veil around her neck, and the necklace with four golden strands intertwined. Holy Salus, everything fits her figure divinely. We still must fit the headpiece and the diadem over her head. Now what else is there? These gloves, and hold this small veil in your hands. Oh, how the gems and ornaments gleam! You would say the very splendor of God is in her. Mistress, pray tell us how you like yourself in your new ensemble now.

ECCLESIA. Since I am pleasing to my bridegroom, I am now pleasing to myself at last.

CHORUS. How happy these things will make the fallen Hierologus and Theosebes when they hear what has happened![1]

EUROPUS. Very much, and I feel sure they'll know about them soon.

ECCLESIA. Now what more must be done here?

CHORUS. Nothing except to celebrate the coming nuptials with some epithalamion.

AFRICUS. I agree.

ALL [*singing the epithalamion*]. Bridegroom, remember us and let your majesty break through the clouds; grant your people that peace will return as you return. Too long are the ages you have been away from the earth, oh savior, while we your people groaned, mangled by wolves. As the rash world rages and burns for our destruction, it allows no safety to your people. On all sides, savage calamities vex us forsaken, and no land but turns

[1] A clear indication that Latimer and Ridley are dead as Foxe is writing; they were executed on October 16, 1555. They will "hear" the news in the next life.

Ista precor uideas, longos miserate labores: [*p. 83*]
    Nec uideas, uenias sed pie sponse precor.
Te sine nulla mihi uita est, mihi nulla uoluptas: 100
    Delicii nihil est te sine. Sponse, ueni.
Spiritus ut uenias, iubet et te sponsa uenire:
    Rumpe uocate moras, sponse, citoque ueni.
Quicquid in orbe patet, tellus pelagusque polusque,
    Fessa petunt reditum quaeque creata tuum.   105
Foelix hora quater, nos qua in tua colla ruamus.
    Inque sinus plaudat sponsa uenire tuos.
Tum noua perpetuae durabunt tempora uitae,
    Tempora tum nullis commaculata malis.
Tergentur lachrymae, luctus gemitusque facesset,   110
    Nulla cadent siccis salsa fluenta genis.
Ergo utinam coelo redeas quo terra quiescat,
    Solus enim miseris anchora sola manes.
Atque age nunc mecum quicquid tegit axis Olympi,
    Cum senibus pueri, cum puerisque senes,   115
Vos seu uita tenet seu mors tenet arida nigris
    Pulueribus, frontes tollite, sponsus adest.
Munera qui reddet uitae, qui iura salutis
    Nunc reparata dabit: plaudite, sponsus adest.
Illa est, illa meis semper memoranda Calendis,   120
    Lumine quae solem uincit et astra, dies,
Dextra potens Domini coelo quam misit ab alto,
    Laetitiae precium principiumque meae.
Quae uox tantarum plusquam miracula rerum   [*p. 84*]
    Exprimet et celsi munera tanta patris?   125
Quum uice iam rerum uersa mundique prioris,
    Stat natura stupens, statque stupendo tacens.
Victaque dat nunc ipsa manus sentitque pudorem,
    Quae noua sit mirans, quae uenit, ista dies.
Mors quoque uicta manus metuens sibi porrigit ultro,   130
    Nunc sua quum fracta cuspide tela uidet.
Irrita fata iacent, iacet inuida Parca suumque
    Scindere nunc stamen cogitur ipsa sibi.
Cedere qui nulli didicit ab origine rerum,
    Cedere iam discet Terminus ille lapis.   135

red with our blood. Look to these things, I pray, and have pity on our long sufferings; and do not merely look, oh holy bridegroom, but come. Without you I have no life, I have no pleasure; nothing is delightful without you. Come, oh bridegroom. Come, the Spirit and the bride bid you come.[1] End the delays, you who are called; come quickly, bridegroom. Whatever is to be seen in the world—land, sea, pole, and every created thing—is weary and begs you to return.

Four-times happy is the hour when we may fall upon your neck, and the bride may clap her hands to come into your embrace. Then will last new times of eternal life, times unblemished with misfortunes. Tears will be wiped away, mourning and lamentation ended, no salt streams will fall on our dry cheeks. Then would that you would return from heaven that the earth might have peace, for you alone remain the only refuge of the wretched. Now come, whatever is with me under the axis of the heavens—youth with elders, elders with youth—whether life still holds you or withered death has you in its black dust, lift up your faces: the bridegroom is near. He will restore the gift of life and renew your rights of salvation: clap your hands, the bridegroom is near. This day must always be remembered as my calends:[2] this day, which surpasses the sun and the stars with its radiance, which the all-powerful right hand of the lord sent from heaven on high, the sum and source of my happiness. What words will express the more than miracles of such events, such great gifts of the exalted father? Since the reversal of things, the overturning of the world as it was, nature stands stupefied, silent in stupefaction. Now overmatched, nature herself surrenders and feels ashamed, wondering what this new day is which is coming. Death too, overmatched and frightened for itself, of its own will surrenders, since it now sees its weapons with their points broken. Helpless, the Fates fall; the envious Parca falls and now is compelled to break her own thread.[3] The famous stone Terminus,[4] which

[1] A note in B cites Apocalypse 22.[17].

[2] The first day of each month in the Roman calendar.

[3] Atropos, who cut the thread of life of each man at the appointed time.

[4] The god of landmarks and boundaries. As the play began with a curious disruption of the temporal order, so it ends with the formal abolition of temporal and spatial order.

Mortua uiuiscunt, redeunt sua membra sepultis,
    Et sua iam cineres taphica scripta legent.
Quos mare, quos morbus, quos abstulit ensis et arma,
    Furca, ferae, fames, carcer et ignis edax:
Quaeque suos reuoment iterum monumenta solutos,   140
    Pontus et unda suos, puluis et urna suos.
Omnia sistentur iusta trutinanda bilance:
    Sola fides stabit, cum pietate manens.
Nunc cadet et Babylon, cadet alta potentia regum:
    Vnus erit toto Christus in orbe potens.   145
Tristia iam laetis uertentur et ultima primis;
    Celsa ruent, stabunt quae cecidere prius.
Quos caro, quos mundus uexant, Sathanaeque furores,
    Foelices mecum plaudite, sponsus adest.

CHORVS VIRGINVM.   [*p. 85*]

Paratam nunc sponsam, spectatores, cuncta ac   150
Parata cernitis. Restat nihil, ipse
Nisi paranymphus summam qui scenae imponat
Catastrophen. Id quum fiet certum nemo
Dicet. Poeta, quod possit, praestitit. Ipse ac
Monet sedulo imparati ne sitis, sponsus   155
Cum ueniet uos ne dormitantes excludat.
Tempus fortasse haud longum est. Mira uidemus
Rerum praeludia: Sathan cum Christo totis
Vt pugnat copiis, ubique terrarum
Hodie, ut cum alias, maxime. Agnus at uincet   160
Triumphans tandem agnique sponsa, Pseudamno
Rumpantur licet ilia. Interim admoniti uos:
Vigilate prudenter precor. El plaudite.

ΤΕΛΟΣ.

---

142. *bilance*] a nonce-word, found in Martianus Minneus Felix Capella (L-S).

from the beginning of time has learned to yield to none, will now learn to yield. The dead come to life; their limbs return to those who were buried; now ashes will read their own epitaphs. Those whom sea or sickness or sword has carried off, or the fork or fierce beasts or famine, or prison or consuming pyre—all the sepulchers, the sea and the wave, the dust and the urn will discharge their victims freed. All things will be arraigned, to be weighed by an honest scale. Only faith abiding with piety will stand firm. Now too Babylon will fall, and the exalted power of kings: Christ alone will have power through all the world. Now the sad will be made happy, and the last, first; the exalted shall fall, and those who fell before shall stand. You whom the flesh and the world and the madnesses of Satan torment, be happy and applaud with me: the bridegroom is near.

CHORUS OF VIRGINS. Spectators, now you see the bride decked out and all things in readiness. Nothing remains except the bridegroom himself, who will bring the final catastrophe to our stage.[1] When that will happen none will say for sure. The poet has shown what he could. And he earnestly advises you not to be unprepared, lest the bridegroom, when he comes, reject you as you sleep. The time is perhaps not long. We see the marvelous preludes: how Satan battles against Christ with all his forces everywhere in the world today, as hard as he did of yore. But the lamb will prevail, triumphant at last, and the bride of the lamb, though her flanks be broken by Pseudamnus. Meantime be warned, be on your guard with prudence, I pray. And do applaud.

THE END.

---

[1] See *Titus et Gesippus*, p. 105, n. 1.

TEXTUAL NOTES

Textual Notes

The apparatus appearing beneath the Latin texts in this edition is very selective, recording mostly my substantive emendations, a few conjectural emendations, and some comments on Foxe's unusual words—matters most immediately useful to the reader of the established texts. The Textual Notes which follow comprise a comprehensive apparatus recording Foxe's revisions, my substantive emendations, and (for *Christus Triumphans*, which alone survives in more than one version) a historical collation.

All words appearing in these notes in roman type are taken from original documents, printed or manuscript; all words appearing in italics are editorial. In each note the lemma normally reproduces the wording of my text and is followed by a bracket]. The copy text should be assumed to agree substantially with the lemma unless its siglum follows a listed variant; the copy text for *Titus et Gesippus* is, of course, the only surviving manuscript version (MST), and that for *Christus Triumphans* is the first printed edition, 1556 (B). All other versions of *Christus Triumphans* not specifically cited should be assumed to agree substantially with the lemma. Normally only substantive variants are recorded. Sometimes minor differences from the lemma are shown in parentheses following the siglum of the edition having the differences.

The following sigla are used in these notes:

MST   The holograph manuscript of *Titus et Gesippus* in British Museum Lansdowne MS. 388, ff. 121-146, 112-116v.

MSC   The holograph manuscript of *Christus Triumphans* in British Museum Lansdowne MS. 1045, ff. 132-155v.

B   Basel edition: *Christus Trivmphans, Comoedia Apocalyptica:* Avtore Ioanne Foxo Anglo. Basileae, per Ioannem Oporinum. [Colophon: Basileae, ex Officina Ioannis Oporini, Anno Salutis humanae M.D.LVI. Mense Martio.] The edition was based on a (probably authorial) manuscript later than MSC. Copies

375

collated are British Museum (BM), University of Illinois (Ill.), Bodleian (Bodl.), and Harvard (Harv.).

Be　　The errata page in B (sig. I5v).

N　　Nuremberg edition: *Christvs Trivmphans, Comoedia Apocalyptica: Autore Ioanne Foxo Anglo.* Noribergae, In officina typographica Gerlachiana [the widow and heirs of Dietrich Gerlach], Anno MDXC. This edition was based on a copy of B; the unknown editor did a careful job and made a few emendations which are proved right by collation with MSC.

L　　London edition: *Christus Triumphans. Comoedia Apocalyptica.* Autore Joanne Foxo, Anglo. Edita est olim Basileae, Anno 1556. Nunc denuo Edita, & Scholarchis, Ludique Literarii Moderatoribus dedicata, ob insignem Styli Elegantiam in Scholas utilissime admittenda. Editore T. C. Sidn. Collegii, S.M. Londini, Impensis Rob. Clavel, apud quem prostant in via vulg. voc. Little Britain. 1672. [Some copies with 1676 on the title page are merely reissues of the same printing.] This edition was based on a copy of B and is carelessly edited. The editor may have been Thomas Comber; see my Introduction, n. 80.

Le　　The errata page in L (p. 123).

PM　　Manuscript notes in the Harvard copy of B. The hand is very early, probably sixteenth-century. Whoever made the notes must have known Oxford, for he corrected Foxe's directions in V.2.28 (see the note to the translation *ad loc.*). His notes are not very sophisticated, but they are interesting because many of them look like a prompter's notes: they list the props needed, or they tidy up entrances, etc. Is it possible that this copy was used for production at Oxford or Cambridge in about 1562 (see p. 34)?

The following abbreviations are used in the notes:

ess.　　essentially

M.H.　　metrical heading (at the beginning of a scene)

Om.　　omitted

P.H.　　persons heading (list at the beginning of a scene)

S.D.　　stage direction

S.H.　　(act and) scene heading

S.P.　　speech prefix

Most of the Textual Notes record authorial revisions. The manuscripts of both plays are heavily revised, and the printed version of *Christus Triumphans* represents a revision of that play later than the surviving manuscript. I have attempted to record all substantive revisions, ignoring false starts caused by manifest *lapsus styli*. If a note records an authorial revision, the final reading of the manuscript is invariably indicated by the placement of its siglum (MST or MSC), whether it agrees with the lemma or not. Following that siglum, the stages of revision are retraced in order, with the earliest reading normally appearing last in the sequence. The direction of revision is indicated by the bold-face symbol < before each earlier stage. (On the rare occasions when some circumstance has made it more convenient to list the earlier readings first, the bold-face symbol > indicates the direction of revision.) Not uncommonly, in a revision involving several words, some stage will have undergone internal revision of, say, one word; rather than treat this as a separate stage of the entire passage, I have normally recorded such internal revision within square brackets at the point of the revision.

Reconstructing the stages of revision has often been very difficult. At times it is hard to read a canceled word; even when it can be read, its place in the revised passage cannot always be determined; the problems were made more difficult by Foxe's careless failure to strike through many canceled words. I am reasonably certain of my readings of revisions involving only one or two words; but more or less doubt attends my readings of many revisions involving longer passages, especially passages which were revised several times. I have, in some of the most troublesome cases, described the difficulty. At other times certain symbols indicate my uncertainty over particular points. A query before the direction symbol (?<) suggests that, although all the words included in the stage appearing after the symbol may be in the manuscript, I am not sure that they were ever combined into one stage. A query in brackets following a variant reading [?] suggests that, although the existence of that stage of revision is not in doubt, my reading of the words is uncertain. When I have been unable to decipher a particular word, or when I have serious doubt that I have read it properly, I have placed my conjectured reading within angle brackets ⟨ ⟩. In a few cases, where an earlier reading can be seen but is utterly illegible, I have shown the fact of revision by an obelisk in brackets following the revised reading [†]. An asterisk (*) following a reading indicates that Foxe abandoned the reading before completing it; the incompleteness may be of a single word or of a grammatical unit; in one or two instances, I have included after the asterisk a conjectural completion of the reading.

In all transcriptions of manuscript readings I have silently regularized punctuation and capitalization according to the principles which I have used in the text itself. I have reproduced original spellings, but have silently expanded abbreviations for -*que*, nasal macrons, and the like. When a note includes both a speech prefix and words from the text, the speech prefix is differentiated by being printed entirely in capitals; otherwise, only the initial letter is capitalized, even in the lemma, where in all other respects the form of my text is reproduced. All speech prefixes are spelled out in full unless the meaning of a manuscript abbreviation is unclear, and, except in the lemma, supplied letters are placed within square brackets.

Notes to *Titus et Gesippus*

[Periocha]. *In MST, this appears (without heading) after III.1 on f. 136v.*
   5. confectus sese] *MST* < s [*]
  10. egregiam] *MST* < tum [*or* tam] ⟨ ⟩
  12. Semproniae] *MST* < omnia [*] [*See l. 14.*]
  14. gratiis] gratis *MST*

[I.1]
  S.H. and P.H.] *Om. MST*
  1. S.P.] *Om. MST*
    Gesippo hodie] *MST* < h [*]
  9. Te appello qui] *MST* < Proh superne deus
 10. est] *MST* < istuc
 14-15. rogem / Autem? Quis] *MST* < rogem autem quis /
 17. Aut dicas] *MST* < Dicas
 18. unquam] *MST* ?< nunquam
 21. pertinere] *MST* (?) < pertinerere
 23-24. speres— / . . . te] *MST* (*ess.*) < speres / Minus torquebit te
 24. Neque] *MST* (?) < Numquam
 25. Quasi] *MST* < Etiam quasi
 27. est] *MST* < sit
    eas] *MST* < ergo
 28. Gesippo] Tito *MST*
 36. Semproniam] *MST* < Mi Phormio
 38-39. Os . . . tibi] *MST* < Atque / Forma quam vndique venusta sit
 40. Gesippus] *MST* < T [*]
    illum vnice] *MST* < v [*]
 41. huic qui] *MST* < qui huic < qui illi

42. esset] *MST* < essem
44. pol] *MST* < profecto
    Tite] Pamphile *MST*
48. miseriis] *MST* < suspiriis
50. Conclamatum] Comclamatum *MST*
51. nuptiae] *MST* < nuptii⟨s⟩
54-55. dare / Lenimen queam] *MST* < tibi / Lenimen parare queam
58. dialecticos] *Apparently a separate line in MST.*

[I.2]
    S.H.] *Om. MST*
    P.H. Pythias. Stephanio.] *Om. MST*
    1. S.P.] *Om MST*
    3. ipsa . . . remisissimi] *In MST there is a faint line through these words,*
but they are not likely to have been canceled.
    4-5. prorsus . . . enecant] *MST* < neque . . . enecent
    5.-6. Nec pater . . . manus] *MST* < neque scio an quisquam [*word
canceled, then rewritten*] meipso magis / Redarguendus, qui meas hisce rebus
manus
    10. S.P.] *MST* (*ess.*) < Tit[us]
        Syre] *MST* < T [*]
    11. S.P. Gesippus] *MST* (*ess.*) < T[itus]
    16. Syre] *MST* < Syr [*] < T [*]
    17. saltitent] *MST* ?< saltitant
    20. componantur ad munditiem] *Added in MST above the words* aedibus
. . . lilia. *It presumably represents an unfinished revision, and I have therefore
accepted it into the line; I cannot determine what portion of the line would have
been canceled to accommodate it or what connective would have been supplied.
Conceivably it should end l. 19, but* Interspergito (*l. 21*) *would then be left
without an object.*
    21. sertis] *MST* < tum sertis

[I.3]
    S.H.] *Om. MST*
    1. S.P.] *Om. MST*
    4. vides] *MST* < sit
        tuis] *MST* < tib [*]
    5. itque] *MST* (*?*); *see note to the Latin text.*
    8. tibi cantionem recino] *MST* < canti recino [*Written above the line,*
cantionem *appears to replace* recino, *but I assume that the verb was intended to
remain, though the resulting line is hypermetrical.*]

9. vbi . . . possumus] *MST* < tibi quod queat referre gratiam

13. Annon] Anno *MST*

15. ita vt decet] *MST* < ut d [*]

19. Insuauem] *MST* < Gesippe insuauem [*Perhaps* Gesippe *was not canceled.*]

21-22. SIMO. Gesippe . . . / En] *MST* < CHR[EMES]. Atque audin' respice rursus ad / me. En [*See l. 23.*]

22. tecum] *MST* < tibi

23. S.P. Simo] *MST* < Chr[emes]

24. S.P. Simo] *MST* (*ess.*) < C[hremes]

25. Viden'] *MST* < Non

29. accersas vbi lubet] *MST* < vbi voles accersas

33. quando] quado *MST*

34. S.P. Simo] *MST* (*ess.*) < C[hremes]
    arbitratu] abitratu *MST*

[I.4]

S.H.] *Om. MST*

1. S.P.] *Om. MST*

6. exalationes Aristotelis] *MST* < A [*]

8-9. fidem . . . hodie] *MST* (?) < fidem! Quantum ego / [*These words, which were construed with l. 10, were not canceled; and l. 8 is metrically defective without them. Perhaps l. 10 was to be deleted, but deletion would leave* Agressus sum (*l. 11*) *without a function.*]

9. coepi ego] *MST* < ego coepi

12. tantam mihi] *MST* < mihi tantam
    potestatem astutiae] *MST* < ast [*]

14. res . . . prorsus] *MST* < p [*]

19. sit difficile] *MST* < difficile

20. oblinendi oculi] *MST* < faciendus fucus

23-25. Etiamnum . . . oporteat] *I have* (*with some uncertainty*) *lineated this passage, which* (*except for the first two words*) *is added in the margin without lineation. The passage is heavily revised. The earliest version was apparently* Quamquam tamen nonnullum / Ceu per nebulas lucis videre videor / Fabula quomodo haec tractari oporteat / *A later stage seems to have been* Quamquam etiamnum / Eius [?] rei nonnullum mihi gustum videor / Capere, id quo confectum iri pacto oporteat / [*In this stage,* Eius < Huius *and* gustum videor / capere < capere videor / < vid [*], *and* mihi *was first written after* Etiamnum]

26-27. Consului . . . dialecticos] Consului . . . consului dialecticos *MST* (*but perhaps the second* consului, *without which l. 27 is metrically deficient,*

should stand; it survives from an earlier stage) < Quippe simulatque locos
meos oraculis / Ceu pro Delphicis consului dialecticos < Quippe simulatque locos illos meos ceu pro / Oraculis consului Delphicis dialecticos

29. Locus mox . . . se] *MST* < Mox . . . sese locus

30-31. meo . . . molimini] *MST* < mihi . . . instituto

34. vt] *MST* < qu [*]

37. hunc . . . sermonem] *MST* < hunc libido est auscultare paululum
< huic prius auscultabo paululum

[I.5]

S.H.] *Om. MST*

1. S.P.] *Om. MST*

profecto] *MST* ?< praefecto

7. Quicquam] *MST* < Q⟨uam⟩

17. illam pulchram] *MST* < pulchram

23. Vel mors vel] *MST* < Mors v⟨–⟩

26. Praeterea diem] *MST* < Diem

27. video] *MST* < miser video

34. Nisi . . . virgula] *MST* < Diuina nisi ipsa quod aiunt succurrat
virgula

36. me heri] *MST* < me heri mei ?< mei heri

37. tu'] *MST* < Audistin'? Tu

Teipsum querito] *MST* < haud prouideram

41. Here hercle] *MST* < Here hercle meo < Hercle

42. Confici] Confeci *MST* (?)

43. Est] *MST* < Nunc sita est

47. mortuo] *MST* < misero

53. id mihi] *MST* < mihi

55. Tum] *MST* < Atque ?< Ve [*]

regione] *MST* < regionem < re⟨t⟩ [*]

61. Exordiar telam] *MST* < Telum [*sic*] exordiar

64-65. vitam . . . suam] *MST* < vitam suam / Magis amauit < ⟨[*two*
illegible words]⟩ / Scio vitam amavit m [*]

66-67. cui . . . potest] *MST* < cui opitulari⟨ ⟩ [*apparently Foxe started
to write* opitularier] ipse tam facile potest / Vnius adeo impendio virgunculae < quem vna queat virguncula [*]

[I.6]

S.H.] *Om. MST*

4. obsecro] *MST* < obsecro te

Dorivm . . . Dorivm] *MST* < Doricum . . . Doricum

5. S.P. Marsias [*his first speech in the line*]] *Added above the line in MST.*
9. illas] *MST* < ellas
    Orphei] Ophei *MST*
   12. quandam inesse] *MST* < inesse
   14. potest] *MST* < post [*?*]
       S.P. Marsias] *MST* (*ess.*) < S. [*In S.P.'s at ll. 6 and 13, there was momentary confusion, as Foxe started to write the wrong initial.*]
   15-16. Rogatur ut / Audire] *MST* < Ergo te rogatum [< rogari] volumus te audire ut liceat ?< Magnopere rogatur ut < Magnopere fas ne igitur [*These stages are not altogether certain, and perhaps* Rogatur ut *should be a part of l. 14.*]
   19. rogatus hoc] *MST* < hoc
   21. tametsi] *MSC* < tamen
   22. ac . . . audies] *MST* < audies
   23. Siquidem . . . licet] *MST* < Etiam permittis saltare
       Ausculta] *MST* < Salta
   24. lapis] *MST* < lapis Lapis [*?or* Lupis]
   25. compos] *MSC* < compons
       Quidum] *MST* < Quiq [*?*] [*]
   29. orbes] *MST* < s [*]
   30. personantes] *MST* < referentes
   32. ita] *MST* < tua ita
       puero tibi] *MST* < puero
   35. Consequamini] *MST* < ⟨ ⟩ consequamini

[I.7]
   S.H.] *Om. MST*
   1. S.P.] *Om. MST*
      illud hercle] *MST* < hercle illud
   6-7. rerum / . . . aiunt] *MST* < aiunt / Rerum est satietas
   7. aliter euenit] *MST* < in hac re aliter / [*?*] Euenit
   9. quin quo magis] *MST* < nec quicquam est nimium, quippe
   10. magis] *MST* < magis magisque
   12. Oris . . . iubar vt] *MST* < [*See next note.*]
   12-13. dixerim / . . . quicquid] *MST* < dixerim / Quicquid vsquam virginum < dixerim, quicquid vsquam / [*] [*presumably abandoned when extra words were added at the beginning of the line; see preceding note*]
   14. formas conferant] *MST* < huic sint conferendae [*Perhaps* huic *was intended to stand, though the revised words were begun above it.*]
   16-17. Exemplar . . . singulare / Idaeae . . . nunquam] *MST* < Cuius ego idaeae obliuiscar / Numquam

18. vis] *MST* < f [?]
22. faciam] *MST* < volui facere
25. In] *MST* < Prae
27. tamue] *MST* [†]
30. Titus meus] *MST* < Hem

[I.8]
S.H.] *Om. MST*
1. S.P.] *Om. MST*
1-2. Bene . . . ratiunculae] *MST* (*except as in subsequent notes*) < Satis
ergo credo [†] Chreme meministi retinere te / Rationem quod deest
conficiundae [*The revised passage is nonmetrical; presumably Foxe did not
complete his work on the passage.*]
1. atque] *MST* ?< ac
   tantum quinque] < quinque
3. non pigeat tantisper hic / Te] *MST* < tantisper hic / Te non pig
[*] < libeat, hic tantisper te / Velim
5. SIMO. Atque . . . redeuntem] *Added above the line in MST* (*with the
additional S.P. for Chremes necessitated by this added speech*).
   Deo nunc] *MST* < Deo
6. cum res mihi] *MST* < quando res meas
7. quod . . . amplius] *MST* < quod ⟨quippe⟩ optem supra < quod
⟨quisquam⟩ queat optare
8-9. vno / Accipimus] *MST* < vno a [*]
9. ei sola est] *MST* < sola ei est filia
14. Solatium] *MST* < Solatium est
    gnati] *MST* < filii
17. minus] *MST* < non
18. sensi magis, magis] *MST* < magis sensi, magis < expertus sum
20. repositas] *MST* < selectas
    Chreme, cape /] *MST* < cape, / Chreme
22. Laudo] *MST* < Bene dicis
24. hunc dicam] *MST* < d [*]
25. omnes prebeant] *MST* < p [*]

[I.9]
S.H.] *Om. MST*
1. S.P.] *Om. MST*
   neque] *MST* < neq⟨uam⟩
7-9. ac . . . In] *MST* < P[HORMIO]. Ah [*?or* At] istuc quaeso Gesippe
ne cogites. G[ESIPPUS]. Non rogitem? / Quidum? P[HORMIO]. Quia num-

quam id, me referente, audies. G[ESIPPUS]. Principio, potin' / Ego illi [†] vt sim auxilio annon? Saltem consilium meum Phormio / Non deerit. P[HORMIO]. Imo vero tandem dicam. In [*Above* Saltem, *or below* referente, *appear three illegible letters.*]

    9. In te] *MST* < Inte

    10-11. dicas . . . Posse] *MST* < aut impetrare id rogando [< rogand⟨ ⟩] / Possis

      11. vti beneficiis] *MST* < b [*]

      impetrando] *MST* [†]

      12. Quid] *MST* < Quid igitur

      15-17.] *In MST, the lines are bracketed.*

      17. vitae . . . cum] *MST* < vitae cum

      18. Recte] *MST* < Sane / Recte [Sane *a part of l. 17*]

      Itaque] *MST* < Atque

      ipsa ferme] *MST* < ipsa

      19. Ne metuas, Phormio] *MST* < Possum egone

      21. Iusiurandum dabam] *MST* < Etiam iuratum sit

      23. vis tibi] *MST* < tibi

      Verumne . . . hodie] *MST* (*added above the line, perhaps intended to supplant* vis . . . carnifex)

      24. Dicas libere] *MST* < *om.*

      26. vnico] *MST* < vno

      Amat] *MST* < Amor

      28. hercle] *MST* < vero

      sese] *MST* ?< se

      29. impauide] *MST* < libere

      32. vt videas] *MST* < permittere

      33. Temporis hoc] *MST* < Temporis

      Phormio] *MST* < Phormio haec tam angusta ratio

      37. Quamquam] Quamque *MST* (?) < Sane

      38. sed] ?*Read* scilicet [*See note to the Latin text.*]

      39. effundenda sit] *MST* < effundenda

      40. esse mihi] *MST* < vniuus [*sic*]

    44. mediusfidius] *MST* < cum superis omnibus [*Such, I think, was Foxe's intention, though he uncharacteristically wrote the revision below the line, so that it appears to replace* hic iurabo *in l. 45. The vertical spacing, however, appears to indicate that* mediusfidius *was already written before Foxe began writing l. 45.*]

    45-47. omnis . . . Potest] *MST* (?) [hoccine vt *appears below* intendere (*l. 46*), *but appears to be of the same inking as l. 45; the words may have been written before l. 46 (see below), for the last two words of that line are apparently dropped to accommodate them. In l. 47, a* non *from an earlier reading was not struck through. But the combination which I have adopted seems to be the only one possible*] < hic scrupus est / Ne possit per senes fieri, qui si resciuerint, numquam ferent. / Scio non

47. Siquidem] *MST* < At si

48. Certe . . . nunc] *MST* < Quid tum cedo? Nam hic nihil dubites?

53-54. ornatu / . . . tuo] *MST* < capiet ornatum hunc / Atque ad Semproniam ingredietur tuam

56. censes facere] *MST* [*?or* facerem] < ita censes [ita *apparently canceled*] < censeres

57. eum intus] *MST* < eum

vestes] *MST* < vestem

60. Nempe] *MST* < Probe

Ipsa] *MST* [†]

62. S.P.] *Om. MST*

mvro] *MST* < atque mvro

64-65. videbitur / A me] *MST* < a me videbitur /

65. opus] *MST* < opus est

67. haec sunt perinde] *MST* < per [*]

69. male] *MST* < mala

71-72. bene / Diuinata] *MST* < bene ⟨d⟩ [*]

76. E ruina . . . per flammam] *MST* < Per flammam . . . e ruina

79. miserrimo] *MST* < miserrimum

84. maioris] *MST* < maloris

secerni solatii] *MST* < solatii

[II.1]

1. S.P.] *Om. MST*

2. tam] *MST* < modo [*see l. 3*]

5-8.] *The passage was revised several times in MST; I believe the sequence was as follows:* Aequa . . . forem] [*see l. 6n.*] < Quippe ita semper persuasi mihi vt illius / Non minus ac meis studeam faueamque commodis / . . . forem < Mihi enim, quicquid est, illi si fit, fierit / Existimo, neque [< q (*)] minus hercle faueo commodis / Cui si quid boni maliue [*this word added above the line*] obictum [*sic*] est, simul / Me [*this word added above the line*] in eandem secum sortem semper numero < Ita enim mihi illi quod fit fieri quicquid est / Existimo, quando ipsum loco animi mei habeam / < Mihi enim quod illi fit fieri quicquid est / Existimo, quando ipsum loco animi mei habeam /

6. omnino commodis] *MST* < commodis

9-12. Quippe . . . debeat] *MST* (*but see following notes*) < Ita enim videtur mihi, quisquis amicitiam / Vere colit, non tam in sese viuere, quam vbi / Amat par est vt putet

    9. Quippe . . . mihi] *MST* (*?*) [Quippe *and* mihi *may be struck through*] < Quippe sic videtur mihi

    11. nec . . . magis] *MST* < non magis in suo

    15. Animus . . . vt] *MTS* < Nam vt [*]

    16. Animi] *MST* < Et [*]

    20. sin] *MST* < qui [*?*]

[II.2]

    S.H.] *Om. MST*

    P.H. Gesippus] *Om. MST*

    1. S.P.] *Om. MST*

    3. O] *Written twice in MST, once (by accident) after the S.P., which is above the song.*

    4. mihi] *MST* < milli

    7. hinc valete] *MST* < ite curae

    8. Iteque] *MST* < Iteque nuc [?*nunc]

    9. Io triumphe] *MST* < Ite, valete

    11. almus] *MST* < faelix

    15-16. cui / Dari] *MST* < cui vno die / Plura euenerunt bona, aut cui [< bona, cui] dari

    17. hodie qui] *MST* < q [*]

    17-18. expugnaui . . . orbaui] *MST* < expugnasse / Videor . . . orbasse

    19-20. quem . . . Atque] *MST* < quem dari nimis cupio, vt agam / Gratias

    23-24. tuum, / Qui me] *MST* < tuum, qui me /

    36. dare] *MST* < mihi dare

    38-39. hunc / Demonstro tuum] *MST* < tuum / Demonstro

    41. Familiis] *MST* < Familia

    46-47. Atque / Ita] *MST* < Itaque / Bene

    47. epithasis] *MST* < ipsa epithasis

    48. S.P. Titus] *MST* (*ess.*) < G.

    52. Tite] Gesippe *MST*

    53. abiere] *MST* < abierunt

    54. te . . . conferas] *MST* < fugam hinc arripias pedibus < fugam aliquam despicias pedibus

    55. vrbis] *MST* < huius vrbis

        quam primulum] *MST* < promptissime

    56. silere diu] *MST* < diu caelarier

58. Sese] *MST* ?< Se
    atque] *MST* ?< ac
61. humeros . . . denique] *MST* < tandem . . . humeros
    vniuersa] vniuesa *MST*
    moles] *MST* < haec moles
62. Cui . . . copia] *MST* < Quando tum effugere nullo pacto
63. incolumes] *MST* < secundae
64. mala] *MST* ?< mali

[II.3]
    S.H.] *Om. MST*
    1. S.P.] *Om. MST*
    2. noster] *MST* < nostrum
    4. Exquirendus] *MST* < Exquirendus est [*Note* est *later in the line.*]
    5. Pultare] *MST* < Has pultare
    12. Nempe] *MST* < Nimirum

[II.4]
    S.H.] *Om. MST*
    1. S.P.] *Om. MST*
    alta] *MST* [†]
    Misene] *MST* < Marsia
    2. produxeris, bellua] *MST* < produxeris
    6.] *Added interlineally in MST.*
    8. S.P. Marsias] M. *MST* (*So also ll. 10, 11, 12* [bis], *13, 16, 17, 19,*
21; *but cf. ll. 25 ff.*)
    18. est] *MST* < est hoc
    22. S.P.] *MST* < *om.*
    24. puerpera] *MST* < puerfera
    25. S.P. Misenus] M. *MST* (*so also ll. 29* [*his second speech in the line*], *30*)
    Ecquid] *MST* < Sed quid
    26. Pythias] *MST* < Nobis Pythias nolit
    S.P. Marsias] M. *MST*
    27. S.P. Pythias [*her second speech in the line*]] *Om. MST*
    32. meministin'] *MST* ?< meministi
    condiximus] condixmus *MST* (?)
    35. S.P. Marsias] M. *MST*
    38. Piscatus . . . bonus] *MST* < huc appulimus, quid ais?
    S.P. Marsias] *MST* [†]
    39. aeque] aequeue *MST* (?)
    S.P. Midas] Mi. *MST*

40. S.P. Misenus] Mi. *MST*
41. assentior] *MST* < assens

[II.5]
  S.H.] *Om. MST*
  1. S.P.] *Om. MST*
  3. nimisque] *MST* < idque adeo nimis
  4. patri palam] *MST* < palam
  5-6. ita . . . iri] *MST* < ita id nunc est ut ignorari nequeat / . . . iri <
  ita necesse est id confessum iri / Nostro potius indicio, quam ex aliis
  [*Though Foxe may not have written this much before changing his plan.*]
  7. Resciuerit] *MST* < Resciuerit ille
  10. permagne] *MST* < permultum
  11. explicandi] *MST* < referendi
  12. exponuntur] *MST* < referuntur
  13. hanc syngrapham] *MST* < hoc epistolium

[II.6]
  S.H.] *Om. MST*
  1. S.P.] *Om. MST*
  2. Vixdum pol] *MST* [*?read* Vix pol] < Vixdum
  4. uenienti] *MST* < aduenienti
  6. ac] *MST* < at
     asportarier] *MST* < nostram
  10. Tito] *MST* < toto
  12. At] *MST* < Sed

[II.7]
  S.H.] *Om. MST*
  P.H. Syrus] *MST* < Sosias
  1. S.P.] *Om. MST*
  4. Verum] *MST* < Sic est
     abductam] *MST* < adductam
  5. pariter] *MST* [†]
  7. ad] *MST* < etiam ad
     maniam] *MST* < insaniam
  18. ludificarier] *MST* < deludier
  21. tuear] *MST* ?< tueo
  23. illum] *MST* < ⟨e⟩llum
  24. haec] *MST* < illa

[II.8]

S.H.] *Om. MST*

P.H. Gesippus] *Om. MST*
     Syrus] *MST* < Ph.

1. S.P.] *Om. MST*

4-5. Simo . . . Aduenis] *MST* < A [*]

7. Quid, Chreme] *MST* < Chreme

10. Assequatur] *MST* < Persentiat

12-13. facinus / Adolescens] *MST* < adolescens / Facinus

14. Istarum] *MST* [†]

15. fuga haec] *MST* < illius fuga
     prius] *MST* < antea

17. peregrinam] peregrina *MST*

18. tibi scio] *MST* < auribus tuis

19. Imo . . . sit] *MST* < Itaque hercle enimuero credidi

19-20. Simo / . . . perlege] *MST* < cape / . . . ac perlege

20. pol] *MST* < hercu [*]

22. polypus] *MST* < miram

25. tandem] *MST* < existimas

28. hoc mihi] *MST* < bone vir

30. Sollicitasti] *MST* ?< Sollicitarier < Adiisti

31-32. apud . . . eam] *MST* < eam / Mansuram aetatem

33-34. paranymphos . . . re] *MST* < quos item [< frequ (*)] /
Paranymphos nihilo

35. postpositos] pospositos *MST*

37. inicis] *In MST, the two dots over the second -i- suggest that Foxe intended the alternate form* injicis.

37-38. At . . . tuo] *MST* < Eam / Tuo si nolles gnato

38. qui vellent] *MST* < habere sibi

40-41. fac . . . respondeas] *MST* < respondeas / Iudici

45. nobis data sunt] *MST* < dedisti nobis

46-47. habe . . . es, / Simo] *MST* < habe. C[HREMES]. Saeuus es,
Simo, / Nimium, nec

48.] *Added interlineally in MST.*

50. Quidem [*a doubtful reading*]] *MST* (?) < Quid [*perhaps still correct*]
     cudetur] *MST* < cundetur

51. hoc . . . devorandum] *MST* < quod intristi, illi devorandum <
intristi [< intristo] hoc, illi devorandum
     innocuo] *MST* [†]

52. Mastygia] *MST* < Sta mastygia

53. quantas] *MST* < has omnes

57-58. ⟨spurium⟩ / Syre] *MST* (*the illegible word, of which* -rium *seems clear, could be a place-name, such as* Sturium *or* Parium *or conceivably* Pyrium [= Pyraeum], *or a pejorative epithet*) < Syre /

　　58. caput hoc] *MST* < hunc
　　　　ciuitate] *MST* < ciuitate hac < ciuitate hanc.
　　58-59. patris / . . . Abeat] *MST* < patrem vt / Querit [< Querat], abeat
　　61. Ita] *MST* [†]
　　61-62. si . . . sit] *MST* < siquid huic fraudi sibi a / Me tibi e
　　64. me conscium esse] *MST* < hic conscium me
　　65. deum] *MST* < supre [*] < deum
　　　　iudicem] *MST* < maximum
　　69. offucias] offusias *MST* < insidias < insidiis
　　70. Ab . . . factas] Ab . . . factus *MST* < ⟨Factas⟩ ab . . . ⟨ ⟩ < [†]
　　72. Gesippo . . . tua ignorante filia] *MST* < Gesippo suo . . . ignorante tua [< tua ignorante] / Etiam filia
　　73. atque] actque *MST*
　　74. audiens] *MST* ?< audies
　　76. Stupor huc] *MST* < Res haec

[III.1]
　　1. S.P.] *Om. MST*
　　5. Refugii iam] *MST* < Iam refugii
　　7. par] *MST* < pars
　　12. Quod . . . exemplar] *MST* < Ex [*]
　　　　hercle] *MST* < nunc [*See l. 13n.*]
　　13. Mirae] *MST* < Hercle < Atque
　　　　interpretor] *MST* < iudico
　　14. Deus . . . huiusmodi] *MST* < Mihi [*cf. l. 13*] consimiles Gesippos vt reperiam / Obtestor superos

[III.2]
　　S.H.] *Om. MST*
　　1. S.P.] *Om. MST*
　　3. caussa] *MST* < tantum caussa
　　5. iussisti] *MST* [†]
　　6. Quid] *MST* < Tandem
　　11. non prohibuisse pol] *MST* < non prohibuisse iam < iam non prohibuisse
　　12. Cedo] *MST* < Cedo et < Cedo
　　　　damnum hoc] *MST* < damnum est < damnum hoc
　　　　hoc totum] *MST* < scilicet < igitur
　　　　vides] *MST* < cogita

13. namque] *MST* < enim

13-15. adolescentulo / . . . suspicor] *MST* (*see following notes*) < adolescentulo vtique / Consulari filio, tum qui in paternos fasces subiit / Adueniens domum, quo nomine multo [< tuas] esse res tibi / Auctiores iudico

14. Et] *MST* ?< ⟨an⟩
   illam] *MST* ?< illum

15. lauto] *MST* < lautiore
   multo . . . satis] *Added above the line in MST* (*perhaps intended to supplant* lauto in).

16. Vero] *MST* < Hoc nunc < Hoc
   incumbit] *MST* < attinet

16-18. qui . . . id] *MST* < cui nisi / Infaelix essem tua hodie affinitas firmo praesidio / Esse potuit, ac familiae stabiliendae

17. mihi praesidio] *MST* < prae [*]

22-23. mihi / Qui] *MST* < qui / [*]

23-24. quamuis haec / Mea . . . sit querimonia] *MST* < iniuria / Tametsi mea . . . quam tua sit

24. id si] *MST* < si id

25. nunc] *MST* < iam

25-26. habet / Frater] *MST* < habet frater /

27-28. Reduc / Filium] *MST* < Reduc filiu [*] /

28. meritis] *MST* [†]

31. S.P. Chremes] *In MST, added after* sapide *was written.*

36. Ad] *MST* < [†]

37-38. nanciscier / Potero] *MST* < nancisci potero /

39. occurrit quidem] *MST* < occurrit nunc < nunc occurrit
   mihi . . . aiebat] *MST* < mihi . . . aiebat dudum < quem dudum ego [*]

40. vicinus Crito] vicinus Stylpho *MST* < Albertus Discus
   frequens] *Perhaps a late addition in MST.*

41. exerceat] *MST* < habet

41-42. Eum / Iam] *MST* < Eum ⟨iam⟩ /

43. domum adveniens] *MST* < ⟨ad⟩

44. Venire ad] *MST* < Ad

45. hercle me praeteriit] *MST* < hoc praeteritum est

46. Simonem] *MST* < C [?]

49-52. Chremes. Curriculo . . . Scilicet] *Perhaps a late addition in MST.*

52. Eam . . . cupio] *MST* < Eam vid⟨i⟩ prebeto < ⟨ ⟩que ipsis [< ipsos] comitari [< comitatum (?)] (*Since no readings were canceled, it is difficult to determine which one Foxe finally settled on.*)

[III.3]

S.H.] *Om. MST*

P.H. Sophrona] Sostrata *MST*

1. S.P.] *Om. MST. Before this line, MST has the following unfinished passage:* Quid sibi hic [< hic sibi] vult vir meus miror, aut / Quam inceptat dementiam? Ah nihilue pudere hominem? / Saltem non os vereri populi, qui postquam [< postea] filium / Funestauit [< fil (*)] adolescentulum, ac familiam / Luctu foedauit miseram [*This is a variation of ll. 10-16 below (with one phrase also echoed in l. 9), and, though Foxe did not cancel the above passage, he must have intended to do so. Although Foxe set off the revised version of the passage (see ll. 10-16 n.), I take it that he did not intend any longer to begin the scene with it; hence, I have followed the MST order.*]

2. Omnes . . . natas] *MST* < Ad liberos natas

3-4. labos / . . . assidet] *MST* < ibi / Quantus obiectus labos [< labor]

4. denique] *MST* < deniquam

5. Siquid tum] *MST* < Siquid

6-7. est aliis / Foemina] *MST* < aliis / Sit

8. vnum . . . reliquere] *MST* < e multis vnum fata reliquerem

9. Fatis . . . patris] *MST* < Hunc etiam patris nunc

10-16.] *See l. 1n. Above l. 10 is a horizontal stroke, together with some markings which appear to be doodles rather than meaningful marks. Ll. 10-16 duplicate the spirit of part of ll. 1-9.*

13. Saltem . . . Tamen] *MST* < Tamen . . . Saltem

17. ineptiam] *MST* < fortitudinem

18. agitat] *MST* < agitans

19. ductat] *MST* < provocat

23-24. Sine . . . obsitus] *MST* < E patria profugus aerumnis obsitus /

24-25. miserum / Illum] *MST* < illum miserum /

27. Hercle si] *MST* < S [*]

29-30. etiam / Pro piaculo] *MST* < pro / Peccato ma [* malo]

30. praecipitem quemquam] *MST* < quemquam praecipitem

31. Pellere plusquam] *MST* < Extundere

33-34. credibile est. / Alioqui] *MST* < alioqui credibile est /

34. adeo] *MST* < ta [*]

36. Sed] *MST* < Atque [†]

hunc ipsum] *MST* < ipsum

hunc . . . video] *MST* < ipsus presto adest < ipsus adest presto

[III.4]

S.H.] *Om. MST*

1. S.P.] *Om. MST*

2. ilico] *MST* < ad me
    venit vt] *MST* < venit ⟨ad⟩
2-3. veniat / . . . caenam] *MST* (in < ad) < veniat / Nobiscum vt
caenet [*this word not struck out*] < veniat [< venit] ad / Caenam scilicet
    4. hodie] *MST* < huc
    5. Accuratum est sedulo] *MST* < Sedulo curatum reddidi < Accuraui
sedulo < At curaui sedulo
    6. Proh] *MST* < Ah
       Proserpina] *MST* < vero mulier
7-8. effecero / . . . sis] *MST* < effecero vt meis / Sis praeceptis
    9. faxis] *MST* < facesseres
    14.] *Above this line, centered at the top of the page, is the word* Iesus; *cf.*
Christus Triumphans V.1n.
    16. sculptae distortissimo] *MST* < admodum sculptae improbo [*Only*
admodum *was struck through.*]
    17. cereos] *MST* < teneros
        animos . . . vostram] *MST* < ad vestram hanc amussim
    18. quod refractarios] *MST* < quod minus obsequentes magis
    19. imitantes] *MST* < imitantur
    22. Potius . . . taceas] *MST* < E porta oportuit. Atque . . . taceas <
Oportuit. [*See the following note.*]
    23. Quod . . . animum] *MST* (*but part of l. 22; I have assumed that Foxe
intended to start a new line after he expanded Chremes' speech*) < Imo [†] si
[< vi] sic inducas animum
    25. Quamobrem quaeso aliam] *MST* < Aliam
25-26. tibi / Quam] *MST* < tibi quam /
    31. haec esset] *MST* < haec
    32. experti] *MST* < expers
        quod loquor] *MST* < sunt satis
    35. Quippe et] *MST* < E [*]
        haud . . . verberat] *MST* < verberat

[III.5]
    S.H.] *Om. MST*
    P.H. Crito] *MST* < Stilpho
    1. S.P.] *Om. MST*
    3. prouiso . . . vespere] *MST* < nunc veni scire
       mi] *MST* < vir
       Crito] Stilpho *MST*
    4. S.P.] Crito] S[tylpho] *MST* (*so throughout the remainder of the scene*)
       optatissime] *MST* < plurimum

6. Crito] Stilpho *MST*

7. Necessum est] *Added interlineally in MST. Perhaps it should be a separate line.*

8. Est, Crito] *MST* < Stilpho est

9. nunc . . . est] *MST* < nunc paululum vtendum est opera ⟨ ⟩

10. profectus illuc] *MST* < illu [*]

13.] *Probably a late addition in MST.*

[III.6]

S.H.] *Om. MST*

1. S.P. Stylpho] S. *MST*

predicas] *MST* < profecto

ideo] *MST* < ob id

4. curamur] *MST* < nitenti sumus

5. Phrygia] Prygia *MST*

6. S.P. Simo] Si. *MST* < S⟨t⟩

7. S.P. Stylpho] S. *MST*

aberunt, credo] *MST* (*?or simply* aberunt) < abesse credo

[III.7]

S.H.] *Om. MST. Above the P.H., at the top of the page, is a small cross; cf. III.4.14n.*

1. S.P.] *Om. MST*

2.] *Added interlineally in MST.*

natus . . . sydere] *MST* < natus syder⟨is⟩

4. cui . . . querimonia] *MST* (*see following note*) < qui aut aeque de fortuna sua queri [< pote (*)] / Poterit [*See l. 5n.*]

queat] *MST* < potest

5. seu] *MST* < aut

8. fidem] *MST* < testo fidem < fidem

9. quisquam possit] *MST* < potest

his] *MST* < meis

11. octauus] *MST* < ⟨sest⟩ [* ?= sextus]

14-15. cui / Porro neque rei neque] *MST* (*the* P *of* Porro *has mostly been lost as the edge of the leaf was torn off*) < cui iam neque / Rei neque < cui / Rei nec

15-16. in . . . meo] *MST* < in meo / Tito tantummodo [< solum] < in meo / Solo

16-17. telum / Adiget me] *MST* < me telum / Adiget

17. neque . . . animus] *MST* < an idem nunc siet < an ipsus sit etiam [*See l. 18n.*]

18. fuerit an] *MST* < fuerit [*written again in revision*] nec ne

19-21. quicquid . . . omnia / . . . / Velit] *MST* < nunc ipsum [< semel] experiri ⟨ ⟩ / Omnia . . . / Quicquid accidat, velit

23. illuc] *MST* < istud

Numquid] *MST* < Hem numquid

quispiam] *MST* < aduenit

26. an . . . nihil] *MST* < nihil dicam

[III.8]

S.H.] *Om. MST*

1. hinc intro] *MST* < intro iam

1-2. Sempronia . . . est] *MST* < Cum Sempronia hic dum paululum / Deambulauero. Haud longe abero

3. Dic . . . placeat] *MST* < Dic nunc meum suauium nostra tandem Roma vt placeat ?< Dic nunc ergo, Roma tibi haec vt placeat, Sempronia < Quid ais ergo, Roma tibi haec vt placet, Sempronia

4. Ecastor pulcherrime] *MST* < Perpulcherrime. T[ITUS]. Quid ergo, patriae numquis te tangit / Affectus forsitan? S[EMPRONIA]. Aliae vt sunt affectae nescio [*This passage, canceled here, was used slightly altered in ll. 6-7 below.*]

multo demum] *MST* < demum

6-7. numquis . . . nescio] *See l. 4n.*

6. interea] *MST* < interim

9-10. immortales . . . tandem] *MST* < non parum sane metuebam ne quod / Aliis [< quod aliis /] fere fit mulierculis ne molestum istud [< istud molestum] accideret / Tibi vbi quid factum sit rescires sic te circumducier / In nuptiis. [*This passage was rewritten in ll. 13-14 below.*]

11-12. Quo . . . simul] *MST* < Quo firmiore dehinc spero a⟨ ⟩ pace atque concordia / Victuros simul < Vnde [< Vi] firmiore [< facilius (†)] nunc spero nos maiori [< spero m⟨ ⟩ < spero maiori] dehinc concordia / Victuros simul [*I am not certain of all details in the stages here recorded.*]

13. Prorsus . . . eram] *MST* < Stimulabat enim me non parum [*See ll. 9-10 n.*]

incertus] *MST* < meritus [?]

17. tenella] *MST* < imperita

18. tibi . . . sum] *MST* < nunc tibi gratulor [*Note gratulor later in the line.*]

19. nunc . . . viro] *MST* < viro contigerim < nunc viro contigerim

20. hoc] *MST* < facis et dicis

21-22. rursum . . . videtur] *MST* < nullum illius / Fomentum est

28. mecum communia puta] *MST* < sunt communia mecum

29. Gesippus. Admouebo me propius] *Added interlineally in MST*.

30.] *Before this line MST has a S.P., T., which was at first placed after l. 29.*

[III.9]

S.H.] *Om. MST*

1. S.P.] *Om. MST*

1-2.] *Transferred in MST, with slight alteration, from its original position after* omnia (*l. 9*); *see l. 9n. Written on one line here in MST, but* In *is capitalized.*

1. Haeccine] *MST* < Haecce [?]

reponis] *MST* < reposis

2. In] *MST* < in

vertas . . . noscere] vertas etc. *MST* (*I have supplied the missing words from the original MST version; see l. 9n.*)

4-5. ope / Indigeant] *MST* < indigeant / Ope

6. Sufflati] *MST* < Sufflati sunt

7. Adeon' . . . fidem] *MST* < Vsquam adeo nemo est cui credas omnium

8. haud triuialem] *MST* < adamantinam < vnice sacram

9. omnia.] *MST* < omnia. O Tite huccine / Spes mea rediit tandem? Hiccine amicis reponis officia / Vt in ardeliones nunc vertas cum piget noscere [*The last line was not struck through here; see ll. 1-2n.*]

10. redeundi] *MST* < huc redeundi

11. funditus ut numquam] *MST* < ut numquam huc

14-15. hisque . . . miseriis] *MST* < hisque me / Miseriis euoluat < meque [< et me < me] eripiat / Seculi huius ingra [*]

15. ilico] *MST* < istuc

18. grauissima] *MST* < ipsissima

20-21. nequeam / Amplius] *MST* < amplius / Nequeam

21. hinc miserum] *MST* < miserum hinc

[III.10]

S.H.] *Om. MST*

1. quaeso te] *MST* < te rogo

4. Tradantur . . . facito] *MST* < Faxis illae tradantur [< tradand (*)] literae

5. S.P. Chremes] C. *MST*

9. Vbi] *MST* < Ibi

[III.11]

S.H.] *Om. MST*

P.H. Martius Sicarius] *MST* < Sicarius

    Gesippus] *Om. MST*

1. S.P.] *Om. MST*

2. me audit] *MST* < audit me

4-5. Quid . . . Miser] *MST* < Quidnam ego / Commisi miser

5. illum] *MST* < miserum illum

6. Nunc hei mihi] *MST* < Nunc [*Perhaps* Nunc *was intended to be canceled.*]

8. Ad . . . Hac] *MST* < Ad elabendum [*; *crossed out and rewritten*] < Hac ad elabendum

    Illac] *MST* < Istac

9-10. Occisus . . . lapide / Scorpius] *MST* (< lapide scorpius /) < Veh occiso mihi. Homo quisue explorator est /

11. quempiam] *MST* < ⟨hunc⟩

14.] *Because of drastic revisions (see ll. 14-15n.),* Indam afabre *and* ipsumque . . . aspergam *stand on separate lines in MST.*

    afabre] *MST* < clanculum

14-15. ipsumque . . . aspergam / Suspitione] *MST* (?) < huicque omnes [*?read* omnem] hanc contraham suspitionem [*This version appears above* ipsumque . . . aspergam *and is not struck through; I have rejected it because it appears to be an alternative to the version which I have adopted and which apparently must stand, in view of the overrun into l. 15; but, despite the duplication of thought, both versions could conceivably have been intended to remain.*] < ita omnem suspitionem in ipsum / Deriuabo facile [in ipsum *not deleted*] < ita suspitionem facile / In ipsum deriuabo < pro cultello scilicet

17.] *Above the line, at the top of the page, is a cross; cf. III.4.14n.*

    Eya vero] *MST* < Bene hercle

19. hoc] *MST* < mihi hoc

21. nec] *MST* < neque

25-26. Obsecro, / Populares] *MST* < Obsecro, / Populares. Subuenite [*cf. IV.1.2*] < Proh / Ciues vestram fidem [*cf. IV.1.1.*]

[IV.1]

    P.H. Martius] *MST* < Sicarius

1, 3. S.P. Martius] S[icarius] *MST*

1. heccine] *MST* [= haeccine] [*?Read* hiccine]

4. Vbinam . . . aut quo peruasit] *MST* < Quonam . . . peruasit

5. S.P. Explorator] *MST* (*ess.*) < om.

    Hem, quid] *MST* < ⟨qui⟩ [*]

6. Sanguinarium] *MST* < Hominem

7. optimos] optimios *MST* < optimius [?]

obstipemus] *MST* ?< obstip⟨imem⟩

9. Vah] *MST* < Heus

10. Stygis mastygia] *MST* (*ess.*) < surge, homicida [homicida *not struck out*]

Omnipotens] *MST* < Proh

11. manibus] *MST* < ⟨Lat⟩

12. Obsecro] *MST* < Proh

13-14. ego / Egi, obsecro] *MST* < ego egi obsecro /

16. Eho . . . hic] *Added interlineally in MST. Though it is above the present l. 17, it was not intended to replace l. 17, the thought of which runs over into l. 18.*

dico diuitem] *MST* < diuitem dico

17.] *Before the addition in l. 16, this line together with* Ciues (*l. 16*) *formed one verse. After that addition, Foxe did not distinguish a new verse, and I have arbitrarily done so.*

non . . . hoc] *MST* < hoc [*]

18. Adhuc recens] *MST* < Recens adhuc [< adhunc]

Supreme] *MST* < p⟨ ⟩

19. Nunc quid] *MST* < q [*]

21-22. Lanio . . . Interfecisse] *MST* < Quid ais, tun' rusticum [< illum] illum propinquum meum / Interfecisse te negabis [*Perhaps* rusticum illum *should stand.*]

22. Tum] *MST* < Atque

23. postea] *MST* < simul

24. vnquam] *MST* < pestis

infitiaveris] *MST* < infitiare ?< infatiare

26. sane] *MST* < prof [*]

27. rapite, trahite] *MST* < ocyus ac pertrahite

[IV.2]

S.H.] *Om. MST*

1. S.P.] *Om. MST*

2. quantum . . . virginem] *MST* (*see following note*) < hic Gesippum quandam [< quandam Gesippum] amare virginem

meum Gesippum] *MST* < Gesippum meum < meum Gesippum

3. consulis hanc] *MST* < hanc consulis nostri < hanc consulis illius

3-4. Quod . . . intellexeram] *MST* ?< Quod . . . resciueram < At istud numquam ego / Resciueram [?< Resciui] hactenus [Resciueram *not struck through*]

4. complacitam] complacitum *MST*

5. simul . . . etiam] *MST* < cum te etiam memorabat [*Perhaps* etiam *should be deleted, but it was not struck through.*]

6. Inter caeteras] *MST* < Omnium post < Omnium sibi post

8. cupio] *MST* (*above the word are two letters,* c *and* i) < ⟨g——⟩ [*apparently not* gestio]

   Tum] *MST* < Iam

9-10. antea . . . experti adeo] *MST* (adeo ?< ta [*]) < adeo . . . experti

10. estis operae] *MST* < estis

12. sum pollicitus illi] *MST* < illi pollicitus sum

13-14. Plane / . . . haec] *MST* < Ita / Plane res haec < Ita / Haec res

14. animi sunt] *MST* < sunt animi

15. aliis . . . aliter] *MST* < alite [*]

    eadem erit] *MST* < erit

16. lactata est vt] *MST* < regina est regi quae

17-18. summum . . . hoc] *MST* ?< summum hoc / Illi amanti < summum hoc / Illi

21. eam videre] *MST* < vi [*]

    ducito] ducuto *MST* (?)

22. obnoxia] *MST* < iuncta

23. Vel . . . debeo] *MST* [debeo *is not certain*] < illi pro pietate me debere fateor

24. bene huic] *MST* < huic bene

[IV.3]

S.H.] *Om. MST. Between the scenes is an unusually wide space; perhaps Foxe was considering an addition.*

P.H. Cratinus et] *Om. MST*

1. S.P.] *Om. MST*

   Licet . . . ciues] *MST* < Legibus nunc licet [*cf. l. 2*]

   siquis] *MST* < siquem

2-3. Cuicumque iam / Lubitum est] *MST* < Iam [< ⟨Nunc⟩ < Iam] quicumque velit / Huic impingere

3. licitum facimus] *MST* < permitto

4. cognatus] *MST* < con [*]

7. qui] *MST* < quem

   hanc illi] *MST* < illi hanc

9. Infitiari] *MST* < Infetiari

   quaeso potius] *MST* < si placet

10-11. Non . . . conscientia] *MST* < Nullos ego arbitror iudices / Testes certiores, quam suam hominis conscientiam

12. alligat] *MST* < alligit

12-13. merito / Labis] *MST* < labis / [*]

15. Dicite] *MST* [†] < Recte, sed numquid < Quid igitur

15-16. hominem? / Cratinus. Non] *MST* < hominem? Cr[atinus]. Non / [*The S.P. still stands at the end of l. 15.*]

16. insectantes] *MST* < insectatus

20-23. Age . . . consul] *MST* < T[itus]. Quid his tu respondeas? Tacet. Ful[vius]. Siquid habes iuuenis / Quo te absoluas [< absoluis], licet loqui. Ges[ippus]. Iudex est qui nouit omnia. / Ful[vius]. Scio, sed hoc nihil respondet aduersariis. Furti huius / Te reum arguunt. Quid huic respondes? G[esippus]. Neque culpam neque / Mortem detrecto, Consul [< iudex] optime. Mart[ius]. Ecce autem confitetur. / T[itus]. Ergo ipse te reum dicis violati rustici

22-23. Neque / Culpam neque] *MST* < Neque culpam neque /

23. dic] *MST* < igitur

28-29. Titus. Ecquos . . . roga] *MST* (*ess.*) < T[itus]. Haud potes hoc te crimine [?< ab (*)] absoluere, quid ais? / Mihi non respondet [< respondes]. Tu roga. Ful[vius]. Dicdum, latrocinium [†] in / Te hoc admittis [< admittit] an non admittis [?< admitto]. G[esippus]. Haud abnuo. / F[ulvius]. Sat est. [*cf. l. 40*] < T[itus]. Dic dum reum te dicis annon? Mihi non respondet /

29. Socii] *MST* < Socios

30. omnium . . . miserimus] *MST* < equidem miserimus omnium

31. haec] *MST* < quod

33, 35. S.P. Gesippus] *MST* (*ess.*) < T.

37. Haud] *MST* < Non

38. Beneficus . . . scilicet] *MST* < Nempe quia in hominem gratus fui / Ingratissimum

hominem] *MST* < hominem satis < hominem plus

39. S.P. Gesippus] *MST* (*ess.*) [†]

41. teneri] *MST* < hunc teneri

morteque dignum] *MST* < quapropter ex

42. nunc pronunciemus] *MST* < pronunciemus

43. Multa ego] *MST* < ⟨Imo i⟩

44-45. arbitror, / Atque . . . etiam] *MST* < arbitror, / Atque etiam < arbitror, atque etiam /

45. Si . . . censeas] *MST* < Tuo [< s] fiat arbitrio

46-47. in . . . reductum] *MST* < atque cras / Huc reductum < atque cras / Reductum

47. praecipimus] *MST* < mandamus

[IV.4]

S.H.] *Om. MST. Again there is an unusually wide space between the scenes.*

1. S.P.] *Om. MST*

1-2. Etsi . . . est] *MST* < Etsi . . . siet / Decretum est adire [? < cadire] tamen < Etsi . . . siet / Non negabo tamen adire hominem < Etsi hercle aegre hoc iter mihi ac animo aduersum siet / Non negabo tamen adire hominem < Etsi hercle aegre hoc [*this* hoc *probably slated for cancellation*] iter hoc suspicio [*] < Etsi ecastor inuita admodum [< inuita huc incedo admodum] / Adibo tamen vt quid velit sciam

3. ires] eris *MST*

5. Quod fecit] *MST* < Candide

6. quam] *MST* < quamcumque

libeat] *MST* < libet

7. Amare, habere illum] *MST* < Illum [†]

8. illud . . . superis] *MST* < hoc aedepol est, quod illi vobisque omnibus

9. viri] *MST* < hominis

11. illum] *MST* ? < i⟨d⟩

13-14. vt possit / Credere] *MST* < poss⟨iet⟩ credere /

14-15. Athenis ille / Torrebat] *MST* < interim / Athenis torrebat

15. ad] *MST* < ⟨in⟩

17. Adcurrisset] *MST* < S [*]

18. ille sua] *MST* < est hac

pietate] pitate *MST*

19. pariter] *MST* < etiam pariter [*or simply* etiam]

21. vos vt] *MST* < vt

22. tc] *MST* [?†]

24. euenire] *MST* ? < quaerite

27. ita res habe] *MST* (habe ? < habe⟨t⟩) < hoc est verissimum

28. iuuenem . . . ipsum] *MST* < ipsum . . . iuuenem

quam] *MST* [†]

29. flore] *MST* < aetate, flore

ac specie] *MST* < as [*]

29-30. specie / Vndique pellicibilem] *MST* < specie vndique / Pellicibilem

32-33. vrbe . . . porro] *MST* < vrbe insuper / Celeberrima, patris porro [*cf. l. 34*]

34. insuper] *MST* < natum

Docte quidem.] *MST* < Numquid aliud?

36. illius esses] *MST* < e [*]

37-38. fabulator. / Phormio. Age . . . nunc] *MST* < fabulator. /

Ph[ormio]. Age dic nunc igitur libera < fabulator. / Ph[ormio]. Age nunc [*] < fabulator. E⟨cce⟩ / Quid praeterea?

    40. cui . . . sentias] *MST* < magis qui te aut minus mallet suam

    41. quandoquidem] *MST* < quoniam

    41-42. amor . . . amorem] Amor . . . Amorem *MST*

    44. potis . . . mutuo] *MST* < modo illum non redamare queas mutuo

    45. dignum haud] *MST* < haud dignum

    47. digniore me] *MST* < me digniore

        duxerim] *MST* < iudico

    48. vxorem] *MST* [†]

    49. vt traduceret] *MST* < traduceret

    50. ille vt] *MST* < quod ille

    51. sit . . . expetens] *MST* < sit mei vt ita [< ad (*adeo)] ut inquis expetens < ita sit, mei vt siet [< sit] ille expetentior

    54. Adesse] *MST* < Adest

    55. nosti mei haudquaquam] *MST* < nosti mei ne utiquam [= utique] < haudquaquam mei

    56. Iuris esse me] *MST* < Me iuris esse < Iuris sum

    57. necesse] *MST* < necessem

        Verum] *MST* < Sed

[IV.5]

    S.H.] *Om. MST*

    1. S.P.] *Om. MST*

    2. sum . . . hercle animi] *MST* < hercle sum . . . animi

    4. ecastor] *MST* < abs te

    6. adero] *MST* < subsequar

    7-8. ilico / . . . iam mihi] *MST* < mihi / . . . tum primum

    8. ominari] *MST* < ominare

    9. Aspexeram] *MST* < Aspect [*]

    11. nec parentes nominat] *MST* ?< suos etiamnum ibi habet < ibi parentes etiamnum habet

    12. Hinc] *MST* < Ab his

        recens] *MST* < nuper

    15. suspicari] *MST* < suspicarier

    16. vbi meus est] *MST* < est meus

    17. Numquam . . . tantam . . . audaciam] *MST* < Hanc numquam . . . tantam . . . audaciam < Id numquam . . . tantum . . . dedecus

    18.] *Added interlineally in MST.*

        scio] *MST* < unquam scio

    22. Ipsam . . . pene] *MST* (*perhaps* ferro *should stand before* emunxit;

the nasal macron of vitam *cuts through it, but so, apparently, does the line striking out* extorsit [*see below*] ; *perhaps also* miser *should be deleted*) < [*several stages of revision which I have conjecturally reconstructed:*] Ipsam etiam irruens vitam extorsit pene miser < Ipsam vitam ferro extorsit pene miser < Pene ipsam simul vitam emunxit miser

24. esse] *MST* ?< est
    quia] *MST* < mihi
25. Haud] *MST* < Non
    subtraxi] *MST* < subtrahi
26. Compertius . . . Sempronia] *MST* < Compertius, nuncque haud dici nunc potest, Sempronia [*one* nunc *presumably to be deleted*] < Certius, neque enim mens prius quit quiescere
28. S.P. Sempronia] *MST* (S.) < P. [*?=* Pamphila]
29. quam mox] *MST* ?< mox
30. renunciet] *MST* < rem renunciet < renunciet [*cf. l. 31*]
    expediat] *MST* < exquirat omnia [*See l. 31n.;* omnia *reads better* here.]

31. ut . . . omnia] *MST* (?) < is sit nec ne monstret omnia [*this* omnia *appears on the level of the original l. 31 and is not struck through;* monstret *appears above* ⟨eliceat⟩ *(of the original line), which has carats before and after it; directly above* monstret *is the canceled* omnia *which I have taken as a part of the original l. 30*] < is sit nec ne vt ⟨eliceat⟩ [*or* eluceat] omnia [*If l. 30 originally ended with the word* omnia, *the* omnia *here must have been written after it was canceled there; or perhaps the wrong* omnia *was canceled.*]

32. Nempe . . . facias] *MST* < Ita ac mature quidem [*This version, presumably complete, written in the margin (and then struck through) after l. 31, with a new S.P.; it is not clear which stage it represents, but it must have been late, after the interlinear space was jammed.*] < Nempe ita facto opus et puto praesentissimum < Nempe [< Nemp⟨ir⟩] puto praesentissimum, ac mature facias

36. Num] *MST* < Nempe
36-37. si vides / Meum] *MST* < si vides / Tu meum < tu meum / [*]
37. Vel] *MST* < Ipsis vel
38. Nisi . . . coniecturae] *MST* < Mirum ni in carcere [*see ll. 41-43n*]
40. Ne dixeris] *MST* < d [*]
41-43. Quapropter . . . scias] *MST* (*I have rejected as excessively repetitious a line which appears uncanceled in the revised version after l. 42:* Is sit vt scias ac diligenter renuncies; *presumably it was read with* Qui sit, *l. 43.*) < Aut meae / Multum errant coniecturae [*cf. l. 38*], at [< s (*sed)] certum non habeo. / Tu nunc curriculo transcurre ad eum is sit ut / Scias.
45. Tenes quid volo] *MST* < Tenes

46-47. Quam . . . pendeo] *MST* < Quanto nunc quam perplexa mens mihi / Tenetur scrupulo

47. quidnam] *MST* < quid⟨ ⟩

50. praesagit] *MST* < praesaget

[IV.6]

S.H.] *Om. MST*

1. S.P.] *Om. MST*

3. Nostris qui] *MST* < Qui nostris

5. simul] *MST* < antehac

13. Sempronia. Est. Crito] *MST* (*ess.*) < *om.*

15. huc veni] *MST* < volebam

18. venit] *MST* < vidisti

18-19. illum . . . abegit] *MST* < ex at / E⟨t⟩ ⟨ ⟩ . . . illum abegit

22. Coepisse] *First written at the bottom of f. 146, then canceled; in a different hand, I believe, a note was added:* Coepisse vide 61. fol. [*referring to an earlier pagination of Lans. MS. 388, corresponding to the present f. 112*].
    id] *MST* [†]

23-24. prouinciam, / Te vt] *MST* < prouinciam, / Vt te < prouinciam vt /

24. literis . . . epistolaribus] *MST* < cum literis his epistolaribus < cum epistol [*]

25. Suum . . . ut] *MST* < Ea gratia vti illis

31. cavssae] *MST* < cap [*] [*cf. l. 32.*]

31-32. video / Capitis quin] *MST* < video quin / Capitis

32. irrefutabilem] *MST* < damnati

32-33. luet / Sententiam] *MST* < luet sententiam /

34. esse] *MST* [†]

36. Iam exitio] *MST* < Iam infortunio < Inf [*]
    dari] dare *MST* [?]

37. in . . . potest] *MST* < po [*]

37-38. mihi / Quod agam] *MST* < mihi quod agam /

38. quodnam . . . malum] *MST* < quae haec noua repentina mala sunt?

39. illum, ain'] *MST* < ain

42-43. vt iret . . . miror] *MST* < adiret, ac hunc abesse tam diu / Miror [*I have made into one verse (l. 42) what in MST appears on two lines.*]

43. Hunc] *MST* < Huc

[IV.7]

S.H.] *Om. MST*

1. S.P.] *Om. MST*
1-2. Nunc . . . doleam] *MST* [*though perhaps* An doleam *was intended for deletion*] < Nunc ego vtrum mirer an doleam magis / < Ita mihi deus faxit bene vtrum mirer magis / An doleam
    4. Hic] *MST* [†]
    sensus] *MST* [†]
    5. sacra numina] *MST* [†]
  10. Praesensi] *MST* < Praesenti
  12. malum] *MST* < nuncium

[V.1]
    1. S.P. Martius] *Om. MST*
    1-2. esse iudicis / Iuditio] *MST* < iudicis / Iuditio esse < iudicis / Iuditio
    4. Velut vmbra comitetur] *MST* < Comitetur
    5. nil prorsus] *MST* < nihil hisce prorsus
    7. proh dolor] *MST* < meum
  10. tormentum] *MST* < tormen⟨ ⟩
  11. Cui] *MST* < Qui
  13. vni] *MST* < illum
  16.] *Added interlineally in MST.*
  17. Boni . . . quanta] *MST* (?) < Vitam dehinc quanta < Vitam hanc nunc quanta [*?Read* Boni superi / Vitam dehinc quanta]
  18. At] *MST* ?< Atque
  18-20. illum . . . Revalescentiae] *MST* < illi [< illum (?)] quod homini [†] / Vitam spemque promittunt reualescentiae /

[V.2]
  S.H.] *Om. MST*
  P.H. Fuluius . . . Romanus] *MST* ?< *om.*
    1. S.P.] *Om. MST*
    2. Modo . . . aliquid] *MST* < Ali [*]
    3. cui] *MST* < illi vt
    deus me] *MST* < m [*]
    4. depacisci] *MST* < depas [*]
    6. nemini] *MST* < nem⟨ ⟩
    7-8. qui saluum magis / Expetat] *MST* < magis qui saluum expetat /
    8-9. supplicabimus / Simul quandoquidem] *MST* < simul supplicabimus / ⟨Q⟩ [*]
    9. solum hoc] *MST* < hoc [?]
  10. forte] *MST* ?< v [*]

10-11. Siquidem ... sit] *MST* < Siquidem mei vsus / Officii sit < Equidem fiet et placet / Sempronia < Equidem fiet, Sempronia, / Et consultum arbitror

  15. tribunali] *MST* [†]
      actum quid] *MST* ?< quid actum < actum
  17. S.P. Fulvius] *MST* (*ess.*) ?< T.
  21. quodque] *MST* < et quod
  22. vestra ... modo ignoscentia] *MST* < vestra ... quaeso ignoscentia < qu [*] ... ig [†]
  23. vestrae] *MST* < vestrae patres < summi patres [*cf. l. 25*]
  24. generique] *MST* < generis
  28. summi] sumi *MST*
  33. si uelim patitur] *MST* < patitur
  38. Cum ... commeruit] *MST* < Hunc esse ego
  40. monstri] *MST* < autem
  42. rectum] *MST* [†]
  43. S.P. Martius] M. *MST* < ⟨F⟩
      Hem, quid] *MST* ?< Quid
  44. mihi] *MST* < mei
      scias suerem] *MST* < suerem scias
  45. dedisse] *MST* < de⟨b⟩ [*]
  46. S.P. Populus Romanus] P. R. *MST* [†]
  47. Itidem] *MST* < Nil ⟨qu⟩
48-49. in / Sopore oppresserint] *MST* < in sopore op [*]
  49. sunt] *MST* ?< sient
      haud] *MST* < ⟨eos⟩
      facile] *MST* < facile ⟨li⟩
  51. ferrum ... si erat] *MST* < si ferrum ... erat
  52. Vagina vbinam] *MST* < Vbinam vagina
  53. nihil minus] *MST* < pariter
  54. fateor] *MST* < ⟨et⟩
  56. S.P. Gesippus] Ges. *MST* < F. < *om.*
  61. Enimvero] *MST* < Imo
      mea est] *MST* < mea
  62. Idemque tu] *MST* < Et tu idem
  64. S.P. Gesippus] T[itus] *MST*
      cuiusdam] *MST* < cuiusdam sub caprifico
  66. prorsus me] *MST* < me
      Senatum] *MST* [†]
66-67. rem ... referam] *MST* < rem recta referam / < id referam /
  67. in ... dederit] *MST* < quod ad hanc rem attinet

68. retinete] *MST* < adducite
    ad] *MST* < mecum ad
    hinc dum] *MST* < inde huc

[V.3]
  S.H.] *Om. MST*
  1. S.P.] *Om. MST*
  5. Nisi] *MST* ?< Ni
     iuuenes quia] *MST* < quia iuuenes
  6. Conflagrant mutuo] *MST* ?< Conflagrant
  7. vnde] *MST* < cuius
  9. animo . . . suam] *MST* ?< animo [*cf. the revision in l. 10*]
  10. antepositam] *MST* < propositam
  15. a me subuenirier adeo] *MST* < ego subuenire ⟨ ⟩
      commode] *MST* ?< commodi
  16. quingentae] *MST* < ⟨sexcentae⟩
  18. Remque] *MST* < Ac rem
  19. Etsi] *MST* < Et
  21. horum] *MST* < totae
  22. prius] *MST* < *om.* < prius

[V.4]
  S.H.] *Om. MST*
  1. S.P.] *Om. MST*
  4. Nimis] *MST* ?< *om.*
  6. illo] *MST* < Gesippo illo
  7. Noxae se huic] *MST* < Noxae sese huic ?< Noxae huic < Noxae

[V.5]
  S.H.] *Om. MST*
  1. S.P.] *Om. MST*
  2. concessit mea] *This reading was replaced in MST by* decreuit imperium;
*I follow the earlier reading because of the extreme awkwardness of the revision,
which must have been made for metrical reasons but left unintegrated with l. 3.*
  4. rogo, consul] *MST* < rogo Tite < Tite rogo
     quam rem] *MST* < quod
  8. Sine apud te] *MST* < Quaeso vt
  11. Porro] *MST* ?< P⟨ro⟩
  13-14. erat . . . Perempturus] *MST* ?< erat perempturus persensi
quantum equidem / < erat perempturus quantum equidem / [*f. 115*]

Persensi < erat perempturus quantum equidem. / [*f. 115*] Ex ipso collegi postea

15-16. hoc . . . ilico] *MST* < hinc arripiens rebus meis / Occasionem, hoc vti visum est consilium reperi

17. vt insinuarem] *MST* < insinuarem

Hem, quid ais?] *MST* < Bona fide

18. res vt] *MST* < vt res

19. omnem] *MST* < hanc

22. atque] *MST* < et

24. numquam animum] *MST* < animum numquam

27. hoc] *MST* < hinc

argumentum dabit] *MST* < dab [*]

dabit] *MST* ?< dabat

spectabile] *MST* < spectabile, ex

28. huic an non] *MST* < an huic

31. S.P. Gesippus] G. *MST* < T.

31-32. vera . . . omnia] *MST* < vt hic edisseruit / Tibi consul

34. diisque . . . gratiae] *MST* < tibique consul collega mi [*cf. l. 35*]

34-35. gratulor. / Conscende] *MST* < gratulor con / [*]

35. huc] *MST* < vero

denuo] *MST* < ⟨vi⟩

liber] *MST* [†]

37. deinde] *MST* < ⟨col⟩

ut par est] *MST* < persoluo

39. miseri te mei] *MST* < mei te

41. ignoscas] *MST* ?< ignoscat

43. nos] *MST* ?< mei

44. te quaeso] *MST* < quaeso

55. clementissime] *MST* < te vti facias

56. omnem] *MST* [?†]

permitto] *MST* < committo

57. Euge. Quoniam] *MST* < Quoniam [*Perhaps* Euge *should be a separate line.*]

iam] *MST* < hic [*Note* hic *later in the line.*]

hic] *MST* < est hic

58. Statuendi . . . statuta] *MST* < Statuta [*]

59. tibi] *MST* < tibi ⟨o⟩

62. in] *MST* [?†]

62-63. fidem meam / Et clientelam] *MST* < fidem meam / Clientelam < clientelam meam /

[V.6]
  S.H.] *Om. MST*
  1. Miranda] *MST* [?†]
     nostris] *MST* < nostris se < nostris
  3. proferte cum pileo] *MST* < cum p [*]
  5. Hic] *MST* < ⟨G⟩
  6. pol verum] *MST* < v [*]
     ita] *MST* < hoc
  7. mi] *MST* < ibi
  8. quandoquidem] *MST* < quonia [*]
  10. diei] *MST* < ⟨dei⟩
  13-14. candidissime / Non] *MST* < candidissime non /
  16. felicissime] *MST* [†]
  19. At] *MST* < Sed
  21-22. ephorum / Illum] *MST* < ephorum illum /
  22. mihi] *MST* [?†]
     patrisque tui antiquum] *MST* < antiquum
  25. serio iam te] *MST* < et tibi
  27. Pamphilam] *MST* < S.
  28. Genus / Aetatem] *MST* < ⟨A⟩ [*]
  30. Polliceor] *MST* < Fului
     hoc solidum] *MST* < hoc / Sol [*]
  31. perficias] *MST* < perficiens
  33. mi] *MST* ?< me⟨ ⟩
  34. S.P. Gesippus] *MST* [†]
  43-45. Deinde . . . introducerem] *MST* < Deinde / Nec micam . . .
introducerem < Alioqui / Huc pariter introduc [*]
  45. Christo] *MST* < dom [*]

Notes to *Christus Triumphans*

[Dramatis Personae.]] *om. MSC; after the Prologue in B*
  Prologus] *N, Bienvenu; om. B*
  Psychephonus] *PM glosses the name* [animi] interfector
  Thanatus] *PM glosses the name* Mors
  Adopylus] *PM glosses the name* [fe]rox lari
  Nomocrates] *PM glosses the name* [?le]x, *and adds (after* tyrannus) legibus
  Psyche] *L;* Psycha *B, N*
  Pseudamnus] *PM glosses the name* fal[sus] ag[nus]
  Populus . . . Parthene] *om. B, N, L. Bienvenu adds the names of several*

characters appearing in his interpolated scenes: Demye, Cardinal; Athee, Euesque; Gastrimargue, Abbé; *and* Anoet [*originally printed here and throughout as* Auret *and corrected with paste-on cancels*], Curé. *All the added characters are identified as* Medicins de la paillarde [*i.e., Pornapolis*], adioustez par le traducteur

[Title.]] Comoedia Christus Triumphans *MSC* (*before I.1*). *A later hand has added:* This is writ by Joh. Fox

[Prologue.] *at the end of the play in MSC, without heading* (*though a corner of the page, apparently containing some letters, has been torn off*)
    1. Salutem] *MSC* < ⟨No⟩ salutem < Salutem
    2-3. Sibi . . . noui] *MSC* (*ess.*) < Nouus optat poeta spectoribus [*sic*] / Suis vicissim studiis a vobis rogat / Silentium
    5-17. Vtinam . . . decet] *MSC* (*except as in following notes*), *all but the first word in the margin* < Res sacra est / Sacris petita ex literis. Sacro igitur / Indulgete silentio sacris uti / In templis suescitis. Oculos enim sacros / Perinde ac aures esse qui minus decet? / Historia tota est Apocalyptica. / Vobis quae lecta saepe est [saepe est < saepe] numquam at visa prius. / Videbimus quidem olim oculis [< oculisque] clare omnia [clare omnia < omnia] / Re ipsa quum mittit nunc quae [< quam] promittit Deus. / Rerum interim per transennam simulachra / Spectare iuvet [< Spectabitis], poeta quae oculis subiicit. / < Res sacra est / Sacris [< Sacros] petita ex literis. Comoedia / Tota fere est Apocalyptica. Saepe forsitan / Res lecta [?< lectae] vobis, numquam at visa prius. Ac / Videbimus quidem olim oculis clare omnia / Re quum ipsa mittit, nunc quae promittit Deus. / Rerum interim per transennam simulachra / Spectabitis poeta quae oculis subiicit [< subiit]. / Aures ut in templo, hic instituantur oculi. / < Res . . . simulachra [*as in the preceding version*] / Vmbrasque ipsus [< Vmbrasque] spectare libeat cur etenim sacrae / Vt conciones sunt [< etenim / Sunt ut conciones sacrae < etenim sunt ut (*)], spectacula haud item / Sacra [< haud / Item sacra] esse deceat [< decet]
    5. Vtinam] *MSC* < Vtinam et
    6-8. Hunc . . . scenici] *MSC* < Caelitus liceat potius in nubibus / Triumphantem cernere ludi quum scenici / < Caelo hunc triumphantem potius cernere / Liceat [*]
    10. mittit] *MSC* < missa
    12. haud . . . praeludimus] iuvet, oculis subiecta quae sient *MSC*
    13. Res tota] Res quippe *MSC*
    14. quae . . . prius] ⟨per⟩saepe at numquam visa est [< est visa] prius *MSC*

15. Sacro . . . sacris] Vos igitur indulgete silentio, sacris *MSC*

18-19. Ecclesiae . . . furias] Ecclesiae Idaeam hic qualemcumque dabimus, / Dabimus Satanae et [< Satanae et dabimus] tumultuantis furias *MSC* < Ecclesiae primum qualemcunque faciem / Dabimus, eius deinde labores haud leues [haud leues < graues] / Satanae [< T (*)] porro tumultuantis furias [*this version apparently written before the main revision of ll. 5-17 was undertaken*]

20-21. Expressum . . . meretricula] Expressum et Antichristum [< Cernitis et A (*)] cum Babylonia / Cernetis meretricula *MSC*

25. ferteque] *MSC* < dateque

27. ualeat] abeat *MSC*

sycophanticus] sycophantica *MSC*

28-29. quicquid . . . Est] nigrumque quid / Quid est *MSC*

29. tristis . . . mordaxque] dentatus Druso, et mordax *MSC*

34. nocere studet nemini] *MSC* < stud⟨io⟩ id habet sibi, / Nocere ccrte vestrum coeptat nemini

38. Et . . . materia] *MSC* < Materia et multiplex

39. fateor] aliquot *MSC* < quasdam

at] sed *MSC*

40. Ast] At *MSC*

42. Habetis ergo officium] Habetis [†] officium modo [officium modo < modo] *MSC*

Rei] Et rei *PM*

44.] *Line om. in MSC.*

[Periocha.]] *In MSC, added late in the margin without a heading.*

4. Ecclesia] Ecclesiae *L*

7. Prehendens] *MSC* < tyrannus < Thanato [*See l. 8*].

11. Vires potessunt] *MSC* < Pote [*]

adest Philanthropos /] *MSC* < ipse subuenit / Philanthropos

12. Nimisque . . . Adamidas] Euaeque [? < Euae] miseram [*this word added interlineally*] adiutat familiam *MSC* < Euam miserosque iuvat Adamidas

15. exoluit] *MSC* < restituit < restit

[I.1]

S.H. *and* M.H.] *Om. MSC*

1. S.P.] *Om. B, MSC, N, L*

1-11.] *Written twice in MSC: ll. 1-2 and 6-11 are the same in both MSC versions.*

3-4.] *In the original MSC version, l. 3 was added interlineally after l. 4. In the rewritten MSC version, the same order was at first retained; then l. 4 was canceled and rewritten to follow l. 3.*

3. Vox . . . sufficit] *MSC* < Vox . . . sufficit [< suppetit] / Amplius [*see l. 5n.*] < [*the first MSC version:*] Vox nec curis, nec spes malis iam suppetit /

4. ita] *MSC* < ubi (*revision made in the rewritten MSC version*)

5. Porro . . . dum] *MSC* (flere < at flere) < [*the first MSC version:*] Amplius [< Heu] quid agam aut quo me vortem? Porro flere dum [*in margin*] < Heu [< ⟨Fl——⟩ quid agam, aut quid spero, aut quo vortem. Flere dum

uortem] uortam *N, L* (*the grammatically correct reading*)

9. at] et *N*

12. non] numquam *MSC*

20-21. Consistam . . . lachrimisque] *MSC* < Maneam aut consistam nusquam scio ut hanc si iuvem / [*f. 132v*] Nihil, at me [< g (*)] gemitu lachrimisque

22. causa] causae *L*

24. mali] malis *L*

25. oppleta] *MSC* < pleta

[I.2]

S.H.] Sc. 2. *MSC*

1. S.P.] *Om. B, MSC, N, L*

2. uita . . . minus?] *MSC* < magis aut cui vita onus siet

8. Quid huic] *MSC* < ⟨Quis hic⟩ / [*cf. l. 9*]; Quid hic *Le*
   turbatum] turbarum *Le*

9. Ehei] *MSC* < Vide

13. tu me] *MSC* < me
    misereri] miserere *N*

21. experta nulla] *MSC* < nulla experta

26. in . . . dimidium] comes in malis dimidium est *MSC*

27. ferat] *MSC* < adferat

28. quod] *MSC* < quid

31.] *N prints as two lines, the first ending* vicem

33. minus istuc] *MSC* < istuc minus

35. scies] scias *N*

40. Psychae] Psyche *MSC, L*

51. modum] *MSC* < finem

58. cruciatus] *MSC* < cruciatos

63-68.] *Perhaps a late addition in MSC; the lines are crowded into the bottom margin.*

63. Sed quid] *MSC* < ⟨Q⟩
66. tradidit] *MSC* **?**< traditum **?**< dedidit **?**< ver [*]
67. tribus domi] *MSC* < domi tribus
74. Serpenti] *MSC* < Serpentis
    tartareum] *MSC* **?**< tartareo
76. S.P. Eva] *MSC* < *om.*
81-82. Cuiusquam . . . meo] *MSC* < Gabriele paranympho ac inter-
nuncio < Cuiusquam, id Gabriele testante
82. tu] *MSC* [†]
86. celatum] *MSC* (caelatum) < dissimulatum
88. supplicium] *MSC* < sus [*]
    infamis] infame *MSC* < infamis
92. hanc tantam . . . tyrannidem] *MSC* < id . . . pontifices
93.] *PM adds a S.D.* [to]nitru
95. e sublimi] *MSC* < superne

[I.3]
    S.H.] Sc. 3 *MSC*
    M.H.] *MSC* < tr. [*trimetri]; Trimetri *N*
    P.H. Adopylus] Theorgilus *MSC*
    1. S.P.] *Om. B, MSC, N, L*
    2. vertam] vortem *MSC*
    4. Pugnando] *MSC* < C [*Cadendo]
    5. Exagitor] *MSC* < Commotus sum
    6. Extorris e] *MSC* < Ita caput me omnesque sensus destituunt. /
Vulneribus atteror e
        eliminor] *MSC* < excutior
    12-13. angelis / Archangelisque] *MSC* < paululum angelis / Vt ego
magnifice [*] < paululum vt ego / Magnifice [*] (*see l. 15*)
    14. Vna licet] *MSC* < Licet vna
    15. Aut . . . his] *MSC* < [*multiple stages of revision unclear:*] Si darentur
praesto vt his [?] < Aut darentur praesto vt his < Nae ego ut hos [*]
?< Nego [*]
    20. caederem] cederem *N*
    24. se dignis] *MSC* < di [*]
    25. Oh] *MSC* < ⟨s—⟩
        Psychephonum] Pseuchephonum *MSC*
        Adopylum] Theomenim *MSC* < Theorgilum
    26. Hic uocem audire] Audire hic uocem audire *B, L;* Audire hic
uocem *MSC, N.* (*I assume that Foxe moved* audire *by writing a second one in*

the manuscript from which Oporinus printed, but that, as often in the surviving manuscripts, he neglected to cross out the first audire.)

πόποι] *MSC, N;* ποποι *B, L*

28. merito fieri] *MSC* < me merito facere

29. S.P. Adopylus] Ps[ychephonus] *MSC*
mastigiae] *B, N, Le;* mastigae *MSC;* magistiae *L*
perfugae] *MSC* ?< perfugi

30. caedem] *MSC* < pugnam

31. hic] *MSC* ?< hoc

32. Non totum] *MSC* < tot [*]

33. S.P. Psychephonus] Ph *MSC*
At, at] *MSC* < At
S.P. Adopylus] Ps[ychephonus] *MSC*

33-34. Here, / Capitis] *MSC* < Eho capitis /

37. Michael] *MSC* < Michaeli
duello] *MSC* < mecum marte

41. sua] *MSC* < suam

42. trophaea] *MSC* < nunc trophaea

50-51. Sequimini / Huc] *MSC* < Sequimini h [*]

51. Huc intro] *MSC* < Huc

52. His] *MSC* < ⟨hun⟩ [*]

54. Reperio] Adueniens reperio *MSC* < Adueniens uideo [*The line is metrically faulty in both MSC and B versions.*]

55. atriis] *L;* atreis *B, MSC, N*

56. meam ductat] ductat *MSC*

[I.4]

P.H. Christus Rediuiuus] Christus *MSC*

Adopylus] *N, L; Om. B, MSC (After listing Theorgilus [the counterpart in MSC of Adopylus] among the characters in I.3 and after referring to him in I.3.25, Foxe seems to have forgotten about him, for he assigned him no speeches in I.3 or 4 and omitted his name from the P.H. of I.4. Foxe evidently renamed Theorgilus [or Theomenes, as he is once called] as Adopylus in a later manuscript and assigned to him some of the speeches which in MSC are given to other characters. But in recopying the opening list of characters in I.4, Foxe neglected to add Adopylus' name.)*

P.H. Raphael Angelus] Raphael *MSC*

1. S.P. Christus] *Om. B, MSC, N, L*

3. sanctitas] faustitas *MSC*

4. THANATUS. Occidor.] *MSC* < om. *(When he added this speech, Foxe recopied the remainder of the line.)*

tuus] *MSC* < tua < tuus [*in the first writing of the line*]

S.P. Adopylus] Th[anatus] *MSC*

5. unquam cuiquam] *MSC* < cuiquam
6. miserae] misero *MSC*
8. O] *MSC* < Proh
     S.P. Adopylus] Psycheph[onus] *MSC*
9. astrata] *MSC* < ⟨ad⟩ [*]
10. mea iam] *MSC* < iam mea
12. dissipet] disspet *MSC* (*sic*) < disspat
14.] *PM adds a S.D.* [Pa]lmarium
16.] *PM adds a S.D.* [L]iber
     libro hoc] cruce hac *MSC*
17.] *PM adds a S.D.* [Ch]irogra[ph]um
18.] *L prints as two lines, the first ending* cedo
     qua] *MSC* ?< quo
22. terra] *MSC* < in terris ?< in terra
23.] *PM adds a S.D.* Claui[s] capistr[um]
23-24. mysanthropum hunc /] *MSC* (*ess.*) < mysanthopum [*sic*] / Hunc
24. Mastigiam] *B, N, Le;* Mastigam *MSC;* Magistiam *L*
     faxis alligatum] faxis illigatum *MSC* < illigatum faxis
     S.P. Thanatus] *MSC* (*ess.*) < P[sychephonus]
25. accurabitur] *MSC* (?ac curabitur) < curabitur
26.] *PM adds a S.D.* Signac[ulum]
28. patrem] Patrem *N*
29. Soma tuum] Sarcobium *MSC*

[II.1]
M.H. Senarii] Trimetri *MSC*
    3. Queisque . . . uinculis] Queisque alios strinxit, vinclis [?< vinctis]
ipse stringitur *MSC* < Quaeque aliis strinxit ipse potitur vinculis
    8. Pornapolis] *MSC* < Abadon
    9. uicariam] *MSC* < uicarium
   10. Vicem . . . illius] *MSC* < Illius . . . vicem
   11. illa] *MSC* < ille
   12. Suo cum Diocte] Suo cum Cosmetore *MSC* < Satanae nuncius
   13. Nihil] Nil *MSC*
   14. Psychae] Psyche *MSC*
   21. Sed . . . rebus] *MSC* < Atque eccas procedere ipsas uideo. Bene /
Habet. Eas quando ita esse video vt volo / Mihi satis est. Iam
    *After II.1, MSC has a scene om. in B. The following is the final version, after
which appear variants to it:*

Act[us] 2.   Sc[ena] 2.
Acatalectici Iambici cum Catalecticis Quibusdam.
Eua.   Maria.

[Eva.]

Iam illud video, nihil tam supra spem ac credibile possiet
Euenire hominibus Dei quin praecedat potentia. Ah
Quam salua nunc sim, hoc ni desiet modo haec cui narrem bona?
Sed Mariam eccam video quam beate.

Maria.   Eua vbi vbi est mihi
Querenda est cui haec feram de filia.

Eva.   Maria, desine,   [5
Noui omnem rem.

Maria.   Nostin' mea tu?

Eva.   Noui, audiui, vidi, credidi
Quae res me humanas supra faelicitates omnes collocat:
Somnians nisi video haec quae volo, te nunc Psyche ex inferis
Rediuiuam cum video.

Maria.   Equidem ita me deus amet gaudeo.

Eva.

Vah quae mihi vocis nunc tanta dari potestas potest   [10
Summe pater numen qua tuum satis atque vt velim ebuccinem?
O charitas, quae haec pietas! Ergo mi Iesu tantum mea
Te causa laboris capere, ac ob Psychen meam, quin et
Sarcobio filio ius insuper regni promittis tui?

Maria.

Dixin' Eua saepe tibi ex puero hoc magni aliquid denique   [15
Mens quod praesagiret mihi?

Eva.   Memini. Atque quo magis Dei in
Hac re recogito, hoc miror magis prudentiam. Ex muliere
Collapsa salus, ex muliere restituta denuo.
In me Natura ad mortem genuit, in te gratia rursus ad
Vitam viguit, ut gratiae havd naturae cuiusque esset salus.   [20
In me peccatum quid valuit ac iram iustissimus
Patefecit deus, in te misericordiae iterum pandit sinus.

Maria.

Alias nescio, me scio nihil meritam vnquam hoc dignum filio
Ita nisi visum deo esset, maxima conferre in homines
Interdum haud maximos beneficia, quae nec sperauerunt.   [25

Eva.

Rectissime dicis. Itaque satis iam vixisse me diu
Arbitror, et discedere volup'st, haec nunc ita quae filiis

Mihique posterisque quae euenere oculis hisce meis
Quum video.
MARIA.   Verum tempus nunc monet ad montem Oreb, filius
Quo condixerat vt properemus cum apostolis reliquisque Eua   [30
Discipulis pariter, vbi nescio quid sese negotii   [*f. 136*]
Velle aiebat paululum, necubi quid in mora simus.
EVA.
Eamus.
MARIA.   At propere, mea tu, eccum enim huc sacerdotum imminet
Princeps, lupus ut aiunt in fabula.

[1. S.P.] *Om. MSC*
[3. desiet modo] < desiet vnum < deesset vnum
[4. vbi est] < ibi est
[5. est cui] ?< cu [*]
     Maria] < Maria mulierum
[7-9. Quae . . . gaudeo] < Quod me supra omnes faelicitates collocat,
Psychen / Meam vna cum gnato tuo rediuiuam ex inferis. M[ARIA]. Ita /
Deus me amet [< Amet me Deus] gaudeo
[12. Quae haec] < Quae
[13. Psychen] < S.
[16. Mens . . . mihi] < Quod expectem omnibus
[17. Ex muliere] < Siquidem
[20. havd] < ⟨non⟩
[20-21. cuiusque . . . me] < sit quod existimus / [*] < hoc quicquid
sumus / Existeret
[21. quid] < patefecit quid (*see l. 22*) ˈ
[25. haud] < ⟨non⟩
[27. volup'st] < volupe est
[30. condixerat] < condixit
     vt] < vti
     reliquisque Eua] < Eua reliquisque
[33. mea tu, eccum] < eccum mea tu

[II.2]
    S.H.] Act. 2. Sc. 3. *MSC*
    M.H.] Eiusdem Ordinis *MSC*
    P.H. Nomologus] Dioctes *MSC* < Machonomus
       Polyharpax Scriba] Polyharpax *MSC*
    1. S.P.] *Om. B, MSC, N, L*
     Nomologe] Dioctes *MSC* < Machonome
    2. S.P. Nomologus] D[ioctes] *MSC* < M[achonomus]

4, 5. S.P. Nomologus] M[achonomus] *MSC* (*so, ess., through the remainder of the scene except as noted*)

6. ut rem ipsam] *MSC* < rem ut

9. fece] faece *L*

11. compitis] competis *MSC*

13. se] *MSC* < ⟨i⟩

17.] *As in MSC; B prints as two verses, broken after* persentio

19. porrigines] *MSC* < bella

21. quid] *MSC* < quid quid

22. agas] *MSC* < agas praesul maxime

nisi] *MSC* < ⟨mi⟩

χειρῶν] χεῖρον *MSC*

νόμῳ] νομω *MSC*

23. flamma ... omnibus /] *MSC* < cruce, igne, terra, aqua / Ac elementis omnibus

24. in primis] *MSC* < autem

sarta] *MSC* < sartam

28. palmarium] *MSC* < arti

32. concilio] consilio *L*

33. honeste fucatur quae] *MSC* < sic quae fucabitur

34. Quid enim] *MSC* < Quide [*]

37. praesto eccum] *MSC* < eccum

39. Nae] *MSC* < Ny

43-44. obuiam it / Audaciae] *MSC* < obuiam / ⟨It⟩ [*]

46. hos] *MSC, Le;* nos *B, N, L*

47. dignum sit] *MSC* < dignum siet < s [*]

48. dicetis] *Be, MSC, L;* dicet is *B, N*

51. plurimum ibi] *MSC* < ibi plurimum

52. S.P. Saulus] *MSC* **?**< ⟨P⟩

54. S.P. Archiereus] *MSC* < ⟨S⟩

Nomologe] *MSC* < Machonome

55. usui siet hic] hic usui siet *MSC*

S.P. Nomologus] *MSC* (*ess.*) < M[achonomus]

56. S.P. Archiereus] *Om. MSC* < Th[anatus]

58. liceat] licet *MSC*

S.P. Archiereus] Th[anatus] *MSC* (*so through the remainder of the scene except as noted*)

59. Tu] Tu' *MSC*

61. S.P. Archiereus] *Om. MSC* < Th[anatus]

62-63. Fiet. ARCHIEREUS. Et / Mature] *MSC* < Fiet. / TH[ANATUS]. Et mature

63. Quin factum] *MSC* < Factum

63-66. Restat . . . una] *MSC (except as in following notes)* < Nunc conuentos mihi / Hac in re sacerdotum primarios volo, quid ferant / Consilii ut sciam. Ades Nomologe mecum vna

64-65. Petrum . . . Nobis] *MSC* < Petru⟨s⟩ nobis quem habet / In neruo ilico [?] < Petru⟨s⟩ nobis quem habet in neruo /

65. oppilabimus] *MSC* < oppilabitur

After II.2, MSC has a scene om. in B. The following is the final version, after which appear variants to it:

Act[us] 2.   Sc[ena] 4.   [*f. 137*]
Trimetri.
Sarcobius.   Rhodus Puer.

[Sarcobius.]

Numquis nam hic Coricaeus siue Melampygus est?
Nemo est. Quid, nullus vsquam hic auritus Midas?
Sub lapide aut dentatus dormiscens scorpio?
Quod hoc seclum, quaenam peruersitas. Adeo
E tectis nulli vt tutum sit prorepere   [5
Sacerdotum ob vesaniam? Sed quid siet
Miror, Marcus tantopere me quod expetit
Domum ad se accersens. Itaque uiso quid velit
Negoti ut videam, etsi haud manere liceat
Euam per genitricem, confecta quac domi   [10
Senio morboque laborat grauiter. At
Eccum obuiam a Marco Rhodum.

RHODUS.   Sarcobie
Oportune. Herus aliquotque cum illo te pridem
Expectat, ut properes.

SARCOBIUS.   Rei p⟨ae⟩disce scin'
Quid sit cur aduentum expetit?

RHODUS.   Nescio nisi   [15
Petrus quia in nervo ab Herode est coniectus ut
Communis fiat apud deum comprecatio.

SARCOBIUS.
Ah intelligo. Eamus ne quid in mora sumus.

[1-3.] *See V.4.10-13*
[1. S.P.] *Om. MSC*
[12. obuiam a] ?< a
[13. Oportune. Herus] < Her [*]

[14. Expectat] < Expectit
[16. est coniectus] < con [*]

[II.3]
   S.H.] Act. 2. Sc. 5. *MSC*
   1. S.P.] *Om. B, MSC, N, L*
   3. Petre, aut] Petre an *MSC*
   8. Spectans templum uorsus] *MSC* < Vorsus
   14. patefecit] patefacit *L*
   16. hodoeporus] oedoporus *MSC*
       libere] libero *MSC*
   20. Memet] *MSC* < Me
   22. Itemque] *MSC* **?**< Item

[II.4]
   S.H.] Act. 2. Sc. 6. *MSC*
   M.H.] Quadrati *MSC*
   1. S.P.] *Om. B, MSC, N, L*
   3. missititiis] *B, N, L;* missitiis *MSC (the correct form of the word)*
       PM adds a S.D. [L]iterae
   4. Obuinctus . . . haec] *MSC* < Ad Abadonem vinctu' [**?**< vinctum]
ipse cum sit hic
   5. Cum . . . obeat] *MSC* < Cum Diocte legatam imperii < Imperii
ut accipiat legatam sibi
   13. amicos . . . quoscunque] *MSC* < quoscunque . . . amicos
   16. hostem] *MSC* < hostes

[II.5]
   S.H.] Act. 2. Sc. 7. *MSC*
   P.H. Populus] *Om. MSC, B, N, L*
   1. S.P.] *Om. B, MSC, N, L*
       PM adds a S.D. Liter[ae]
   2. At] Ac *MSC*
   5. obiectum ni] *MSC* < ni obiectum
       praeuortissem] *MSC* < antevortissem
   8. pol] *MSC* < sane
   9. ut dissoluar] *MSC* < dissoluar
   10. Saule, ac] *MSC* < ac Saule *or simply* ac
   13. Vsuuenire . . . scio] *MSC* < Sc [*]
   23. articuli] *MSC* < dactyli

24. Polyharpax, me tenes] *MSC* < Polyharpax me accipis < Me Polyharpax acc [*]

    pigmenta] *MSC* < ⟨vnguen⟩

    nescio] *MSC* < non tracto

24-25. Age / Satis] *MSC* < Age / Age *or simply* / Age

26. quicquam] *MSC* (*A second* quicquam *was canceled.*)

27.] *PM adds a S.D.* Drachm[a]

28. modo] *MSC* < hoc

    Quid hoc] *MSC* < Quid quaeso hoc

    pro] *MSC* < quidem pro

31. Fert] *MSC* ?< T

34. cedo] *MSC* < tibi cedo

    Imo harum tibi] *MSC* < Nugas agis

36. sis] *MSC* < sies

38. nil pudet *MSC* < p [*]

40. modo] *MSC* < mi⟨hi⟩

    quos] quas *MSC*

48-49. mihi / Vnum ut] *MSC* < mihi ut / Vnum

53. At] *MSC* < Sed

55.] *PM adds a S.D.* pecunia

58. hercule] hercle *MSC*

59. conuicium] conuitium *MSC*

    scrobae] *B, MSC, L;* scrofae *N*

62-63. irruite, / Obruite] *MSC* < irruite, obruite /

63. Iam si] *MSC* < Si

64. modo] *MSC* < Abite inquam [*See the end of the line.*]

[III.1]

    M.H.] Trimetri *MSC*

    P.H. Ecclesia] *MSC* < Sarcobius

    1. S.P.] *Om. B, MSC, N, L*

    8. indigetauit] *MSC* < cum indigetauit; indigitauit *Le*

    9-21.] *MSC* (*except as in following notes*) < [*the following written for Sarcobius:*]

        Nunc ego relictus solus sum ex illa miser

        Familia paruulis cum filiolis tribus

        Asia, Aphrica, et Europaeho [< Europaeo], coniunx mihi

        Quos peperit Ecclesia, mulier vero optima

        Atque hinc quantum mihi esse nunc solatii

        Et quam vera voluptas posset. Sed quum nihil

        In rebus vndique est faelix mortalium,

Hos tyrannus nunc [< nunc tyrannus] Dicologus in carcerem
Desperationis trusit sordidissimum
Bufonibus, anguibus, ac faetore obsitum.
Quod ni esset quid mea vita venustius,
Melle aut esset plenius? Atque ipsus adeo adest
Dicologus. Quid agam?

11. spolior] *MSC* < ⟨No⟩

15. aliqua . . . solatii] *MSC* < sol [*]

17. Ac orba] *MSC* < Orbaque
    terraeque] *MSC* ?< terrae

18. ni] *MSC, Be, L;* in *B, N*

19.] *PM adds a S.D.* Exit Nomocrat

[III.2]

P.H. Nomocrates. Ecclesia] *MSC* < Dicologus. Sarcobius
        Desmophylax. Dromo] *Om. B, MSC, N, L*

1. S.P.] *Om. B, MSC, N, L*

1-4. Me . . . Euae] *MSC* < Nisi me fallunt argumenta omnia, hominem
eccum ipsum / Inuenire quem volui reperi. S[ARCOBIUS]. Men' petit?
D[ICOLOGUS]. Quisquis es / Edico tibi, tun' Sarcobius ille es Adamitica / Satus stirpe Euae ac

4. S.P. Ecclesia] *MSC (ess.)* < S[arcobius].

5. quae] *MSC* < qui

6. consciam] *MSC* < conscium
   feret] *MSC* < foret

7. S.P. Nomocrates] *MSC (ess.)* < D[icologus].
   S.P. Ecclesia] *MSC (ess.)* < S[arcobius].

8-23. NOMOCRATES. Scin' . . . uideo] *MSC (except as in subsequent notes)* <

DICOLOGUS.   Cuius pridem apud me tres cum matre in
    Vinculis desperant liberi?
SARCOBIUS.   Quid num reddere cogitat
    Captiuas mihi?
DICOLOGUS.   Quid ais?
SARCOBIUS.   Ipsissimus [< Ipsus] equidem Sarcobius
    Egomet sum, Dicologe optime.
DICOLOGUS.   Abi Dromo, Desmophylax,
    Ac Theorgile, parati cum loris fulsite [*sic*] propius [?] [< propius /] vt
    Vbi [†] iussero. Abripiatur recta hinc [< hinc mox < recta hinc] in
    carcerem.

SARCOBIUS.   In
    Carcerem innocens?
DICOLOGUS.   Iniustum in te nihil a nobis fiet.
    Id primum predico [?< prec (*)] tibi.
SARCOBIUS.   Quid egi?
DICOLOGUS.   Tune? Pessime a fasciis
    Cui ad malum omnes cogitatus accliues sient.
SARCOBIUS.   Mei?
DICOLOGUS.
    Recte id quia nescis. Abi curriculo Dromo ad Psychephonum
    Vt chirographum huc quam mox remittat nuncia, quod huic
    Satanaeque pridem permiseram. Atque eccum foras exire video.

   10. Desmophylax] Desmophylax, Theorgile *MSC*
   12. postulat] *MSC* < postulat et necessitas
   13. uero liberam] *MSC* < liberam vero
   15. fiet] *MSC* < hic fiet < fiet hic
       tibi praedictum] *MSC* < praedico tibi
   16. Bene . . . arbitror] *MSC* (quid admisi < adm [*]) < Recte quid
commisi [(†) < commisi] igitur vobis [< vobis igit (*) < igitur vobis]
fas explanare mihi
   17. sorore una] *MSC* < vna sorore
  18-19.] *MSC* < *reverse order*
   18. Cuius . . . sient] Cuius tum omnes cogitatus accliues in malum sient
MSC < Cuius porro cogitatus [< Cuius cog (*)] accliues omnes sient
   19. Denique . . . ancillula] Denique quid recens egeris id [*or* iam]
Synidesis ancillula *MSC* < Denique nuper quid [< quid nuper] patraris
tua Synidesis ancillula [*For* tua *see l. 20.*]
   20. fecit tua] fecist *MSC* (*See l. 19n.*)
       uerbis] verbis opus *MSC* < verbis moror ?< opus moror
   21. sis] *MSC* < tota sies
   22. remittat] *MSC* < remitta⟨re⟩ < remittat
  22-23. huic / Satanaeque quod] quod huic / Satanaeque pridem *MSC*
   23. exire] foras exire *MSC*

[III.3]
   P.H. Nomocrates] *MSC* < Dicologus
       Lictor] *B* (lict.); *om. MSC*
       Adopylus] *Om. MSC* (*his speeches being divided between Psychephonus
and Thanatus*)
       Ecclesia.] *MSC* < Ecclesia. Dromo < Sarcobius. Dromo.

1. S.P.] *Om. B, MSC, N, L*
   circumcurso] circumcursa *MSC*
3. S.P. Nomocrates] *MSC (ess.)* < Dic[ologus] [*so, ess., throughout the scene except as noted*]
4. Nomocrates] *MSC* < Dicologe
7-9. Psychephone . . . Nos] *MSC (ess.)*; Nos *B, N, L* [*I assume that Foxe or the compositor of B accidentally skipped from* Quid . . . *in l. 7 to* Quid . . . *in l. 9. Scansion is improved with the words supplied.*]
8. Nomocrates] *MSC* < Dicologe
9. S.P. Adopylus . . . Adopylus] Ps[ychephonus] . . . Th[anatus] *MSC*
   NOMOCRATES. Quis?] Quis? *MSC* < DIC[OLOGUS]. Quis? < *om.*
10.] *As in MSC; B, N, and L print as two verses, the first ending* occideram.
   istic] istuc *MSC*
11. addixeram] *MSC* < ⟨ade⟩
13. S.P. Adopylus [*bis*]] Thanatus [*bis*] *MSC*
   S.P. Nomocrates] Dic[ologus] *MSC*
13-14. opes-/que omnes] *MSC*; opesque/Omnes *B, N, L*
15. auexit secum] *MSC* < auexit simul < vna auexit
   certa . . . nuncias] *MSC* < haec certa si mihi [*]
16. S.P. Psychephonus] *MSC (ess.)* < ⟨P⟩h.
17. Antigraphen] *MSC (?)* ?< Autigraphen
19. S.P. Ecclesia] *MSC (ess.)* < Sar[cobius]
   S.P. Adopylus] Th[anatus] *MSC*
   Nos] *MSC;* Hos *B, N, L*
21. S.P. Thanatus] *Om. MSC (continuing the speech to Nomocrates)*
   ostentat] *MSC* < ostentitat
   Psychae] Psyche *MSC*
22. occidi] *L;* óccidi *B, N;* occîdi *MSC*
   ego] *MSC* < quod aiunt
23. S.P. Ecclesia] *MSC (ess.)* < Sar[cobius]
24. Pancratistes] Pancratiastes *Le*
25. nisi quia] *MSC* < qu [*]
30-31. S.P. Adopylus] Ps[ychephonus] *MSC*
31. maledictionis tuae] *MSC* < desperationis tui [*sic*]
32. Qua . . . libera] *MSC* ?< Qua Ecclesiae huius nunc expediat liberos
   < Qua Ecclesiam huius coniugem cum liberis manu expediet liberam
33. S.P. Adopylus] Ps[ychephonus] *MSC*
   illos] *MSC* ?< illas
   certo] certe *MSC*
34. me] pol *MSC*
   S.P. Psychephonus] *MSC (ess.)* [†]

35. Nomocrates] *MSC* < Dicologe
36. Vah, siccine] *MSC* < Sicci [*]
37. Nomocrates] *MSC* < Dicologe
   Hinc] TH[ANATUS]. Hinc *MSC* (T *heavily rewritten* [*?over* P])
38. S.P. Ecclesia] *MSC* (*ess.*) < Sar[cobius]
39. exanimata] *MSC* < exanimatus
   ut] uti *MSC*
41.] *PM adds a note, so heavily cropped as to be illegible,* [Qu]i sunt isti
[ ]⟨g⟩riti hos [ ]itos
   Qui . . . incedunt] Quis tragicus hic satrapas tam magnifice qui
incedit *MSC*
42. nimis . . . gaudia] cesso vxori [< ad (?* ad vxorem)] haec natisque
impartire nuncia
   After l. 42, PM adds a note, Hic interponatur Scena. *Perhaps he envisioned
a dramatization of the reunion of Ecclesia and her children.*

[III.4]
   P.H.] Pornapolis. Dioctes. Anabasius. *MSC* (*though this order misassigns
the first speech, in the absence of a S.P.*) < Abadon. Anabasius
   1. S.P.] *Om.* B, *MSC* (*assigning the speech to Abadon*), *N*, L
   7. Mihi . . . meae] Mihi simul ac Diocti amasio meo *MSC. The line,
not in the earliest version, was added interlineally here after first being added before
l. 6, where it appears as above after originally reading* Mihi atque Diocti
amasio meo
   9. et] & B, *N*, L; ac *MSC*
   12-13. Heus . . . putes] *MSC* < Heus, Pornapolis, tuque Dioctes, cui
haec loquor maxime [*or simply* loquor] / < Heus, Abadon, priusquam
incipias sic primum putes /
   15. duras] B, *MSC*, *N;* diras L
   17. Quippe hanc] *MSC* < Hanc quippe
   censeo] sentio *MSC*
   19. S.P. Dioctes] *MSC* (*ess.*) < Ab[adon]
   22. aut me Christum] *MSC* < me aut Christum
   persequi] *MSC* < prosequi
   26. aliud nihil] *MSC* < nihil aliud
   27. S.P. Anabasius] *MSC* (*ess.*) < Ab[adon]
   euadet] euadat *MSC*
   28, 29. S.P. Dioctes] *MSC* (*ess.*) < Ab[adon]
   28. instruis] *MSC* < instruit
   31-33. Christicolas . . . Domitianus] *MSC* < Christicolas prope ac /

Habere me spero ad sententiam. Heus, Nero / Ad me euocetur [< Nero huc / Evocetur, Domi (*)] [*] < Christocelas impetu [*]

    34. Maximinus] *MSC* < Maximinius

    35. Cletianus] Clesianus *MSC*
        His] Iis *MSC*

    38. S.P.] *Om. MSC* (*See the following note.*)

    38-40. Imo . . . Anabasi] At mane. Egomet eos ut conueniam satius est / Praeceptisque instruam domi accuratius. / Ibo, Anabasi [Ibo, Anabasi < Anabasi] *MSC*

    39. instruemus] *B, L;* instruamus *N*

[III.5]

    M.H.] Eiusdem Numeri *MSC;* Senarii *N*

    P.H. Ecclesia] *MSC* < Sarcobius

    1. S.P.] *Om. B, MSC* (*first assigning the speech to Sarcobius*), *N, L*

    1-2. liberos meos . . . eductos] *MSC* < coniugem meam . . . eductam

    3-4. Certe . . . refers] *MSC* (*ess.*) < Tribus una cum liberis Asia, Aphrica, et / Europaeo [*perhaps originally a continuation of Sarcobius' speech*]. S[ARCOBIUS] [?< P (*)]. Ipsaque ipse in re adfuistin'?

    7. S.P. Ecclesia] *MSC* (*ess.*) < Sa[rcobius] (*so throughout the scene except as noted*]

        coniicias] *MSC;* conniicias *B*

    8. duran' . . . fide] *MSC* (te ?< se) < adeon' dura esse te fide hominem

    9. Ast] *MSC* < Verum
        Nomocrates] *MSC* < Dicologus

    10. S.P. Ecclesia] S[arcobius] *MSC*

    12. obligatorio] *MSC* < obligatu

    13. Ecclesia] *MSC* < Sarcobie

    19. eundem] *B, MSC, N, L;* eandem *Le*

    22. at uero] atenim *MSC*

    30. iuri datum] *MSC* < factum iuri

    31. totam] *MSC* < tutam

    33. his] iis *MSC*

    36. Ecclesia] *MSC* < Sarcobie < Sarbo
        S.P. Ecclesia] S[arcobius] *MSC*

    37. metuis] *MSC* < queritas

    39. maxuma] maxima *MSC*

    42. dicenda est] dicenda *MSC*

    44. Corpus . . . paucarum] *MSC* < Corpus id at paucarum [*]

    47-48. Psychen . . . Scilicet] Animam ex inferis [< Erebo], idem quin

corpora / Simul restituet, quid dubii est? E[ecclesia] [< S(arcobius)].
Ita predicant / *MSC*

  50. uerba fere] scripturae *MSC*
  51. resurrectio] resurrexio *MSC*
  53. Nitidius] *MSC* < Nitius
  54. e terra ut] *MSC* < ⟨ut⟩ [*]
        pullulat] *MSC* < pullulet
  55. queam] *MSC* ?< queo
  56. scripturis cum] *MSC* < cum scripturis
  57. S.P. Paulus] *MSC* < S
  58. Mihi quae dixti] Quae dixti mihi *MSC*

[III.6]

  M.H.] Senarii *N*
  1. S.P.] *Om. B, MSC, N, L*
  3. Nomocrati] Dicologo *MSC*
  5. θεῶν] θεων *MSC*
  6. χείρ] χείρ *MSC*
  7. empiritici] empirici *Le*
  9. his] iis *MSC*
  15. Spirans] Spirat *MSC*
  16.] *PM adds a S.D.* Exit Ana[basius]
  19. nuncius] nuncius nuncius *MSC*
  20. puero particeps] *MSC (with a very long space between the words)*

[III.7]

  P.H. Psychephonus] Pseuchephonus *MSC*
  1. S.P.] *Om. B, MSC, N, L*
  2. in hac re quoscunque] *MSC* < quosc [*]
  5. Psychephone] *MSC* < Ps[eu]chephone [*erased letters illegible*]
        Christicolae] *MSC* < Christocolae
  6. cornicibus ut] *MSC* < ut cornicibus
  10. Hinc] Huic *MSC* (?)
  11-15. Herus ... Asiam] *MSC* < Herus satis hunc si / Nosti meus
Nomocrates [< Dicologus]. A[nabasius]. Quid is? Ps[ychephonus].
Ecclesiam hic modo quandam [?< Ecclesiae hic modo quosdam (*)] /
Non in Trophonii antro at desperationis in Labirinthis / Vinctam habuit.
A[nabasius]. Ah illocne in purulento carcere? Ps[ychephonus]. Tresque
simul cum / Illa alios: Asiam, Afrum [?= Africum] [< Lybicum] ac

[< et] Europum [< Europaeum] eius opinor pignora [< gnatos].
Certum / Non habeo

17. sutela] *MSC* < arte

Quid] *MSC* < Clauem mihi miram / Predicas, seram at mvtatam
oportuit. Ps[YCHEPHONUS]. Atqui tantundem fieret si / Quidem ad
omnia clauis aeque versatilis est. A[NABASIUS]. Quid < Nae tu mihi
miram / Clauem predicas, prius at seram mvtatam [< matatam] oportuit. Ps[YCHEPHONUS]. Atqui tantundem fieret clauis. / [*]

herus? Non-] *MSC* ?< Non- < igitur, non-

18. illis] *MSC* < illo
    hos] *MSC* < hunc

21. molestant iam? Cedo] molestant, iam cedo. *MSC*

27. Victoriam post] *MSC* < P [*]
    magis miror] *MSC* < mir [*]

29. obstant] *MSC* ?< obstent

30-34. Quod . . . Praesto] Quod struimus, quo obnixius hos nunc
sudores suffero nostro / Pro Diocte hos ut obtorto collo ad cruces rapiam.
Atque [*?lineation thus; after revision, the words appear in two lines, broken after*
obtorto] / Vide, pene quod exierat. Ps[YCHEPHONUS]. Quid? A[NABASIUS].
Psychephone uti sies / Praesto *MSC* < Quod struimus, quo obnixius hos
nunc sudores suffero nostro / Pro Nerone, Traiano, ac Decio hos ut
obtorto quod aiunt / Collo ad cruces [< f] rapiam. Atque quod per-
commode mihi venit / Nunc in mentem pene exierat. Ps[YCHEPHONES].
Quid? A[NABASIUS]. Psychephone uti presto sies /

30. quem . . . timent] *Be, L;* qui . . . timet *B, N*

33. exierat] *B, MSC, L;* exciderat *N*

35. Opera] *MSC* ?< S
    opus ad quaedam] *MSC* < opus

36. manubias] *MSC* [†]
    recuperare se] recuperare / Se *MSC*

37-38. Sed . . . dixero.] *Om. MSC. More than half of the page is left blank.*

[IV.1]

P.H. Dioctes] Abadon *MSC*

1. S.P.] *Om. B, MSC, N, L*

8. Maximinus] *MSC*; maximus *B, N, L*.

10. addidit] *MSC* [†]

13. Etsi] *B (Ill., BM), MSC;* Et si *B (Harv.);* Et si *B (Bodl.)*

15-16. tamen . . . Sedulo] *MSC* < ab eo est sedulo / Tamen

17. Sunt . . . sufficiam] *MSC* < Sunt, alios restat nunc monarchas in
loco / Vt sufficiam < Sunt vna nunc res restat conficiunda

18.] *PM adds a S.D.* Exit Anab.
20. uideo] *MSC* < accedere / Video

[IV.2]
   P.H. Dioctes] *MSC* < Abadon
   1. S.P.] *Om. B, MSC, N, L*
      nihil] nil *MSC*
   2. S.P. Dioctes] *MSC (ess.)* < Ab[adon] [*so throughout the scene*]
      S.P. Anabasius] *MSC (ess.)* < Ab.
   6. Nempe] *MSC* < Qui
   9. mortem] morte *L*
      ANABASIUS. Eius] Eius *MSC*
  11. inimicus'st] inimicu'st *MSC*
  13. Dioctes] *MSC* < Abadon
  17. occipit] *MSC;* accipit *B, N, L*
  19. Quid . . . supputa] *MSC* < Nobis quid reliquum sit tuted vide
  21. At] *MSC* < At at
  23. futurorum spe praesentia] *MSC* < praesentia futurorum spe
      Dioctes] *MSC* < Abadon
  25. ita personam geras] *MSC* < personam induas
  31. autem, quem] *MSC* < quem autem

[IV.3]
   1. S.P.] *Om. B, MSC, N, L*
  1-11. Qvanquam . . . exoluerit] *MSC (except as in following note) (ll. 1-10 in margin)* <

       Soma nunc vir defunctus est [*labeled* dimeter]
       Mulierque relicta sola Ecclesia sum [< sum Ecclesia] tribus
       Cum gnatis. Porro tum Asiam a Turcis insuper
       Periclitarier audio. Cui haec mulieri
       Non extundant animum, animus qui non stipes
       Est, fortunae tot vnam tundier ictibus?
       Primum viri in funere, quem persecutio
       Absumpsit. In aerumnis tum gnatae hoc aliud est
       Quae adhuc an viuit incertum est. Vt interim
       Quanta obsidet egestas nunc me ne refricem.
       Ob Christum adeo bona cui direpta [< derepta] sunt [< sunt /
         Quae habui omnia (*)]
       Vsque redacta adeo prorsus sum inter Symplegadas

Vidua, orba, et egens, domo eiecta et patria,
Curis ac odiis hominum obsita, cui
Praeter vitam nil superest, haec si tamen
Dicenda est vita, invita quam circumfero.
Quamquam vtrumque mihi tot circumstrepunt cruces
Vnum hoc animo penitus persuasi mihi,
Nihil vita haec vnquam feret tam felleum
Quod non ferendo patiar, Christus cum meus
Gehennali hoc me ⟨animae⟩ exoluerit

1. Soma] *B and MSC agree on this reading; if this page belonged to the earliest draft, we would expect the name in MSC to be Sarcobius.*
  2. nihil] nil *MSC*
   13. tempori' est] *MSC;* tempori, est *B, N;* tempori est *L*
   17. pulso tandem] tandem pulso *MSC*
      Diocte] *Om. MSC* < Abadone
  22-24.] *PM adds a S.D.* Tonitru & [stre]pitus subt[er]raneus
   25. hem] *MSC* < ehem
   26. quos] *MSC* < nisi quos
   27. leue] *MSC;* bene *B, N, L*
   29. ni me] *MSC* < mi ni
   30. Adest iam] *MSC* < Ipsum iam [*]

[IV.4]
  M.H.] *MSC* < Tetrametri
  P.H. Dioctes] *MSC* < Abadon
      Pseudamnus] *MSC* < Psydamnus
  1. S.P.] *Om. B, MSC, N, L*
  2. Itan'] *MSC* < Itane
  4. uinclis] vinculis *L*
  6. Dioctes] *MSC* < Abadon
  14. nostra] *MSC, N;* nostro *B, L*
  15. S.P. Dioctes] Ab[adon] *MSC*
  16. Diocten] *MSC* < Abadonem
  17. S.P. Dioctes] *MSC* < Ab[adon]
      gratulor] *MSC* < graut [*]
  21. S.P. Dioctes] *MSC* < Ab[adon]
  24. Pseudamnum] *MSC* < Pseudamne
      exire] *MSC* < huc exire foras
  31. robur] *MSC* < robus

33. conficiamus] *MSC* < perficiamus

36. astu] *MSC* ?< est (*See* 'st *later in the line.*)

38. no' omnem] *MSC;* non omnem *B* (*presumably mistaking the apostrophe for a nasal macron, though the line can be made to make sense reading* non); nos omnem *N;* omnem *L*

45. Tentamine quo] *MSC* < Quo tentamine

49. Probe] *MSC* ?< Probo

50. dynastias] deinastias *MSC*

53. saccharum] *MSC;* saccarum *B, N, L*

56. Eosdem] Rursus *MSC*

57. nemo] mihi nemo *MSC*

60. cur ad] *MSC* < cur huc ad

62. Babylona] *MSC* < Babylonem

63.] *PM adds a S.D.* Gazula [pe]cuniari[a]

65. hanc] hac *MSC* (*a tempting reading, except that the gender is wrong*)

66. Quid] *MSC* < ⟨Cui⟩ [*or* Sic (?)]

71. potius] *MSC* < magis

72. desunt] *MSC* < dee [*]

75. terris] *MSC* < terra

82. exornetur] *MSC;* ornetur *B, N, L*

84.] *PM adds a S.D.* Cyathus fo[r]nicationis

90. uindices] hunc vindices *MSC*

91-122. Dei ... Sed] *The original MSC version, omitting most of this passage, read as follows:* Dei. / SA[TAN]. Nec refert, modo sub nutum hos [< hos modo ... hoc] quocumque subigas / Opibus [< Tr] illi, fruemur [< fruemus] nos victoria. / Sed [*This passage was not crossed out. A version of the omitted lines was added in the margin with no indication of where it belonged. See subsequent notes.*]

92-95. Porro ... vbi] In rebus publicis priuatisque omnium / Tum vero in comitiis suffragiisque ordinum / Te praecipue Pseudamne immisceas. Vbi [*the last line* < Illic te imprimis inger (*)] *MSC* [*perhaps the missing line was cropped, or perhaps it was accidentally struck out of the earlier version*] < Porro ausculta [< Non quid is (*)] insuper auremque vtramque arrige. / In comitiis imperatoriis [< impetoriis] vbi

98. Falx ... posita] Leo suam ut partitur praedam Aesopicus / Tui [< Pars (*)] ut electionis [< electorum] pars sit maior gregis *MSC*

101. te ut] *MSC* < te

102. libidine] *MSC* ?< libido

103-104. quid ... Mouerier] *MSC* < quis te aduersum quid mouerit /[*]

105. Bellum aut Turcis] *MSC* < Turcis bellum

106-107. tu ... aderit] tu tendito. Victa pars / Mox supplex aderit

MSC < tu haec tendito. Victa pars / Mox supplex aderit < eo tute intendito. / Victus ilico supplex aderit < tu semper tendito. / Victus ilico supplex aderit

107-108. erit . . . ipse] erit commodum. / Sic etenim *MSC* < commodum / Erit. Sic etenim < commodum / Fuerit. Sic etenim

108-109. gratiam . . . te] *MSC* [fidem *at first moved* (? *by accident*) *to the end of l. 107*] < gratiam. / Fidem seruare

    109. res] *MSC* < res cum [*see l. 110*]
        monuerim] *MSC* < moneo
    110. cum haereticis] haereticis *MSC* < cum haereticis
        nuspiam] *MSC* < numquam
    111. Fiscum . . . pecunia] *MSC* < Pecunia . . . fiscum
        interim] quid mones *MSC*
    117. suo hinc uentri] *MSC* < hinc culinae

118-129.] *In MSC, the order is as follows* (*following the two lines om. in B which are quoted in the note to ll. 91-122*): *122-127, followed by two more lines om. in B* (Facilius esse huiusmodi te, ex eo, arguant. / Talis quisque est, ut sint quibuscum victitat), *then 118-121, 128-129, and another line om. in B* (*see note to ll. 128-129*). *A few lines are variant; see notes ad loc.*

    120. S.P. Dioctes] *MSC* < Ab[adon].
    124. Nomocratem] *MSC* < Dicologum
    125. sentio] censeo *MSC*
    128. Congredere] *MSC* < S [? = S(ATAN)]. [*Because of line rearrangements, MSC has a S.P. Sa[TAN] before this line.*]
        Dioctes] *MSC* < Abadon

128-129. Imperium . . . redintegret.] cui is imperium, caput / Ac exertum redintegrabit denuo, / Nomen sed cum habitu mutes peropus est, capin'? / *MSC* (*Before the last line is an* X, *presumably marking the line for deletion; beneath the line is a short stroke, perhaps showing the end of the rearrangements.*)

    130. Nomocratem] *MSC* < Dicologum
    131. huicque] *MSC* < ad eumque
        addictum] adductum *MSC*
        uide] *MSC* < ut cures
    132.] *PM adds a S.D.* Auri[ ]
        accipe] arripe *MSC* (?)
    133. seu] *MSC;* ceu B, N, L
    136. holosericas] *MSC* < holosericas / Cum pellibus Zebellinis, Madauricis [*a marginal* X *marking the line for deletion*]
    140.] *PM adds a S.D.* [E]xeunt
    145. Moxque] Mox *MSC*

[IV.5]

P.H. Europus] Europeus *MSC*

1. S.P.] *Om. B, MSC, N, L*
   bene] benet *MSC*
6. quam misere] Iam miserae *MSC* (*part of the following sentence*)
8. malum malus] *MSC* < malus [*]
9. mater, est] *MSC* < est, mater
13. potessunt] potessuvnt *MSC*
    magis] *MSC* < ⟨magis⟩ magis
17. est] *MSC* < se offert
18. S.P. Africus] *MSC* < Afer
19. Nomocratis] *MSC* < Dicologi
21. irrumpens] erumpens *MSC*

[IV.6]

P.H.] Dioctes] *MSC* < Abadon
      Europus] Europaeus *MSC*

1. S.P.] *Om. B, MSC, N, L*
   hic] *MSC* < nunc
5. irruimus] *MSC* ? < iniuimus
6-7. ex . . . ilico] *MSC* < noster occasionem illico / ⟨At⟩ [< ⟨In⟩]
8. pingam] hic pingam *MSC*
   hypocrisim] hypocrisin *MSC*
9. S.P. Dioctes] *MSC* < Aba[don] [*so throughout the scene except as noted*].
A D *was written in the margin before* est fabula (*l. 8*), *then erased.*
   12. Nomocratem] *MSC* < Dicologum
       secum semper] *MSC* < numquam non secum
   14. gratiam] *MSC* ? < gratium
   19. Comitia adsunt] *MSC* < Adsunt comitia
   21. panegyricos] panagericos *MSC*
   24. Prior] *MSC* < ABA[DON]. Prior
   29. S.P. Dioctes] Aba[don] *MSC*
   33. Quid] *MSC, L;* Ev[ROPUS]. Quid *B, N* (*Perhaps Foxe intended to
assign the speech to Africus and wrote the wrong name; more likely, he accidentally
wrote the S.P. in the wrong place and neglected to cancel it in correction.*)
   34. Quid] Quod *MSC* < At qui [*?or* Quid *MSC* < At quod]
       inquam] *MSC* < volui
   34-35. ut . . . Dei] *MSC* < vti siet / Haud vspiam agnoteros quisquam,
agnum dei / Ipso non tam loco quam natura exprimens /
   36. S.P. Dioctes] Aba[don] *MSC*
   38. suffragiis quin cederet] *MSC* < quin ce [*]

40. foras] foris *MSC*

45. Mecum] *MSC* < Quibus mecum

46-47.] *PM adds a S.D.* [Ex]it Pseu[da]mnus

[IV.7]

M.H.] Iambici Acatale. *MSC (but a marginal note calls l. 10 a Senarius)*

P.H. Dioctes] *MSC* < Abadon

　　　Europus] Europaeus *MSC*

　　　Africus] Afer *MSC (see l. 8)*

1. S.P.] *Om. B, MSC, N, L*

2. Et] *MSC* < Ac [?]

5. S.P. Dioctes] *MSC* < Ab[adon]

　　Here salue] *MSC* < S [*]

6. queis] *MSC* < pol qu⟨o⟩

7. sati] *MSC* < sati⟨s⟩

9. es] *MSC* ?< et < st [?= 'st]

12-14. pauonia . . . Hac] *MSC* < pauoniam [?< panoniam] hanc tibi plumigatam coronulam / Cape [< Sumito], stellulis emblematisque fulgurantem inaureis. / Fidei defensor [< Fidei pariter defensor] esto. Tu cum romphaea hac Afer, / Quid?

　　　PM adds a S.D. pauoni[a,] coronu[la,] Rhomph[aea]

14-15. hac uos . . . face] *MSC* < hinc intro. Dioctes [< Abadon]. / Dioc[tes] [< Ab(adon)]. Hem. Pseu[damnus]. Ah quem volui? Atriensis inquam introductos ad me face /

17-19. At . . . prius] *MSC* < At vbinam Porna, vbi tam diu / [*f. 149*] Cessat ita aduentum . . . prius < ac vt volui. Et vbi restat id, / [*f. 149*] Nomocrates [< Dicologus], cui ut dixi ius restituam carceris? Psy[chephonus]. Atenim caue / Faxis here. Pse[udamnus]. Cur non? Psy[chephonus]. Ipse iumento [< corio] ne tuo vapules [< vapl]. Pse[udamnus]. Tace, / Sufficit an non Scriptura claues cum volumus? Psy[chephonus]. At vera sit / Vt clauis [< clauit] quae prosit vereor. Pseu[damnus]. Non quid verum sit refert, / Populus at quid verum [< at verum] censeat, referre censeo. / Capin'? Psy[chephonus]. Probe. Pseu-[damnus]. At Porna vbinam cessat tam diu, / Aduentum ut dixit cur non adproperat? [< diu, cur non ita / Aduentum ut dixit adproperat < diu, cur non ita ut (*)]. Salta Psychephone in cubiculum / [> in / Cub(*)] Cito. Atque eia, prius [*or* Atque (*)] [*Apparently at an intermediate stage a version of* At Porna vbinam cessat *etc. stood for ll. 17-19.*]

[IV.8]

This scene was printed as a sample of the work by [Josiah Pratt] in The Church Historians of England: Reformation Period, I.1 (London, 1870), Appendix, 14]-[15.

P.H. Pornapolis Meretrix] Ponapolis [*sic*] seu meretrix *MSC*
    Chorus] *Om. MSC, B, N, L*
1. S.P.] *Om. B, MSC, N, L*
    in hac] *MSC* < ex hac
3. Pseudamno] *MSC* < Pseudamne
    χαίρεν] χάρειν *MSC* < Salue
4. gestiens adeo quod] *MSC* < quod gestiens adeo
11. ueritatis] *MSC* < veritatisque
12. opido] oppido *MSC* < sedulo
14.] *PM adds a S.D.* Cyathus fornicari[us]
16. submoueam] *MSC* (-veam) < submoneam *or* submoueam
17. sumus] simus *MSC*
18. Mea . . . siet] *MSC* < Mea . . . sit < Mea sit
19. id esse] *MSC* < e [*]
26. Sueuimus] *MSC* ?< Sueuimur
27. ubi] *MSC* < q [*]
    magis] *MSC* < satis
28. His] *MSC* < Illis
29-31. diem . . . lux] *MSC* < diem / Tibi ut dixi, hunc Pseudamne
datura sum. Pseu[DAMNUS]. Vah ut ut dulci te osculo / Nunc capio mea
lux
34. pergas, Porna, hanc] *MSC* < hanc pergas, Porna
37. At] *MSC* < Sed
    illinc] *MSC* ?< hinc
38. aiunt] *MSC* < ⟨q⟩ aiunt
39. inuasse] *B* (*Harv.*), *MSC* (< ingress [*]); iuuasse *B* (*Ill., BM,
Bodl.*), *L;* jurasse *N*
44. Commorsit] *MSC* < Commordit
45. Mihi] *MSC* < Mihin'
46. Anabaptistica] *MSC* < Anabaptista
52. Ecclesiamne] *MSC, N, Pratt;* Ecclesia'ne *B;* Ecclesiáne *L*
54. hos] *MSC* ?< nos
56. S.P. Psychephonus] *MSC* < Pse[udamnus]
57. S.P.] *MSC; om. B, N, L* (*continuing the speech to Psychephonus*)
57-64. Ac . . . Corybantica] *MSC* (*except as in following notes*) <
Psy[CHEPHONUS]. Here, prorsus haec / Insanit Corybantic [*]
58. decretistae] *MSC* < decretisti
    Cosmosophoi] *MSC* < cosmosoph⟨i⟩
59. holoporphyri] *MSC* < holoporphyr⟨ae⟩
    uos] vosque *MSC*
60. Copistae, Sigilliferi] *Om. MSC*

62-63. Ecclesia. Stat . . . Pseudamnus. Quid ais] *MSC (though, because of revisions, l. 62 appears to be a continuation of Pseudamnus' speech)* < Quid tune Ecclesiam id credis catholicam? [*this a continuation of Pseudamnus' speech*] Ecc[lesia]. Credo. Pse[udamnus]. Quid / Hanccine num credis esse? E[cclesia]. Non credo. *B reads* Ecc[lesia]. Stat . . . Pseu[damnus]. Quid ait

63. S.P. Psychephonus] *In MSC, this S.P. was evidently struck through by accident during the revision of this line.*

64. inquam repagulis] *MSC* < repagulis

65. Lunaticam hanc] *MSC* < Hanc lunaticam

  atque] ac *MSC*

  ad] *MSC* ?< in

  abducite] *MSC (but its position in the line is unclear because of the revision recorded in the next note)*

65-66. atque . . . sequimini] *MSC (except as noted above)* < abducite iam [< hanc] ac me sequimini hinc / Intro

66. hinc] *MSC (see preceding note)* < huc [?or huic]

[V.1]

In MSC appears a cross at the top of the page, above the S.H. Foxe often made such prayerful markings in his manuscripts.

P.H. Lictor] *Om. MSC (The name* Thanatus *and the following names look like late additions.*

  Adopylus] *Om. MSC*

  Europus] Europlethius *MSC (Through the scene, MSC abbreviates S.P.'s ambiguously.)*

  Hierologus] Ierologus *MSC*

1. S.P.] *Om. B, MSC, N, L*

1-2. rursus . . . me] *MSC* < ego me / Rursus in Europam

6. minime modo sumus] *MSC* < iam non sumus

7. mutanda] *MSC* < flectenda

10. veste] *MSC* < veste hac

  tegam] *MSC* ?< tego

  PM adds a S.D. vestis

12. Mihi quos] *MSC* < Quos mihi

13. Adopyle] *Om. MSC*

  estis] sitis *MSC*

15. Ornamenta haec] *MSC* < Induuias hic < Orna [*]

  S.P. Adopylus] Psyc[hephonus] *MSC*

16. haud] *MSC* < non

18. hoc sub Francisci] *MSC* < sub Francisci hoc

18-19.] *PM adds a S.D.* [Fr]ancisci [p]allium

19. Tu] Tum *MSC* (*?*)

    re et] *MSC* < et re et

19-20. nomine . . . uere] *MSC* < nomine / Sies. Quemcumque nactus sis vere

21. teneas] *MSC* < scias

22.] *Om. MSC*

23. Inde] *MSC* < Dehinc

24-26.] *PM adds a S.D.* [E]xeunt [E]uro. Hier.

25-26. per . . . Spargite] *MSC* < late per omnia spargite /

29. Hierologe] Ierologe *MSC*

31. S.P. Hierologus] Ier[ologus] *MSC* (*so throughout the scene*)

    Non . . . magis] *MSC* < Non magis ficus est ficus < Non tam ficus est ficus

34. Meretriculam] *MSC* < Catholicam quam dicunt meretriculam

37. Europe mi] *MSC* < Europlethe

38. irruimus?] *MSC* < irruimus. S[ATAN]. Cantem tamen. In principio erat / Verbum, et verbum erat apud Deum. IER[OLOGUS]. Quae oratio haec? / SA[TAN]. Pax hic Dei [< Dei et]. PSY[CHEPHONUS]. Et sancti Francisci [< Et Francisci]. TH[ANATUS]. Et sancti / Carmeli. EUR[OPUS]. Quos camelos hic video? S[ATAN]. Adsumus / E Grynwico serui Dei, atque filii / Beati Francisci [*]

    amabo] *MSC* < obsecro

39-40.] *L prints as one verse*

40-41. Abominatio . . . succurite] *Assigned to Thanatus in MSC.*

    in . . . stans] *MSC* < hic / Stans in loco sancto

41. Quidnam] *MSC* < Quid

42. pseudopontificem] speudopontificem *MSC*

49. Europe] Europlethe *MSC*

    procul] *MSC* < tibi procul

50. S.P. Evropus] *B prints at the end of l. 49* (*in a passage which seems to have been undergoing typographical compression*).

51. Tu hic] *MSC* < Hic

    quo is] *MSC* < hic quo

52. haec si] *MSC* < si [*?*]

    Satanae] Satane *MSC*

53. Id . . . ut] *MSC* < Omnibus id restat iis vt < Id re [*]

54. ea in] *MSC* < in ea

55. haec ita] *MSC* < ita [*]

    diu'] *B* (*?*); diu *MSC*

56. in urbe haud] numquam *MSC*

58. tandem euaserit] *MSC* < nam euaserit < euadet denique < nam euaserit < nam euadet < euadet denique

60. Arietis . . . nescio] *MSC* < Ariete ominosum nescio / Quid [*before ominosum is* -is de, *apparently a first start on the final reading*] < Arietis decimo quid nescio / Omi [*]

62. Signum . . . Atenim] *MSC* < Marte ipso radiante in signo foemineo / [*f. 152*] Sed

62-63. *PM adds a S.D.* [Str]epitus

63. audire] haurire *MSC*

64. inseruiat] seruiat *MSC* (?) < inseruiat

66-67.] *As in MSC; B and L seem to start a new verse with* Francisci.

[V.2]

1. S.P.] *Om. B, MSC, N, L*

2. Papam uti] *MSC* < Ut papam

3. Card'nalium] *MSC* (?); Cardualium *B, N;* Cardinalium *L*

4. audi nos] *MSC;* &c. *B, N, L*

4-5. Episcopos. / Satan. Satis] *MSC* (epis.) < epis. S[atan]. Satis / Iam

5. respice] *MSC* < respo [*]
    intercipit] hic intercipit *MSC* < inter [*]

7. In] *MSC* < Prorsus in
    atque] *MSC* < a⟨c——⟩
    audin] *MSC* < audin' Deus [*See l. 8.*]

7-8. quae ibi / Vidi] *MSC* < quae ego / Illic vidi < quae ego ibi / Vi [*]

9. quam immaniter] *MSC* < diro duello < implacabiliter

10. umbrarum . . . obortus] *MSC* < qu [*] < vmbrarum ob [*]

12-14. iam . . . Myriades] *MSC* < Inde haereticorum psammocotiae / Myriades [< myriae psammocotiae / (*)]

14-16. scintillitus . . . placent] *MSC* (*see the following note*) < ⟨omne id⟩ scintillitus / Mergunt [< Extinguunt] purgatorium. S[atan]. Ominosa haec mihi parum placent. / Pseu[damnus]. [*]

15. Aethnam] *MSC* < culinam

16. Papae] Pape *MSC*

17. Interim tun'] *MSC* ?< Tun'
    esse] *MSC* ?< here esse < here nostrum [*probably connected with revisions recorded in the following note*]

17-18. iusque . . . nephas] *MSC. The passage was heavily revised, and I can make no sense of the earlier stages. The earliest seems to have been* quod tam late / Quam rem agis. *Above* Quam *is* qu⟨am⟩. *Above* quod tam late (*and* *below* iusque concilii) *is* vide quid ⟨ius⟩ [?†] modo; *apparently* quid ⟨ius⟩ *was cancelled separately. Perhaps the intermediate stages were somewhat as follows:* ?< vide quid ius ?< vide modo / Quam rem agis ?< iusque concilii [< cons (*)] violas /

18. Haud] *MSC* ?< Ne

S.P. Pseudamnus] *MSC. Originally it was in the margin as though* Violas . . . nephas *were the end of a verse.*

dico . . . modo] *MSC* < illum dico modo / Qui praeteriit

19. Hierologum] Ierologum *MSC*

20. Europo] Europletho *MSC*

20-21. Collegium / Vbi] *MSC* < Collegium vbi /

21. sit] *MSC* < est

pone] *MSC* < ilico < porro

23-24. Ad . . . ualet] *MSC* < Tandem quando [< quoniam] [< Ad phanum donec] instare me uidet nec desistere, viam / [*f. 152v*] Is vorat pedibus quantum valet

25. uicit] *MSC* < me vicit

26. hariolor] *MSC* < intell [*]

28. dextra . . . laeuam] leua . . . dextram *PM*

uergite] tendite *MSC*

29. decliuis] *MSC* < decil < decll [*]

30. Illic secus] *MSC* < Secus

adeoque uel in] ad dextram, vel in *MSC* < ad dextram haud procul, in

31. porta potius] *MSC* < potius porta ?< potius potius

32. vt fortes] *MSC* < fo [*]

34. Gymnopodes] *MSC* < Gymnopodes pulpifices < Sarbonarii

35. est] *MSC* < sit

Hierologum] Ierologum *MSC*

auditis? ad] *MSC* < ad

35-36.] *PM adds a S.D.* [In]trat Por[n]opolis

36. Diocten] *MSC* < Abadona

abducite] *MSC* < adduciter

probe] *MSC* < *om.* < probe

37. Sed . . . abite] Interim [< Interea] haec utcumque sint, illud mihi cordi est, quod que ego et / Pornapolis meros triumphemus panegyricos: cap⟨ut⟩ulum a / Nobis gladii uerbere resectum prius. Postquam regnet / Denuo, ut Nesiarchum hunc nunquam [?< nunc] pro meritis laudem satis. / Sed illa egreditur *MSC (this passage altered from earlier MSC versions which appeared in V.3; see notes to V.3.14-15 and 20)* < Vos abite. Sed Pornapolim video. Abite

[V.3]

    P.H. Zenodorus . . . Colax] *Om. B, MSC, N, L*

    1. S.P.] *Om. B, MSC, N, L*

       tam . . . impudens] *MSC* < cuiusquam tam impudens

    3. fulmine?] *MSC* (fulmine!) < fulmine! / Ac Pseudamnum bestiam esse apocalypticam?

    9. coepit] occoepit *MSC*

       Quin] *MSC* < Porro.

       insuper] *MSC* < cum insuper.

    14-15. Zenodore . . . blanditer] *MSC* (Blanditer) < Zenodore abi / Cum rosa hac aurea [*] < Zenodore abi / Mature ad [*] < Sed hoc bene / Me habet interim, caput [?< quod] hoc quod occisum est prius / Nunc postquam reuixit denuo, ut eum numquam ego / [*f. 153*] Nesiarchen pro [< satis pro] meritis laudem satis. Por[NAPOLIS]. Bene / [*See V.2.37n.*]

    15.] *PM adds a S.D.* rosa aurea. ensis cum vagina aurea. Linolaneum pallium.

    16. ensem] *MSC* < gladium.

    17. hoc] *MSC* ?< g [*].

    20. Quid . . . Colax] *MSC* < Nuncque id [< Atque id] non parum iuuat / Caput hoc gladii uerberem resectum prius / Postquam reuiguit modo, eum ut numquam satis / Nesiarchum [< Nesiarchen] pro virtutibus laudem. Por[NAPOLIS]. Bene / Profecto factum [*] (*See V.2.37n.*)

    21. Tu ad] *MSC* < Ad.

       Diocten] Abadonem *MSC*.

       PM adds a S.D. [Ann]ulus gem[m]eus.

    23. face] *MSC* < fac⟨io⟩.

       Virum . . . gerat] *MSC* (*but above* Virum *and not canceled is what looks like* rem) < Virum ut strennue [*] < Quid restat modo?

    29. Hierologo] Ierologo *MSC*.

    31-37. quia . . . temnier] *MSC* (*see following notes*) < quia oculis / Captus Pseudamne tam diu videre iam / Coepit, naribus nec [< ⟨i⟩] ducitur amplius. / Linguae atque literae passim perpoliunt. / Fuco iam nil proficitur. Imperio tuo / Vbique oppeditur, claues uilescere, / Bullas pro bullis concacari ab omnibus [< Vbique oppeditur, concacantur bullae /]. / Fulmen ceu ex vitro frigere vndique /

    32. oculis captus] *MSC* ?< captus oculis

    33. homines literae ac] *MSC* < ac literae homines

    35. undique] *MSC* < vbique

    38-39. Corpus . . . Alit] Monstrum hoc corpus, bina [< s] quod / Alit *MSC* < Monstrum hoc corpus quod duo [< s] / Simul alit

    40-41. doctrinam . . . fumos] *MSC* < doctrinam [< s(*)] fumos fuc [*]

43-44. credier . . . ais] *MSC* < credier. Pse[udamnus.] Quid ais [*] < credier, quem bestia / [*f. 153v*] Praefert apocalyptica [*See l. 47.*]

44. Pseudamne, esseque] *MSC* < Pseudamne esse, esseque

46. Magis] *MSC* < Magis ipso

48. mirum ut] *MSC* < prorsus

48-49. bestia / Turcam haec] *MSC* < bestia haec / Turcam

51. haud pote] *MSC* < haud pote id < id haud pote

Quidum] *MSC* < Quinam < Qui ⟨ ⟩

52. fateor] *MSC* < fateor / Quod nusquam vsu vestra nisi in tyrannide

53. vobis] *MSC;* nobis *B, N, L*

53-54. haud . . . Res] *MSC* ?< haud Turcis res certa est / < res certa est modo /

56. haec sit] *MSC* < sit

bestia] *MSC* < bellua

57. sanescet denuo] *MSC* < resanescet tamen < sanescet denuo

58. Id . . . liquidum] *MSC* < Id ⟨iam⟩ quod [< Id quod] . . . liquidum < Nimis in Triagonesa [< Tv (*)] est iam id [< Triagonesa id iam (*)] gente liquidum < Idque ad Triagonesam omne [< ⟨iam⟩] referunt insulam < Idque ad Tr. [*] < Idque inquiunt omne expletum iam cernimus / Triagonesa illa in insula [< In Triagoneso in (*)]

60. Eoque] *MSC* < Ac proin

62. putant] *MSC* < sic

62-63. Vitae . . . imaginem] *MSC* ?< Vitae quia inanimem / vocique [*] < Vitae quia bestiam / Vocique [< Ac voci] inanimem eius reddidit imaginem < Quia priorem is bestiam / Istinc abolitam voci ac vitae reddidit

64. agni dum] *MSC* < dum agni

65. immanior] *B, N;* imanior *MSC, L*

66. Remque ita] *MSC* < Itaque rem

ipsa res] *MSC* < res satis ipsa

68. Europaeus] *MSC* < Europlethus

69. Insuper] *MSC* < Equidem

71. perculsa] *MSC* < uict [*]

71-72. muliebriter? / Pornapolis. Non] *MSC* < leuiter [*or* leniter]. Por[napolis]. Haud /

78. me hic] *MSC* < me

vix . . . compos] *MSC* < vix pedes capio /

Compos] *As in MSC; B, N, and L print as a continuation of l. 79.*

[V.4]

P.H. Africus] *MSC* (*originally intended as the last name in the list, an order which would have assigned the first speech to Europus*)

　　　Europus] *MSC* < Europlethus

1. S.P.] *Om. B, MSC, N, L*

1-2. Ecclesiam ... uisos] *MSC* < tota iam urbe quaerendo / Sum sessus [? = fessus], quos diu non uisos impense /

10-13.] *See the draft scene after II.2 in MSC.*

10. Articulo] *MSC* < Tempore

　　　seu] ceu *MSC* [*but* siue *in the draft in Act II; see p. 419*]

12. uel] *MSC* < aut

13. mater, pericli] *MSC* < per [*]

16. tutum ut] *MSC* < vt tutum

17. ego nunc] *MSC* < ego

18-20. Aut ... serpentibus] *MSC* (*except as in subsequent notes*) ?< Quum desertum iam ipsum nec quicquam / Tutum sit a serpentibus < quum nec desertum iam ipsum sit tutum [< tutum sit] a / Serpentibus

18. quo] quo me *MSC*

20. mater] *MSC* < parens < ma [*]

21. gnate] *MSC* < fili

22. me merito] *MSC* < me simul

23. recipio] *MSC* < accipio

23-24. saluum / Atque ualidum] *MSC* < saluum / Ac validum tete < saluum / Te ac validum < saluum ac / Te [*] [*See following note.*]

24. restitutum te] *MSC* < te restitutum

25. Nobis ... mater] *MSC* < Gaudeo. Eccl[esia]. Quid ergo nouarum ex Affrica? Af[rica]. Haud quicquam. / Eur[opus]. At hic malarum satis [*] < Nobis gaudeo. E[cclesia]. Quando venisti? Af[rica]. Modo mater.

27. Ac ... nil] *MSC* < Ac stygmaticam adeo vnquam conspici [?< vid (*)], sed nil < Stygmatisque obsitam adeo conspici, sed nil < Ac stygmatis obsitam [< obsessam < ade (*)] adeo conspici [< vider (*)]

30. mihi ut] *MSC* < uti [*See following note.*]

31. tutum quicquam siet] tutum iam quicquam sit *MSC* < tutum iam quicquam mihi sit [*see preceding note*] < quicquam tutum sit < quicquam sit tutum

35-36. Quam ... gestio] *MSC* < Quam mox monstrari / Mihi hominem gestio < mihi quam mox monstrari [*] < *om.* (*since, immediately after* sacrilegus, *Foxe wrote* Eu[ropus]. Pseu [*], *the beginning of the speech in l. 36*)

36. S.P. Europus] Ec[clesia] *B, N, L; E. MSC* [*I emend on the assumption that Foxe's ambiguous S.P. survived into the later manuscript and that B mis-*

interpreted it. Foxe's intention, I think, is shown, though not beyond dispute, by what he wrote before he added Quam . . . gestio *(see the preceding note).*]

Christi] *MSC* < Antichristi [*but probably intended to be* Antichristus]

36-37. atque . . . omnium] atque bonorum / Hostis hominum *MSC* < atque / Bonorum omnium inimicus

37-38. Vah . . . in] *MSC* < Quid qui me extrusit / In

40. ipsi] ipse *MSC* (*?*)

41-44. At . . . inuasero] *MSC* (*except as in following notes*) ?< [*the following reading perhaps preceded by some part of the original reading, below*] Dein scripto / Milite atria arcesque eius [< ill (*)] fundam omnes. Eamus. / E[CCLESIA]. Quam tu rem inceptas, nate, cedo? < Haeccine quemquam [< Nequeo (*)] / Pati. Eamus pugno hoc cerebrum ilico [< ill (*)] extundam / Venefico. Dein scripto milite [< mite] atria arcesque / Illius fundam omnes [< Omnes fundam]. Ecc[LESIA]. Minime gentium [*See ll. 47-48.*]

42. mastygiae] mastygae *MSC*

43. Cerbero] *Be, MSC* [< cerebro], *L;* cerebro *B, N*

extundam] *MSC* < huic extundam

cani ilico] *MSC* < ilico cani

44-45. ac . . . quid] *MSC* (*?ac partially struck through when* peste *was canceled*) < peste ac / Vomica hac Europam [< Vomica Europam] exonerabo actutum / Boni ex Hydra hac nequid

46. mali hinc] *MSC* < hinc mali

47. liceat] *MSC* ?< ⟨tu⟩

48. Patiar . . . unquam] *MSC* < Vnquam patiar [< Vnquam vim] vim hic ullam [*See following note.*]

48-53. non . . . iniusta] *MSC* ?< non . . . rectius [*as in text*] et melius: nos vim [?< melius: vim hanc ut / ?< rectius: vires (*)] / Faccssat omnium in patientiam et vires in / Preces vertemus. Telum oratione vna / Nullum potentius. Machina haec perrumpit coelum. / Illorum inferre est, nostrum ferre iniurias < non? / Ecc[LESIA]. Quia enim vobis dabo consilium rectius: / Vim [< Patientiam (*)] in patientiam armaque [< ac arma] in preces ista / Vertemus. Telum oratione nullum usquam / Potentius. Machina haec coelum ipsa [?< ipsum] perrumpit. / Illorum inferre, nostrum ferre est iniurias

54. Sors quippe haec] *MSC* < Sors haec quippe < Haec sors [*]

54-55. Christi . . . est] *MSC* < bellua / Aliter bellua [< quam bellua], haec aliter haec quam [< quam haec] aduentu Christi extingui nequit (*?*)

56-59. Illi . . . sumus] *MSC* (*except as in following notes*) < Haec si ferimus, quid magni est? Ille maiora / Subiit dux et coryphaeus noster. Maiores / Illo non sumus. Quae ferimus Christi haud (*?*) [*] [*This last sentence was heavily revised; see subsequent notes.*]

56. ergo trophaeum hoc] *MSC* < trophaeum ergo < trophaeum hoc
    permittemus] *MSC* < ⟨pro⟩mittemus
57-59. Nam . . . ille] Nam ad me quidem quod attinet, sic inducor:
/ Quae fero Christi quum fero causa [*or* causa fero], lubens ferre [< fero].
/ Maiora ille *MSC* < [*a complicated revision, the stages of which were perhaps
as follows:*] Nam ad me quidem quod attinet: quae fero Christi / Quum
fero causa lubens fero: maiora [†] ille / < Quae fero Christi quum fero
causa [< haud mea causa fero]. Maiora / Ille
    59. illo maiores] illo nos maiores *MSC* < atque nos illo maiores
    59-60. sumus . . . stigmata] *MSC* < sumus. / Illius stigmata sunt
?< sumus. Illius [*]
    60. suam is causam] *MSC* < causam is suam
        arbitratu] voluntate *MSC*
    61. Vindicet] *MSC* < Vendicet
        diu iam pertulerim] *MSC* < iam diu per [*]
        pertulerim] *MSC* < pertulimus
    62. aberit] iam aberit *MSC*
        imponet] imponat *MSC*
    64. Iunctis] Iuctis *MSC*
        At] *MSC* < Sed
    65. lychnophorae] hae lychnophorae *MSC*
    66. Praetensis . . . miror] *MSC* < Miror praetensis huc [< huc facib
(*)] quae facibus affectant
    67-68.] *Squeezed into the bottom margin of MSC, as though a late addition.*
    68. Ad nuptias expectant] *MSC* < Expectant ad nuptias

[V.5]
    P.H. Chorus Quinque Virginum] Chorus Uirginum *MSC*
        Europus] Europlethus *MSC*
    1. S.P.] *om. B, N, L;* Ch. *MSC*
        etsi . . . sit] *MSC* < etsi sera sit p [*] < perquam etsi sera siet
    3-6. Vigilando . . . salue] *MSC* (*except as in subsequent notes*) **?<**
Vigilando haud tamen defatigarier sponsus / Dum . . . salue **?<** Vigilando
tamen numquam defatigarier / Sponsus dum . . . salue < Propositum
tamen vsque persequi prorsus / Vigilando sponsus dum redeat ad nuptias.
/ Sed sponsam ipsam video. Hera salue
    4. S.P.] 2 *MSC*
        cantu noctis] *MSC* **?<** cantu nox < cantu noctis
    5. trudamus] *MSC* < fallamur
    7. amoque] *MSC* < et amo
        quae] quum *MSC*

11. id] *MSC* < hoc

12-13. Stigmata . . . sponsi] *MSC* < Imo stigmata haec si nescitis, / Mihi margaritae ac vniones merae sunt, / Sponsi

14. circumfero] *MSC* < suffero

17. tu] num *MSC*

19. obtemperetis] *MSC* < ⟨ex⟩temperetis

20. S.P. Africus] *MSC* < *om.*

21. Manemus] *MSC* < Manebimus

    preces] ?< pro [*]

22. Capessite] Capescite *MSC* < Capi [*]

23. primum] precor *MSC*

23-24. nosque . . . tuam] vocem / Voto sequemur nos tacito tuam. Eur[opus]. Fiat. / *MSC*

26-28. tua . . . praesidia] tua . . . nos quando [< quando nos] / Praesidia destituunt omnia *MSC* ?< tua vt dextra / Opem ferat diuina [< Opem diuina (*)] humanae quum destituunt nos [*] < Opem vt dextra / Diuinam iam ferat tua humanae quando / Opes nos omnes destituunt

31. ferro] fero *MSC*

33-38. nusquam . . . abs] nusquam vt / Loci ut quicquam tuis sit reliquum in desertis / [< numquam vt / Loci nihil vsquam tuis relictum sit (< nihil sit vsquam t [*]) /] In desertis [†] etiam ultimis [< ultimos]. Dioctes sic / Cuncta penetrat, rabiesque Pseudamnica. Et / Quem tandem miseriae pones modum? Mundus / Olim abs *MSC*

39-40. At . . . facies] Flectant te miseranda / Haec rerum [?] [?< Rerum haec] facies *MSC* < Quum te flectat rerum / Miseranda haec facies

40-41. sponsae . . . rumpe] sponsae / Haec stigmata, sponse voluptas [< volun (*)] mihi ⟨rumpe⟩ [?†] *MSC* < sponsae / Tuae toto haec in corpore stigmata [?*] [*see next note*] < sponsae haec / Tuae tuto [*]

42-43. Age . . . ueni] *MSC* (*ess.*) < sueta tua te flectat pietas, preces si
        nil / Proficiunt nostrae
        PM adds a S.D. fulg[or] & od[or]

43. Cito ueni] *MSC* < Veni cito
    cito, Domine] Domine *MSC*

44. quae . . . mira] *MSC* < quaenam noua odoris quaedam

45. adspirat] aspirat *MSC*

46. Tum] Ac *MSC*
    S.D.] *Om. N*
        theatri] *MSC* < theatri par [*]
        ostendunt se] *MSC* < se [*]
        Above demittuntur *in MSC is a canceled word* (*illegible*).

Ergo] *MSC* (?) < Euge [*Not manifestly a part of l. 46.*]

46-49 (including S.D.).] *Crowded onto the page in MSC, as though a late addition.*

48. iam] iam iam *MSC*

49. apertos] abertos *MSC*

50-67.] *Added in the margin of MSC.*

50-52. Porro . . . uideo] *MSC* (*except as in subsequent notes*) < Porro delapsae, sponsa queis se paret agni. [< Porro delapsae queis (*) < Porro queis sponsa se ornet agni.] E[cclesia]. Mira / Vero praeter supraque spem oculis hodie ipsa / Quae video

51. uero] haec vero *MSC*

52. ego] hodie ego *MSC* < ego ⟨vid⟩ [*]

52-53. magna . . . miror] *MSC* ?< magna / Haec miracula quid volunt miror [< quid volunt] < magna / Haec quid volunt miracula miror

55. Atqui] *MSC* ?< Atque

56. insculptum] inscriptum *MSC*

58-61. Hierusalem . . . &c.] *Om. MSC* (Sententiam *being on a line by itself*); *perhaps Foxe skipped the passage temporarily until he could check the passage in Apocalypse.*

67. Bombycina . . . palla] Hoc byssino, hasque sordes exuere *MSC*

67-163. Ast . . . plaudite] *Om. MSC*

76. corpori] corporii *L*

88-89.] *L prints as one verse.*

163. *ΤΕΛΟΣ*] *B, L; om. MSC;* Finis *N*

TWO LATIN COMEDIES BY
JOHN FOXE THE MARTYROLOGIST

Designed by R. E. Rosenbaum.
Composed by The St. Catherine Press, Ltd.
in 11 point monotype Baskerville, 3 points leaded,
with display lines in monotype Baskerville.
Printed offset by Valley Offset, Inc.
on Warren's 1854 text, 60 pound basis,
with the Cornell University Press watermark.
Bound by Vail-Ballou Press.

Library of Congress Cataloging in Publication Data
(For library cataloging purposes only)

Foxe, John, 1516-1587.
   Two Latin comedies by John Foxe the martyrologist.

   (Renaissance text series, 4)
   Latin and English.
   "Copy text for Titus et Gesippus [written in 1544-1545] is ... the only known version of that play, in British Museum Lansdowne MS. 388."
   "Copy text [for Christus triumphans is] the octavo edition printed in March, 1556." Includes bibliographical references.
   I. Foxe, John, 1516-1587. Christus triumphans. English and Latin. 1972. II. Smith, John Hazel, date.   ed. III. Title. IV. Title: Titus et Gesippus. V. Title: Christus triumphans. VI. Series.
PA8520.F67T5 1972   872'.04   72-3950 ISBN 0-8014-0730-3.